FONTANUS MONOGRAPH SERIES
XV

ETHNOGRAPHY

AND

DEVELOPMENT

THE WORK OF
RICHARD F. SALISBURY

The FONTANUS MONOGRAPH SERIES
and the annual journal FONTANUS,
published by the McGill University Libraries,
are devoted to the exploration
and presentation of the collections
of the McGill University
libraries, museums and archives

General Editor
Hans Möller

XV. Marilyn Silverman,
Ethnography and Development: The Work of Richard F. Salisbury,
2004

FONTANUS MONOGRAPH SERIES
XV

ETHNOGRAPHY

AND

DEVELOPMENT

THE WORK OF
RICHARD F. SALISBURY

Edited by

Marilyn Silverman

with contributions by

Harvey A. Feit
Henry J. Rutz
Colin H. Scott
Marilyn Silverman

McGill University Libraries
Montréal, 2004

Canadian Cataloguing in Publication Data

Main Entry under title:
Ethnography and Development: The Work of Richard F. Salisbury

ISBN 0-7717-0622-7
ISSN 1183 – 1774

General Editor: Hans Möller

Editor: Marilyn Silverman

with contributions by
Harvey A. Feit
Henry J. Rutz
Colin H. Scott
Marilyn Silverman

Design: Andrew Ensslen

Printing: AGMV Marquis, Montréal

RICHARD F. SALISBURY
(1926 – 1989)

Acknowledgements

Generous support from McGill University Faculty of Arts and the Department of Anthropology, as well as additional support from various anonymous donors, made the publication of this volume possible.

TABLE OF CONTENTS

Editor's Note

Typographical errors in the original publications, when found, have been corrected. References have been added at the end of Salisbury's articles in cases where such references were originally appended at the end of entire edited volume. The occasional grammatical error, when found, has been corrected.

The article, "An Anthropologist's Use of Historical Methods," was originally an oral presentation. The version here has been edited to enhance clarity in its written form.

Typographical and stylistic differences, which typified the various publications in which Salisbury's articles were published, have been partly modified to create some uniformity of style in the present volume.

My thanks to Professor P.H. Gulliver, York University, for his help in preparing this manuscript; and to Professors Hans Möller and Bruce Trigger, both of McGill University, for their help in expediting the publication of this memorial volume.

Marilyn Silverman
Toronto, 2004

The following have kindly given permission to reproduce materials:

American Anthropologist
>   "Asymmetrical Marriage Systems" (1956), *American Anthropologist* 58, pp. 639-655.

Anthropologica
>   "Structuring Ignorance: The Genesis of a Myth in New Guinea" (1966), *Anthropologica* N.S., Vol. VIII, No. 2, pp.315-328.

>   "Non-equilibrium Models in New Guinea Ecology" (1975), *Anthropologica* 17(2), pp. 127-147.

Institute for Social and Economic Research (ISER), Memorial University of Newfoundland
>   "Transactional Politics: Factions and Beyond" (1977), from Marilyn Silverman and Richard F. Salisbury (eds.), *A House Divided: Anthropological Studies of Factionalism*, pp. 111-127.

Man

> "New Guinea Highland Models and Descent Theory" (1964), *Man* 64 (Nov.-Dec.), pp. 168-171.

McGill University Programme in the Anthropology of Development

> "The Nature of the Present Study" (1972), from *Development and James Bay: Social Implications of the Hydro-electric Proposals*, pp. 1-15.

Royal Society of Canada

> "Application and Theory in Canadian Anthropology: The James Bay Agreement" (1979), from *Transactions of the Royal Society of Canada*, Series IV, Vol. XVII, pp. 229-241.

Salisbury, Mary

> "Siane: The Social Structure of the Siane People, Eastern Highlands, New Guinea" (1954), unpublished report; and "An Anthropologist's Use of Historical Methods" (1967), unpublished paper.

University of California Press

> "Introduction," pp. 1-16; and Chapter X: "Political Consolidation and Economic Development," pp.334-351, from *Vunamami: Economic Transformation in a Traditional Society* (1970).

University of Pittsburgh Press

> "Formal Analysis and Anthropological Economics: The Rossel Island Case" (1968), from Ira R. Buchler and Hugo G. Nutini (eds.), *Game Theory in the Behavioural Sciences.*

> "Anthropology and Economics" (1968), from Otto von Maring and Leonard Kasdan (eds.), *Anthropology and Neighboring Disciplines.*

University Press of America

> "The Economics of Development Through Services: Findings of the McGill Programme Among the Cree" (1988), from John Bennett (ed.), *Production and Autonomy: Anthropological Studies and Critiques of Development.* Society for Economic Anthropology Monographs No. 5, pp. 239-256.

I

IN MEMORIAM ET AD FUTURAM:

THE ANTHROPOLOGY OF RICHARD F. SALISBURY

(1926-1989)

by

Marilyn Silverman

> Crees believe that all honourable men belong to
> the same tribe. Richard Salisbury was an hon-
> ourable man (Philip Aashish, Executive Chief
> of the Grand Council of the Crees of Quebec,
> Memorial service for Richard F. Salisbury,
> September 28, 1989).

It sometimes happens that a profoundly influential and extremely active anthropologist emerges who gains international renown and respect. Such anthropologists spend years in the field, publish widely and intensively, and profoundly affect those around them and those who come after through their writings, teaching, personal dedication and organizational acumen. One such anthropologist was Richard F. Salisbury.

Born in Chelsea, England, in 1926, Salisbury served in the Royal Marines between 1945 and 1948. He then studied Modern Languages at Cambridge University (B.A. 1949), received a certificate in Spanish in 1950 and studied anthropology with Meyer Fortes during 1950-1. He went on to do graduate work in Anthropology at Harvard University (A.M. 1955) and the Australian National University (PhD. 1957). While studying at Harvard, he married Mary Roseborough, a fellow graduate student from Toronto. He taught at the Harvard School of Public Health, Tufts University and the University of California before coming to McGill University in 1962 as an Associate Professor. He remained at McGill for the rest of his life. He was appointed Full Professor in 1966 and, in 1967 and 1984, he held Visiting Professorships at the University of Papua and New Guinea. He was elected to the Royal Society of Canada in 1974, and was awarded the prestigious Killam Foundation Senior Research Fellowship for 1980-82.

During this time, Salisbury was the author (or co-author) of 20 books, monographs and reports, more than 60 articles, and numerous other reviews and commentaries. This immense corpus spanned several locales (New Guinea, Guyana, Canada) and a wide spectrum of anthropological topics: economics, kinship, religion, linguistics, politics, development, and human rights. His numerous insights, theoretical ideas, and applied concerns helped to shape how his generation of scholars around the world did anthropology. They also underlie much of contemporary Canadian anthropology in particular and social anthropology in general. Moreover, Salisbury was not simply a highly productive and influential scholar. He also was a fine teacher who supervised over 30 graduate theses. Through them, and their subsequent careers in anthropology, Salisbury helped to reproduce the discipline both in Canada and abroad.

Salisbury also was extraordinarily active in promoting the organizational and institutional infrastructure of the discipline. The list of his administrative involvements is daunting: from chair of McGill's anthropology department and Dean of Arts to president of five anthropology associations.[1] He served also on the Social Science Research Council of Canada (1969-72), the Academic Advisory Panel of the Canada Council (1974-1978), the Board of the *Institut Québécois de la Recherche sur la Culture* (1979-84), and as Programme Chair for the Eleventh International Congress of Anthropological and Ethnological Sciences (1983). He was co-founder, and later director, of the Centre for Developing Area Studies at McGill, he served on the board of the Canadian Human Rights Foundation, and he was a member of the Quebec Commission on Higher Education (1977). Throughout, he

> combined a career of high-quality scholarly research and active publication with a devotion to teaching, promoting the scholarly growth of social science organizations, and service to the people of Canada and New Guinea. His brilliant intellect, personal integrity, and the energy with which he worked to help others won him widespread admiration (Trigger 1989:3).

****

I enrolled at McGill for graduate studies in anthropology in 1976, drawn mainly by the work of Dick Salisbury and his students at the Programme in the Anthropology of Development. ... As Dick let me know in our

very first conversation, he thought that my
view of the politics of development was overly polarized. ... I thought Dick's view of the
world was too optimistic, assumed too much
liberal *decency* on the part of social actors; and I
certainly let him know. If this ever taxed his
patience, he never lost his humour. He was
adept at seizing the right opportunity to inject
an unsettling comment, question or fact that as
often as not left me with the feeling that *he* was
the realist, not I (Scott 1990:18).

When graduate students returned from the
field, our discussions ... [often] ... took place in
each other's apartments. ... Dick Salisbury was
a frequent visitor at these gatherings, usually
sitting on the floor with four or five students
gathered around. Who can forget those
sparkling eyes, wavy black hair combed straight
back, the omnipresent bow tie, or those large
hands poised in mid-air? (Hedican 1990:16)

****

An academic whose career has spanned 27 years has necessarily
touched many people who retain stories, recollections and memories. Perhaps the
most insightful are those of his students. As both an undergraduate and graduate student at McGill, I have many recollections of Dick. Like others, they offer glimpses
into the style and essence of a fine scholar and mentor.

I recall, for example, how disconcerting it was as an undergraduate
to sit in a small class with a professor who knew so much. In a fourth-year theory class,
in 1966, we were discussing Lévi-Strauss. A question was asked, and Dick proceeded
to answer it. To do so, he gave an impromptu, one-hour lecture on culture and personality theory, Freud and Jung. I remember looking around the room. In typical fashion, we undergraduates had put down our pens for this stuff obviously would not be
on the exam. Yet I remember being profoundly struck, and still am, with the breadth
of his knowledge, with his ability to move into other disciplines, and with his capacity
to pursue issues laterally, into adjacent theoretical areas. This marked not only his
teaching but was an essential part of his ability to contribute theoretically to the
discipline.

But it sometimes made it difficult to follow his thinking. Most of Dick's students can recall his "quizzical look" – which usually followed what the student thought was a particularly erudite question. This look, as I recall it now, came about because, for Dick, the answer was so often self-evident. I remember taking away with me several of his responses which followed on his quizzical look: answers which seemingly were off-topic and not at all self-evident. It would take about 48 hours, a lot of thinking, and occasionally a trip to the library. Then the penny would drop. "Why," I asked one day, "did American acculturation studies move in such a sterile direction?" With a quizzical look, Dick told me that it was the influence of Fred Eggan. I was already on my way to the library before he had finished his sentence.

Sometimes, though, the quizzical look was because Dick genuinely did not understand the student's logic, motivation or, more often, his or her desperate fear of failure. The quizzical look, as I see it now, always meant that he had more faith in us than we had in ourselves. Just before my PhD defence in 1973, I went to his office for some reassurance. I said, trying to be light, that I was very nervous about being able to answer the questions which would be asked. With his quizzical look, Dick blurted out: "But you're the world's expert on the topic. You're the only one who knows the answers!"

Dick taught anthropology, however, not only by in-depth lateral extrapolations and by quizzical looks. He also taught by example; and there was no better model than Dick Salisbury in the field. The Research Institute for the Study of Man (RISM) in New York provided funding for M.A. students from four universities to do field work for the summer of 1966 in the Caribbean. The McGill team, along with Dick, went to Guyana – to a bauxite mining town which he had chosen in the interior, accessible only after an eight-hour boat ride. We all met up in Georgetown, at a hotel. The first afternoon, we met for drinks. At the bar were several West Indian literati. Amongst them, as I remember, were novelists George Lamming and Jan Carew and McGill economist Kari Levitt. The students, along with Dick, joined their group. The students listened in silence to the conversation, feeling tentative, and preferring to explore the taste of real rum. After an hour, the group broke up. Dick disappeared, the students went for a walk. Two hours later we were back in the bar. Dick emerged, waving a sheaf of about a dozen, single-spaced, typed papers. He sat down, handed the papers to us and announced: "These are field notes of the conversation!" And we had thought that he had retired for a nap!

The next day, we went up the Demerara River, to Mackenzie, the mining town. At the time, we wondered why we were going to that particular place. Looking back, the answer is obvious. Dick was concerned with indigenous local development. And Mackenzie, under the aegis of the Alcan Aluminum company, had literally been carved out of the jungle and set up as a company town. Dick saw this as a perfect opportunity to investigate socio-economic change. The students, in the politicized late-1960s, saw it as a case of Canadian colonialism. Dick saw our point, but his quizzical look, which he often wore as we argued this point over the weeks, was that it still provided the chance for original research. The students took the line that, by simply being there, we were lackeys of western imperialism. So Dick was the only one who talked to the expatriate company officials that summer while the students studiously maintained a boycott and talked only to Guyanese. Looking back, I realize that Dick had to exercise the patience of Job that summer and, most importantly, the patience that came from a man secure in his own convictions.

Such generational and political differences, however, were highly instructive – both in theory and practice. In Mackenzie, the students had all moved into a house which Dick had rented from the company. The first morning, Dick arrived – in khaki bermudas and a sports-shirt, carrying a clipboard. Immediately, the thought crossed my mind that the field was clearly a different and liminal place: I had never before seen Dick without a bow tie, and certainly never in shorts. The lesson continued beyond the etiquette of dress in liminal places, however. We students were sitting around, drinking coffee, vaguely thinking that, now that we were in the field, we ought to do field work, and wondering if we were experiencing sufficient culture shock to be allowed to stay home all day. Dick joined us for a cup of coffee. He then stood bolt upright, announced that he had three interviews with Alcan executives set up for the morning, and had to be off. He marched out. A few of us struggled out a few hours later, for our own initial forays, following his example.

An anthropological colleague has since observed that "the hardest thing about field work is getting out of the house in the morning." Dick was a sublime researcher. It came out of the particular kind of detachment, and engagement, which he carried with him to the field and with which he approached other people and places. He became, for many – both students and others – a model to emulate.

> I ended up on the Gazelle Peninsula ... half way between Matupit and Vunamami, where about 25 years earlier Bill Epstein and Richard Salisbury had worked. Frequently I travelled to both places to listen to Tolai telling me their histories. In order to explain what I was doing I only had to refer to my predecessors, who were both held in high esteem, by elders, and by people who had never met them, alike. ... In Vunamami I first elicited no recollections when

I mentioned the name of the scholar who made the village known among anthropologists and historians working in the South Pacific. Soon I found out that Richard Salisbury called himself (or was called?) ToMas. "Oh yes, ToMas, of course." And I was told where he had lived, I was told about his two kids, and that his wife had been such a good dancer of the customary *malagene*. Most of the men ToMas had interviewed were long dead in 1986/88. ...

During ToMas' stay, Vunamami was probably indeed "the most advanced village in New Guinea" (*Vunamami*, p.15). When he wrote about the achievements of Vunamami villagers, his writing reflects their pride. And, in a way, his pride to have been accepted, if only temporarily, as one of them. As one of them, ToMas was a committed advocate of their interests and rights (Neumann 1989:23-4).

Dick also was a model thesis advisor: one who could find money for a graduate student whose funds had run out or who had missed a deadline for a grant competition. He also was extraordinarily prompt and sensitive to the needs of students. Harvey Feit recalls that he gave the final draft of his 1000-page thesis to Dick, for his comments, on a Friday afternoon. The next Monday, Dick gave it back to him, with comments duly written in the margins, along with several, tightly-typed pages of additional comment.

Such commitment to students, whilst respecting always their rights to independent thought and their own visions of their own work, was accompanied, however, by explicit techniques for getting students on-line. Several of us arrived back from the field in 1970, after a year or so of research for our doctorates. We naturally went to see him for the first of what we thought were to be a series of meetings for discussing our theses. He told each of us that he was very glad to see us back, and wondered had we written our Conclusions yet. The response of a surprised "no" elicited his comment that we should begin our theses with the Conclusions and that we should come back to see him when they were done. I disappeared for three months, struggling, as he knew I would, with the central issue of what exactly I was going to do with a trunk full of data and only a vague idea of what it all added up to. I never did write the Conclusions at that time. But I was forced into doing a lot of thinking about what exactly I wanted my thesis to be. I now use the technique with my own graduate students. They also never write the Conclusions first and, in fact, I don't really expect them to. But the task, especially if I keep a stern face while setting it, certainly centres their thinking. I have often wondered though, but never remembered to ask, if Dick wrote his Conclusions first.

****

In academia today, the pressure for theoretical novelty is so great that intellectual approaches are old before their implications have been thoroughly explored and young followers of particular gurus barely have time to write their dissertations before their modes of reasoning have been rendered obsolete. In such an atmosphere of rapid change, the new must be quickly and dramatically legitimized and, for this to happen, dialectical reasoning requires that the old must be trashed. Indeed, "as each successive approach carries the ax to its predecessors, anthropology comes to resemble a project in intellectual deforestation" (Wolf 1990:588). In such a context, a discipline is in great danger of losing sight of its roots, of its own history – as the new not only displaces the old but also designates the past as irrelevant, ignores its essential place in the present, and denies it a role for the future. The present volume is in small part an effort to restore some balance: to take the opportunity to explore our shared anthropological past, to bring that past forward into the present, and to try to ensure that the past will extend into our future.

When Dick Salisbury died at the very untimely age of 62, he left behind not only a massive corpus of work, but also a younger generation of social anthropologists whom he had trained at McGill. Four of us, all academic anthropologists, decided that his life and work should be celebrated. In the ordinary course of time, had Dick enjoyed a normal span of years, we would have prepared a festschrift in his honour. Now that he was gone, we asked ourselves what we might do to honour his work, express thanks for his accomplishments and speak to his present place in anthropology. A book made up of our own articles on diverse topics, *in memoriam*, would not have accomplished this: it would have shown too little of Dick, the depth of his work, and the extent of his contribution to contemporary anthropology. So we decided on something different. Given his extraordinary influence on anthropology, and given his extensive publications and the facts that a few pieces have never been published while others are scattered in difficult-to-get-at places, we decided that it was important to produce a readily-available collection of his writings.

We also decided, however, that we did not want the book to be seen as having only an antiquarian value. Rather, we wanted to show how Dick's work,

7

and the issues which he confronted and raised, are also relevant to anthropology, to the academy, and to a younger generation in the present. We therefore decided to contextualise his writings: to provide background essays on the kind of anthropology which he did, the context in which he did it, and the implications which it has for contemporary anthropology.

To do this, we divided the volume into five sections, each reflecting one of Dick's major analytical or empirical areas and each reflecting as well a period of his career. Each section was assigned to a contributor(s) who chose which of Dick's many writings to include and who wrote an introductory essay for the section. Our aim was to bring together the most representative materials and to bring out, as well, those which have never been published. Our concern also was to produce a volume which had an historical authenticity: about an anthropologist who worked at a particular time and in particular socio-historical contexts, who had an impact on another generation, and who confronted theoretical and applied issues which still are central to the discipline. Finally, our goal was to provide a volume which would be of interest to numerous constituencies: to those who are involved in economic and/or political anthropology; to those who are concerned with the anthropology of development and public policy; to those who work in Melanesia and amongst Native Peoples; and to those who wish to learn something about what it was like to be a social anthropologist in Quebec and Canada in the 1960s, 1970s and 1980s.

NOTES

1. Salisbury served as Chair of the Anthropology Department at McGill (1966-70) and as Dean of Arts (1986-89). He served, *inter alia*, as President of the Canadian Sociology and Anthropology Association (1968-1970), the Northeastern Anthropological Association (1968), the American Ethnological Society (1980), the Society for Economic Anthropology (1982), and the Society for Applied Anthropology in Canada (1986). See Scott's essay, section VI of this volume for a more detailed rendering of Salisbury's immense contribution.

REFERENCES

Aronson, Dan. 1989/90. "In Memoriam: Richard F. Salisbury, 1926-1989." *McGill News*, Winter.

Feit, Harvey. A. 1983. "An Anthropologist as Primitive Man." Unpublished address. May.

Hedican, Edward. 1990. "Richard Salisbury's Anthropology: A Personal Account." *Culture* X(1).

Neumann, Klaus. 1989. "Richard Salisbury." *Anthropology Today* 5(6).

Salzman, Philip. 1989. "Richard F. Salisbury: An Appreciation." *Newsletter*, Faculty of Arts, McGill University. Fall.

Scott, Colin. 1990. "Some Thoughts on Regional Development and the Canadian North in the Work of Richard F. Salisbury." *Culture* X(1).

Tremblay, Marc Adélard. 1989. "In Memoriam: Richard Frank Salisbury, 1926-1989." Address given September 28, McGill University.

Trigger, Bruce C. 1989. "In Memoriam: Richard Frank Salisbury." *Proactive: Society of Applied Anthropology in Canada* 8(2).

Wolf, Eric R. 1990. "Distinguished Lecture: Facing Power - Old Insights, New Questions." *American Anthropologist* 92(3).

II

ETHNOGRAPHY AND SOCIAL STRUCTURE

IN NEW GUINEA: THE EARLY YEARS

by

Henry J. Rutz

There is no more abstract and formal part of anthropological science than kinship, or so it would seem. Irrelevant and out of reach to undergraduate minds, confounding to graduate students for whom kinship is a dry academic *rite de passage* on their way to becoming a Ph.D., the promise of every paradigm in the history of anthropological ideas nevertheless has been etched in debates about kinship. Kinship's favourite word is 'structure.' Indeed, 'social structure' is virtually synonymous with kinship in the anthropological literature, denoting principles from which patterned social meaning and action are derived. In 1952, when a young and uninitiated Richard Salisbury went to do fieldwork in the New Guinea highlands, the French anthropologist Lévi-Strauss (1969 [1949]) had recently published his monumental contribution to kinship studies, in which he attempted to show that patterns of marriage alliance resulting from an exchange of women could be deduced by following through the logic of different *marriage rules*. In contrast, several decades of British anthropologists' work on kinship in Africa was about to be summed up in the publication of Fortes' (1953) seminal paper, in which he argued that *descent principles* were the foundation of social structure, from which marriage practices were derived. The stage was set for a prolonged debate, from the mid-1950s to the mid-1960s, between so-called 'descent' and 'alliance' theorists over the best way to solve a number of cultural puzzles in apparently disparate 'systems of consanguinity and affinity in the human family.'[1] But the greater relevance of the debate on kinship lay in its promise of clarifying the epistemological foundations of a generalizing science of culture by working through a tangle of problems in phenomena of primordial significance to every human society. In little more than a decade, every practitioner with a claim to leadership in the field of social theory carved out a position on the implications of alliance or descent theory for solving the complex cultural puzzles in apparently disparate 'systems of consanguinity and affinity.'

Richard Salisbury was no exception. His very first publications, entitled "Unilineal Descent Groups in the New Guinea Highlands" (1956a) and "Asymmetrical Marriage Systems" (1956b), appeared in *Man* and *American*

11

Anthropologist, the flagship journals of the Royal Anthropological Institute of Great Britain and Ireland and of the American Anthropological Association, respectively. His other contribution was a clarification of his earlier position, published several years later in *Man* under the title "New Guinea Highland Models and Descent Theory" (1964). This kind of exposure assured Salisbury of a wide readership among anthropologists on both sides of the Atlantic, one which would be receptive to *From Stone to Steel* (1962), his book-length ethnography on the Siane of the New Guinea Highlands.

Today, a subject so full of promise for a generalizing science has lost its appeal for most practitioners. In marked contrast to the quest for grand kinship theory that would discover general, if not universal, rules or principles underlying diverse kinship practices, anthropologists now are intent on particularizing social practices, taking the arbitrariness of the 'sign' as a point of departure for discovering ever more ambiguity and ambivalence in social action, requiring 'deeper' (more contextualized) interpretations that result in multiple competing voices, none of which are presumed to be authoritative, either on the part of the anthropologist or his/her native informants. The ethnography of kinship, denoting some of the most prosaic practices in every society, such as being a 'bachelor,' having a 'spouse,' sharing the 'same blood,' knowing your 'kin,' learning all the categories of 'person' to which people attach social meanings such as 'friend,' 'stranger' or 'enemy,' or toward whom they express such emotions as 'love,' 'sympathy,' 'affection,' 'trust,' and 'pride,' is alive and well, if only because every anthropologist's encounter with real people in a fieldwork setting brings her/him literally face to face with the problems of learning not only kin categories and meanings but also the sentiments and emotions that accompany such acts as 'generosity,' 'selfishness,' and claims of 'possession' or 'propriety' which constitute people's everyday lives. And when an anthropologist writes about one culture for an audience from another, problems of ambiguity in interpretation are unavoidable. Emphasis in the ethnography of kinship has shifted from rules and relationships to perception, feeling, and experience. Along with that shift has come new methodological problems of interpretation in the process of fieldwork, theory and ethnography.

It so happens that Salisbury also was intensely interested in the interplay among fieldwork, ethnography and theory, but he would never imagine the task of ethnography to be interpretation without evaluation, nor would he think there was any other purpose for the particularistic than to advance a generalizing science of culture. His methodological tenets and writings on social structure in the 1950s and 60s do not seem out of place with the temperament of the 1990s, but there has been a definite shift in emphasis that would baffle him. Notwithstanding his contributions to kinship theory, the importance today of his early years lies primarily in what they reveal about how Salisbury wrestled with problems of interpretation and analysis.

12

While writing about social structure in the context of a 'distant' theoretical debate on kinship and the 'nearness' of his recently completed fieldwork, Salisbury settled on methodological tenets that later would guide his most significant contributions, those which helped to shape emerging sub-disciplines of political (Part III), economic (Part IV), and development anthropology (Part V), the subject of the remainder of this volume.

Salisbury maintained that bad kinship theory was the result of bad fieldwork. This dictum later became a refrain played out in his contributions to other sub-disciplines of anthropology and may be considered to be his main methodological tenet. To put it positively, 'ethnography' was the medium through which theory and fact reached their own accommodation, the validity of which rested primarily on the authority of the fieldworker and her/his familiarity with categories and concepts of those among whom s/he lived, whether that was the Siane people or colleagues 'back home.' For Salisbury, numbers also 'count.' His interpretations and analyses are sprinkled with the significance of numbers, and he exhorted his students not to ignore them in their own fieldwork. Whenever possible, statistics should be collected in the light of native cultural models, which were themselves first order abstractions from patterns of social action. He sided unequivocally with Lévi-Strauss and Leach, however, when he said 'I feel that the empirical reality is best understood in the light of a model so derived [as a formal abstraction from the rules], rather than vice versa' (1964:171). The anthropologist had an obligation to draw her/his own inferences, including those which contradicted native models when these contradicted their own behaviour. Ethnography was something more than the interpretation of others' interpretations of themselves. It was also an evaluation of those interpretations in the light of non-self-evident statements about possible or probable practices that were not actual, i.e., did not appear directly in the actions observed or ideas elicited. Salisbury's contributions to studies of social structure rest squarely on fieldwork practices among the Siane and strategies he adopted for writing about Siane culture. At the same time, he urged theorists to build models that would raise questions about actual systems from the standpoint of possible ones.

This complicated but coherent view of the task of writing about social structure, one in which 'ethnography' is the product of an interpretive process by which empirically-informed theory and theory-guided fieldwork are hammered out *and evaluated by the anthropologist*, informs us about Salisbury's approach to the debate on kinship.[2]

ETHNOGRAPHY OF SIANE SOCIAL STRUCTURE

To illustrate this, and to situate Salisbury's theoretical contributions to kinship in the context of fieldwork and ethnography, I have chosen for inclusion in this volume, first, an excerpt from a very early, unpublished report (Chapter II.1) and, second, a published article on the making of a Siane myth (Chapter II.2).

The report, written by Salisbury for S.F. Nadel at the Australian National University in 1954, was entitled *Siane: The Social Structure of the Siane People, Eastern Highlands, New Guinea*. In it, the central chapters concern "Internal Structure of the Clan," "Inter-group Relationships" and "Marriage." Other chapters on ritual and spirit beliefs, the symbolism of ceremonies, property ownership and the economics of distribution describe various Siane practices within the framework of analysis he adopted in chapters on marriage and descent.[3] I have selected for this volume a section entitled "Kinship," excerpted from Chapter 3, "Internal Structure of the Clan and the Child's Adaptation to It." This first attempt at writing about Siane kinship, at a moment when Salisbury was still close to his fieldwork experience, contrasts sharply with his first published articles on the subject two years later, when he was more distant from fieldwork but closer to his professional audience. In "Kinship," he adopts an ethnographic strategy of introducing his readers to Siane culture through the experience of an everychild who must learn to feel and comprehend what is conceptualized as 'kinship.'

I first saw this unpublished report when Marilyn Silverman sent me a copy and asked me to consider making a selection from it for this volume. My initial reaction was negative. It was 'too discursive,' not sufficiently 'analytical' to warrant inclusion. At that time, I saw no point to including material from a first fieldwork experience, most of which needed to be rewritten, edited, and reworked for publication in a professional style and format suitable for the best journals. Presumably, Salisbury himself had similar thoughts. It sat on my shelf for over a year as I began to think about how Dick kept going back to the insights he gained in the field for building models that would improve the analytical and interpretive power of ethnography. His published work is full of details from the field, so much so that the reader cannot miss the point that getting it right at 'ground zero' was of paramount importance to him. He loved bringing out his field journal and giving a lecture from it on specific events, persons, places, and dates. On my first meeting with him after I returned to Montreal from fieldwork in Fiji in April of 1970, he took his notebook, on which there was a list of questions, and immediately quizzed me about details concerning Fijian grammar and vocabulary, which he wanted to compare with Tolai, a language spoken by a people of New Britain about whom he wrote in *Vunamami* (1970), his most ambitious ethnography.

So I reread the report from the viewpoint of an ethnography 'closer' to the source of fieldwork, more akin to a field journal than to a published ethnography, and at the greatest 'distance' from a professional journal article; and it took on a new life. The writing is plain English, uncomplicated, free from jargon, and unmediated by methodological considerations or complicated analyses that distance an author from his fieldwork and from his readers. In short, it was entirely different from the demands of 'theory' and the standards of publication in professional journals. His writing style gives the reader an impression, a confidence one might say, that the author is 'on the scene,' surrounded by Siane going about their daily lives while he is there to record in minute detail every act and utterance. The narrator, however, is not in the text except to inform the reader of an omission or incompleteness of detail. Salisbury helps the reader's sense of being there by avoiding distantiating techniques such as inducing culture shock, indulging romantic dispositions, or persuading by rhetorical flourish. The most important way in which the reader is drawn into the concreteness of Siane life, however, is Salisbury's imagining of an everychild's experience of growing up among those around her/him. Early childhood experiences are shaped by the significance of 'kinship' as the child first feels, and only later becomes cognizant of, what every Siane adult 'knows' about her/his world of significant social relations.

In "Kinship," the specific topic is one of the driest and most formal of all topics in social structure, to wit, kinship terminology. The normal way in which this subject is introduced in most anthropological monographs is to present a synoptic chart which shows the various categories of person ('mother,' 'aunt,' 'cousin,' etc.), assign a type name from a taxonomy of anthropological types according to features (sex, generation, seniority, etc.), and offer an explanation by reference to the descent and marriage rules that make sense of the categories in terms of the social relationships they express. Alternatively, the categories of person may be abstracted and analysed 'ethno-semantically' as a coherent system of meaning and communication, free from encumbering practices. But Salisbury backgrounds all the terms and relationships of 'structure,' choosing instead to evoke for the reader a Siane child's-eye-view of the concrete experiences of learning how to feel and what to think about members of her/his own clan. He succeeds in this artifice only to the extent that he already has cognized Siane social structure sufficiently to allow the reader to learn categorical distinctions slowly, the way a child might – one concrete experience at a time.

The child-reader at first feels that her/his needs for affection and attention are met by specific others. The concrete modality of learning is affect, or what some might now call a 'structure of feeling' (Williams 1973: 35). The child slowly learns that 'love,' 'respect,' and other sentiments are *social*, i.e., they are distributed unevenly among persons and mapped onto *named* categories of person. The child of Salisbury's narrative is not a real child, one whom he can follow through socialization, anymore than he can have direct knowledge of a child's cognitive or emotional development. Rather, it is an imaginative rendering of a thousand detailed observations and elicitations, influenced by Salisbury's theoretical predispositions, hidden from view. He allows the reader to learn about this aspect of Siane social structure as if s/he were like a Siane everychild. What makes it all work is the description, at every point in the process, of concrete experiences about emotions that will later be cognized as *socially* distributed by generalized rules, norms, and values.

The sequence begins with the child's concrete experiences with a woman who will become known to the child as 'true mother' (to be distinguished from other women who will be called 'mother'). Later, the needs fulfilled by the true mother are transferred to a girl who will become known to the child as 'older true sister' (to be distinguished from all 'sisters' who, although they fulfill the same need, do so with different intensities of emotional involvement). A little later, a child learns that one boy is particularly protective, one who will come to be known as 'older brother' (to be distinguished from all 'brothers' by becoming a father surrogate). And so on through a general and gradual shift from family-centred to peer group-centred experiences transformed into relationships for both boys and girls who, by age six, feel and know the significance of 'age-mate' terms. As the sequence unfolds, 'the kinship structure of our clan is simply understood by the child.' And, one might add, by the reader. At this point Salisbury introduces a Siane kin terminology chart, and from that point he proceeds to an account of how the male child maps names of gardens onto categories of person by following his father around all day, learns to be more generous with small gifts toward some men than others, distinguishes a 'namesake' as someone who, like certain 'elders,' is deserving of special affection and respect, and so on through the permutations of the kin classification system. Around age six, each Siane feels and knows that s/he has a personal identity (affective, cognitive, moral, material, and meaningful) as a member of a group of 'kin.' In the following sections of the chapter, the reader learns that what makes sense of all this concrete experience, which is what Mauss explored in *The Gift* (1967 [1925]) as a total social fact, is the concept of 'unilineal descent group.'

Along the way, Salisbury reveals a great deal about how kin terminologies are practised in ways absent from most orthodox ethnographic accounts. He never lets the coherence of the classification system take precedence over the varieties of experience that are a part of context and situation. The terminology remains partial and must be 'filled in' by the exigencies of experience. One cannot deduce the whole range of observed practices from the rules of using kin terms, which always remain contextualized and partially coherent. For Salisbury, situation and action take methodological precedence over rule.

16

In "Structuring Ignorance: The Genesis of a Myth in New Guinea" (1966), an article Salisbury placed in a Canadian journal at a time when he was helping to establish Canadian anthropology as an independent tradition, Salisbury is at his ethnographic best (Chapter II.2, this volume). The article ostensibly is about how myths originate, couched in the context of a critique of explanations of myth put forward by French and British structuralists, mostly the same persons who enter into the debate on kinship. As the title suggests, however, the relevant question is "How do social phenomena become 'structured'?" This question underlies much of Salisbury's theorizing about social and economic development. It is not about the elementary structures of the unconscious mind as revealed in the myth and its given variants, as Lévi-Strauss would have it, nor is it merely about how given myths perform the function of a charter, legitimizing the social structure, as British social anthropologists would have it. It is, rather, about the process of myth-making itself, conceived as a process of 'structuring.'[4] In a word, it is post-structuralist, more in tune with the current trend than with a debate in which both sides shared the idea that rules were given features of the explanatory frameworks of analysis. Most of the article is about the interests and intentions of the myth-makers and their shifting audiences, and about the social construction of the presuppositions that go into the telling of a 'true' story. The structuring takes place during the retelling of the story, augmenting and modifying it as events unfold.[5] Even more in keeping with the present fashion rather than with that of his contemporaries, Salisbury-the-author places himself squarely in the process of improvisation, telling the reader that he asked to accompany his informants on a visit to an area a day's walk from his residence to see the site of a salt spring that was rumoured to have been discovered. The day for the visit was changed to accommodate his plans. In fact, as Salisbury-the-fieldworker, he becomes at times the main audience for the developing myth, someone who can and does influence the selection process.

The reader is told the date and exact location of the rumoured discovery, the name of the person who comes to tell Salisbury about it, and the residence of the fieldworker when the latter first hears the story. All these details take on their significance later, when the author steps back from the narrative sequence of events to analyse and interpret the process of myth-making. Salisbury-the-ethnographer tells his story about how the original myth is modified as Salisbury-the-fieldworker traverses the space between his own residence and a neighbouring linguistic area where the spring is located.[6] All the details of where he is, whom he encounters, and who makes additions, modifications, and corrections to the original myth add to the cultural puzzle of how a myth becomes structured.

Not only is the fieldworker present in the text as a member of the myth-makers' audience, but he also influences their story by his interrogation. The

17

ethnographer reappears in the narrative portion of his own text when he tells his readers that the fieldworker became 'impatient' with the behaviour of his hosts and 'suspicious' about one myth-maker's radical corrections to other versions. At this point, to his Siane audience the ethnographer appears to be obsessed by 'the facts' and driven to raise questions about the veracity of different accounts in ways that are irrelevant to them.

Salisbury-the-ethnographer divides the non-narrative portion of the text into 'analysis' and 'interpretation.' In his analysis, he points out that the owners of the salt spring were not the inventors of the myth. Owners not only rejected myth-makers' beliefs about supernatural intervention in its discovery, thereby rejecting those beliefs as a charter for legitimate ownership, they also denied the very existence of a salt spring. But the Siane, who were ignorant of the discovery (literally, at some distance from 'the facts') were more easily convinced of its existence and made myths about how the discovery came about. The Siane showed 'intense interest' in establishing the 'true' story and meaning of every event, but ignorance of events close to the source allowed them rhetorical sway. The process was one of arguing different versions before successive audiences, which then selected a 'true' version. Salisbury noticed that the rhetorical story-teller had an advantage over a 'factual reporter.' The audience, with the exception of Salisbury-the-fieldworker, was never very interested in getting the details about the discovery of the salt spring. They were satisfied merely in confirmation of the rumour about its existence. 'As the story was repeated, elements taken as true became more and more like myths already familiar to the listeners.' Salisbury goes on to describe how the audience listened for symbolic elements and fantastic relations that make intelligible 'real' events in the myth-makers' stories, events such as finding a real salt spring, real death payments, real animals killed in a hunt, deaths of real persons, and real accidents that happen along paths on mountain ridges.

Salisbury's interpretation of the structuring of ignorance is based on his assertion that Siane make no clear distinction between 'fact' and 'imagination.' The relevant differentiation upon which the selection of a story is based is between story-tellers who have the 'true' (*ona*) story and those who 'lie' (*suki*), i.e., those who do not use recognizable symbolic codes to make plausible connections. Story-tellers make incremental additions and modifications to previous story-tellers' versions, and some are so bold as to make 'corrections.' But there is no point to criticism beyond fitting the story to often vague symbolic relations, nor do audiences question 'the facts.' They do, however, recognize the 'correctness' of a myth when they hear one. And some are more 'correct' than others because they include the necessary symbolic connections to supernatural phenomena that confirm Siane beliefs about what must be 'true' for such a discovery to occur.

Aside from the processes of discovery and experience in fieldwork and writing, Salisbury's contributions to the most abstract and formal aspects of kinship theory involve Siane ethnography and middle range model-building for purposes of comparative generalization. Such models go beyond the empirical reality to explore relationships that are possible as well as actual. They aspire to both the complexity and intelligibility of the diversity of kinship practices that get underneath a deductive logic of practices that 'must' follow from stipulated marriage rules or descent principles, as well as rising above an empiricist approach that would limit its inferences to what is actual at a given moment. Salisbury's immediate aim was to make more coherent and intelligible the Melanesian literature as variants of supposedly universal rules of social structure. In "Asymmetrical Marriage Systems"(1956b), included here as Chapter II.3, and in "New Guinea Highlands Models and Descent Theory" (1962), Chapter II.4, Salisbury drew on all three methodological tenets – that bad theory is the result of bad fieldwork, the primacy of action over rule, the relation between behaviour and culture is complex – to find his own intellectual space within the debate on kinship theory.[7]

Salisbury admired Lévi-Strauss's tour de force of marriage systems (1969 [1949]), but he pointed out in "Asymmetrical Marriage Systems" that Lévi-Strauss had conflated a *rule* for marriage with the *transactions* that occur in it. This had led Lévi-Strauss to make generalizations about how such systems *must* work. Leach (1951) had already discovered one counter-case in the Kachin of Burma, and Salisbury claimed that the Siane were another, but different, counter-case.

A very brief overview of alliance theory is necessary to grasp the direction in which Salisbury took Lévi-Strauss. Lévi-Strauss had focussed on marriage systems he termed 'elementary,' by which he meant the exchange of sisters, unmediated by prestations of another kind or order. He further viewed these systems in terms of their 'structure.' This led him to define and analyse the systems as systems of *rules*. There were two types of structure for elementary systems. One was 'restricted' exchange, by which he meant a prescriptive marriage rule that would result in the *direct* exchange of sisters, the group that received sisters sending its own sisters to the group that gave sisters. The other was 'generalized' exchange, by which he meant a prescriptive rule that would result in the *indirect* exchange of sisters, the group that received sisters sending its own sisters to at least a third group, which in turn would give sisters to the first group. To create a *symmetrical* generalized system, Lévi-Strauss reasoned, the system must be circular, i.e., specific groups had to exchange with each other in such a way that the 'first' group which gave wives would receive them from the 'last' group in the sequence. Because Lévi-Strauss thought about these systems abstractly, as systems of marriage rules (e.g., matrilateral cross-cousin marriage [MCCM] or patrilateral cross-cousin marriage [PCCM]), the number of marriages didn't matter, nor did the particularities of the transactions of women for goods. So long as the rule was fulfilled by at least one marriage between specific groups in at least one generation, with or without 'prestations,' the system was 'symmetrical.' An 'asymmetrical' system was one in which that chain was broken, leaving, as it were, every group exposed to an uncertain future about where they would receive or send women.

By following through the logical implications of MCCM and PCCM rules, with limited data on actual marriage practices, including number of women, number of groups, number of goods, and degree of exposure *over time*, Lévi-Strauss was led to conclude that a prescriptive MCCM rule would maintain a symmetrical system through every generation, but that a prescriptive PCCM rule would do so only for alternate generations. Leach (1951) applied these conclusions to the Kachin of Burma, who had a MCCM rule but, he concluded, an asymmetrical marriage system. Leach suggested that the answer lay in looking at the political and economic context of marriage, including hierarchical relations of wife-givers and wife-receivers, and the counter-flow of prestations against the exchange of women, in order to think through the implications of a system of generalized marriage exchange based on a prescriptive MCCM rule.

Salisbury jumped into the breach created by Leach and carried his implications to their logical conclusion, ultimately concluding in "Asymmetrical Marriage Systems" that the Siane marriage system was another variant of a set of complementary models that needed to be formulated to increase the power of Lévi-Strauss's initial insights. Along the way, however, he refined Lévi-Strauss's concepts and substituted a transactional approach to the problems posed by Lévi-Strauss's Cartesian kinship. Space does not allow me to develop this approach in sufficient depth to show how his nuanced and sensitive handling of Siane marriage practices is used to refine Lévi-Strauss's whole framework of analysis. Suffice to say that Salisbury's empirical analysis of Siane marriage transactions is among the most precise and detailed in all the literature on kinship. And he deployed a political economy of kinship approach to the Siane marriage system that he later developed for all his other contributions to political, economic and applied anthropology: for Lévi-Strauss to draw his conclusions, he would have to analyse the 'distribution of women, power, and goods,' all of which are 'commodities that can be used as prestations.'

The Siane system of commodity exchange was kin-ordered (Wolf 1981), not capitalist, and Salisbury not only provided the conceptual framework for concluding that the Siane had a variant of a prescriptive PCCM system *in practice*, he also had sufficiently detailed quantitative data on marriage transactions, including the number of marriages to different specific groups over time, and the counter prestations in goods, to conclude that the *actual* marriage practices contradicted the Siane cultural model premised on a MCCM rule along with their deeply held belief that they practised it. He might have left it as a matter of fact, but he went on to explain this contradiction by showing that Siane have been caught in a particular political position within the larger regional commodity system. This bit of ethnography done, he then presents the reader with a plausible model of regional instability that would result in further variants in the marriage systems of other societies within the regional system, one that would account for the empirical distribution of women, power, and goods that he thinks exists but for which he has insufficient documentation from fieldwork.

As for Lévi-Strauss's claim that rules are necessary for marriage systems to be either symmetrical or asymmetrical, and his claim that different systems are derived from the rules, Salisbury used Siane ethnography to show that a particular pattern of practices does not *necessarily* require a rule. Instead, he attempted to show that they did have a rule, but that it was the wrong one to understand their marriage transactions. The more likely model was one which took into account the pattern of resource distribution, including the distribution of political power (not all of which is in the hands of men when it comes to marriage choices). The Siane had only partial information because of their place in a regional commodity system which included the exchange of women. Further, Lévi-Strauss and Leach both show that there *may* be rules but, in their respective cases, similar rules operate in significantly different circumstances and contexts to produce opposite results (MCCM associated with a symmetrical system in the case of Lévi-Strauss, an asymmetrical system in the case of Leach).

Despite Salisbury's detailed description of a marriage system with a prescribed patrilateral cross-cousin marriage rule, some theorists in the alliance vs. descent debate continued to assert on logical grounds of inconsistency that a prescriptive PCCM rule was 'impossible.' Salisbury published "New Guinea Highlands Models and Descent Theory" (1964) in response to their 'failure to consider the ethnographical evidence.' He makes clear in the article (Chapter II.4) that the failure is due to rethinking kinship theory as an exercise in logic to be performed on some formal and abstract system of rules. The prevailing scholarly mood of that time prevented this privileged domain of analysis from opening up to currents of intellectual change.

The article is reprinted here for two reasons. Drawing on his ethnography of Siane marriage transactions in "Asymmetrical Marriage Systems," and combining it with his ethnography of descent groups in "Unilineal Descent Groups in the New Guinea Highlands" (1956a), he brought the issues of the alliance and descent debate together by showing how both are deficient for building models of kinship that account for marriage practices given in ethnographic descriptions based on careful fieldwork. The more important reason for making this article more widely accessible, however, is that it reflects Salisbury's determination to 'stay the course' by encouraging a more comparative and generalizing framework for kinship based on models that would capture all the variants of a system, actual and possible. This was his last published work specifically on kinship, but he continued for two more decades to use models to make better ethnography (in this volume, see section III, especially III.5, and Part IV, especially IV.9 and IV.11).

Aknowledgement

I am grateful to Doris Rutz for helping to shape some of the ideas in this essay and to Marilyn Silverman for encouraging me to look more closely at some of Salisbury's early writings.

Notes

1. The third main entrant to the kinship debate was a book co-authored by an American sociologist and anthropologist. Homans and Schneider (1955) attempted to mediate the debate between two kinds of structuralism, French and British. This work is important in the present context because Salisbury acknowledged the suggestions given him by David Schneider in "Asymmetrical Marriage Systems" (1956b) and the latter's great influence on his argument in "New Guinea Highland Models and Descent Theory." (1964) Schneider (1965) published his own account of the debate on kinship, in which he reciprocated by saying that he had profited from the suggestions of Salisbury. They were colleagues at the University of California at Berkeley from 1957-62, and both shared the common experience of having been at the Harvard School of Social Relations when Talcott Parsons was developing his social systems approach to society, culture and personality in the early 1950s. In his "Preface" to *From Stone to Steel* (1962: xiii), Salisbury recounts how he joined a group headed by Parsons and Smelser, who were working on the final revision of *Economy and Society.* (1965 [1957]) Salisbury stated 'It immediately became apparent that the substance of my study was an independent confirmation of many of the analyses contained in their work. It was arrived at inductively from the consideration of the economic concepts used by the Siane, whereas their analyses had been deductive starting from Dr. Parsons' general theory of action.' Salisbury was a postgraduate student of S.F. Nadel at the Australian National University when he did his fieldwork among the Siane people. Nadel (1951, 1957) at that time was making his own contributions to studies of social structure, and it was he who encouraged Salisbury to use his fieldwork data on Siane marriage practices to rethink Lévi-Strauss's theory of marriage systems. After Salisbury had published his initial contributions, influential works by Leach (1961) and Needham (1962) appeared, prompting Salisbury to write his 1964 article on modelling kinship.

2.   For some contemporaries, the debate on kinship seemed less about abstract theories and more about the cultures that influenced them. Lewis (1973) wondered aloud whether the difference between alliance and descent *theories* might not really be a difference between kinship practices in the culture areas where theoreticians had done fieldwork. Those who favoured marriage alliance theories had done fieldwork primarily in Latin America or Southeast Asia, whereas those who favoured descent theories had worked primarily in Africa. Scholte (1966) took a slightly different tack by pointing out that the differences seemed to be less about the consistency and coherence of the theories than about differences between Anglo-empirical and French cartesian world views.

3.   Stanner (1962: v), in his "Foreword" to *From Stone to Steel*, records that 'the Siane project' was part of S.F. Nadel's plan to do the social structure and religion of little known groups living in the New Guinea Highlands. The Siane were first sighted by explorers in 1933, 'but no other Europeans did so until after the war,' when the Australian administration sent patrol officers into Siane territory. Salisbury was the first anthropologist to live among Siane people. The organization of his dissertation reflects the demands of a comparative project and the constraints of documenting the life of an uncharted human group.

4.   The methodology developed here, which is also apparent in the section on "Kinship" in his dissertation, parallels, to a remarkable degree, that which J. Piaget referred to in "Genesis and Structure in the Psychology of Intelligence." (1968 [1956]). Piaget laments the absence of genesis in theories of structure and of structure in theories of genesis in the field of developmental psychology.

5.   The main argument of "Structuring Ignorance" is an excellent example of what P. Bourdieu was searching for and found in his concept of 'habitus', which appeared in translation as "Structures and Habitus" in *Outline of a Theory of Practice* (1977 [1972]: 72-95) too late for Salisbury to make note of it.

6.   The narrative of traversing symbolically rich topography while retelling stories of supernatural influence on social facts is reminiscent of the beginning of Lévi-Strauss's justly famous structural analysis of myth in "The Story of Asdiwal." (1976) The contrasting analyses, however, are revealing. Lévi-Strauss argued that all the variants of a myth must be used to discover the unconscious patterning of culture that takes place in the human mind. Salisbury argued that variants of a myth had to be understood processually by knowing the context for the genesis of a myth, but he acknowledged that the Siane interpretation of 'myth' in general was framed by a Siane concept of 'truth.'

7.   Salisbury meant by 'complex' the shared beliefs informants held about their own actions and the apparent contradiction between those beliefs and the observations recorded by the anthropologist. The empirical content of both beliefs and observations may be too incomplete to support the knowledge claims of either the informant or anthropologist. Because this problem plagued all social phenomena, Salisbury sided with Leach and Lévi-Strauss in their claim that valid generalizations had to be derived from models which went beyond mere patterns that were realized and empirically verifiable to those that were possible but unrealized. Lévi-Strauss used this methodology to support arguments about the unconscious patterning of culture by the human mind. Salisbury interpreted the variants of myth as the product of a process of structuring that, in the final analysis, left structure open to contingent variation and structural change.

References

Barnes, J.A. 1962. "African Models in the New Guinea Highlands." *Man* 62, 2.

Bourdieu, Pierre. 1977 [1972]. "Structures and the Habitus." *Outline of a Theory of Practice*. New York: Cambridge University Press: 72-95.

Fortes, Meyer. 1953. "The Structure of Unilineal Descent Groups." *American Anthropologist* 55:17-41.

Homans, G.C. and D. M. Schneider. 1955. *Marriage, Authority and Final Causes*. Glencoe: The Free Press.

Leach, E.R. 1951. "Structural Implications of Matrilateral Cross-cousin Marriage." *Journal of the Royal Anthropological Institute* 81:23.

------------1961. *Rethinking Anthropology*. London: Athlone Press.

Lévi-Strauss, Claude. 1969 [1949]. *The Elementary Structures of Kinship*. Boston: Beacon Press.

------------1976. "The Story of Asdiwal." *Structural Anthropology*, Vol. 2. New York: Basic Books: 459-81.

Lewis, Ioan. 1973. "The Anthropologist's Muse. An Inaugural Lecture." London School of Economics and Political Science. Welwyn Garden City, Hertfordshire: The Broadwater Press Ltd.

Mauss, Marcel. 1967 [1925] . *The Gift*. New York: W.W. Norton.

Nadel, S.F. 1951. *The Foundations of Social Anthropology*. New York: Free Press.

------------1957. *The Theory of Social Structure*. New York: Free Press.

Needham, R. 1962. *Structure and Sentiment*. Chicago: University of Chicago Press.

Piaget, Jean. 1967 [1964]. "Genesis and Structure in the Psychology of Intelligence," in Elkind, David (ed.), *Six Psychological Studies*. New York: Random House: 143-58.

Parsons, Talcott and Neil Smelser. 1965. *Economy and Society*. New York: Free Press.

Salisbury, R. F. 1954. The Social Structure of the Siane People, Eastern Highlands, New Guinea. Unpublished PhD Dissertation. Canberra: Australian National University. May 1954

------------1956a. "Unilineal Descent Groups in the New Guinea Highlands." *Man* 55, 2.

------------1956b. "Asymmetrical Marriage Systems." *American Anthropologist* 58: 639-55.

------------1962. *From Stone to Steel*. London: Cambridge University Press.

------------1964. "New Guinea Highland Models and Descent Theory." *Man* 64: 215-19.

------------1966. "Structuring Ignorance: The Genesis of a Myth in New Guinea." *Anthropologica* 8: 315-28.

------------1970. *Vunamami: Economic Transformation in a Traditional Society*. Berkeley: University of California Press.

Schneider, David. 1965. "Some Muddles in the Models." in Banton, Michael (ed.), *The Relevance of Models for Social Anthropology*. ASA Monographs No. 1. London: Tavistock: 25-85.

Scholte, Robert. 1966. "Epistemic Paradigms: Some Problems in Cross-cultural Research on Social Anthropological History and Theory." *American Anthropologist*: 1192-1201.

Stanner, W.E.H. 1962. "Foreword," in R.F Salisbury, *From Stone to Steel*. New York: Cambridge University Press.

Williams, Raymond. 1975 [1973]. *The Country and the City*. New York: Oxford University Press.

Wolf, Eric. 1982 . "Modes of Production." *Europe and the People Without History*. Berkeley: University of California Press: 73-100.

1.

SIANE KINSHIP:

THE INTERNAL STRUCTURE OF THE CLAN

AND THE CHILD'S ADAPTATION TO IT

by

Richard F. Salisbury

Source: "Siane: The Social Structure of the Siane People,
Eastern Highlands, New Guinea."
Unpublished Report, 1954.

Into the patrilineally organised village group, the clan, the child is born and to its organisation it is adapted. First of all the child learns behaviour patterns and expectations within the family to which it is born, and then these patterns and expectations are generalised and extended to all the members of the group in which it lives. This then is the kinship structure of the clan, and the introduction to it is through specific behaviour patterns learnt in infancy.

(i) INFANT BEHAVIOUR PATTERNS

Before the birth of the child, the mother will continue work until the last moment. A mother may be working in the gardens, digging up the food for the evening meal, when she feels her labour pains commencing. She will go home and possibly manage to cook the evening meal before she retires to her house to give birth. One other women, possibly her mother but more probably the wife of some classificatory brother of her husband, will be there as midwife, cutting the umbilical cord, washing the new-born child, disposing of the after-birth, and attending to the mother. Birth is an affair for the women only, and it is not till the second day after birth that the husband first signifies his concern by bringing food, animal food, to his wife. It is to the woman's world therefore that the child first becomes adapted, being carried about almost continually by the mother, and being given the breast at the least indication of discomfort. The carriage of the baby is inside one of mats of sewn pandanus palm leaves, folded to give a U-shape and housed inside one of the net-bags which all women carry suspended from their foreheads. This bag and mat provide a firm enclosure for the child but his movements are not tightly restricted.

In it he lies naked and on his back. The mother will go to work in the gardens almost immediately after the birth, usually hanging the net-bag on the fence while she works, but often carrying the baby with her, either in its mat and bag, or resting it on one thigh as she digs with the opposite hand.

The evening is felt to be the time for a regular feed, although in actual fact the child will be given the breast whenever it cries. If the mother dies during these first few months, the father will feed the child on masticated sugar-cane, but will always leave the baby outside the house, suspended in its net-bag, in the early evening. Then, if the child cries, the ghost of the mother will hear those cries and come to feed the baby. Foster mothers are rare, and the natives would not admit that failure of milk in a mother ever occurs.

In this way the child soon becomes used to its own mother, and to the affectionate care which typifies the mother-child relationship. In fact during the first two or three months, which the child spends in the mat and bag, it has contact with no person other than the 'own mother,' and this is the kin relationship it adapts to first.

On emerging from the mat, the child makes contact with the other women of the village – other wives of the same father, or the wives of other men of the same village – and it is to these women that the term 'mother' is primarily extended. They will pick the child up, handle it, fondle it, and kiss its penis or vulva with an admiring gesture, but they will not normally give it food or discipline it in any way. Contact with the father's mother is not so frequent – the grandmother will probably not go to the fields with the younger women, and she will usually be at the house her husband has given her, when the cooking is taking place. She is just seen as one of the vague elder relatives, friendly and interested in one's welfare, but not of great importance in day to day life. It is only when she is seen as the mother of one's father that she assumes an individual importance; otherwise the category 'grandparent' is only dimly apprehended by the child.

As the child begins to move about of its own accord it increases its range of contacts. The mother will no longer always leave it in its mat as she works or cooks the evening meal. The child may be given to another 'mother' to be held, but if there are any older siblings, the child will be most frequently 'looked after' by them.[1] The eldest sister will be the most frequent 'substitute mother,' whatever the sex of the child. As soon as the baby has any teeth at all – say at the age of six months – it will be given small portions of adult food. Masticated sugar-cane or edible *pitpit*[2] (with a texture not unlike asparagus) will be among the first foods given, but soon the child is nibbling at all the commoner foods like sweet potatoes, yams or taro. The giving of food is mainly the task of the mother, but the elder siblings will do so too. Especially is this the case with the eldest sister, while the eldest brother will 'look after' the child by preventing it wandering away and hurting itself. He will not contribute so much to the nurturing of the child as will an eldest sister.

The father's interest in the child is intense from birth onwards, but his actual contacts with the child are few until the baby has begun to be more active. The father will carry the child around, will be eager to show it to other people, and will be extremely demonstrative in his affection for the child – with hugging and kissing. There is no question of physical punishment for the child, for it is not thought possible that parents could strike their own children. Nor have I ever seen any children struck except perhaps in momentary spasms of anger (e.g. when the mother's nipple was bitten during nursing). The only form of discipline used is to say that the 'spirits' will hurt the child if he does certain things, including straying too far away. The reaction of the child is to cling all the tighter to its parent, from whom it receives floods of affection, hugs and kisses. This use of the spirits as 'bogey-men' is extended now to include the use of white-men, for the 'spirits' are visualised as white-skinned. It is normal to see children, when they are frightened or when white men appear, run to their parents and hide their faces against the tightly-clasped legs of the parent, until they are picked up and comforted. In this connection, it is always the 'own mother' or 'own father' who is run to, and comfort from one of the other men or women of the clan, who would be called by the same kinship term, is of little use in calming the child.

In the context of lack of punishments, toilet training is easy and mild. At first the child's excretion is a matter of little importance. It is naked, and when it excretes, the person who is holding it, holds it at arms' length, and lets the excreta fall where it may. No disgust is shown, and mothers will unconcernedly wipe soil off themselves, and will remove other soil at their leisure. Just as the child begins to walk, it will be encouraged to follow the example of other adults and walk off into the bush to perform its toilet. Stories are told of the small children who did this on their own initiative, and the desirability of so doing is marked, although failure so to do meets with no punishment. The rewards used are profuse affection on the part of the mother and general praise on the part of the spectators, male and female. This is also the pattern for the rewarding of meritorious acts by young children in other systems of behaviour, and always the child is made to feel the warmth and affection of its own group – especially of the parents – as opposed to the possible dangers from the spirits or from other humans who are not members of the group. In actual fact, the handling the child receives, especially the way of picking it up by one arm and swinging it into a carrying position, is not gentle, but the affection expressed is both warm and demonstrative.

31

It is in the toilet training however that the first sharp division for the child of the world into male and female occurs. When the child begins to understand speech, it is told by the parent of the same sex, where to go for its toilet. Before white contact men would merely go off into the bush in one direction, and women in the other, but nowadays there are latrines dug for either sex. One talk, and the child is supposed to have been taught finally. The occurrence of lapses, once the talk has been given, is not conceived as possible. This did not prevent informants explaining the use of very short aprons by young girls, as being to avoid soiling the apron with urine. The complete nakedness of boys up to the age of six or seven was sometimes explained as being for the same reason. But in any case, punishment for lapses would be unthinkable, and only on one occasion did I see such a thing occur. A young boy was too timid to get up and walk out of the house when adults were talking there, and the parents' reaction seemed to be a compound of sympathy with the child for its timidity, and annoyance at disgusting the other adults present.

Siblings of the same sex would also assist the young child in finding its way to the latrines for that sex, and from this age the activities of the child, who can now walk quite competently, become more and more associated with his siblings of the same sex. Reflecting this interaction, there is one term for 'sibling of the same sex,' and another one meaning 'sibling of the opposite sex,' both of which are used reciprocally. On the other hand, the eldest sister, with her nurturing role, has a specific term. So also does the eldest brother with his protective role.

Weaning has been described as starting within a few months of birth, with the offering to the child of the softer items of adult diet. This process of adapting the child to adult foods continues for years. The child eats these foods as they are offered to it when adults eat – even to the chewing of sugar cane, which needs strong jaws and teeth for the removal of the skin – but it still continues to nurse. Native theory attributes great powers of causing growth to milk,[3] and the child is given the breast on all possible occasions. Theoretically there is a ceremony which is given at the end of weaning and this should occur after the second Pig Feast following the birth of the child. During this interval which would be between 3 and 6 years, there is also a tabu on intercourse between the mother and the father. The spacing of pregnancies at about 3-yearly intervals would support the belief that the tabu is widely observed. In one case I did observe the end of weaning ceremony[4] for a child, and six months later when I left the field the mother appeared to be six months pregnant. On the other hand, there does not seem to be a clustering of births at three-yearly intervals, as would be expected from the simultaneous removal of a rigidly observed tabu on intercourse. The age of weaning does however, sometimes reach the upper limit for I have seen children aged 6, run to their mothers and seize the breast, and start to nurse while both mother and child were standing up.

This occurred even though the mother's breasts were obviously dry and seemed much more as though the child ran to the mother for emotional support rather than for material food. The use of tobacco juice on the nipples, to relieve mothers of the trouble of ceremonially 'weaned' children who continue to want to nurse, is not unknown.

Perhaps the most striking change in the child's relationships which accompanies the weaning ceremony, is the classing of the child on many occasions, with its sex mates – with the boys, or with the females – rather than with the mother. The change is noticeable in everyday life in the composition of play groups, where children tend more and more to be found in groups of age-mates of the same sex. However the change was most strongly marked in the ceremonial usage after the one weaning ceremony I saw. Soon after the ceremony there was a distribution of pork to cure a sick man of the clan, and in this ceremony the categories of the society – boys, adult men, old men, women, etc. – are distinguished, both by position of seating, and in the type of meat that is given to each category. The newly 'weaned' boy went with his mother at first, but she sent him away to sit with the other boys. One of the older boys came over and led him across, and he took his place, sitting on some of the leaves which a boy of his own age had spread on the ground for himself. This boy then showed him how to take the meat in the ceremonial fashion when it was offered.

At this time too, comes the independent training of the boy. Now he will play with his age-mates, and when he cries he will be ignored, whereas before he would have received immediate attention from a parent or older sibling. The play is generally rough – unorganised ball games, fighting, a game where each boy tries to knock the others over by kicking them on the thighs, and bow and arrow shooting. Crying is frequent when the friendliness is not apparent, but it is ignored by elders, and a pattern seems to develop in which the aggrieved individual wanders off by himself, crying ostentatiously, but being ignored. In fact during childhood, little attention is paid to aggression in any form – it is just ignored by adults, and is usually accepted in good part by the other children who are the objects of it. If it is directed to someone who is unable to accept it, the object merely withdraws crying, or, if it is a young child, is removed by a parent or elder brother.

This increase in peer group activity is accompanied by continued accompanying of the parent or siblings of the same sex. This is not demanded, but the young child will follow its parent to the gardens, or to work inside the village. Spontaneously it does the same things as the parent, and when one of the older men or boys issues one of their random commanding statements – "Bring a light" – it is one of the younger boys who goes and executes the action, although the command may not have been directed to him. All the time the child is slowly and incidentally learning the skills necessary in the native society; learning to use chopping tools; playing with a bow and arrow; helping weed the gardens; helping to unpack the tree-trunk ovens. It is not forced to do anything, nor is it permitted to do the skilled tasks, which it may only watch, but it is present at the performance of all the economic tasks.

This outline of the learning of economic skills, and the gradual shift from a family-centred life to a peer-group centred life is valid both for boys and for girls. The girl, it is true, is still within the same category – 'the women' – after her 'weaning' but the only way this differentiates girls from boys is in terms of degree. The girl spends more time with the mother and elder sisters, while the boy spends more time with the peers; both become more attached to their group of age-mates. For both sexes there is the term 'age-mate' – very similar to, but definitely distinct from, the term for 'sibling of the same sex.' Among older boys the term is used for the group who were initiated at the same time, but the same term is used by girls for their peers, and for boys of the same age by uninitiated boys. Its primary significance is not in terms of initiation.

Thus by the age of 5 or 6, the child is adapted to the kinship system of the older members of its own clan; it has expectations as regards the behaviour of other members of its clan; it has developed patterns of behaviour towards older members and it is acquiring the skills and techniques of everyday life. By now, too, the child has probably a younger sibling and it is being trained in its duties towards the younger members of the clan. It sees the parent caring for, or feeding, the new baby, and the baby is sometimes left in its elder sibling's charge. The lessons of protecting, nurturing, or 'looking after' the young child are told to the elder sibling verbally, and it is rewarded by parental praise when it carries out those duties well. More especially, the eldest son or daughter would frequently be left in charge, while a second sibling would find the job already done, vis-a-vis the third, youngest sibling. So the eldest sibling of either sex receives the most training in protecting or nurturing the youngest child, and becomes differentiated from the intermediate siblings, who only perform those duties when the eldest sibling is not there. The first child is always made a great fuss of, and then, when the fuss is being made of the new child, it is treated more as a companion and help of the parent. When the youngest son of 3 is still with its mother, the eldest son of 6 is with its father, helping him in the gardens and incidentally learning to know the sites where the father owns ground. While the young daughter of 3 is still playing near the fire, distracting the mother as she loads the oven, the eldest daughter of 6 is quietening the baby by offering sweet corn roasted in the ashes.

(ii) TERMINOLOGY

In this way the kinship structure of its own clan is simply understood by the child. It has organised the world of its own clan into a series of categories, on the lines of generation division, but with two categories, those of eldest brother and eldest sister, which are distinguished on grounds of seniority. The terms it uses for these categories are listed below, and included on the attached chart. In addition it has heard these terms used by others, and so been enabled to complete the picture. The terms are:

menefo	father
onefo	mother
aunefo	grandparent or grandchild
nanefo	son
orunefo	daughter
yanefo .	eldest brother
atanefo	eldest sister
kunanefo	sibling of the same sex
nemona	sibling of the opposite sex
koinanefo	age-mate of the same sex

These terms, as given, all include the first person singular possessive (-*ne*-) and are all the terms of reference. There are different terms of address for most crucial relationships: mother – *moiyo*; father – *veano* or *fafau*;[5] and eldest brother – *yato*. When addressing other people, the personal name is used. It is possible to use the term of reference as a term of address, but it is unusual and means one particularly wishes to emphasise what relationship one wishes to stand in, during the ensuing conversation.

Another use of kinship terms of address is when there are strangers present. There is a convention that one does not know the personal names of people in other clans, and a dislike of 'betraying' one's own personal names to others, connected to some extent with the sorcery beliefs. Thus namesakes will use the term 'my namesake' – *rinefo* – when addressing or referring to someone of the same name, especially if strangers are present.

The 'namesake' relationship does create sentimental bonds between the individuals concerned. There is some pattern of naming children after their grandfathers – to perpetuate the name – and the naming of a child after another adult is a compliment to that adult. Stories will be told to the child of the great deeds of previous namesakes, and the sense of 'identification' with those previous

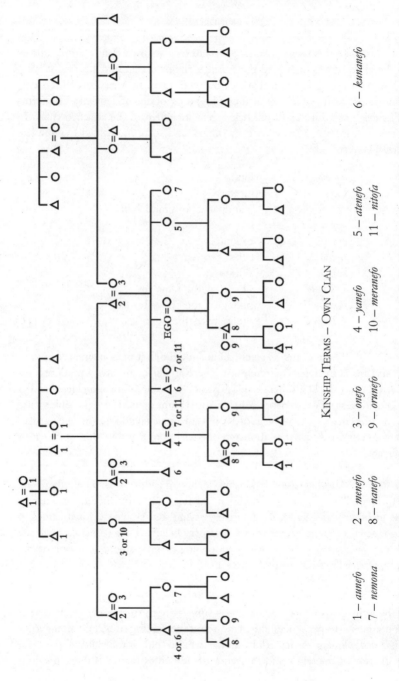

Kinship Terms – Own Clan

1 – aunefo	2 – menefo	3 – onefo	4 – yanefo	5 – atenefo	6 – kunanefo
7 – nemona	8 – nanefo	9 – orunefo	10 – meranefo	11 – nitofa	

Note: (1) For ego female, the terms are the same except that the usage of the terms *kunanefo* and *nemona* are reversed to apply to siblings of the other sex. (2) Ego's own children and descendants will not be of Ego's own clan.

namesakes is also extended to the sphere of property. To say 'I would like that object of yours,' to a namesake is tantamount to an irrefusable demand for a gift. In fact the person after whom the child is named will give gifts freely and unasked. As soon as natives were sure I was aware of this custom, children, dogs and pigs were named after me. I then had to use the term 'father of my namesake' to the fathers or owners, and they expected the least mention of the needs of the child or animal to be met by gifts from me. The term 'father of my namesake' is also loosely used to any individual as an honorific term of address, whether that person has the appropriately named child or not.

The other most common form of address, and also occasionally of reference, is to call a person by his teknonymic name, 'father or mother of so-and-so.' For the purpose of this type of naming it is usually the eldest son who is taken as the point of reference. A man is 'father of his eldest son,' but since the youngest child is also a special target for its parents' affections (especially when the child is newly born), one can also use the phrase 'father of his youngest child.' For women too it is usual and honorific to call them 'mother of so-and-so,' and a man will often use such a term when referring to his wife.[6]

(iii) DYADIC RELATIONSHIPS

We have seen the child's early relationships to the agents of socialisation, and the terms that are used. The study of the dyadic relationships, as they occur in society at large, brings out the connection between the infant experiences and the social reality of adulthood.

Teknonymy illustrates the importance of the father-son relationship in Siane society. To call a man 'father of so-and-so' means that he is an adult man and so of consequence in the society. He is also a man who is 'looking after' a family, is providing cleared garden sites for his wife, is contributing to the clan store of male children, and is taking a full part in the ceremonial payments incurred by every clan member.

In his relationships with his son, the pride the man feels is shown, together with his strong affection, in the way he will walk round holding the hand of his son, until the boy is 7 or 8; by the way the father will have the boy sleeping next to him in the men's house, even though the boy has not yet been initiated, and will have to return to his mother if there are any esoteric ceremonies in progress; and in the interest he displays in the son's progress, either in his courting or in his introduction to his life of the white man through indentured labour. He has the duty of 'looking after' the son, and does not expect any return for his care, although the son will, in the course of his general introduction into society, do the incidental errands of fetching lights for cigarettes, of throwing away rubbish, of fetching drinking water, etc. for the older man. The father, when he receives his food from his wife at the men's house, will give food to his sons, immediately he has given to guests and near-by adults. The father uses no compulsion to make the boy accompany him to the gardens, to make him learn, or to make him 'help'[7] him with the work, but in actual fact the young boy will spend about half his time with the father. This amount of time declines as the boy reaches the age of 11 or 12, and as he participates more in the activities of his age-group. At this age too, the father will leave the son to fend for himself more as regards food, etc. At the same time, the group of age-mates becomes included as a whole in the larger size work groups, making large new gardens or new men's houses. All the boys will be there, and each will be helping on his own father's plot of land. As the boy gets old enough, his main assistance with his bride-price will come from his father, and this assistance will not be regarded as a repayable debt, as is the case with assistance from other clan members.

However, in old age, the father may 'retire' and distribute his property; and then it is the duty of the sons and heirs to 'look after' him in their turn.

The son at all times respects, and has pride in, his father; he will tell stories of his father's doings, comment on his special skills, and make a point of doing things for him without being asked.

Especially is this the case with the eldest son. He is, in theory, the sole heir of his father,[8] and the father gives more time and attention to him, than he gives to other sons. The father instructs the boy in the boundaries of his various plots of land, and also instructs him in the various ceremonial 'talks' which he knows, and has the right to repeat in the men's house on the appropriate occasions. Later the eldest son will inherit the land of the father, and will also have the privilege of repeating the 'talks' which the father has taught him, and which are property which no one else may use. In this way the eldest son is trained to take over the role of the father. When the father retires or dies, his land and property will go to the eldest son, but in addition, the eldest son takes over the duty of 'looking after' the younger children. This he does by distributing the property among all those who have claims upon the father, by freely giving assistance in ceremonial payments, by providing cleared garden sites and a house for his father's wife, and by attending to the needs of his father's daughters – giving them land if their husbands cannot provide enough, and ensuring that they are not ill-treated. He also has the duty of 'looking after' his father. If the father has merely 'retired,' he attends to his daily wants, and may well delay the final distribution of the property until the father's death, acting rather as his manager in the interim.

On the father's death, however, the 'looking after' takes the form of attending to the burial. The eldest son must recompense the mourners, must pay those who actually carried the body or dug the grave, and he must give the necessary payments to the mother's brother's people of the dead man. This is perhaps the most important duty of the eldest son, and it is on his performance of this duty that his right to the inheritance depends.

His other most important duty, both symbolically and in the way in which it binds the society together, though it may not involve much action, is the eldest son's responsibility for 'looking after' his sisters. During the girl's first menses ceremony, he it is who builds the wall behind which she is secluded. At marriage, although it may well be the father who arranges the details, in all the speeches and in the appropriate parts of the ceremonial, it is the eldest son who plays the important role. He formally receives the bride-price and distributes it to the boys of the clan; nominally he decorates the bride with the valuables she will take with her, and he provides the pigs for the wedding distribution; he has charge of the *'gerua'* board which symbolises her soul and remains in her natal village.

Younger sons defer to the wishes of their eldest brothers, and these eldest brothers seem much more peremptory, in their demands that the younger brothers satisfy their wishes, than do the fathers. They even use physical force where the fathers would not, but this does not preclude strong emotional ties between elder and younger brothers. The eldest brother will always come to the defence of his younger brother if any accusation is made against him, while the younger brother will expatiate on how big, strong, and important his eldest brother is. In general he will regard his eldest brother as his role-model.

Towards their sisters, brothers are magnanimously protective in public, although in their informal interaction there is much friendly teasing and fighting. The girls take great delight in provoking their brothers, running away when chased, laughing at them and teasing them. The boys never use physical violence to their sisters, but they will joke with them, laugh at them, and tell them that they are just stupid girls. Never did I detect ambivalent overtones however, except perhaps in the frustration of boys who are teased and pushed about by a bigger, elder sister, to whom they should feel protective, but who is actually more powerful physically than they are. Later when the girl has married into another clan, it is to the brothers that she flees, if she is cruelly treated; it is the brothers who receive claims for the return of the bride-price if she is unfaithful; it is the brothers who receive payment for the children she bears.

The girls themselves spend much more time with their mothers, than boys do with their fathers. In fact the girl's peer-group activities are exceeded by her family activities. As a group of peers, the girls may be seen playing cat's cradles together, or sometimes even, football (to the amused scorn of the boys), but it is more usual to see them in groups, going to fetch water for the cooking, or doing other household tasks to 'help' their mothers, but doing them in the company of age-mates who also come within the category 'women.' They group themselves with their age-mates, but their activities are usually directed to 'helping' or learning from the mother. There is a steady progression of the learning of female skills right up till the time of the girl's first menses. Then she is freed from any tacit obligation to help her mother, by the advice her mother gives her, 'Soon you are going to be a married woman, and your life will be one of work. Now is the time to enjoy yourself.' This advice actually goes counter to one of the main themes of the first menses ceremony, where the girl is ceremonially and symbolically told what are the tasks of a woman. However, observation shows that the girls, up till this age, do much more work helping their mothers in the fields, and with cooking and child-care, than they do in the period between the ceremony and their marriage, although even then they do help. This period is, par excellence, the period when girls form peer-groups for their activities. In some villages they have girls' club houses, while in other villages they use the women's house of one of the girls' mothers as a club house. In these houses they entertain, each night, boys from other villages, in informal courting 'sing-sings.' Elder sisters do take their younger sisters into these sing-sings, although few girls under the age of 10 would go inside. This introduction to courting does however form part of the general educational, protective, and nurturing role of eldest sisters vis-a-vis their younger sisters, and it is an occasion when the older married women cannot exert influence, as they are forbidden to enter the club houses. After marriage the girls go to other villages, but the link with their home clans is exceedingly strong, especially with their eldest brother. If one wishes to ask from what clan a wife comes, one always asks 'Whose sister are you?', while if one asks a man, during a distribution, to whom he is sending goods, he will almost invariably reply 'To my married sister.'

The relationship of a child with its mother, is the closest of all relationships, and the cry of 'Moiyo, moiyo' ('Mummy, Mummy') is the one most frequently heard. The child is secure in its expectation of warmth and of affection, of food and care, whenever it needs them. The loss of one's true mother is irreplaceable. One calls the wives of other 'fathers,' or later wives of one's true father, by the term 'Mother,' but a big distinction is made between the true and 'later' mothers. Children say "If we go to them and say 'Moiyo, moiyo I am hungry,' they will give us food; but grudgingly and we would be ashamed! To our true mother we go, and she will always give us food." If the true mother dies, it is the father who takes over the whole task of looking after the children, and the children will prefer to wait with their peers, and be given their scraps, rather than be shamed by depending on women who are not their true mothers.

The child returns the affection of its mother by doing everything it can to 'help,' or even to 'look after' her, when it is old enough. Young boys whose fathers have died, are proud of the way they themselves build houses or clear garden sites for their mothers, even though the mother may have remarried and have a husband to provide for her. Elderly women have their every whim treated as law by their affectionate sons, while they joke with them much as they would if they were still young children. In fact, the old women seem to enjoy life immensely – they are strong personalities who can expect to be obeyed, are well-cared for, and well-fed, wiry and active, and able to do just as much work as they wish to – they lead a care-free existence.

Though most elderly women will be with their husbands, widows seem to spend about half their time with their sons and half their time with their daughters. In the villages of their daughters, just as in the villages of their sons, they may be sure of a welcome, a place to sleep, every comfort, and all the affection that is involved in the mother-child relationship. The strength of this bond is perhaps illustrated by the custom of calling a man by the name of his mother's clan. His equals, and older men will address him by his proper name, or use teknonymy etc., but younger boys of his own clan must show him more respect, and there is nothing a man likes more, than to be reminded of his mother and her place of origin. An emotional tie is felt between people whose mothers come from the same clan – they say 'We are one mother' – and though there are no specific duties connected with this tie, they will look after each other and assist each other, much as a mother would her own child.

The closeness of the mother-son bond is also illustrated by the custom of adoption. The bride-price that is paid for a woman is regarded as a payment by the husband's clan for the children that the woman will bear, but this does not prevent the children of a divorced couple usually going with the mother. Only if the mother goes with the child is there any possibility of adopting a child into a clan other than the clan of the mother or of the father. Then, and it is extremely rare, a man from some other clan may marry the divorced or widowed woman, and take the child as his own by paying to the first husband's clan, a sum which balances the purchased rights of the first husband to the child. In actual fact divorce is rare if there are children to a marriage; many of the men and women have had one or more spouses before they have children, while almost none have divorced when there have been two children to the marriage; the mother is tied to the children. The cases where the custody of a child has been in question, have been instances where there is one child who has gone off with the mother. The husband's people, in such a case, maintain that the child will come back to their village when it is old enough to be independent of the mother, but this does not seem to happen. By the time the child has reached that age, it has formed other ties with age-mates, etc., in the village of its nurturance. Widows too normally retain custody of their children, and since the husband's people have paid for those children in the bride-price, the leviratic solution, of the widow being looked after by another man of the dead husband's clan, is the one which satisfies both parties. It permits the strong emotional bond between the children and their mother to be retained, without destroying the contractual bond implied in the bride-price.

(iv) Wider Extensions of Terminology

The distinctive relationship with the true mother as compared with the relationship with other 'mothers,' is somewhat exceptional in the kinship system. In other cases where kinship terms are used in a classificatory sense, it is a sign that the relationship is qualitatively the same as the original 'true' relationship, though quantitatively less close.

In their widest extensions the terms for mother, father, grandparent, son, daughter, and sibling of either sex, may be used for any member of the same clan as the speaker, who thus divides his own clan by age, sex and generation. This use however is one that is not frequently heard, and when it is heard it is usually to stress the fact that two people are clansmates, when a person from another clan is being spoken to. In a similar context it is even possible to refer to all members of the same clan or tribe as brothers, though the person spoken to, would have to be from some very distant tribe, to whom the distinction between clans would be of little importance. Much more common is the usage where the men's house is the unit of widest extension for classificatory kin terminology. This group will, however, be composed of about 10 or 12 small 'lineages' between which no true genealogical connection can be traced. Each of these 'lineages' will have a remembered depth of about 4 generations – from the present young boys to their grandfather's father. The distinctive feature of these 'lineages,' is the fact that, when you ask an individual 'Who is your father?', he will give you a list of 'fathers' – number one, number two, number three, etc. This list will not include all the classificatory fathers in the men's house, but the the group so delineated is the group I call a 'lineage.' In point of fact, these fathers cannot all be linked by traceable genealogies, and it might be more correct to call this grouping a pseudo-lineage. I will retain the inverted commas round the term lineage, to indicate that this is not a true lineage, but the sociologically important unit. This unit is the one which normally determines the extension of use of classificatory terms, and it is far more important than the true, traceable lineage. In the mechanism of inheritance, and in the perpetuation of the kinship and political organisation, it is crucial.

(v) SUCCESSION

Within this 'lineage' group, kinship terms are applied to whomever performs the duties appropriate to that kinship status. Thus, if the father of a boy dies, his second father will perform the duties of 'looking after' the son, who will then call him father. This second father is the obvious choice as the man to 'look after' the widow of the first father (although it is for the widow to decide if she will stay with him or not), and if the son of the dead man is still young, the second father will be the man who takes over the property of the dead man, managing it and eventually handing it over to the boy, as though he were his own son. In fact, for all practical purposes, it is as though the dead man had never existed, and the second father had had two wives. This complete taking over of the social personality of the dead man, was graphically brought home to me in the taking of genealogies. At first I was compelled to work with young informants, and in one case obtained a genealogy with a depth of four generations, and four members of the grandfathers' generation. From the way I obtained the genealogy, I am sure that the informants did not know the names of any other members of the grandfathers' generation, but I was later able to check the genealogy with the oldest man of the fathers' generation. As he gave it, the genealogy went two more generations back, had three names in the grandfathers' fathers' generation, and eight in the grandfathers' generation, all of whom had issue still alive. In the genealogy as first obtained, these eight had been grouped together in four 'social personalities' with four names, and the other four names had been forgotten. Four names in the grandparental generation were enough to explain the spread of the present generation, and the rest had been ignored. This principle of continuously ignoring, through time, the names of men whose social personalities have become merged with those of others, applies through each 'lineage.' If I had started by asking each native "Whom do you call 'father,' 'brother,' etc.?", and had not made it clear that I was trying to discover true parentage, I would have got a simple picture of each of these 'lineages' as true lineages, each with a neat depth of four generations and pyramiding to a single ancestor. As it was, I worked from true parentage, taking great pains to get beyond the simple pictures I was given at first. Only gradually did I begin to amalgamate the tiny minimal, but true lineages, into the larger 'lineages' which the natives themselves think of automatically.

Inside each 'lineage,' each generation has its 'eldest brother' and it is through this 'eldest brother' that the inheritance system works. Each nuclear family has its own 'eldest brother' and it is only when he is not the 'eldest brother' of the 'lineage' that the term 'yanefo' has any ambiguity. Otherwise it is a defining term, referring to the oldest male of one's own generation within the 'lineage,' and the need for a special defining term indicates the special importance of this role. This is the man in each generation who will 'look after' all his classificatory younger brothers, and normally he is the eldest son of an eldest son. In particular, he is the person to whom is given the custody of all the ceremonial knowledge and speeches, and eventually the privilege of repeating them on the appropriate occasions. This makes him an important man in the community, and, in so far as there is any succession to statuses, he is the person most likely to succeed to the position of *bosboi* of his men's house.

If he is killed however, it will be the next oldest son who becomes 'yanefo,' and he may not be the son of an eldest brother. Though this does occur quite frequently, the genealogy would become so 'collapsed' by the omission of names through two or three generations, that he would soon appear to be the eldest son of an eldest son. Since he would now be carrying out the duties of this status, the fictitious genealogy, the kinship terminology and the actual behavior would then all be consonant.

The inheritance by the son is not automatic on the death of the oldest man of the fathers' generation. It is always open to the next oldest of that generation to step into the 'father' status of the dead man. He becomes the 'eldest brother' of his own generation. In practice, this is what normally happens when the sons are not fully adult, especially as regards the ceremonial knowledge of the dead man. It also happens when an old man decides to retire – he passes out of public life and his status of 'looking after' the children and younger brothers is taken over by the next of the brothers. The land or material property may either be passed on in the same way, or, if his true son is old enough, may be passed on to the son who becomes a quasi-father to the younger sons.

This taking-over of the social personality of others thus keeps the 'lineage' a stable group of approximately constant size. Each generation is large enough to ensure that there will be some sons born to it, at least to one of the 'fathers.' Grandparents are forgotten if their names are more numerous than the number of personalities needed to 'justify' the existing personnel of the 'lineage.' Each single generation is made to feel as though they are the children of one father, through the possibility of each individual moving into the status of 'eldest brother,' although there may be no actual traceable kinship with the person occupying that status at the moment. They are all dependent on the eldest brother of each generation, and thus there is not the tendency to fission on the lines of sibling rivalry, with pairs of brothers fighting for the heritage from the father. The 'holes' in the kinship system caused by deaths – and death in war seems to have been the most common single cause of death in the old days – are easily 'plugged' with the minimum of distur-bance, and there is always someone of mature age to succeed on the death of an eld-est brother. If the dead man left only young sons, his next brother takes over; when there are no more of the fathers' generation left, then the eldest son of the original eldest son will certainly be mature.

To cement the various 'lineages' together, within this kinship structure, is the age-mate relationship. This relationship, between individuals of dif-ferent 'lineages,' is not merely one of potential taking-over of the social personality of others, but of an actual identification. In ceremonies where ego is disqualified from performing an action, ego's age-mates are also disqualified. In the weaning cer-emony, a man may not cut the hair of his own children; the ceremony must be per-formed by a clansmate, but must not be performed by an age-mate. In native terms "the age-mate would see the child and say 'this is my own child,' and he would not be able to do the cutting."

Within the clan therefore, solidarity is achieved through the ties of brothers or age-mates. The ties between brothers and sisters, which form the con-necting kinship link between clans, is the subject of a later chapter.

Notes

1.   I use this word in inverted commas to translate the native term 'kiamfaiye' (pidgin *lukautim*) which describes one of the key types of relationship in the kinship structure. The content of this relationship will be apparent from the occasions on which the term is used.

2.   Probably *saccharum arundinaceum*. Murphy 1949, p.87 [editor's note: detailed reference not given].

3.   The natives are puzzled by the contradiction between this belief, their belief that white women do not suckle their children, and the great size of white children.

4.   On the departure of the father for indentured labour.

5.   This term may have been derived from pidgin 'papa' but its use is widespread, especially among young children and may well be 'baby-talk' for veano.

6.   This also illustrates the way a woman obtains status in her husband's clan, as the mother of his children.

7.   I use the term 'help' in inverted commas to translate the native term 'umaiye' (pidgin *alivim*). It is the type of relationship reciprocating 'looking after.' In addition to the English senses of help, it has connotations of 'contributing to a larger task' and 'continuing where another has left off.'

8.   See below for the way he inherits obligations as well as rights and the way this prevents the accumulation of power in the hands of eldest sons.

2.

STRUCTURING IGNORANCE:

THE GENESIS OF A MYTH IN NEW GUINEA[1]

by

Richard F. Salisbury

Source: *Anthropologica* N.S. VIII, No. 2, 1966.

RÉSUMÉ

En 1953, on découvrait une source saline sur le territoire d'une tribu Déné habitant les Hautes-Terres de la Nouvelle-Guinée. Les Dénés eurent soin de cacher les circonstances de la nouvelle découverte, mais des rumeurs naquirent chez les Siane voisins qui donnaient de cette événement une certaine explication qui devint un mythe assez généralement accepté.

L'analyse du mythe et de ses développements démontrent que les bénéficiaires d'un mythe n'en devraient pas être en même temps les inventeurs. Ce sont les auditeurs eux-mêmes qui, en cherchant à comprendre, vont structurer et standardiser en termes mythiques les événements inexplicables.

Since the early 1900's it has been out of fashion to theorize about the origin of myths: people have stressed functional interpretations of the relations between myths and the current activities of a society. Malinowski's discussion of myths as "charters" exemplifies this, as does Firth's (1961:175) detailed analysis of how variant forms of traditional tales are "pressure instruments (used by different groups) for keeping alive competing claims" and reflect "not so much ... differential memory as ... differential interests." Yet such analyses, like those of how far myths reflect history, all imply a view of how myths originate. Crudely phrased, they imply that myth-makers have a vested interest in justifying their own present behaviour by making it appear to be the outcome of important events in the past. Myth-makers are the prototype propagandists.

A second series of interpretations of myths stresses their internal structure (cf. Lévi-Strauss 1958), and how this structure symbolizes some fundamental aspect of relationships in the society. Such interpretations, applied to highly standardized narratives or versions collected from single informants, provide dramatic insights, but suffer from an over-static view of myth. Some elaboration of the structural position is needed to account for the existence of variation, over time and synchronically, as well as for regularity.

The present paper seeks to contribute to these two areas by considering a specific historical event of 1953 – the discovery of a salt spring in the Highlands of New Guinea. It discusses how, in the week following the discovery, a relatively standarized (though mythical) account of it developed. It will be shown that the mythmakers were not the individuals owning the spring, who might be expected to have tried to justify their possession of it. Rather, the myth evolved progressively among people with little accurate knowledge of the facts, each person adding details that appeared to make the story more "true" for him. It is argued that the audiences for such story-telling, with their existing cognitive structures of religion and myths, then select versions which they approve, and so give them a structuring.

Discovery of the Spring

On February 15th 1953, I was told in my house at Pira in Siane[2] territory that a new salt spring had just come up in Keu, a Dene-speaking village some seven miles away, across the precipitous divide of which Mt. Erimbari forms part. The first man to tell me was the local Government interpreter who ostensibly came to say that the Agricultural Extension officer was due to visit my house. But he seemed more excited by the news of the salt spring, and by the fact that the headmen of several Siane villages had decided to travel to Keu to claim plots of land. The plots he said, would be the site of workshops which their villages would use for purifying salt. Their trip would be on February 17th. I said I would like to go.

The Agricultural Officer's presence made it impracticable for me to go then, but without prompting, headmen (*luluai*) from several Siane villages came in to say that they would like to accompany me on the 18th instead. Each one, with his accompanying villagers, stayed to talk about the salt spring, so that for three days I was subject to an increasing spate of rumours, some cumulative and many conflicting. These form the subject of this paper.

Besides the luluais and the Government interpreter, 12 men and three women of my own village said they wished to accompany me. All the men, except the village headman, were young adults, newly married or actively searching for wives: the women were two wives, married in from Dene-speaking groups, and a girl with mother's brothers living in Keu. It turned out that all had other business near Keu – the new wife of one man had run home to a nearby village, and the group was going to secure her return. En route the luluais later mentioned no interest in building workshops, but stressed that they were coming on a trip, and had other business to perform-taking pork to a sister, or settling a long outstanding court case in Keu village.

The first rumour changed the site of the discovery from near the village of Keu, in Duma tribe, to near a village four miles further west at the Government Rest House of Gun. Then the story was elaborated that a man had been walking in the bush and had seen an area of discoloured kunai grass, and as he wondered about it, he had been struck by water bubbling out and had tasted the water. It had been "sweet" (i.e. salt). Next I heard discussion of where the man had come from, and it was agreed that he was "from a long way away." At this point I asked both the Government interpreter and the luluai of Roanti, the last Siane village before Keu, about property rights in the new spring – salt being a precious commodity in Highland New Guinea – and they reconfirmed that people from foreign tribes would not be barred from working the salt. By the evening of the 16th an agreed version of the story seemed to have emerged. "A man from a long way away was walking along, far from his home, when he saw a woman on the path in front of him. When he caught up with her, she had disappeared, but then she reappeared further ahead on the path. After several recurrences of disappearances and reappearances further ahead, he finally got to a spot where, when she disappeared, strange murmurings underground were heard. He fell down on the ground and began praying. When he finished praying he struck a stick in the ground. Through the hole in the ground came bubbling up a white liquid like milk. He tasted it and found that it was salt, and so began to work the salt."

On the 17th, the luluai from Rofaifo a Siane village halfway to Keu arrived, and told me that I had only part of the story. The thing that had attracted the man to the woman was the way in which she had tossed her head so that her hair shook like kunai-grass in the wind (yet most Siane and Dene-speaking women now have very short hair). When the woman disappeared he had picked up a stick, and had been plunging it into the ground all over the place to discover the hole through which she had disappeared. The strange sound he had heard had been a rhythmical beating like that of a *kudu* drum. The luluai laughed at my suggestion that the discoverer had prayed, asserting only that he was a mission helper by the name of Pis.

From him too I tried to obtain details of the process of salt manufacture and trade. (I had previously read Vial's (1941) descriptions of the process some eight miles west of Gun, and knew the outlines of how roughly a year elapses between initial collection of brine and eventual production of a large salt cake). He said that a house was already built for salt manufacture, watched over continuously by one man. At the start of manufacture they had killed three pigs, and mixed the blood of the pigs with the brine. Now those who came to get salt would have to contribute pigs. I could not obtain from him a clear statement of whether these pigs would give the right to work the salt, or would be in exchange for salt cakes manufactured by the Gun people.

Talking over this version of the story I tried to establish what the meaning of the woman's tossing hair was. Several people said that to shake one's head from side to side is the common way to show that food is good, and that the incident indicated that she was telling him about the salt. Others disagreed and said that it was the way some women seduce men.

On the 18th the party from my own village set out for the ten mile walk, and by the time we had climbed the pass several luluais from other villages had joined us. In Keu, the first Dene-speaking village over the divide, everyone sat down and was entertained by friends, while several court cases were discussed. As the hours dragged on I became impatient, and accompanied by the men from my own village, (most of whom were bilingual in Dene) and a Government interpreter from a Dene village in Gomia tribe four miles to the north, who was also going to Gun, we pushed on. The interpreter had a slightly different story. The discovery of the spring had originally been reported by a Seventh Day Adventist mission helper, and on hearing his story, several luluais had searched for the spring, but without success. He insisted there was no spring. Yet when I asked him who would manufacture the salt, if one *were* found, he was adamant that only Dene-speakers could work it. Villagers at Gun would ask friends and relatives nearby villages to help. When the salt was eventually ready he would come and tell me and I could come to the feast, bringing a pig perhaps. He was not trying to hide anything from me. He was only angry that I had heard such a deceitful story from a mission helper, causing me to come all this way. He had never heard the name Pis. This behaviour did not inspire my confidence and I wondered what interest he, a foreign Dene-speaker, might have in secrecy.

Nearing Gun Rest House it became clear that my own villagers were beyond the range of friendship or affinities; house styles had changed, and no one knew the way. When we reached the village, the *tultul*, or assistant headman, was the only person present. He also denied that there was any spring. No one offered hospitality to my accompanying Siane. We waited an hour and no local villagers came bringing food or firewood to sell. All my questions were answered in the negative. Against such stolid refusal to assist in any way, I realized that staying would collect no information and would mean a cold and hungry night. I turned and left for home.

In Keu I met the other luluais ready to return to Siane, together with the paramount luluai of Duma tribe, whose jurisdiction covered Gum village. The latter was quite straightforward but said he didn't know how the spring was discovered. He had two men guarding the spring, and was directing the operations of soaking grass in the brine, letting the grass dry and then burning it. The collected ash would then be dissolved in water and dried in clay cylinders placed over heated rocks, but the workshop for this task had not yet been built. It would be allowed to see it, when he sent word that the first cakes were ready for sale. With that I had to be satisfied, and hurried home, leaving my own villagers to amorous adventures in Keu, and a search for an errant wife in the next Dene village to the south.

Needless to say, no word arrived to invite me to Gun, before I left the field in November.

ANALYSIS

In the first place it is clear that the owners of the spring, who, presumably, would gain by having a myth to validate their ownership as resulting from a supernatural gift, were not the inventors of the myth. They either denied the existence of the spring, or, in the case of the paramount luluai, denied any knowledge of supernatural intervention and discussed only practical matters. These people, although in the best position to know what the facts of the discovery were, were unwilling to tell the facts.

The myth originators were the people who did not know the facts – who were, perhaps, deliberately kept from knowing the facts, except for a few hints that a spring existed. In such a situation rumours spread like wildfire, as Firth (1956) has shown for Tikopia. Yet rumours tend to have a cyclical life; either they are rapidly proved true by events, or, if they are not confirmed they gradually die for lack of supporting evidence. In this case occasional admissions (e.g. by the paramount luluai) that a spring existed were enough to keep rumours alive, and the refusal by the Gun people to discuss the actual discovery meant that the rumours could proliferate unchecked.

Yet the rumours also developed cumulatively. Several practical details mentioned by early reporters – notably the grass discolouration, the praying and the existence of bubbling brine before the discoverer arrived – all were finally rejected, in favour of details with more supernatural connotations. To me the prosaicness of these details and the internal consistency of the praying and the consensus that the discoverer was a mission helper, indicated that here was the kernel of fact. But, to quote Shaw, prosaicness is too true to be good; large departures from fact often have a greater ring of "truth."

There was in my experience intense interest among the Siane in establishing what the "true" story was, and in discussing the true meaning of each event of the story. As people narrated the version they had heard, others, with different versions would argue. No one appealed to the authority of first-hand evidence which was unavailable. Favourable audience reactions to the version determined which version was repeated to succeeding audiences. In such a situation the raconteur has the advantage over the factual reporter.

The audience reactions also structured the accepted version in a predictable way – as the repetitions progressed the elements taken as true became more and more like myths already familiar to the listeners.

The name of the mission helper – Pis (the pidgin spelling for "fish") – is an element of this type. The origin story of Emenyo tribe in Siane (Salisbury 1956:470-2) tells how the two (or in some version, three) clans of Emenyo tribe resulted from the cutting up of a water creature (a fish, eel, or tadpole) by the original ancestor. To have the spring discovered by a man, named for an exotic creature, would make this into the same sort of quasi-totemic story. The vagueness of description of the discoverer, merely walking along, coming from a vague distance, and apparently going to no particular place as no Seventh Day Adventist mission was located near Gun, adds to the sense of myth.

The vision of the woman preceding him along the track is a common theme in Siane stories. During my year of residence in Siane two of the sixty men of the nearest village claimed to have visions of this type while walking home from distant gardens around nightfall. One had restrained himself from following the woman, but thought he had recognized a dead "mother." The other man had been heard screaming hideously in the darkness from the valley bottom near the village. Next morning he was found, scratched by thorns and bruised but still alive, and told of seeing a shadowy female figure on the track ahead as he came home late from the gardens. He had hurried behind her but had missed a turning in the track and fallen into a limestone hollow where the thorns had ripped him. The woman had beaten him with sticks until he lost consciousness.

A youth told me how, after his mother had died when he was aged about five, he had seen her walking along a path near the village and had followed her into the bush. While so doing he had fallen into a limestone hollow, and had rolled over and over to the bottom. There he had come face to face with his mother's body. Adults had told him that it could not have been her body for she had been buried properly elsewhere, but he was uncertain whether the traumatic experience had been an affair of the spirits or a material one. He volunteered this story, soon after the body of a woman who had died of a wasting illness had been summarily thrown down a limestone fissure, before her kinsmen could arrive from her natal village to weep over her and so claim larger death payments. In this case too, the husband's lineage publicly denied that she had been improperly buried.

Most common are varied stories of men hunting opossums, at evening. Commonly the man saw a woman on the track ahead of him, and on following her into the bush found that she had disappeared near a particular tree. On searching he found opossum droppings, and by remaining on watch he was able to shoot several animals. Alternatively stories describe hunters waiting near trees known to contain opossums, and just as they are about to fire, being hit on the head by a female spirit, being torn by her nails, and having their arrows turned aside in flight.

Even the prosaic practical details of the early versions of the story – the discolouration of the grass, the bubbling of stagnant water in it, and the prodding of the ground which appear as rationally connected to the Western observer, also have a supernatural aspect in terms of Siane belief. Swampy areas, where seepage occurs at the foot of slopes and methane gas bubbles intermittently are well known in Siane country. They are widely believed to be the abodes of "nature demons" (pidgin *masalai*) (cf. Bulmer 1965:153) materially visualized as a form of snake (*reyana*) and also evidenced by smells or lights at night. Only an insane or supernaturally inspired person would deliberately risk death or disease by disturbing a *reyana* by prodding the ground. Increasing supernatural significance is attached to the discovery as first the discoverer was said to have prayed, then to have prodded once, and finally to have prodded repeatedly.

The last major element, the recognition that the spring was salt closely parallels a well-known Siane myth, that of the migration of Komunku tribe from their place of emergence to their present territory. Coincidentally the place of emergence is supposed to have been near Gun, in what is now a Dene-speaking area, although Komunku is now the largest Siane-speaking tribe (cf. Salisbury 1962b:10-11). A Komunku man was hunting in the primary forest southeast of where Chuave now is.[3] He shot a bird and cut it open to eat it, but when he ate the crop, he found that it was sweet (i.e. salt). He watched and when another bird flew by, he followed it, and found where it drank at a spring on the east side of the valley. When he tasted the spring he found that it was sweet too. On his return to Gun he told the rest of Komunku tribe and they all moved to live near the spring. It may parenthetically be noted that the spring is no longer salt, and that salt was never manufactured there.

The founding clans of Komunku tribe have moved at least twice since the salt-spring episode, once to the south-east towards Emenyo territory, and once, some fifty years ago, to the north into another side-valley of the Mai River. This myth does not validate ownership of a salt spring, nor does it explain the present residence of Komunku tribe.

INTERPRETATION

To the Western observer the preceding narrative and analysis may be divided into a factual description of actual events, and a series of superimposed supernatural imaginings. Among local informants no such division is made into "fact" and "imagination," or into reality and supernatural. The differentiation is between story-tellers who have the "true" story (*ona*), and those who lie (*suki*) or who "do not hear/understand correctly." The criterion for truth is not objective fact. Although the Siane expressed great interest and excitement in going to Gun, when there I was the only person who questioned about fact; merely to have been to Gun was sufficient for most Siane, who then showed more interest in humdrum affairs.

Truth in Siane is partly a matter of appearing an authoritative inside dopester; partly it comes from a belief that there is some power derived from a precise knowledge of ritual formulae. It is these formulae and their inner meanings that are sought in discussions. Lawrence (1964) and Burridge (1961) have described this intense search for "truth" and inner meaning in other areas of New Guinea and have shown how the search lies behind the development of beliefs in the supernatural origin of manufactured goods, or *Kago*. Virtually any European factual statement about factory production or any missionary discussion of sin can be seen as a distortion of a hidden deeper meaning. If one knew that hidden meaning, the ultimate truth, then one would have power to control the flow of manufactured goods. In the same way those who knew only a few facts about the salt spring sought for the inner meaning of those facts – invented rumours in our terms; sought the truth in Siane terms, in a normal Siane way.[4]

Knowledge of the "real facts" may even hinder the search for "truth" and hidden meaning. The men of Gun, with the most facts available (but with no ties to my friends of Emenyo), and other Dene-speakers with less knowledge but more ties to Emenyo, alike chose to conceal their knowledge, denying that anything had happened. To a Western observer their reasons are obscure; it would seem more rational and prestigeful to advertise the existence of the spring, and so draw customers, even if no salt were yet available. It may be that such promise of wealth would have resulted in excessive demands from fortune-seeking affines. Yet it may also be rational to deny the facts and let other people invent "facts" as a better "soft sell" advertisement. Denial of a rumour has, in technologically advanced countries, become one of the best ways of evoking interest in an already-decided but secret government or business policy decision. In short, ignorance may produce better myths than does historical knowledge; the people who are likely to benefit by a myth (the beneficiaries of the charter) are likely to have historical knowledge, but their interest may be to keep quiet, and to let myths be created by those who know less.

How then do the ignorant make their myths? A substratum of historical fact is needed – in this case knowledge of the discovery, its general location, and an indication that the discovery had been made by an outsider. The first step is to fill in the elements of the story that are practically predictable – the way in which salt would kill the grass, the need to taste the salt etc. The story then has a structure of practical experience but the added detail does not add to the "credibility" of the story as any story-teller could invent these items, and their meaning is obvious.

Next follows an effort to fit the inherently unpredictable elements of the story – "why did he happen to be walking where he did?", "why did the event happen at that particular time?" – into a framework of cultural understandings of human motivation and the nature of chance events – the man wandered in there because a female ghost enticed him, and (being a mission helper) the spring emerged because he prayed. The elements added at this point may be those of other myths, but clearly any one of a number of elements can be inserted to provide each explanation. Prayer was clearly appropriate for a mission-helper to use, yet his merely prodding the ground was the alternative explanation which most people accepted. At this stage it is the reaction of the audience which crystallizes the form of the myth.

A final stage would seem to involve aesthetic and formal re-structuring – the myth is fitted into new frames, elements are added to complete the "balance" of those frames, and other "embroidery" elements enter, which nevertheless have an important relationship with the cruder form of the myth. Thus in the present case the motif of appearance and disappearance, common in stories of seduction by female ghosts, is linked coherently with the prodding of the ground. The murmurings underground then become, not a threat which the discoverer had to pray to avert, but an incitement to prod – they sounded like *kudu* drums being beaten for an imminent religious ritual. The entire story therefore is re-phrased as a single incident, with indications of spiritual influences becoming steadily more explicit, and climaxing with the drum beating and the disturbing of the spirits by prodding. The bubbling up of the salt is then only the epilogue, the practical moral of a supernatural story.

But such a neat story, I would also maintain, leaves no room for doubts about its meaning. The really skilful raconteur introduces new elements both to make a more exciting story, and to add something that is not immediately explicable – something truer, as it has more hidden meanings. The mention of hair waving as the spirit tossed her head seemed to do this for my evening audience of February 17th, who argued about the meaning of this new motif.

Their arguments did not exhaust the potential significances. The most seductive female action is usually said to be the motion of her *konto*, the strip of barkcloth hanging from the back of her belt, which swirls like a kilt as she walks. For a man to grab her *konto* is to accept seduction; to walk behind a woman along a path is to expose oneself to seduction. But in this story it is her hair that waves, not her skirt, and it is said to wave like kunai grass. To me the mention of kunai evokes the report explicitly placing the spring in a kunai-grass seepage area. It suggests, perhaps, that the distracted discoverer could not distinguish between the wind in the kunai, and the spirit figure movements.

For the Siane too, long hair on women has certain connotations. It is a pre-mission influence style, worn by independent-minded women, especially at times of religious ceremonials when the ringlets hang down heavy and matted with pig grease. Young girls taking part in Yam taro dances knot lengths of shredded bark fibres into their hair and oil them with red pandanus oil to appear like waist-length hair. This style, paralleling styles more common for boys elsewhere in the Highlands (cf. Read 1952), has implications both of sexual attractiveness and of contact with spirits (Salisbury 1965). Any one (or several) of these connotations might be implied by the added phrase that the mission helper was attracted by her tossing hair. This embroidery of the story is "true" for a Siane audience, not as clarifying the story, but for the additional hidden meanings it implies – it maintains ambiguity in the story, and a sense of ignorance in the audience.

In summary, the present analysis would suggest that the common assumption that myths are created by the groups which use the myths to support claims, is not necessarily correct. It ignores the potentialities for myth-creation implied by imperfect factual knowledge in audiences, and the interest audiences have in fitting ambiguous untoward events within their frames of cognitive understanding.

The present study confirms Firth's (1961) discussion of how traditional tales are told in many variant forms, and suggests that his finding, (p. 176) that the greatest degree of variation occurs in tales about the most distant past, may be generalized – most variation occurs where factual accuracy is least checkable. In the present case deliberate concealment of facts was the cause. The existence of variation and change, while throwing doubt on *structural* analyses which appear to account for every detail of a particular version, nevertheless provides the basis for explanations in terms of dynamic principles of *structuring*. Tales are seen in the present case as undergoing continuous elaboration by their tellers in three main directions – amplification of detail deduced from what is known, reorganization and additions to give structural form, and "embroidery" to add hidden meanings. It is the reactions of different audiences which give the stamp of approval to different versions, accepting those structurings which fit audience needs. In those areas where there is most ignorance, structuring is most likely to be effective.

Notes

1. The fieldwork on which this study is based was supported by the Australian National University.

2. For an ethnography of the Siane and a map of tribal and linguistic areas see Salisbury (1962a). Salisbury (1965) gives a somewhat fuller outline of religious beliefs.

3. The myth asserts that this land was unoccupied. It is, however, the same side valley investigated by S. Bulmer (1964) and White (1965) both of whom report a virtually continuous archaeological sequence back to paleolithic times. Their evidence comes mainly from cave mouths and rocks shelters. On the evidence of bones White concludes that until fairly recently the area was inhabited by migrant hunters. The myth suggests that the primary forest was used for hunting by nearby agricultural groups, using rock shelters for cooking picnic meals of game. It is unfortunate that no closer correlation of archeological sites and traditions is possible, as archaeological reports cite only recurrent site names, and not the clan or tribal names within whose territories the sites occur.

4. This is also the Tikopian way of truth-seeking through rumour elaboration. See Firth (1956).

References

Bulmer, S.E. 1964. "Prehistoric Stone Implements from the N.G. Highlands." *Oceania* 34:246-248.

Bulmer, R.N.H. 1965. *The Kyaka in Gods, Ghosts and Men in Melanesia*. Melbourne and Oxford: The University Presses: 132-161.

Burridge, K.O.L. 1960. *Mambu*. London: Methuen.

Firth, R. 1956. "Rumour in a Primitive Society." *Journal of Abnormal and Social Psychology*, 53:122-132.

------------1961. *History and Traditions of Tikopia*. Memoir, No. 32. Wellington: The
    Polynesian Society.

Lawrence, P. 1964. *Road Belong Cargo*. Manchester: The University Press.

Lévi-Strauss, C. 1958. "La Structure des Mythes." *Anthropologie Structurale*. Paris:
    Librairie Plon: 227-256.

Read, K.E. 1952. "The Nama Cult of the Gahuku-Gama." *Oceania*. 23:125.

Salisbury, R.F. 1956. "The Siane Language." *Anthropos* 51:447-480.

------------1962a. *From Stone to Steel*. Cambridge and Melbourne: The University Presses.

------------1962b. "Notes on Bilingualism and Linguistic Change in New Guinea."
    Anthropological Linguistics, Oct. 1962 1-13.

------------1965. *The Siane in Gods, Ghosts and Men in Melanesia*: 50-77. Melbourne and
    Oxford: The University Presses.

Vial, L.G. 1941. "Down the Waghi." *Walkabout* 7(a):16.

White, J-P. 1965. "Archaeological Investigations in New Guinea." *Journal of the Polynesian
    Society*, 71:40-56.

3.

Asymmetrical Marriage Systems[1]

by

Richard F. Salisbury

Source: *American Anthropologist* 58, 1956.

This paper is a consideration of the association between the system of marriage relationships between groups, and their economic system of production and exchange. It is based on ethnographic material collected by the author in New Guinea, and on material from secondary sources. I try to show that where marriage is accompanied by prestations or payments of any kind, an asymmetrical marriage system can occur. Such a system exists when there is an unreciprocated flow of women going in one direction and a flow of goods going in the opposite direction. This asymmetry can exist despite the fact that the people themselves view the marriage relationships as symmetrical or reciprocally balanced. It can also exist without there being any recognition of the asymmetry in the form of a kinship rule of preferential marriage.

There has recently been much interest in the subject of kinship systems which prescribe who shall marry whom, and which thereby structure an asymmetry in the marriage relationships (Lévi-Strauss 1949; Leach 1951; de Josselin de Jong 1952; Schneider and Homans 1955). I wish to distinguish between these rules of preferential marriage and the pattern of marriages actually taking place in a society, which I shall call its "marriage system." I show that it is possible for the marriage system to operate in opposition to the marriage rules of a society.

Marriage systems can be of many forms. They can be reciprocating when two groups exchange women; they can be circular when a large number of groups intermarry and, on balance, each group receives as many women for wives, as it gives[2] out women in marriage to other groups; they can be asymmetrical when certain groups give out significantly more women in marriage than they receive, while other groups receive more women than they give. By considering some of the general properties of an asymmetrical system, I wish to clarify the differences between the reports of Lévi-Strauss (1949) and Leach (1951), and to show that their views of preferential marriage rules, although different, are actually complementary since one is referring to circular marriage systems and the other is dealing with asymmetrical ones.

In his *Structures Elémentaires de la Parenté* (1949), Lévi-Strauss demonstrated the existence of two sorts of sister-exchange underlying the marriage rules of many primitive societies – the direct exchange of sisters between two groups (*échange restreint*) and the more general exchange of sisters where at least three groups are involved. This form, which he terms *échange généralisé*, in its simplest expression means that the groups are formed into a chain; each group gives wives to the next group in such a way that the first group receives its wives from the last group in the chain. The system which such a marriage rule creates is a circular one, since all groups receive as many wives as they give out sisters. If, however, there is no gift of wives from the last group to the first group, then the system becomes an asymmetrical one.

In an *échange généralisé* it is usual for the first group to receive a bride-price or, as Mauss (1924) would call it, a *prestation*, in exchange for the women it gives to the second group. The first group then passes the *prestation* on to the last group when it receives wives from them, and in a similar way the bride-price is passed through the circular system. There is a flow of women going in one direction around the circle, and a flow of prestations going in the opposite direction.

For such a formal circular system to work requires that the marriage rules compel the members of each group to give wives to, and to take wives from, specified other groups. Lévi-Strauss uses the term *mariage privilegié* to refer to such a compulsory rule, and I propose to use "obligatory marriage" as a translation of his term. "Preferential marriage rules" is a term that has commonly been used to refer both to obligatory marriage rules and to those types of marriage which are preferred but which comprise only a proportion of all the marriages contracted. I shall use "preferential marriage" to refer only to the latter type.

Lévi-Strauss deals mainly with obligatory marriage rules. He shows how, in generalized exchange systems, unilateral cross-cousin marriage is typical. If it is matrilateral in a patrilineal society – if Ego marries his mother's brother's daughter – then one group is continuously giving women to a specific other group, and this involves what he calls "structural continuities" (p. 554); if the marriage rule is to marry a father's sister's daughter, then Ego's group will give a woman (father's sister) in one generation and will receive a woman (Ego's wife) in the next generation. This involves no "structural continuities," or permanent wife-giving/wife-receiving relationships between groups. Both of these generalizations hold to a limited extent if the marriage rules are only preferential and not obligatory.

Leach's paper *Structural Implications of Matrilateral Cross-Cousin Marriage* takes up the implications of marriage rules that are only preferential. He shows that a circular marriage system does not result from a matrilateral cross-cousin marriage rule unless the total society is made up of defined marriage classes, each of which is exogamous but which are, as a totality, endogamous. In fact, he goes on to show how, among the Kachin of Burma, who have such a marriage rule and localized clans, the marriage system which results is an asymmetrical one. He also shows that there is a status difference between groups of wife-givers and groups of wife-receivers, and this results, in the asymmetrical system, in a flow of prestations – which can be variously bride-wealth, services, protection, or prestige – going in the opposite direction to the flow of women.

In his analysis of this system, Leach takes as his starting point the existence of a marriage rule stated in the kinship idiom of matrilateral cross-cousin marriage, and he then goes on to show how the rest of the social structure of an asymmetrical marriage system, status differentiation, and a flow of prestations, can be derived from a knowledge of the type of marriage rule. The first point I wish to make in the present paper is that a preferential marriage rule is not essential if an asymmetrical system is to persist; it is, I maintain, common for asymmetrical systems to arise in societies possessing either status differentiation or differences in the distribution of economic resources, and this asymmetry may persist without ever being expressed as a preferential rule of marriage. Leach's analysis, in other words, is of a special type of asymmetrical system; Lévi-Strauss' analysis is of the mechanics of circular or closed marriage systems, and in this sense their contributions are complementary. The conflict in their analyses comes from the fact that both deal with similar marriage rules, stated in a kinship idiom, and they do not spell out the fact that these rules apply to different kinds of marriage systems.

My second point is that I wish to generalize further Leach's analysis of the Kachin asymmetrical system, when he shows that to understand the working of such a system one must study the articulation of the small society with a wider social context than is usually treated by anthropologists. I will show that this context must extend over a wider geographical area than the sovereign group, and must consider the relationship between the marriage system, the political system, and the economic system. These systems deal with the distribution of women, power, and material goods. Any of these commodities can be used as a prestation, and if all prestations are taken account of, the principle of reciprocity applies. An asymmetry in the possession of power or wealth can lead to an asymmetry in the marriage system, which in turn acts to distribute power or wealth through the whole society.

My first example of an asymmetrical system is that of the Siane[3] people of the Eastern Highlands of New Guinea, among whom I worked for twelve months in 1952-1953.[4] These people are a congeries of tribes practicing slash and burn agriculture and living in villages on the mountain ridges at about 6,000 feet altitude. Typically, each village is composed of one patrilineal, patrilocal, localized clan of about 250 individuals, and is surrounded by similar clan-villages, two miles distant in every direction. The tribal unit is loosely organized and consists of from two to nine clans. It often coincides with the largest exogamous unit, composed of two or three neighboring clans. This unit has some religious functions and is the largest unit within which warfare to kill is theoretically prohibited. The clan-village forms a corporate exogamous unit which, to outsiders, is internally undifferentiated, although internal segments are recognized in dispute situations within the clan. Lineages within the clan are important in inheritance, land-ownership, and in the range of use of certain kinship terms, but they do not regulate marriage. Each marriage between two clans is a relation between two corporate groups as wholes, but neither clan is permanently in a wife-giving or wife-receiving status. In native eyes, the ideal is one of exact reciprocity within each pair of clans. As some girls of an Emenyo clan expressed it to me, when a distant Yamofwe clan had not reciprocated a wife they had received from Emenyo, "They do not give their vulvas to our penises; we will not marry a Yamofwe man." The corporate relationship between clans, which this expresses, means that every clan (except clans within the same exogamic group) is thus in an affinal relationship with every other clan. As the Siane say "We call them 'wife's-father'; with them we fight."

Warfare is one aspect of the affinal relationship. Another more important expression of it is in the exchange of nonutilitarian valuables which takes place at marriage and at the rites of passage for the children of the marriage, as well as at peace-making ceremonies at the end of wars. Although both sides make payments, there is a large balance going from the husband's clan to the wife's clan, and this balance is regarded as payment for the offspring. The "valuables" which are exchanged consist of shells of many shapes and sizes, principally gold-lip shell cut into crescents or small cowries sewn onto bark headdresses, and also bird-of-paradise plumes, pigs, fine axes, and lengths of colored cloth. In precontact times these valuables were traded in from the coast, which is here about 70 miles away to the northeast (or over a week's walk through enemy territory).

The trading was in the form of the ceremonial gift-exchange between affines, and relatively small numbers of broken shells reached the Siane area. Pigs were raised locally, but their meat was quickly consumed, while but a few birds-of-paradise can be shot locally. With these two exceptions, the only way of obtaining valuables was through ceremonial exchanges, and to replenish one's stock after making a ceremonial payment, one usually had to give a sister in marriage to another group. The general picture is thus of the circulation of a limited stock of valuables between the various groups in the society, with this flow being matched by the movement of women in the opposite direction.

As I have indicated above, the natives picture their marriage system as composed of a symmetrical exchange of sisters between individual clans. I collected data on all marriages involving members of one clan which had taken place in the last three generations, including the numbers involved and the clan of the spouse. The figures are as complete as I could make them, but the number of "women went married to" is substantially lower than the number of "wives obtained" in the grandparental generation. This difference does not necessarily imply an imbalance in the numbers of women involved at that time. It occurs because individuals remember ties through their mothers, and this ensures that all the women marrying in are remembered. Sisters marrying out are less socially significant and tend to be forgotten over time, rendering these figures less complete. I have no reason to believe that such forgetting is anything but random with respect to where the sisters went, and so it does not distort the analysis below. These figures are given in Table 1.

Chi square calculated from this table is 3.72 and indicates that there is a probability of less than 10 percent that the pattern of marriages is random and balanced, as is implied by the native theory of reciprocity and symmetry in the marriage system. It is clear from the figures that there is actually a marked trend for wives to be obtained from clans to the south and west, and for sisters to go out in marriage to the north and east.

Table 1. Marriages involving members of Antomona clan, Emenyo tribe.
(All marriages through three generations tabulated by clan of spouse.)

	Antomona clan	
	Man obtained wife from	Women went married to
Clans to north and east	43	42
Clans to south and west	63	33

It is possible that the system might be of the kind described by Lévi-Strauss, where each generation returns women to the clans from which their fathers acquired wives. If this were so, then the greater number of marriages listed for the parental generation would make it appear as though there were an over-all flow in one direction, although there might really be only a flow in one direction in one generation, balanced by a return flow in the next generation. To test this possibility I divided the marriages into generation groups, using the complete genealogies for each lineage. The native system of informal age-grading of the males renders this division fairly reliable in terms of the absolute dates of the marriages. Since many marriages were of people who had died, or of sisters whose ages I could not check, and since the division into generations does not give much overlap in age-distributions in those cases where I did have an outside estimate of age, I feel that such a division is the most reliable one. It gives a picture of the marriage patterns in the parental and grandparental generations, and also of the patterns in two successive periods of twenty years. Table 2 lists this information.

When the marriages in the parental generation alone are considered, the calculated x^2 of 3.46 is a significant departure from the expected random distribution at the 10 percent level, and the trend is for women to come in from the south and west and to go out to the north and east. For the grandparental generation the x^2 of 1.91 is only significant at the 20 percent level, but the trend is in the same direction. There is at least no reversal of the trend between the generations, as would be expected if the marriage rule were of the patrilateral cross-cousin type.

It is possible to test whether there has been any change in the pattern of obtaining wives by comparing the third column of Table 2 with the first column. The x^2 of 1.46 is not significant at the 20 percent level, indicating no significant change. Similarly, we can test whether there has been a change in the areas to which sisters are sent, and we obtain a x^2 of .41 which is not significant at any level. There is no reason to reject the null hypothesis that there has been no change in either pattern between the two generations. In other words, there is some evidence that the asymmetrical marriage system has continued for at least the past forty years, although the pattern of a general drift of women from the south and west towards the north-east has become, if anything, more marked in the Siane area during the last twenty years.

Table 2.—Marriages involving members of Antomona clan, Emenyo Tribe. (Tabulated by generations and by clan of spouse.)

	Antomona clan			
	Grandparental generation		Parental generation	
	Men obtained wives from	Women went married to	Men obtained wives from	Women went married to
Clans to north and east	28	13	15	29
Clans to south and west	35	8	28	25

This drift of women I wish to associate with a drift, in the ceremonial exchange of valuables, of goods going in the opposite direction. In grandparental times the source of shell valuables was on the coast, and old men would point to the northeast-the direction where the coast comes nearest to Siane – as the source of shell ornaments. The amount which came in was small, however, and most of the exchanging of valuables for women entailed only the circulation of a relatively fixed stock of valuables, and not the introduction of new valuables. Since the differential possession of new valuables by northeastern groups played so little part in the exchange system, it becomes all the more surprising that the drift of women was perceptible in the figures.

Since 1934 there have been Europeans in the Highlands, with the nearest settlements to Siane being in Goroka and Asaroka, 30 miles to the east and north. The natives near the settlements quickly became wealthy in shells and cloth which the Europeans brought in. The Siane area was not entered by government patrols until 1945, and until then the way in which European-type valuables entered the area was through the channels of ceremonial payments and exchanges. In other words, the presence of Europeans served to accentuate the difference in wealth as between Siane and the north and east, and gave the contacted groups an advantage in the trading for women.

A measure of that advantage is provided by the detailed figures I kept during my year of stay, of all the commodities which natives took from me in payment for food, wood or services. I was the sole source of European goods for a radius of about eight miles around my house. Natives came from all over this area, and in return for their services they could choose between payments in cash, payments in articles like beads or shells (which could be used as native valuables), payments in consumable goods such as salt, paper, or trade tobacco, or payment in hard goods such as nails or razor blades. The amount of payments of the fourth kind were negligible for present purposes, but the percentages of compensation accepted in the various other media are shown in Table 3.

Table 3.—Payments taken by various Siane clans. (Payments are for services rendered to author. Antomona clan, Emenyo tribe, has been omitted.)

	Percentages of			Total
	valuables	cash	consumables	payments
Clans to north and east	27	14	59	100
Clans to south and west	57	10	33	100

The demand for cash is ambiguous since cash could be used for consumption, as a valuable, or as saving for a large capital purchase. Leaving out this demand, it is clear that the northern and eastern clans more often chose consumables; the southern and western clans seized the opportunity to earn valuables. Such a pattern is consistent with the idea that the northern and eastern clans were already well supplied with valuables since they took fewer of them; the southern and western clans would appear to have had less originally, and so there was a tendency for the valuables to move in that direction. This confirms the statement that there is a tendency for valuables to move towards the south and west – the direction from which women come – rather than toward the north and east. This movement was marked when my presence made it possible to obtain valuables without giving women in exchange; it confirms the existence of differences in the amounts of wealth possessed, even though a Siane man would deny that there were such differences within the 180 square mile area. As an outside observer I could find only small differences between villages fifteen miles apart, although villages twenty-five miles apart were noticeably different. The natives' assertion that clans are equally wealthy must be considered as a case where the native ideal of equality repudiates the actual inequalities of wealth; just as the native ideal of the marriage system as being reciprocating repudiates the actual asymmetry.

In short, for the Siane area of about 180 square miles, it has been shown that there is a tendency for women to pass from the south and west towards the north and east, and for valuables to move in the opposite direction. There is suggestive evidence that this same pattern existed in the grandparental generation, though to a less pronounced degree. In the grandparental generation the northern and eastern clans had a slight wealth advantage because they were nearer the coast; since the coming of the Europeans they have had a more marked wealth advantage, and the movement of women is also more pronounced. Neither the wealth difference nor the movement of women is recognized in Siane ideology.

Nor is the asymmetrical marriage system recognized in the kinship structure by its statement in the form of a marriage rule. There is definitely no obligatory marriage rule in Siane, and the only preference for marrying a definite category of kin acts against the asymmetry and towards the establishment of a reciprocating system. This preference is that girls favor marriage into the clan of their mother (though they may not marry into her lineage). This means that their mother's brother will live in the village into which they marry, and will give support in marital quarrels. I have data on thirty women of the Antomona clan for whom both the clan they married into and the clan of their mother is available. Seven of these women married into their mother's clan. There are nine surrounding clans with whom Antomona clan marries, and thus the chance expectation would be that one-ninth of all girls would marry into the clan of their mother. Using the method of the standard error of a proportion, the difference between one-ninth and 7/30 is significant at the 5 percent level. In other words, the type of marriage involving the return of a woman to the clan from which the father took a wife is a preferred type in fact as well as in theory.

Marriage of a man into his mother's clan is forbidden. For both men and women, marriage with a true father's sister's child is also forbidden. But in the wider classificatory sense of the term, "father's sister's child" could be applied to every member of all other clans. A classificatory father's-sister has married into every surrounding clan, so that all senior male members of every other clan can technically be called "father's sister's husband." This is because both the avoidance of affines and the corporate nature of clans mean that, technically, Ego does not know which individual of the clan his father's sister has married. All the children of the other clans are the children of father's sister's husbands and Ego can, if he so desires, call them *novonefo* or "my cross-cousin." Ego must marry a classificatory father's sister's daughter. A boy will claim such kinship to ensure hospitality when he goes on a courting visit to any other clan. On the other hand, there is one clan which the child visits with his mother and where he learns to use the term *momonefo*, "my mother's brother." The boy learns that he cannot marry into this clan; the girl learns that marriage into this clan, but not into the lineage of her mother, is desirable. In short, the marriage rules favor patrilateral cross-cousin marriage (in a classificatory sense) and forbid matrilateral cross-cousin marriage. They favor the marriage which tends to form a reciprocating system of delayed sister-exchange, and act to discourage an asymmetrical system such as is found among the Burmese Kachin. It becomes all the more remarkable that an asymmetrical system should have persisted through at least two generations.

To understand how this asymmetrical system could have persisted it is necessary, as Leach has shown, to examine the wider social context in which the asymmetrical system occurs. This social context involves other aspects of the group's social structure, as well as the structure of nearby groups.

The first possible way in which an asymmetrical system could maintain itself in a small society would be if the small society was in fact only one segment of a larger society in which the marriage system was circular. If this were so, the groups at the wife-giving end of the small chain would obtain wives from groups at the wife-receiving end of the chain, giving in return the valuables which they had received.

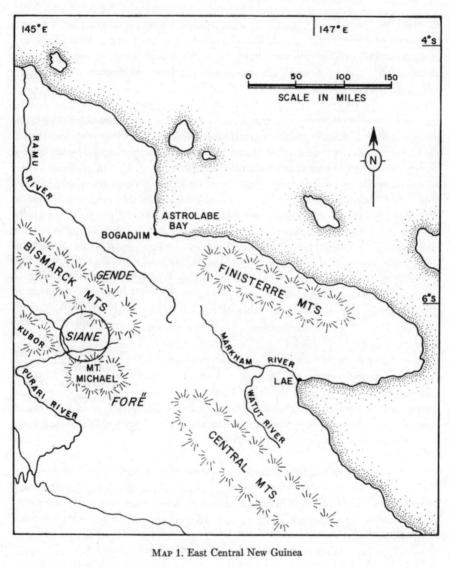

MAP 1. East Central New Guinea

A study of the map shows that this is a virtual geographic impossibility for the Siane area. The marriage chain is in existence some 40 miles to the north, on the far side of the 10,000 foot Bismarck Mountains which divide Siane from the Ramu River and the sea. These people to the north are the Gende, described by Aufenanger (1940). He states (p. 54) that the Gende obtained the trade commodity of women from the Arawa, their nearest neighbors on the southern side of the mountains. From the Ramu people to the north and east they obtained shells of various kinds, which they traded with groups further south. There is definite evidence in support of the continuance of the chain, although in this area other commodities entered into the system of exchanges. Axes are obtained from further west, and are handed on to the northeast in return for salt and pottery. But if the marriage chain stretches 40 miles to the north, it is extremely unlikely that it turns in the opposite direction and links up with the wife-giving groups some 60 miles away across two mountain ranges to the south. We may safely say that the Siane system is not merely one sector of a large circular marriage system involving several groups.

Another possibility Leach cites as helping to support an asymmetrical system occurs when there is also a general drift of males accompanying the females, and the local descent groups participating in the system are not stable. The Siane evidence points in the opposite direction. After prolonged genealogical study I could find only 2 percent of marriages that were other than virilocal – men stay in their own villages on marriage. This agrees with the society's emphasis on patrilineality and residence on land which was owned by the ancestors, and out of which the first ancestors emerged. Of 36 clans whose legendary history is known, only 14 do not claim descent from ancestors who "came out of holes in the ground," and the immigration of those 14 is not within remembered history.

Another possibility is that the asymmetrical system is supported by other features of the social organization of the societies in different parts of the chain. One would expect an asymmetrical marriage system to cause strains in a homogeneous society if it persisted for long. Certain adaptations would minimize the effect of those strains.

These strains can be understood by imagining what would happen if a group of societies, all of equal size, similar sex composition, and equal wealth, formed an asymmetrical marriage system isolated from the outside world. The system would work so that the group at the wife-giving end would, in the course of time, be deprived of women, while the group at the wife-receiving end would have a large number of women. Contrariwise, the first group would tend to accumulate the valuables which were offered in exchange for wives, while the last group would be deprived of its wealth. The groups in the middle of the chain, although they would be giving and receiving wives and valuables from different groups, would give and receive the same amount of valuables and wives. The groups at either end of the chain would have other difficulties in addition to their surpluses of wives or valuables. They would each have marriage relationships with only one other group, but these groups next to them would be in relationship with two groups and would be unable to provide sufficient marriage partners to satisfy the needs of the groups at the ends of the chain. The end groups would be left with numbers of marriageable men and women for whom they could not obtain marriage partners.

This problem of an excess of both marriageable men and women could be obviated in two ways. Either the groups at the ends of the chain could be smaller than the groups in other parts of the chain, or they could permit endogamy as well as exogamy. The problem of the drift of valuables from one end of the chain to the other has two aspects. The problem of how the valuables-deficient group could recoup its losses would be solved if it had a permanent source of supply of new valuables; the problem of how the valuables-acquiring group could avoid amassing a stock of valuables would be solved if progressively less and less valuables were given in each payment, as the distance from the source of supply increased; in other words, if the exchange value of a valuable increased and if less were needed as a payment for each woman. This is what would be expected on classical economic grounds, since the supply of valuables decreases the further from the source of production, while the demand remains constant.

The over-all surplus of women remaining in the wife-receiving group could be reduced either by female infanticide or by an increase in polygyny. The over-all deficit of women remaining in the wife-giving group could be mitigate by male infanticide (which would be unusual), by warfare and the killing of numbers of adolescent males, or by a late age of marriage. Warfare and a late age of marriage, to be sure, create strains in their turn, but such strains are dealt with in several common institutional ways. One such way is by an initiation period during which the boys are denied sexual access to women when they are warriors, or by strictly enforced religious sanctions preventing them from competing with the older men for the sexual favors of women. The more an initiation period is a technique used by the older men to control the younger unmarried men, the more concern we would expect to find on the part of the married men over the possible desertion of wives to the unmarried men. Sexual anxiety would be common in the legal code, while the younger men would try to stress their sexual attractiveness.

The diagram shows a hypothetical model of three societies in which the social structures are of the kind sketched above, and which together form an asymmetrical marriage system. Society A is a wife-giving society and is smaller than the others for the reasons stated above. It gives its four sisters to society B in exchange for two units of valuables; it obtains two wives from society B in exchange for one valuable. The net result is that society A has one more valuable than it started with, two of its men have obtained wives, but there is no surplus of marriageable sisters. If the society is to maintain itself, it is clear that the two wives must produce large numbers of children.

Composition of the societies before marriage exchanges take place, with women and goods to be exchanged circled

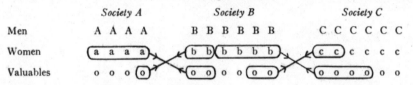

Composition of the societies after the exchanges of women for valuables

	Society A	Society B	Society C
Men	A A A A	B B B B B B	C C C C C C
Wives	b b	a a a a c c	b b b b c c c c
Valuables	o o o o o	o o o o o o o	o o o o

Hypothetical Model of an asymmetrical marriage system involving three societies. (Each symbol represents one individual man, woman, or valuable. The marriages which have taken place in the second situation are indicated by pairs of lines joining men and women. The rules on which the model is built are explained in the text.)

Society B has exchanged four sisters for four valuables with society C; in return it has obtained two wives from C in exchange for two valuables. In its relations with society A it has obtained four wives in exchange for two valuables, and received one valuable in exchange for two sisters. The exchange rate in transactions with C was one valuable equalling one woman; with A it was one valuable equalling two women. The net result is that society B has given all its sisters in marriage and obtained wives for all its men; it has also gained one valuable – probably just sufficient to replace breakages.

Society C is a wife-receiving society, in which endogamy is permitted (possibly through some moiety system) and polygyny is common. It has given out four valuables to obtain four wives from society B, and has given two of its sisters to B in exchange for two valuables. The men in the society who did not obtain wives from B, have obtained wives from within their own society. The net result has been that the group has gained two women and lost two valuables. This loss is negligible, since we have posited that society C is situated at the source of valuables and can manufacture replacements.

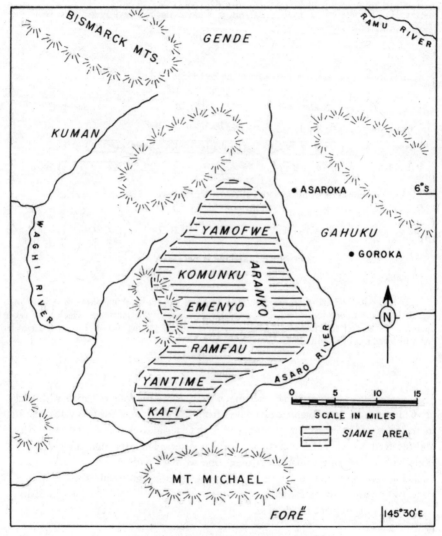

MAP 2. Eastern Highlands of New Guinea

In the New Guinea situation, this hypothetical model could be applied to the concrete societies. The Siane area would then be occupied by type B societies – there is a drift of women in one direction, but the society does not seem to suffer any net loss or gain of women. The model would lead one to look for type

A and type C societies in distant areas having some contact with Siane, and together forming a long marriage chain.

The fact that the source of valuables used to be the coast would suggest that societies of the C type would be found on the nearest section of the coast near Bogadjim on Astrolabe Bay. Type A societies would be expected further south in the Highlands, notably south of Mount Michael (see map 2).

The area south of Mount Michael is as yet unexplored, but some material is available from the texts collected by R. M. and C. Berndt in a nearby area farther east. The main emphasis in this society – the Forë – seems to be on warfare and physical aggression (C. H. Berndt 1953:133). The men's houses there are larger and more ornate ceremonial centers than are those further north (Read 1954:12), though the villages themselves are smaller and consist of from 12 to 20 houses (C. H. Berndt 1953:114). In spite of the incessant fighting and the practice of cannibalism, there is an over-all preponderance of males over females (C. H. Berndt 1953:126). Sexual anxiety in the area is evidenced by the ferocity of the punishment fur adulterous women, sticks being thrust into their vaginas (Read 1954:23). Read also quotes R.M. Berndt as saying that it is not unknown for men to have intercourse with dead bodies. It is interesting to note that some small villages far to the south permit endogamy (R.M. Berndt 1953:201 note). Endogamy has previously been adduced as one possible way of disposing of a surplus of marriageable men and women within the village. The hypothetical model did not consider this as a way of organizing societies at the wife-giving end of the marriage chain, but it can be seen here as an alternative (and additional) method of dealing with the problem of a surplus of marriageable sisters.[5] In any case, there is prima facie evidence that southern societies are of type A.

There are no anthropological reports for the area around Bogadjim (see map 2) where we would expect to find type C societies, but there are notes by numerous early German visitors to the area. Lauterbach describes (1898:147) how the villages near the coast are composed of two or three hamlets, each of which consists of some 20 houses. These groups of hamlets intermarry (Zoller 1891:62), "but sometimes wives are taken from the mountain tribes, and these marriages are the occasion for special arrangements." What these arrangements are is not described, but presumably it means that large payments are made.

Lauterbach (1898:147) confirms the intermarrying of coastal and mountain villages, but also connects the villages through trade relationships in a complex which extends to the mountainous hinterland, and to the coastal island of Bili-Bili. All observers agree that the valuables of the coastal people were boar and dog teeth. On the other hand, as the explorers got further inland they found that shells were increasingly highly prized (Lauterbach 1898:158). Tappenbeck (1901:42 et. seq.) mentions that in some coastal villages women are in the majority, although this is unusual for New Guinea; that there is polygyny and that there is no long wait before getting married; that bride-prices are low and consist of only one pig; that infanticide is not infrequent. This could be seen as a means of controlling the population increase that would be expected from an influx of women. In short, the picture seems to be exactly what would be predicted for a type C society. There is internal differentiation, polygyny, and a constant source of valuables, whose worth increases the further they travel from their source. There are other ways in which the coastal societies adjust to their wealthy wife-receiving position – their relations with the trading islanders being one – but there is no space to discuss this problem here.

It remains to show that the long marriage chain system which I have tentatively described as stretching for over 100 miles, and of which the Siane form only a small sector, is not an isolated example. In fact there is suggestive evidence that similar chains are common in New Guinea. Hogbin and Wedgewood (1954:65) show that for most coastal regions "multi-carpellary parishes" (internally differentiated villages) are the most common form of social organization.

> "Monocarpellary parishes in which marriage is necessarily exogamous are exceptional ... Marriage is both intra-parishional and extra-parishional ... [but] most women on marriage only move from one part of the settlement to another."

The "rope" system described by Mead (1938:321-22) for the Arapesh suggests a marriage chain such as I have described, although as Mead describes it, it is purely a matter of trade. However, she says,

> "There is a vague feeling that such [trade-friend] relationships were originally set up by marriage of women ... and that a continuance of the marriage ties is not inappropriate."

The Abelam described by Kaberry (1941) are the next people inland from the Arapesh, and they have a social organization more closely resembling the Siane than do the Arapesh. Villages are more important units and are "geographically exclusive" (p. 239); clans, which are the exogamous units, tend to be localized in one or two hamlets, and hamlets usually (though not exclusively) are composed of one clan. In all, the pattern is one of localized descent groups which are usually exogamous, and which are definitely corporate (p. 241). Mead shows (1935:102) how women from these southern groups do go to the northern groups in marriage, but the opposite process does not seem to occur – further evidence that the marriage system is asymmetrical.

Examples of type A societies are hard to find since they are in inaccessible central areas, but Blackwood (1939:18) describes a mountain group on the Watut river which resembles the Mount Michael peoples in its small village groups and incessant warfare. The examples of marriage which she cites are all of women from inland groups marrying men from groups nearer the coast. In all these areas then, the material is suggestive of asymmetrical marriage chains, but the evidence is inconclusive since the appropriate statistics have not been collected. Theory would suggest that the differences between coastal and inland New Guinea societies, noted in passing by Hogbin and Wedgewood (1953:246), are functionally determined by the greater wealth of the coast and by the existence of asymmetrical marriage chains.

Asymmetrical marriage systems are not peculiar to New Guinea. Caste hypergamy in India is an obvious case of such a system associated with differences in political power and religious "purity." The material collected by Hulstaert (1938) for the Nkundo of the Congo region of Africa suggests such a system. Marriage preferences among the Nkundo seem largely to be a matter of sisters being given in marriage to clans that are wealthier than their own clan. It can be seen that this would result in the sisters of the wealthiest clans not being able to marry any one. For these women there is a special form of marriage called *bolumbo*, whereby suitors come from very distant areas and are selected on the basis of their being rich enough to give presents to every clan which intervened between their own home and that of the girl (Hulstaert 1938:30 et. seq.). Again the evidence is suggestive rather than conclusive, but it would appear that this special marriage form is an adaptation of the social structure to cope with the strain of an asymmetrical system. Here the asymmetry is clearly caused through differences in wealth.

Ireland is one of the few areas where statistics were collected which show an asymmetrical system (Arensberg and Kimball 1940:226-27).Their description of the social structure of County Clare shows how many of the tensions consequent upon being a wife-giving society are dealt with in institutional ways.

In short, the purpose of this paper has been to show that asymmetrical marriage systems can exist without there necessarily being any rule of preferential marriage. The existence of such systems is suggested by much data, but the marriage statistics necessary to prove this have rarely been collected. It is hoped that this paper will prove a stimulus for the collection of more such data. Asymmetrical marriage systems, of which the Kachin type described by Leach is one special case, occur when there is also some difference – of wealth, prestige, or power – between the various groups involved. In such a situation the giving of wives becomes one of the many prestations between the various groups. The rules of reciprocity outlined by Mauss and Lévi-Strauss act to distribute the wealth, prestige, or power more evenly through the society. Such asymmetrical marriage systems require that societies in different parts of the marriage chain be organized in distinctive ways. On the basis of the analyses made by Leach (1951), I describe in hypothetical terms one possible way in which such societies can be organized and then show that this model applies in New Guinea.

NOTES

1. The writer wishes to thank Dr. D. M. Schneider for his critical reading and helpful suggestions during the writing of this paper, and to thank Professor S. F. Nadel for posing the questions from which this paper grew.

2. Throughout this paper I use such phrases as "give women" or "payment for women." In fact what are given, or paid for in a *bride-price*, are certain specific rights over the woman and her offspring; women are rarely if ever transferred absolutely as a chattel or filiated completely with their husband's group. They are, however, the concrete object whose movement one can observe, and to use the phrase "exchange of women for valuables" gives a more concrete picture. Such phrases are used throughout the paper for vividness and convenience; the proviso that what is referred to is actually rights over women should be borne in mind throughout.

3. For further ethnographic material on these people, and especially on their kinship system, the reader is referred to Read (1954) and Salisbury (1956a and 1956b).

4. The fieldwork on which this study is based was carried out with the aid of a grant from the Australian National University, while the author was a Research Scholar at that University. Grateful acknowledgment is made of their support.

5. This surplus would appear in society A of the hypothetical model if the society had been composed of 6 men and 6 women, as were societies B and C. In that case only four sisters would have gone in marriage to B which could not absorb more, leaving two unmarried girls in A. There would also be four unmarried men in A. In this situation, permitted endogamy would solve the problem of unmarried girls, but late marriage would still be needed to solve the problem of the excess number of males.

References

Arensberg, C.M. and S.T. Kimball. 1940. *Family and Community in Ireland*. Cambridge, Mass.: Harvard University Press.

Aufenanger, H. and G. Holtker. 1940. *Die Gende in Zentral NeuGuinea*. Wien-Mödling.

Berndt, C. H. 1953. "Sociocultural change in the Eastern Highlands of New Guinea." *Southwestern Journal of Anthropology* 9: 114.

Berndt R. M. 1953. "Reaction to contact in the Eastern Highlands of New Guinea." *Oceania* 24:190.

Blackwood, B. 1939. "Life on the Upper Watut in New Guinea." *Geographical Journal* 94:11.

Hogbin, H.I. and C. Wedgewood. 1954. "Local grouping in Melanesia." *Oceania* 24:58 and 23:241.

Hulstaert, G. 1938. *Le Mariage des Nkundo*. Institut Royal Colonial Belge, Section Sciences Morales, Mémoires tome 8:3.

De Josselin de Jong, J.P.B. 1952. "Lévi-Strauss' Theory on Kinship and Marriage." *Mededelingen van het Rijks-museum voor Volkenkunde* 10. Leiden: E. J. Brill.

Kaberry, P.M. 1941. "The Abelam tribe." *Oceania* 11:233.

Lauterbach, C. 1898. "Die Geographische Ergebnisse der Kaiser-Wilhelmsland Expedition." *Zeitschrift der Gesellschaft für Erdkunde zu Berlin* 33:141.

Leach, E.R. 1951. "Structural implications of matrilateral crosscousin marriage." *Journal of the Royal Anthropological Institute* 81:23.

Lévi-Strauss, C. 1949. *Structures Elémentaires de la Parenté*. Paris: Presses Universitaires de France.

Mauss, M. 1924. "Essai sur le Don." *L'Annee Sociologique 1923-24*.

Mead, M. 1935. *Sex and Temperament*. New York: William Morrow, Inc.

------------1938. "The Mountain Arapesh; an importing culture." American Museum of Natural History, *Anthropological Papers* 36:141.

Read, K.E. 1954. "Cultures of the Central Highlands, New Guinea." *Southwestern Journal of Anthropology* 10:1.

Salisbury, R.F. 1956a. *Outline Grammar and Wordlist of the Siane Language, Eastern Highlands of New Guinea*. Fribourg: MikroBibliotheka Anthropos Monographs.

------------1956b. "Unilineal descent groups in the New Guinea Highlands." *Man* 56: January, 1956.

Schneider, D.M. and G.C. Homans. 1955. *Authority, Marriage, and Final Causes*. Glencoe, Illinois: Free Press.

Tappenbeck, E. 1901. *Deutsch NeuGuinea*. Berlin.

Zoller, H. 1891. *Deutsch NeuGuinea, und meine Ersteigung des FinisterreGebirges*. Stuttgart: Union deutscher Verlagsgesellschaft.

4.

NEW GUINEA HIGHLAND MODELS AND DESCENT THEORY

by

Richard F. Salisbury

Source: *Man* 64 (Nov-Dec), 1964.

In 1956 I described the existence of an obligatory patrilateral cross-cousin-marriage rule among the patrilineal Siane of the New Guinea Highlands (Salisbury, 1956b). In view of some theorists' failure to consider the ethnographical evidence when they assert that an obligatory patrilateral cross-cousin-marriage rule is impossible, it is perhaps appropriate to restate the ethnography in model form.[1] I hope to show that this model is one variant of a general model of corporate descent groups, and to assist in explaining why African models are inadequate for the understanding of New Guinea society (cf. Barnes 1962).

The Siane group of tribes number some 15,000 individuals; the group has no boundaries beyond those assigned to it by administrators and ethnographers using geographical and linguistic criteria. It is an aggregate of numbers of independent clans of about 250 individuals, and similar clans exist on all sides of the Siane. Clans are grouped into phratries and tribes, the term 'phratry' applying when the clans may not intermarry and the term 'tribe' indicating only that the grouping of clans has a defined territory and that it is named. A tribe may consist of only one phratry, or of several unnamed phratries. Clans are segmented into varying numbers of wards (sub-clans) and lineages.

It is, however, the relations *between* clans that will concern us first. The few non-intermarrying clans of a phratry consider themselves as *nenta wenena* ('close people') or *kunarafo* ('brothers'). Towards all other clans there is a multiple and distributive opposition. This takes the form of marriage, of formal presentations of valuables, and of warfare with other clans. The shifting empirical pattern of alliances, wars and neutralities with specific other clans merely accentuates the continuity of the opposition, which is predicated on an equality of prestige and power between clans (cf. Salisbury, 1960), when in fact there are constant but varying inequalities. In one sense, then, all marriages occur between clans which are already in a state of corporate affinity with all other marriageable clans; reciprocity by clan B giving a 'sister' to clan A should follow within a year or so after clan A gives a 'sister' to clan B.

83

When a particular marriage is due to take place between a man of clan A and a girl of clan B, however, the bride is not viewed as an affine whose status is being reaffirmed but as a *komorafo* ('sister's child') or a *hovorafo* ('cross-cousin'). This may be because the girl's own mother was of clan A,[2] but it may equally well be because a woman of A married a man of clan B in the distant past. In short the ideology of the relationship between clans at the time when the marriage occurs is that clan B are corporately fa-sis-children to clan A. Ideologically it is appropriate that fa-sis-da should marry into the clan of her mo-br, as this produces reciprocity over the generations; in practice the reciprocity is an almost immediate exchange of 'sisters.' The marriage rule is obligatory as all men, when they marry, must be and are (with modern exceptions of those marrying foreign women) marrying a 'father's sister's daughter.' The rule should not be called 'prescriptive,' as nothing is 'prescribed.' A young man does not have to search for a girl who falls into a specific kinship category, but when he has found an attractive girl, he sees how she fits into the category which all brides fit into. Alternatively, and this is common in Siane, a girl decides which clan she can most appropriately claim 'mother's-brothers' in, and then chooses a particular husband who is not a son of one of her true 'mother's-brothers.' Patrilateral cross-cousin-marriage does not 'produce a lasting structural arrangement between (specific) clans,' but constitutes an excellent ideology for expressing relations of reciprocity in total prestations between large numbers of distributively opposed and politically equal clans.[3]

After the marriage has taken place the relationship between clans A and B reverts to its normal state of corporate affinity, of polite antagonisms and suspicion alternating with overt hostility. But for the principals to the marriage and their immediate kin (and offspring) the fields of personal ego-centred kinship are changed. The bride from clan B, after a period of marginality, takes over her husband's viewpoint towards his clan, clan A. He now treats her parents exclusively as *niamfa* ('close affines') and her clan as *nitofa* ('distant affines'). The parents-in-law (and possibly also siblings of the spouses) call each other *emonawe* ('sister-men'), thereby further emphasizing the aspect of reciprocity. For the children of the marriage, all the men of clan B become either *momorafo* ('mother's-brothers') or *hovorafo* ('cross-cousins'). A male child may not marry into clan B, though a female child may, and I have no cases in my genealogies of transgressions against this rule. Thus both the positive and negative aspects of an obligatory rule of patrilateral cross-cousin marriage exist.[4]

Let us now turn to the formal model of patrilateral cross-cousin marriage (fig. 1), and its implications. Bilateral cross-cousin-marriage involves only two types of intermarrying groups, type A and type B, although as Romney and Epling (1958) have pointed out, each type of group may comprise numerous separate local populations within a tribal 'universe.' The formal model in which only two groups are shown on a single genealogy is an adequate representation if it is understood that type A includes specific populations A1, A2, A3, ... Specific populations Ai and Aj are related to each other as identical or as 'siblings'; this relationship is assumed and need not be indicated. In the formal model of patrilateral cross-cousin marriage systems three types of intermarrying groups are indicated – Ego's own group A, and other groups B and C. The relation between groups B and C is necessarily one of non-identity; symmetry would lead one to expect that the relation should be one of possible intermarriage, of the same nature as that between A and B. When one interprets the formal model in terms of specific populations, it is important to note that the tribal 'universe' is not necessarily split into only three types of groups, but into many types, B, C, D, ... which share the properties of being distinct from A and also distinct from one another. Indicating only three types in the formal model is conventional. Type A groups may indeed comprise more than one local population, as may each other Type, and these populations may stand in a relation of identity to each other. This does not affect their opposition to populations of other Types.

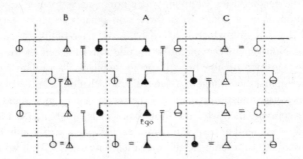

FIG. I. MODEL OF OBLIGATORY PATRILATERAL CROSS-COUSIN
MARRIAGE, WITH PATRILINEAL DESCENT AND VIRILOCAL
RESIDENCE

Shading indicates descent-group membership; dotted lines indicate common residence.

The conventional formal model in fact illustrates the orthodox marriage patterns within one lineage of a local population of type A, in which marriages are alternately with local populations of type B and type C. By extension it implies that some other lineages of the same local population will marry alternately wives from groups B and D; other lineages will marry alternately wives from groups C and D; yet others will marry wives from groups B and E, and so on. The absence of any clear-cut generation divisions within the various lineages of the local population of type A will mean that at any one time some lineages are giving wives to a particular local population of type B, while other lineages are receiving wives from that population. The small size of individual lineages and the consequent unpredictability of sex balance within them, means that lineages cannot be the units for exact reciprocity. Larger populations can be, and can balance exchanges in the short term rather than in delayed exchange as predicated by Lévi-Strauss (1951).

The preceding analysis concerns the relations between numbers of independent types of groups. Let us now return to considering the internal organization of groups, and of local populations. First the empirical Siane ethnography must be cited. I have previously (1956a) described their organization as being one of 'unilineal descent groups.' In terms of the cohesion and opposition between segments and the use of genealogies as a charter for the organization of lineages, Siane clans fit the analytical model of 'corporate unilineal descent group' (Fortes, 1953). In terms of the more recent discussion of 'filiation' and 'descent,' Siane clans are neither unilineal, nor are they organized in terms of descent, though they are corporate groups possessing a stock of land and of ancestral spirit. Except in degree they closely resemble the neighbouring Chimbu, where non-agnates form a large part of any local population (Brown, 1962). Most Siane non-agnates are, however, regarded as members of the clan with which they are living and have rights to demand land for their own use. Non-agnatic clan members include sons of sisters of the clan (and any men, whether kinsmen or not, brought up in the clan-village) who have eaten the food of the clan, had their initiation financed by the clan or had their bride price paid by the clan. No discrimination is made between these clan members and agnatic clan-members. By contrast, men who are living uxorilocally, are treated as temporary visitors, allowed to use land as a special favour even though their children (as sons of clan sisters) may be clan members, and they themselves may have lived in the village since marriage.

In most cases, it is true, a child is a member of the same clan as is its father, and the majority of the exceptional cases are of children who are members of the clan of their mothers. But it is not the fact of parenthood that establishes a claim on the allegiance of the child-filiation is not the relationship which establishes clan membership. This can be seen in those few cases where there are conflicting claims on the allegiance of a child. Thus Antomona clan of Emenyo tribe claimed as a member a man who in 1952 was living in Aranko tribe. His mother from Komunku tribe had borne him in Emenyo shortly before her Emenyo husband and the child's father was killed in warfare. She returned home to Komunku rather than re-marry leviratically. She took the child with her when she re-married an Aranko man. Antomona said he was an Antomona man because Antomona had paid the mother's bride-price, and because it had paid for the child's hair-cutting ceremonies at age 3.

Aranko claimed him because they had paid for his initiation and for his bride-price. In 1952 he visited Antomona periodically; by 1961 he had planted several acres of coffee in Antomona (Aranko is land-short) and lived most of his time there, but visited in Aranko frequently. The ceremonies are the crucial symbolic statement of group membership, and it is the payment for the ceremonies which determines clan membership.

In religious terms what occurs at each of the ceremonies is that more ancestral *korova* or 'spirit' of the clan giving the ceremony is infused into the child, to replace spirit already there. This spirit may come from the blood or milk of the mother, the father's semen, food eaten during childhood which contains spirit from the land on which it is grown, from pork, from a name, or from proximity to objects such as sacred flutes which symbolize *korova*. *Korova* may be lost in the form of bodily secretions or blood through exorcism, or through sorcery, and such loss is a permanent loss to the whole clan depleting the stock of *korova* which can be periodically reincarnated.[5] The individual has a direct relationship with the original clan ancestors, sharing their material essence, some of which he may have acquired through his genitors, but most of which is acquired through ceremonial and growth. It is not acquired by 'cumulative filiation' or descent in the usual definition of the term.

I feel, however, that it is appropriate to call such a relationship with the ancestors one of descent, and that if existing definitions of 'descent' do not fit the Siane case, then the definitions should be modified. In fact, if one goes back to Rivers' (1914, Vol. 1, p.15) original formulation no modification is needed. Rivers arrived at his definition of descent not in order to contrast it with either filiation or affinity, but from a consideration of Melanesian ethnography. Group membership in Melanesia, as among the Siane, is a clearly evident phenomenon with the groups being named and being corporate with respect to some property rights. The titles and rights of particular individuals are obtained through different mechanisms. Inheritance and succession for Rivers were two such mechanisms, while descent was the acquisition of rights through membership in social groups defined in terms of kinship.

Rivers also attempted to spell out what is meant by 'kinship' in terms of 'genealogical demonstration,' but, I submit, neither he nor subsequent butterfly-collectors have succeeded in doing so. On the one hand there is an assumption that everyone knows what kinship is, and that this knowledge is similar for all peoples of the world; secondly there is the assumption that it is related to the process of procreation, and that there is such a thing as 'real kinship' which can be contrasted with 'fictive or conventional kinship'; finally there is the recognition that what anthropologists study is actually 'socially recognized kinship' and that peoples differ widely in what they recognize as 'kin' relationships. With Leach (1962), I feel that the third position should be taken more seriously and that there should be an examination of different peoples' conceptions of the category 'kinship.' The Siane concepts outlined above fit closely with what Leach analyses for Kachin and Trobriands as belief in a 'relationship of common substance.' I would reverse Leach's phrasing of the nature of this relationship, when he says that such a relationship is commonly felt to exist among kinsmen, and say that 'when people define the relations between individuals A and B as being one where they share some common substance, then we can call such a relation one of kinship.' Descent then refers to the transmission of group membership through kinship, or the way in which an individual is categorized as a member of a group because he is felt to have within him some substance which previously existed in another member of that group.

What the Siane case (and, I believe, the full analysis of other New Guinea Highland ethnographies) indicates is that formal models, based on the general theory of corporate descent groups, are indeed relevant. African models are special cases where inter-group relations are phrased in the same terms (agnation) as are intra-group relations; the Siane and other Pacific and South-east Asian people conceptualize inter-group relations in terms of corporate affinity. The Siane model shows how a model of patrilateral cross-cousin marriage, held by the people themselves, conceptualizes an organisation of numerous sovereign egalitarian but opposed local groups.[6] This model is only an ideal one; it needs different transformation rules from a matrilateral cross-cousin marriage rule, in order to apply it to concrete groupings of individuals; it also demands the existence among the people of another model of relationships based not on corporate kinship and corporate affinity (or 'clanship') but on ego-centric network relationships. A treatment of ego-centric relationship models needs concepts other than those provided by descent theory, and is beyond the scope of the present note.

NOTES

1. Salisbury (1962) expands the ethnography, citing the cultural rules as these are given by the Siane, rather than citing statistics on residence, etc. The model here given is a formal abstraction from the rules. With Leach and Lévi-Strauss, I feel that the empirical reality is best understood in the light of a model so derived, rather than vice versa. The 1952-53 fieldwork on which this analysis is based was supported by the Australian National University. Discussions with David M. Schneider have greatly influenced the formulation.

2. Such marriages occur at a rate statistically significantly greater than chance but still represent only 23 per cent of all marriages (Salisbury, 1956b, p.646).

3. The fact that persistent economic inequality results in an asymmetry in the system of marriages actually occurring and that such asymmetry need not be reflected in the marriage rule was the central topic of discussion in Salisbury (1956a).

4. The Siane thus constitute a negative case for the theory of Homans and Schneider (1955). This may well be explained by the fact that Homans and Schneider, insofar as they treat personal choice as influential in selecting marriage partners, always consider that it is the choice of the prospective groom that is crucial. In Siane girls are 'forward' and elope to boys; boys are 'moral' and would not choose a *mo-brda* as a sweetheart as they would feel she was 'like a mother' to them.

5. For a fuller treatment of the religious concepts involved see Salisbury (forthcoming).

6. Livingstone's (1964) insightful analysis of the generality of such social organizations is the stimulus for publication of this paper, which was originally written in response to Barnes (1962).

References

Barnes, J.A. 1962. "African Models in the New Guinea Highlands." *Man* 2.

Brown, P. 1962. "Nonagnates among the Patrilineal Chimbu." *Journal of the Polynesian Society.* LXXI (1962):57-69.

Fortes, M. 1953. "The Structure of Unilineal Descent Groups." *American Anthropologist* LV (1953):17-41.

Homans, G.C. and D.M. Schneider. 1955. *Marriage, Authority and Final Cause.* Glencoe, Illinois: The Free Press.

Leach, E. R. 1962. *On Rethinking Anthropology.* L.S.E. Publications in Social Anthropology 22.

Lévi-Strauss, C. 1951. *Les structures élémentaires de la parenté.* Paris.

Livingstone, F.B. 1964 . "Prescriptive Patrilateral Cross-Cousin Marriage." *Man* 59.

Rivers, W.H.R. 1914. *The History of Melanesian Society.* London: Cambridge University Press.

Romney, A.K. and P.J. Epling. 1958. "A Simplified Model of Kariera Kinship." *American Anthropologist* LX:59-74.

Salisbury, R.F. 1956a. "Unilineal Descent Groups in the New Guinea Highlands." *Man* 2.

-----------1956b. "Asymmetrical Marriage Systems." *American Anthropologist* LVIII:639-55.

-----------1960. "Ceremonial Economics and Political Equilibrium." *Proceedings of the VI International Congress of Anthropolgical and Ethnological Sciences.* Paris, 1960, Vol. 11:255-259.

-----------1962. *From Stone to Steel.* Melbourne: Melbourne University Press.

-----------forthcoming. "Siane Religion and Society," in P. Lawrence, M. Meggitt and R. Glasse (eds.), *New Guinea Religious Systems.*

III

POLITICAL ANTHROPOLOGY:

SYSTEMS, TRANSACTIONS AND REGIONS

by

Marilyn Silverman

Richard F. Salisbury saw himself as an economic anthropologist and, later, as an applied anthropologist. However, in pursuing the empirical and analytical agenda which underlay such designations, Dick invariably explored the political dimensions of social and economic life. This was because of several factors. In part, it came out of an anthropological holism which typified the structural-functional paradigm that dominated social anthropology in his formative years: the economic system, and the *political system*, were seen as unquestionably interconnected. In part, too, it resulted from the ethnographic context in which Dick did field work. In his earliest field research, the nature of Highland New Guinea societies made the analysis of *local-level politics* a necessary component of any ethnographic endeavour. In part, also, Dick's concern with the political emerged from the way in which he constructed economic anthropology. His early commitment to formalist theory and the central role played by individual decision-making and entrepreneurship led him to analyse *leadership*, that is, the political dimensions of economic activity. In part, as well, his exploration of the political sphere developed logically out of his interest in applied and development anthropology. His concerns with innovation, economic change, and the conditions which permit indigenous, self-sustained development led him to consider the role of *regional political structures*.

In this essay, I explore the changing ways in which Salisbury approached the political sphere during his anthropological career. In so doing, however, I must also construct a more general history of political anthropology itself. This is because Dick's work is an integral part of that story: his research and writing both reflected and created it. What is perhaps most striking about this is that the analysis of the political sphere was never Dick's primary concern. He remained, throughout, an economic and development anthropologist.

What then did Dick do that was seminal to political anthropology? A way to answer this is to view the history of political anthropology as a movement through successive paradigms: from structural-functionalism in the 1940s and 1950s to transactionalism in the 1960s and 1970s and, thence, to regional analysis in the 1980s. Dick, in his efforts to understand economic innovation and development, began first by exploring political systems (via structural-functionalism), then local-level/transactional politics and political leadership (via transactionalism), and then, finally, regional political structures. He became, as a result, an integral player in the growth of political anthropology.

POLITICAL SYSTEMS AND THE STRUCTURAL-FUNCTIONAL PARADIGM

When Dick did field work for his doctorate among the Siane of Highland New Guinea during 1952 and 1953, the viewpoints in *African Political Systems* (Fortes & Evans-Pritchard, 1940), the first effort by British social anthropologists to define the nature and scope of non-western political systems, were highly influential. These viewpoints were rooted in a structural-functional paradigm in which the political sphere was conceptualized as a system which functioned to maintain order within society. As Salisbury worked within this paradigm, and as he taught an undergraduate course on political organization to budding Canadian anthropologists at McGill in the mid-1960s, he approached the analysis of political systems through four issues: how disputes were settled and order enforced in society; the ideologies which underlay legitimacy and authority; the kinds of representative headship which typified the groups which made up the society; and the way inter-group relations were managed. Underlying any political system, however, its structure and functions, was the economy: modes of livelihood profoundly affected these components of the political system.

Such viewpoints both drove and constrained his political analysis in his earliest ethnography, *From Stone to Steel* (1962). On the one hand, in *From Stone to Steel*, Dick described the Siane political system in a formulaic way which mirrored most anthropological analyses of stateless societies at the time: formal, kin-based levels of territorial segmentation, of ever-more inclusive layers (lineage, clan, phratry and tribe),[1] each with representative heads, formed a structural skeleton upon which hung both the system of land tenure and the political system – that is, the formal mechanisms for settling disputes and enforcing order within and between groups.

On the other hand, because Dick conceptualized the Siane economic system in a somewhat radical way for his times, and because of Siane life itself, Dick intuitively recognized that such a description of the political system was insufficient. He saw the economy not simply as the systematic allocation of resources for production, distribution and consumption, but also as the sphere within which individual choice and decision-making operated. With a concern for the extent to which Sianes' activities were "based on a rational calculation of quantities so that scarce resources are allocated between competing ends" (1962:83), Salisbury concluded that three, independent "nexuses of economic activity" co-existed (1962:105-6). First, in subsistence activities, most decisions were "made on traditional or technological grounds." In contrast, in the second and third nexuses, rational calculation was key. Thus, there was much competition between ends in the production, distribution and consumption of luxury goods (tobacco, nuts, oil, salt) and of valuables (pigs, shells) (1962:84). In the former, it was individuals, not groups, who were involved in the exchanges of what were in effect personal goods; and they acted in terms of personal self-interest in a way which "almost parallelled a system of free market exchanges" (1962:90). In the latter, entire groups were involved in public, large-scale exchanges of these valuables on ceremonial occasions (*gimaiye* exchanges). Through success at these exchanges, and by setting up reciprocal exchange obligations both between clans and among men within clans, "men gain power within their community, a reputation for public spiritedness, and indirectly, more relations outside their own clan" (1962:104).

Such men were called "big men," and they spent a great deal of time "in corporate clan work" (1962:110). Indeed, the presence of such big men in economic exchanges brought to the fore, for Salisbury, an essential problem with structural-functional interpretations of political systems. How could these big men be fitted in? They were individuals with influence in economic and political affairs whose positions, titles and authority were achieved – through knowledge, age, industry, wealth and bravery. Each men's house and each clan had several such big men, "all equals and all jealous of the power of others" (1962:30). In other words, men's houses and clans were represented not by those who inherited headships but by the most successful political and economic entrepreneurs. Moreover, it was not norms and custom which were central for settling disputes, enforcing order and mediating inter-group relations, but the entrepreneurial actions of big men.

A second contradiction, and limitation of structural-functional interpretation, also surfaced out of the Siane data. At the local level were cross-cutting, inter-personal relations which also had a direct impact on dispute settlement, order and inter-group relations.

> The individual has a network of personal kin-
> ship ties which cross-cut the clanship relations.
> ... These relationships are close and affection-
> ate, and often involve the giving of mutual gifts
> and assistance. It need hardly be pointed out
> that any conflict between two clans involves
> many individuals of those clans in a conflict

between their loyalty to their clan and their affection for friends in the enemy clan (1962:38).

Underlying Siane political organization, and the interplay between group dynamics and individual choice, was ideology. It too contained contradictions which created, for Salisbury, other analytical dilemmas. On the one hand, because the Siane had an ideology of clan unity and because they "set great store by maintaining good relations with other people" (1962:31), the pressure to settle intra-clan disputes was strong. This meant, too, that in inter-clan relations, lineage heads and big men represented their groups. This was classic structural-functional interpretation. On the other hand though, Dick also recognized that the Siane ideology had a deep-seated notion of "individual autonomy": an ideology "that all individuals are their own masters, acting autonomously and subject to no man" (1962:31-2).

These contradictions, on both the ideological and material planes, and the tension between conventional political analyses of group relations as distinct from a view of the machinations of individuals, emerged both because of Salisbury's approach to Siane economics and because of the Siane themselves. In *From Stone to Steel*, however, Dick aimed to explore economic change. He therefore was led to analyse the nature of political development associated with such change and, yet again, of individual machinations.

Specifically, it was big men who, according to Salisbury, made the first "indirect contact" with Europeans, received the new valuables which penetrated, and introduced these into ceremonial exchanges. Simultaneously, the introduction of steel axes allowed more leisure and enabled the Siane to expand their ceremonial and political activities. A "greater velocity of circulation" for an increased number of valuables ensued (1962:121-2). This

> strengthened the position of the "big men." Previously, a young man could hope to "produce" a few valuables, through the pigs his wife raised, and these would steadily repay the contributions he had received towards his brideprice. Now the numbers he could produce were swamped by the disproportionate numbers flowing in as ceremonial payments to those already participating in *gimaiye* activities – the "big men." They could make larger payments, and more grandiose gestures of reconciliation

at peace makings, from what they received. Their reputations for generosity increased, and as result they received even larger payments from others. Their stocks of valuables grew as the inflation grew, while the stocks of less venturesome, younger men remained static. Although the "big men" produced nothing, their wealth and power grew (1962:117).

Later contact with Europeans, and the introduction of indentured labour on the coast, brought "other goods, new attitudes, and new habits" into the central highlands (1962:126). However, resources brought back from the coast by labourers were again absorbed into the *gima* system (1962:126) and benefited "those who are active in *gima* activities" (1962:132), that is, the big men. Indeed, the continuing dependence of youth on older men to procure bridewealth payments not only allowed big men to maintain control over youths, but also forced the young "to distribute the very valuables which [were] the basis of the older men's power" (1962:133). The political future, as Salisbury saw it, was ever increasing power for big men.

Thus, in the tension between the systemic, normative viewpoints of structural-functionalism and the analysis of individual decision-making in the political sphere, it gradually becomes apparent, in hindsight, that in *From Stone to Steel*, Salisbury was moving towards favouring the latter. However, the tension highlighted the interpretative problem of how choice intersected with structure and how the individual was located in society. It was a problem which engaged not only Salisbury but most of his generation and, until the late 1980s, most of my own.

TRANSACTIONAL POLITICS, BIG MEN AND POLITICAL PROCESSES

The dependence of the political on the economic persisted as a central theme throughout Salisbury's career. What did change, however, after the publication of *From Stone to Steel*, was the importance which he gave to the individual's place in both spheres. In this, Dick helped to wean social anthropology away from the structural-functional paradigm and to a transactional one.[2] In the political sphere, it meant that he helped to displace the analysis of the so-called political system with what became known as "local level-politics." This was manifested in two interrelated ways: first, in detailed discussions on the nature of big men and, second, in analyses of local-level "political processes" (Swartz et al. 1966:1).

Already in the 1950s, it was becoming apparent that so-called African models of segmentary lineage systems, as defined in structural-functionalism, did not quite fit the New Guinea Highlands. Segmentary levels did not seem to dovetail neatly with Highland territorial groups; Highland descent ideologies were poorly developed; inter-group relations were far more complex than segmentary, fission-fusion models allowed; warfare was endemic; and leaders were not the representative heads of pre-existing groups but men who achieved their roles and who recruited groups of followers, often beyond the boundaries of their own group. Salisbury's very early concern with delineating the similarities and differences (1956) was soon superseded by clear evidence and argument that New Guinea social systems were different in kind: segmentation was not inevitable; choice about group affiliation was key; and cognatic (rather than patrilineal) principles operated (Barnes 1962). In addition, residence was more important than descent as a basic organizing principle; warfare directly affected local group composition; and, ultimately, big men were the pivots of the system. As the decisions-makers, it was they who recruited followers and so created local groups whilst managing external relations through warfare and exchange (de Lepervanche 1967; 1968).

Central to this formulation was Salisbury's work, particularly as the focus on big men became more explicit, leading to explorations into their political careers and into their authority – as consensus (Read 1959; Strathern 1966), as anarchy/satrapy (Brown 1963), or as serial despotism and bureaucracy (Salisbury 1964). These issues also became linked at this time to questions of social change: how contact and Australian administration had affected leadership in the Highlands (e.g. Brown 1963; Salisbury 1964). As part of this discussion, Salisbury (1964), with Sahlins (1963) and Meggitt (1967), pointed to the wider political implications of big men activities. They showed that the rise and fall of big men occurred in cycles, and that these cyclical patterns, over time, directly affected the structure of the political sphere as political groups, or factions, (re)formed and (re)dissolved according to the dynamics of inter-group and intra-group exchanges which big men organized. In this way, some of the more insightful analysts, such as Salisbury, were able to reincorporate individual leadership back into a broad view of how the political structure worked.[3] This view was one which Dick, in latter years, attempted to expand.

At the time, though, this work on big men articulated with a second major field project which Dick carried out amongst the Tolai of New Britain in 1960-61. It also articulated with the growing influence of the transactional paradigm through which leading anthropologists not only analysed the machinations of leaders but also explored, more broadly, local-level political processes. And there were none better than Melanesian politics, and Dick's work, to serve as exemplars.

In a 1966 article for a volume on political anthropology which aimed to explore the "wind of change [which] was invading political theory" (Swartz et al 1966:1), Dick provided a classic description of those economic machinations of Tolai big men in exchange networks which underwrote their political leadership and, in so doing, perpetuated a system of economic inequality through which "the rich become richer and the poor remain poor." This political process was rationalized by an ideology which promised success to the individual efforts of the many whilst masking the ways in which resources actually were appropriated by the few.

This focus on entrepreneurial strategies and on local political processes comprised essential elements of the transactional paradigm in the field of political anthropology during the 1960s and 1970s. Salisbury was more and more drawn in, through his own interests and through those of his doctoral students at McGill. With their concerns with leader-follower relations, the "game"of politicking and the nature of factions (Salisbury & Silverman 1977:2), Dick himself began to explore more deeply the world of micro-political processes. He did so, however, in a theoretical way, using the data from a burgeoning number of ethnographies, mainly by his own students, in order to find regularities in what he labelled "transactional politics" (Salisbury 1977; Chapter III.7, this volume).

> Transactional politics [is] the study of how individuals within particular institutional systems, exercise political power through transactional behaviour which may be described as the transmission of goods and services by leaders in exchange for acceptance of their power by supporters who grant them authority (1977:111).

In seeking regularities, Dick focussed on factionalism, a political phenomenon which had by then become a central topic, and on developing typologies of "factional sequences" (Salisbury & Silverman 1977:2) and of the "institutional environments" which affected factionalism and local politics (1977:111-2). For Dick, factionalism, like the careers of big men, had "an inherent dynamic." Factional "confrontations were rarely balanced," factional cycles ensued as a result and the cycles could propel the society (Salisbury & Silverman 1977).

For the Introduction to *A House Divided: Anthropological Studies of Factionalism*, which Dick and I wrote (Salisbury & Silverman 1977), it was he who suggested that we look at the different ways factions had been studied within the transactional paradigm: through the analysis of networks, of political strategies and of their class bases. For Dick, these seemingly distinct ways were not only interdependent but, he argued, by viewing them as such, factional patterns and, then, "factional sequences" could be extracted.

Thus, factions could be built using one of three types of network structure (establishment-opposition; multiple clusters; open), of transactional strategies (patronage; group mobilization; opportunistic) and of class participation (elite; class-based; bourgeois). The most common patterns were as follows:

> We could classify factionalism as *conservative* if it is marked by establishment-opposition networks, by patronage transactions and by elite participation; as *revolutionary* if it combines group mobilization transactions, participation by class and multiple clustering of networks; and as *progressive* where strategies are opportunistic, participation bourgeois and networks open (Salisbury & Silverman 1977:16).

Each pattern, however, was only to be found at particular junctures because each was invariably succeeded, in dialectical response, by a different one. That is, depending on what actors do, and how they respond to the networks, strategies and class recruitment patterns of others, a different pattern will emerge. Factionalism, and political processes more generally, therefore, moved in cycles, propelled by the dialectical responses of the actors. In so doing, predictable sequences emerged which could give a "net movement to the whole society."

In true transactionalist mode, however, Dick never argued that actors were free agents. Rather, goal-based behaviour, competitive relationships and micro-political processes were always dependent on, and constrained by, the environment or context. Dick in fact became particularly concerned to describe the resources, rules and stratification patterns which comprised the environment (1977; Chapter III.7, this volume). This is not surprising. For despite Dick's central place in political anthropology through his innovative work, he remained an economic anthropologist who was drawn to the political because it was a key variable in the issues which most interested him: the economy and development.

HISTORICAL ANALYSES AND REGIONAL POLITICAL STRUCTURES

In *Vunamami: Economic Transformation in a Traditional Society*, published in 1970, Salisbury expanded on the economic concerns which he had first explored in *From Stone to Steel*: economic innovation, development models derived from the micro-analysis of small societies, and how non-industrial countries can "achieve sustained economic development using their own resources." For Dick, Vunamami town and region was yet another example of successful indigenous development, in this case, among the Tolai of New Britain (Papua-New Guinea). To explain why, he was again led into politics: because "pre-existing local political organization contributed to economic development" (1970:13), that is, "internal political changes" turned "conditions conducive to development, and available technological knowledge, into the reality of development" (1970:1). To show this, not only did he collect economic data, as for the Siane, but also "the changing political structure needed to be reconstructed" as did "the history of each technological innovation" (1970:14; see Chapter IV.11, this volume).

Salisbury thus moved into history: into exploring the chronology of change among the Tolai as it had been recorded by Europeans, and into exploring Tolai history as it would have been "written by the people themselves" as they are seen "trying to make rational choices in situations of great novelty" (1970:7,8). It was the interplay of history, ethnohistory and an economic anthropology that used formal micro-analysis which, together, concerned Salisbury: for "these techniques ... give insights that are not available to workers relying on written history, on macro-economic analysis, or on descriptions utilizing only the concepts of the discipline of economics" (1970:9). Indeed, in a 1967 conference paper which he never published, and which is included in this volume (Chapter III.6), Salisbury provided cogent arguments about the value of introducing historical work into anthropology. It presaged what would become a fundamental part of socio-cultural anthropology two decades later.

At the time, however, Dick was concerned with history for a particular reason: "to relate [the Tolai] pattern of successful economic development to the political events that accompanied each economic change." Thus, whilst using historical and ethnohistorical data, Dick was concerned with two interrelated issues. First, on a micro-level, he used life histories of economic innovators to show "how their innovations fitted within their political careers, and within the options of choice open to them at different ages." He therefore explored the ascent of big men in the system of "shell money [*tabu*] finance." Seen as a "quaint survival" by Europeans, Salisbury argued that shell-money finance was "the mainspring, not only of inter-Tolai trade and business enterprise, but of a critical area of entrepreneurship." Traditional "entrepreneurs are 'big businessmen.' They also are politicians, and their skills are those of organizing people and finance to realize large collective projects" (1970:275). Thus, Vunamami big men were innovators who "appear[ed] as staunch traditionalists," who "*always* occupied positions of importance ... within their clans; ... in ... rituals; ... in land matters; ... [as the] foci of residential groups of clansmen and [as the] upholders of tradition." (1970:313). Salisbury thus showed how "pre-existing local political organization contributed to economic development, or to phrase it more dramatically, the way in which 'tradition' ensured successful change" (1970:13-14).

However, a more macro-level view of successful development was also necessary; and Dick located the political innovations of entrepreneurial big men in the context of "changes within a total political" structure (see Chapter III.5, this volume).

> Economic factors are ... vital [in] providing the possibility for self-sustained growth. ... But the main precipitant cause, triggering off the growth made potential by technological innovations in societies which, like Vunamami, are relatively affluent and not agriculturally involuted ... is, I maintain, one of *organization*. By this term I mean much more than merely economic entrepreneurship. ... Growth requires that individuals must be able to invent organizational forms. ... In a word, growth requires political development. On the broad level, this may well be a matter of the consolidation of small, quasi-autonomous political units into larger wholes. ... [It could also] imply the involvement of a greater number of people in the policy decisions of that society, by means of an improvement in the administrative structure. In either case, political activity provides the improved security and communications that are required for economic development. It is also vital in providing the spur of leadership, the opportunities for mobility, and the managers to cope with organizing economic production (italics mine)(1970:349).

It was this latter idea, particularly on political organization, which Dick used when trying to explain successful economic development amongst the Cree in the James Bay area of Canada. Here again, in *A Homeland for the Cree* (1986), he used secondary materials. In this case, a massive amount of field data were available from the numerous anthropological studies which came out of the so-called McGill Cree Project which had begun in the mid-1960s. What Dick drew out from this material was a description of how Cree society had changed, between 1971 and 1981, from being fragmented, and based on relatively unconnected village-bands, to a "regional society." It was a process of continuity combined with growing complexity through which the "mechanical solidarity" which had typified the Cree region in 1971 was transformed into "organic solidarity."

Central for this change were two factors. First, in 1971, the very survival of the Cree was threatened by the building of a hydro-electric dam. Negotiations ensued, the state proved ready to decentralize, and the James Bay Agreement, which provided money and use rights in exchange for allowing natural resource development on Cree land, was signed. Second, the crisis provided the necessary ideological shift.

> For regionalism to exist, as it did by 1981, ... people had to become conscious of regional unity, to feel that they were "Cree," and to feel that they had common interests. The crisis of 1971 ... created unity because for the first time an issue emerged in which the interests of the previously fragmented Cree villages were all alike. ... [A]nd it used a highly valued traditional symbolic language, that of the animals, the land and the hunter, to articulate ... opposition. Without a crisis it would have been impossible for the Cree to rise above factionalism and the everyday problems of existence, and to proceed to the creative and innovative activity which ensued (1986:147).

The growth of the regional society was characterized by the growth of an indigenous regional bureaucracy, an indigenous, social-services economy, and an "ethnic strategy" focussed on Cree political-administrative structures, language and culture. In the political sphere in 1971, "informal politics," typical of "a stateless society," predominated: "factions" and transactional politics, led by "important men exercising authority" and managing brokerage relations between the village-band and state were key. Collective action was precluded. As of 1981, the political sphere had been transformed. Numerous pan-regional administrative bodies had been founded, and village councils and policy-making committees formed the local nodes of regional administration. All were run by Cree. For Salisbury, this signalled a change from informal to formal politics, from "traditional politics" to "modern bureaucracy." A "single political society" had been created.

Though these viewpoints, in this final major work, can be seen the essential threads which had been developing since Dick's earliest work: the search for the reasons behind successful innovation and for models of economic development through the analysis of micro-phenomenon and the role of the political sphere. In this final vision in 1986 of how the economy and political structure had to be constructed, Dick explicitly opted for a wide regional structure, dependent on organizational innovation and collective consciousness. It was an elegant viewpoint which had long been implicit in his work. It represented the culmination of his thinking about the political sphere – always in the context of economic and applied anthropology.

CONCLUSION

In the context of how ethnography was conceptualised in the late 1950s and early 1960s, little criticism had yet been made of the dominant structural-functional approach which typified social anthropology. One of the earliest and major critiques, by Leach on Highland Burma, was published in 1954; Turner's classic Ndembu study came out in 1957. Richard Salisbury had already been in the field and, as of 1956, had begun to publish. By the time that Barnes' seminal article was published in 1962, Salisbury too was a major agent in what was to become a major paradigm shift in social anthropology: from structural-functionalism to transactionalism. If Barnes' article suggested ways in which New Guinea ethnography might articulate with, and differ from, the dominant Africanist tradition, it was Salisbury's work which provided a good part of the ethnographic and analytical base from which both the African-Melanesian distinction could be made and the paradigm shift accomplished.

In the domain of political anthropology, Salisbury's work reflected and advanced this change in several, inter-related ways. Most generally, he provided a way by which anthropologists could make the crucial connection between the allocation of economic resources and the structure of the political sphere. He did this by focussing on entrepreneurial careers and by showing how the individual actions involved in career-building were related to the emergence of leadership, the allocation and use of power, the structuring of socio-political groups, and the development of society. His work was (and is) an exemplar. The notion of "big man" is a classic concept which came out of this viewpoint and Salisbury's work provided for much of its elaboration. Indeed, so central are big men for understanding not only Melanesia but also other areas that, if they are not found in a particular locale, today's ethnographer has to explain why.

Once, when speaking with him about my own PhD work in a Guyanese village (1979; 1980), I said that I was somewhat dissatisfied with my study of local politics because it seemed to involve only the elites, only the big men, only the entrepreneurs. Dick looked at me quizzically and said what clearly to him had long been self-evident: "But these are the people who get involved in politics." Clearly Dick saw the political sphere as too small: his concerns were broader – with "the politically weak" as well as with "the power of the politically strong" (1966:127). He also was guided by a more holistic ethnographic tradition and the view that close and detailed ethnographic description made no sense if compartmentalized, *a priori*, into discrete pieces. As a result, when political anthropology declined as a sub-field in the 1980s, precisely because it was seen as too elitist, Dick had already taken his political interests in another direction. He had always been concerned with the wider society, with context, with the economic bases of political behaviour and with development. These interests ultimately led him to explore the ways in which regional political systems – their growth and structure – were related to successful, sustained economic development. It was a distinctively novel approach, and it remains so today.

Most generally though, Dick was an anthropologist who was able to move between the political and the economic, between social structure and individual choice, and between the local and the regional with an ease and comfort which, today in socio-cultural anthropology, remains a goal for most of us. His theoretical contributions were immense; his ethnographic insights irreplaceable; and his legacy, through and to his discipline and students, profound.

NOTES

1.   The lineage was the basic economic unit; the clan, coterminous with the corpo-
        rate village, was the sovereign, blood-feud unit; the phratry was the exogamous
        and ceremonial unit within which warfare was forbidden; and the tribe was a ter-
        ritorial unit within which all members had land-use rights.

2.   In general, transactionalism posited the view that structure was generated by
        individual choices made within the constraints of previous and/or external struc-
        tures, norms, rules, ideas, resource availability, and so on. A key figure in defin-
        ing the contours of the paradigm was Frederik Barth (1959; 1963; 1966)."

3.   I am grateful to Malcolm Blincow, Department of Anthropology at York, for the
        long discussions which culminated in much of the above analysis of big men.

REFERENCES

Barnes, J.A., 1962. "African Models in the New Guinea Highlands." *Man* 62:5-9.

Barth, Frederik, 1959. *Political Leadership among the Swat Pathans*. London: Athlone.

------------1963. *The Role of the Entrepreneur in Social Change in Rural Norway*. Bergen:
        Arbok for Universitet i Bergen.

------------1966. *Models of Social Organization*. London: Royal Anthropological Institute,
        Occasional Paper 23.

Brown, Paula, 1963. "From Anarchy to Satrapy." *American Anthropologist* 65 (1):1-15.

de Lepervanche, Marie, 1967/8. "Descent, Residence, and Leadership in the New Guinea
        Highlands." *Oceania* xxxviii, No. 2:135-158 and *Oceania* xxxviii, No.3:163-189.

Fortes, M. and E.E. Evans-Pritchard (eds.), 1940. *African Political Systems*. Oxford: Oxford
        University Press.

Leach, E.R., 1954. *Political Systems of Highland Burma*. Boston: Beacon Press.

Meggitt, M.J., 1967. "The Pattern of Leadership Among the Mae-Enga of New Guinea." *Anthropological Forum* 2(1): 20-35.

Read, K.E., 1959. "Leadership and Consensus in a New Guinea Society." *American Anthropologist* 61: 524-36.

Sahlins, M.D., 1963. "Poor Man, Rich Man, Big Man, Chief." *Comparative Studies in Society and History* 5:285-303.

Salisbury, Richard F., 1956. "Unilineal Descent Groups in the New Guinea Highlands." *Man* 55(2).

-----------1962. *From Stone to Steel: Economic Consequences of Technological Change in New Guinea*. Melbourne: Melbourne University Press.

-----------1964. "Despotism and Australian Administration in the New Guinea Highlands." *American Anthropologist* 66(2), Special Issue on New Guinea: 225-39.

-----------1966. "Politics and Shell-Money Finance in New Britain." in Swartz, Marc J., Victor W. Turner and Arthur Tuden (eds.), *Political Anthropology*. Chicago: Aldine.

-----------1967. "An Anthropologist's Use of Historical Methods." Paper presented to History Seminar, University of Papua and New Guinea, 7 July.

-----------1970. *Vunamami: Economic Transformation in a Traditional Society*. Berkeley: University of California Press.

-----------1977. Transactional Politics: "Factions and Beyond." in Silverman, M. and R.F. Salisbury (eds.), *A House Divided: Anthropological Studies of Factionalism*. St John's: Institute for Social and Economic Research (ISER), Memorial University of Newfoundland.

-----------1986. *A Homeland for the Cree: Regional Development in James Bay, 1971-1981*. Montreal: McGill-Queen's.

Salisbury, Richard F. and Marilyn Silverman, 1977. "An Introduction: Factions and the Dialectic." in Silverman, M. and R.F. Salisbury (eds.), *A House Divided: Anthropological Studies of Factionalism*. St John's: Institute for Social and Economic Research (ISER), Memorial University of Newfoundland.

Silverman, Marilyn, 1979. "Dependency, Mediation and Class Formation in Rural Guyana." *American Ethnologist* 6(3):466-490.

------------1980. *Rich People and Rice: Factional Politics in Rural Guyana*. Leiden: Brill.

Strathern, Andrew, 1966. "Despots and Directors in the New Guinea Highlands." *Man*, n.s.1(3):356-67.

Swartz, Marc J., Victor W. Turner and Arthur Tuden, 1966. "Introduction." in Swartz, Marc J., Victor W. Turner and Arthur Tuden (eds.), *Political Anthropology*. Chicago: Aldine.

Turner, Victor W., 1957. *Schism and Continuity in an African Society*. Manchester: Manchester University Press.

5.

POLITICAL CONSOLIDATION AND ECONOMIC DEVELOPMENT

by

Richard F. Salisbury

Source: Chapter 10, *Vunamami: Economic Transformation in a Traditional Society*,
Berkeley: University of California Press, 1970.

Four main themes have run through this book. Here I shall try to
bring them together in relation to the central underlying aim of the work – the understanding of the meaning of economic development.

Two of the themes have been primarily ethnographic. First, in
describing how economic change looks from a village point of view, I have tried to
analyse for each activity the economic concepts used by the local people in making
their allocational choices. The result has been, I believe, to show that in each activity there is economic rationality, not always in the short term but in the long run, and
bearing in mind the "costs" of operating in a small-scale society. Thus "delayed
barter" may seem inexplicable to an observer accustomed to short-term profit-mak-
ing in highly complex and diversified markets; it becomes entirely rational when
viewed in a context of highly variable supplies in a market where there are essential-
ly only two groups which alternate the roles of buyers and sellers. The indigenous
concepts provide a vocabulary for understanding bilateral negotiated trade, though
not open-market trade. Or in the case of copra production methods, the peasant producers appear rational in terms of output per man-day – their major cost – while at
the same time plantations, calculating in terms of output per acre of land, can maintain that they are rationally organized, only because a distorted wage structure exists.

The second ethnographic theme has been to show how different-
ly a change process looks from the inside and from the outside. In seeking to establish this point I have, perhaps, made too sharp a distinction between the two views.
It is not in fact necessary to regard one as true and the other as false, but rather to
recognize that the truth lies in a combination of both views. Outside observers too
readily assume that their view of change is right, and that the inside view is distorted. I have stressed the reverse position to redress the balance somewhat. The balanced view, with which I should hope to conclude, is that change is a complex
process. Without stimuli, usually from outside, and without a spread of knowledge

from the vast reservoir that exists in the world as a whole, a local society is unlikely to develop. Yet the mere giving of stimuli, "encouraging development" or "teaching new crops," is as inadequate for producing development as is the mere availability of knowledge. The process by which such developments are accepted and then adapted to local conditions, and, in turn, bring about a reinterpretation of existing practices, is at least as important for the success of development. Yet understanding the local view of economic change is possible only if one is prepared to accept the earlier conclusion – that the local economy has a rationality that needs detailed analysis and a use of indigenous economic concepts.

These two ethnographic themes are so fundamental that they will not be further discussed here. Instead I shall concentrate on the two analytic themes: the relationship between a continuity of tradition and successful economic change, and the nature of the social reorganization that economic change requires. The two are closely interwoven. Thus, to take one change as a specific example, that of cocoa growing and processing, the *content* of the change was entirely introduced from outside – the crop itself, the techniques of fermenting, the bank that gave the loan, the registration of the Tolai Cocoa Project with the national government. Yet the attitudes and concepts brought to bear on this content were all long standing ones – "traditional," from the short-term perspective of both Europeans and New Guineans, for whom what happened five years ago is ancient. Cocoa in the local context was another cash crop like the "traditional" copra crop. The highly flexible matrilineal system of land ownership meant that it was easy to get rapid planting of large areas, using "traditional" means of labour recruitment such as the granting of rights to garden use of land while shade coconuts were being established. Crop processing, though more complicated, was still a variation of the kind of processing used "traditionally" for copra. Subscribing for a jointly owned *kivung* drier was already "traditional," although the composition of *kivung* had changed markedly since 1875 when they were exclusively clan-based. Accepting a loan to finance a project was also traditional, and the traditional attitudes (of desiring to pay off a loan as quickly as possible so that the material assets would become the property of the subscribers themselves, and also of removing the stigma of indebtedness) were also originally applied to the bank loan. Cocoa fitted easily into patterns of local thought. People could more easily learn new techniques with a familiar model to work from.

Another aspect of the importance of familiarity was that the people could evaluate the likely profitability of the new crop in the same way that they evaluated copra. The delay in obtaining returns was not an important disadvantage, as it would have been in a subsistence cropping area; in fact, the shorter establishment period for cocoa may have been an attraction for copra growers. The possibility of building up lasting assets for the benefit of future generations by planting cocoa would seem to have been in growers' minds from the start, to judge by the way in which they registered their trees. This is a traditional way of judging how successful a business enterprise is likely to be. Although labour requirements for harvesting could not be accurately foreseen, wealthy landowners could afford to take a risk on them, even if smaller landowners held back until the yields were clear.

Many writers have commented on how readily technical innovations are adopted when they are seen to have a clear and immediate advantage: the advantage of steel axes over stone, or of penicillin over herbs. Yet these are only simpler examples of my general point, that when an innovation retains some continuity with the past, people can compare it with a known standard and to that extent are better able to judge its likely profitability. Only if it is likely to be profitable will it be accepted. An understanding of pre-existing means of estimating profitability – the underlying structure of local costs – is needed before one can predict local reaction to an innovation.

Yet another element of continuity is the role played by leaders in ensuring the acceptance of change. Most people do not go through all the calculations implied above, but they assume that respected individuals who accept the change have calculated. They copy leaders. Rogers (1962) has referred to this as the two stage process in the adoption of innovations. But it implies that some structure of leadership exists prior to the change, although the relationship between the first stage leaders – the innovators – and their followers – the accepters – may well not be one of formal authority. Some studies of innovation stress that innovators communicate best through informal channels. A pre existing structure of leadership where people with recognized positions (but not necessarily formal authority) readily communicate informally throughout the society, would seem to favour the rapid spread of behaviours adopted by leaders. A readiness by such leaders to make changes would seem to provide the ideal condition for the adoption of innovations.

Even so, to continue with the example of Vunamami cocoa adoption, the long-term profitability of cocoa growing could not be accurately foreseen in advance. Returns now obviously depend on world market prices, and on climatic and disease conditions. Yet even within these unpredictable limits, the return to the peasant grower could still be greatly increased if less time were wasted in numbers of people individually bringing beans to centralized fermenteries. In other words, reorganization of the process of production continues long after the adoption of an innovation, and may not be completed for many years. For productive organization to change, there must be a degree of flexibility in other social groupings; and in this case it would seem that rigidity has begun to set in, following Administration control of the Project, with great pressure from the top for further centralization. This would make the crop even less profitable for the peasant grower, unless some channel for the expression of grower opinion emerges. It could well kill the cocoa industry entirely while curing inefficiencies in marketing and fermenting. Adoption of innovations without the accompaniment of social organizational change can be self-limiting; the appropriate changes do not necessarily follow automatically.

Yet in Vunamami the important technological changes up to 1950 have all been followed by social reorganizations that have successfully institutionalized the innovations or made them profitable. The central problem of this work is to try and explain why.

The first reason is that the statement contains a tautology. Only those technological changes that have been followed by social reorganization are ones that have been "important." Numerous changes have been introduced that have not been economical or have not been followed by the requisite social changes, and they have either remained unimportant or have disappeared entirely. Kapok trees were introduced by the Germans; without the marketing arrangements to use the product in local upholstery, they remain unimportant trees. Rice, repeatedly introduced by Agricultural Officers and by the Japanese, is an uneconomic crop in New Guinea because of its high labour requirements unless machinery can be used; problems of milling and marketing have ensured its failure except at times of extreme starvation or depression. Centralized village copra driers in the 1930's proved uneconomic because of the costs of transport, although village feelings of patriotism got them started; social reorganization in the late 1940's and 1950's ensured the success of small copra driers, however, although reforms in the transport system are now making larger driers profitable for store owners living along the main roads. Whether any of the unsuccessful crops might have been successful if the necessary social changes had also occurred is a meaningless speculation. All that can be said is that a certain number of the plethora of innovations that are constantly occurring are not successful, are not adopted over wide areas, and are unimportant. They occasion or involve no social changes. They must be considered different from those where economic profitability was present, given the cost structure of peasant society, and where social changes occurred. The calculations of economic profitability, and its principal dependence on the labour inputs needed by peasant farmers, have already been discussed. Let us now turn to the social and political processes involved in successful economic changes.

As described in the Introduction, four such changes can be isolated: the development of trading in coconuts, the planting of coconuts, the development of copra processing, and the development of the more complicated cocoa growing and marketing organization. Dates for each change can be given: 1878 for the first reign of King Copra; 1897 for the start of coconut planting on a large scale following the adoption of the Reserve policy; 1948 as the beginning of successful copra processing, after a false start in the 1930's; and 1953, the year of the Vunamami Cacao Marketing Account, as the start of cocoa processing and marketing. A first point to note is that each of these economic changes *followed* fairly closely a preceding political change. By 1878 the pre-contact situation, in which the effective political units had been the small hamlets of about thirty persons, had changed dramatically in Vunamami on the coast. Before 1875 these hamlets had often fought one another, even within the boundaries of the same larger unit, the village, that periodically combined under a strong fighting leader (*a luluai na winarubu*). The hamlet leaders, rich men and clan *lualua*, were the significant politicians. During 1875-1876 the presence of both missionaries and traders served to bring the village units into greater prominence, and to concentrate power in the hands of village heads. Church-building could be done only on a basis of units of two hundred individuals – that is, villages – and the hamlet head who sponsored the church became, for church purposes, the village head. The several big men of a coastal village tended to monopolize trade with Europeans, and with their increasing wealth they acquired the guns that established them as village leaders. Guns were used against inland villages, and the fighting was organized and conducted by village units rather than being the petty ambushing and killing practised between hamlets. The infrequently activated "crisis" form of indigenous organization came to be the regular form for everyday action, under a single leader.

A similar political change took place before 1897. Both the war of 1890 and that of 1893 had involved *ad hoc* alliances of several villages, numbering up to two thousand men, against the Europeans. These had emerged, during the years preceding, as groupings allied by a large degree of intermarriage, by common links along a chain of trade running inland, and presumably by the alliances of *tubuan* owners, but with no formal political unity aside from that provided by the needs of the moment and by the energy of the man who organized the alliance. But in 1893 the defeat of the alliance and the killing of its leader did not destroy it, as had been the case heretofore. The alliance was established as a permanent grouping under the recognized leadership of a *lualua* or *nambawan*, ToBobo, when Judge Hahl arrived in 1896. A new level of lasting political unity had emerged.

The Mandate of 1921 marked a political retrogression for the local people, until an office of Paramount Luluai was reinstituted in place of the *lualua* in 1929. The Paramountcies may have been somewhat larger than the jurisdictions of the *lualua* before 1921, but this is not entirely clear. There were, in the Kokopo Sub-district, exactly the same number of each, and they were based on the same villages, Vunamami, Birara, Raluana, Toma, and so on – though now the populations were larger, ranging up to four thousand. The units of the 1893 alliance persisted as the largest effective local units, though it was not until 1937, the beginning of "Village Councils" as local courts in Rabaul District, and the appointment of an effective Paramount in Vunamami, that the units began to take over new activities.

In 1950, with the establishment of Local Government Councils, the area advanced again in political organization. The councils were in many ways a continuation of the Paramountcies, but their jurisdictions were enlarged. Vunadidir, Toma, and Nangananga Paracountcies combined to form one council; Vunamami was joined by a few villages from outside, and over the next ten years most of Birara Paramountcy joined it, though Raluana remained aloof. Six thousand became an average council size. In their powers, too, particularly that of collecting tax money, the councils continued a practice that had been under way for the preceding thirteen years under the Paramounts and the village *Komiti*, but this *ad hoc* informal arrangement became formally recognized. And where the Paramount had occasionally been able to force his own decisions through unofficially but without any question, as a result of his own personal drive, now the authority of the Council president was validated by an election, and was universally accepted. With the emergence in 1952 of a new president, raised within the system, this wider political consolidation was further stabilized.

Further consolidation occurred in 1964, during the writing of this book, in which all the councils throughout the Gazelle Peninsula combined to form a Gazelle Council embracing 40,000 people. What economic change is presaged by this political consolidation will have to be the subject of a later study, as will the eventual consolidation of Papua and New Guinea into a single unified country. Enough has been said to make a *prima facie* case for linking wider political consolidation and economic change.

A third element of each political change must also be recalled from chapter 9: both the political consolidation and the subsequent economic innovations are, in local thinking at least if not exactly in fact, identified with a single dynamic leader.

Are these four cases to be dismissed as just coincidence? Or even if the interaction of political consolidation and economic change is accepted as one of cause and effect, are they to be viewed as resulting from the fortuitous emergence of a rare dynamic leader at a particular stage of history? I do not believe such a coincidence could occur four times within a single village, especially when four other coincidences would also have to be explained – namely, the availability of the external stimuli of knowledge, of traders, of administrative policies, and of agricultural extension at exactly the same time that the leaders emerged.

I prefer to try and connect the various observed events common to each of the four cycles, to show how they could be seen as part of a single logically related process, all interrelated with no one element as primary cause. I shall attempt to describe this process in generalized terms, as a hypothetical model of successful economic change in a wealthy agricultural society (i.e., one with more land and more jobs available than people to fill them). I shall refer back to Vunamami as a concrete example of the working of the model.

In the first place the elements of such a model must fit a society that was never stagnant and unchanging, though at any one time the dynamic forces that could provide movement might have been in balance, so that no over all movement might be visible from the outside. I should thus postulate a continual flow of innovations as occurring, but virtually all of them proving uneconomic. I should also postulate a political system in which, at any one time, many persons are competing for the limited number of political and organizational offices available within any politically sovereign or quasi autonomous unit. I shall refer to such individuals, in accordance with a terminology described in Salisbury (1964), as "executives." At the same time, the individuals who obtain the headships of each unit – "directors" in my 1964 terminology – are continually trying to expand their jurisdictions by influencing other groups, making alliances, and so on. A local "director" may be successful in combining units for a short time, but the larger units that he controls usually tend to fall apart when he dies, or when the emergency that called them into being declines. Politically there is a dynamic equilibrium.

I thus see the competition between "directors" (including aspirants to directorship) as the impetus towards political consolidation. In a situation of crisis, consolidation can be realized, taking a form very like those that have arisen in similar crisis situations in the past. But when the crisis is greater than usual, or lasts longer, the larger political unit of consolidation does not immediately fall apart, and allow the system to return to a low-level equilibrium.

The leader of such a successful consolidation has extremely wide powers. As I have shown (Salisbury 1964),[1] directors tend to have a different order of power from that exercised by their executives. The latter are seeking promotion by trying to please their superiors and their supporters, and their actions are bound by the rules or customary expectations and sanctions of both sides, A director is to some degree limited in power by the need to placate his followers, but the best way of satisfying his followers is for him to gain material benefits and prestige for them

113

by his leadership. If he can do that, then he is granted a wide freedom to ignore normal canons of behaviour and to act as he sees fit. He can, in other words, be despotic; he can act according to his own wishes. These may not involve oppression of followers, though success in some of his actions may lead to the acceptance of a degree of oppression in others. Over a long period of time, however, the limits of acceptance and the spheres of potential autonomous action by a director come to be more closely defined. He is more and more bound by the precedents of his own behaviour and that of his predecessors. There develop expectations regarding the director role.

But the director who emerges at the head of a newly (if temporarily) consolidated political unit is not so limited. There are few, if any, pre-existing expectations about his position; even oppression by him is tolerated in the light of anticipated benefits that will accrue from the actions of a wider unit, under his leadership, and, for a short time at least, people suspend judgement about the wisdom of many of his actions. The crucial issue is whether the crisis that brought him to power is resolved. If it is, he will be remembered as a successful leader, who unified his people and brought lasting benefits. If it is not, he will either be largely forgotten, or he will be remembered as a self-seeking aspirant to power, whom the people rejected as a despot – though he may at the same time anticipate successful unification of society under another leader.

But if it is a successful political consolidation that makes a man remembered as a leader, rather than any extraordinary inherent personal abilities, we need to consider what makes for political success One aspect has been indicated in chapter 9 – the need to be able to mobilize some loyalty to or pride in the consolidated larger unit. A second attempt to consolidate a unit is thus more likely to succeed than the first, since the first attempt is likely to have produced some awareness of the possibility of the wider unit's existing. It is likely to have thrown up a name or slogan expressing loyalty to the wider unit that a politician can use to gain support at the second attempt.

A second aspect, one that is most central to this book, is that if an economically profitable technological innovation is introduced concurrently with a successful political consolidation, the material benefits accruing are likely to be attributed to the consolidation. Its disadvantages are more likely to be forgotten, and only its advantages remembered. Reciprocally, the fact of political consolidation makes the success of a technological innovation more likely.

In the first place, the leader in a unification has all the ideal characteristics of an economic innovator: he is personally respected as more than merely the occupant of a defined political position; in order to have effected the unification he must have a wide network of informal communication links; his judgements of what is the right course to be taken are likely to be accepted on trust by followers, at least for a trial period. Initial costs, such as the cost of new tools to replace those rendered obsolete by the change, may be ignored in a flush of enthusiasm for following such a leader, when, without that enthusiasm, these costs might be felt to make a desirable long-term change unprofitable in the short run.

This does not mean that the political leader must be an inventor, or even the first to recognize the merits of an innovation brought from outside. As with the acceptance of copra driers in Vunamami in the late 1930's, he may merely advocate something that has been invented elsewhere, or, as with the growing of cocoa, the merits of the innovation may already have been widely recognized. But giving his approval to the innovation transforms it; instead of being known but impractical, it becomes popular and possible. In popular thought at least, the name of the politician becomes identified with the technological innovation.

In the second place, the fact of unification provides the degree of social organizational flexibility that is desirable if the most efficient means of arranging production is to emerge. Thus the new Vunamami Local Government Council was ready to experiment with running its own fermentery at Ngatur, but when an improved organization for financing and marketing was suggested in the form of the Tolai Cocoa Project, no rigid commitment to the Vunamami Cacao Marketing Account had developed. Further experimentation was still acceptable, and in many ways people were interested in explicitly trying out new organizational forms – committees, co-operatives, budgeting – as a result of the success of the political change.

On a third, more material, level we can also see that wider political unity tends to make profitable economic enterprises that would not have been profitable within smaller political units. This is not simply a matter of economies of scale, although these do enter in. Many of the innovations, such as the small copra driers, required neither larger work forces nor a mass-marketing system for their success. They would have been technically possible before the political consolidations of the 1930's. Even the central fermenteries of the Tolai Cocoa Project could have been paid for (though not so rapidly) out of growers' revenues. My own calculations of the labour and capital requirements for running Ravalien plantation and its fermentery showed that they were all technically within the capabilities of Vunamami village in 1961.

But with wider political unity the market for raising capital is less restricted; a village would not have to devote its entire resources to a single project if

115

it had access to support from a Council. For Vunamami village to buy and operate Ravalien plantation would have meant that all other projects would have had to be ignored, and that if that one project had failed (perhaps for extraneous or petty reasons like the dishonesty of one man) then the village would have suffered immeasurably. The village's capital resources could not justify the risk; for such a major purchase the capital market provided by a Council, and its reserve funds, was the minimal one that could finance it.

The form of the capital holding corporation is also important, as the discussion of businesses in chapter 7 showed. In establishing public support for such corporations, whether co-operative or private, it is of utmost importance that the people should feel that they have some control over the leaders, or some participation in planning the future use of the resources of the corporation. People should feel that if their interests are ignored, there is a superior authority to which they can appeal. The suspicion of businesses run by important political figures, who may with impunity exploit the ordinary public, has been noted. By their political connections these men can get away with exploitation. In a colonial situation there is little faith that the foreign administering power will support an ordinary person against politically powerful figures; only at levels of grouping at which political decisions are made by New Guineans is there a feeling that such support will be guaranteed. Within a politically autonomous village, the lineage may remain the largest important capital-holding unit (see Plotnicov and Befu 1961), with the village providing sanctions in case of disputes. Within the framework of a regional political structure village enterprises may be possible. With supra-village political groupings, *kivung* recruiting from several clans develop. The size of the largest economic grouping in a society tends, in short, to be somewhat below the size of the largest political grouping. Unification permits larger capital-holding units.[2]

A fourth contribution of political unification to economic success may be generally described as being in the field of communications. By this I do not mean simply the building of roads or bridges or other items that are listed in the capital requirements budgets for developing countries under the heading "communications." Rather, I include communication in the broad sense, that is, the development of group unity by bringing people together who formerly were isolated. We have seen how eliminating inter-hamlet feuding and consolidating the powers of village leaders combined with the presence of missions and traders to open the way for copra trading inland. The changing emphasis of trading, from inter-village delayed barter to open-market cash trading with bargaining, was a consequence of political consolidation. Political consolidation made it possible for individuals to roam widely and to meet from the supply side the opportunities which the presence of traders presented in providing a mass demand. So, too, the expansion of possibilities for recruiting workers and acquiring new knowledge are a matter of communications. The presence of large teams of workers was vital in resettlement schemes that involved clearing virgin forest. The recruitment and support of teams of village workers for the Council scheme was as dependent on the development of better and more extensive communications as was the hiring of workers from western New Britain and the New Guinea Highlands to work on the individual landlord schemes promoted by the Department of Agriculture. Yet another aspect of widened communications with political consolidation was the way in which new political bodies or offices provided channels for disseminating information about innovations. ToBobo, as representative of an enlarged social grouping, had direct contacts with higher levels of the German administration than his predecessors who had led only villages. These channels of communication permitted the land situation to be clarified and information about coconut planting to be disseminated. In 1950 the use by the Agricultural Extension Officer of the forum provided by the new council was an important way of acquainting the people with the details of the new crop, cocoa.

A final and perhaps most fundamental connection between the success of moves for political consolidation and the success of technological innovations lies in the area of education and the provision of skilled managerial manpower. First let us take the situation before unification, at, for example, the time when villages consolidated under ToBobo or into Paramountcies. As managers each village had its own "director" in the form of a *luluai* or big man; there may have been in each village a single contender for his directorship. There may also have been another eight executives at various levels, men who were active organizers but who were unlikely to lead their villages or to give *matamatam*. Each village had perhaps ten politically active men in its population of two hundred (or 5 percent), with only one percent being top-level directors. After unification, it would not be necessary for the new single director of the emergent Paramountcy to remove any of the existing leaders of village units from their positions, because all the former tasks would still have to be performed. His position would be an additional one, while a whole new range of executive positions would be opened-up – the people working directly under the newly emerged director, co-ordinating activities throughout the Paramountcy, most of which had not existed under the previous system of independent villages. If as many jobs were created for each director as previously existed in the villages, it would mean an addition of eight central bureaucrats plus the director (and one rival). For the population of 2,000 the number of politically active persons would rise from 100 to 110. The overhead "organizational" costs of running a political grouping of this size would increase, but not so fast as its effectiveness in facilitating economic productivity. Provided an appropriate economic innovation was in prospect, similar gains could be expected at each unification.

The opening up of this type of position would have a double importance, however. These positions are ones that would likely be available for patronage gift by the new director. To them he would presumably appoint individuals representing several key areas. Some of them would be progressive former directors of villages whom he could rely on to support his economic and political innovations. Their promotion would then leave vacancies for the mobility of younger executives to lead villages. At the same time, if the pattern of patronage appointments described in chapters 8 and 9 were followed, still other young men would be selected out for direct appointment to assist the director, to be trained to succeed him. In this way political unification would open up opportunities for social mobility at all levels.

Yet if there were economic prosperity at the same time, the less successful village headmen who had not been promoted but who had not lost their jobs would not feel slighted, for additional work of organization would devolve on them. They would be better off financially and would not at first realize that they were now executives and not directors. They would not be an inevitable nucleus of a dissatisfied "conservative" wing, especially if the new leader could, as Vunamami leaders all did, maintain that he had a claim to being a "traditional" leader. Conservatives could see the new leader as the defender of tradition against overwhelming modern corruption, and could ascribe the success of his actions to the way in which he preserved continuity with the past. "Radicals" might, at the same time, praise him for his innovations. The result would be an upsurge of patriotism throughout the wider group, a recognition that "we," a newly unified single body, achieved success together. Each social segment would be satisfied and all would focus their satisfaction on the political leader who would be seen as the cause of prosperity. Increased efficiency in local management by existing leaders could be accompanied by the emergence of new managers at the wider group level.

Such managers would need training. Traditional activities like those connected with shell money and the *tubuan*, if continued, would still train many organizational entrepreneurs. The new political positions would offer comparable training, and the same motivation for success, in both financial and prestige terms. It would be at a somewhat higher level, however. Thus when Vunamami Council was formed there was a group of young men whom Enos had previously patronized and organized to run a volunteer school. These men he appointed as the junior Council executives right at the start; they became skilled in the new organizational techniques along with the old, presiding over meetings, organizing committees, writing minutes, preparing budgets, handling complaints, getting formal Administration approval of decisions, and so on.

But when the technological innovations began to require organizational changes and flexible new-style managers, a small supply of appropriately trained people would be at hand. As happened in Vunamami some of the original political appointees could transfer to the new enterprises, taking their training with them and retaining personal ties with their old colleagues. Their departure would open up further vacancies in the political hierarchy, with possibilities of more rapid promotion all round. Economic expansion would continue the general satisfaction and keep the same leader in power.

Expansion may not continue indefinitely and the model's course may break down. The supply of trained managers may be inadequate, although the Vunamami experience suggests that a gap of three years between the commencement of managerial training through politics, and the need for reform of the productive organization may be enough to start the flow. This assumes the presence, however, of a pool of generally educated young men. The number trained in three years can provide the cadre to train more in a steady flow for the future. Expansion may also slow down for economic reasons – declining world market prices for copra and cocoa are examples for Vunamami – but some slowing down may not negate all support for the leader and the new regime. As long as there are still some rungs free on the executive ladder and the leader can promote more of his supporters without demoting other people, opposition will be negligible. But as soon as the ladder is full, and the only alternative to waiting for a senior person to die or retire is to depose him (or get his superior to dismiss him), unrest is likely to occur. The leader will depart (or become oppressive). The political structure will become rigidified and politics will become a jockeying for limited positions, not a struggle to create imaginative policy.

But the process of self-sustained growth is the one that most concerns us here. The picture of this process that has emerged in this final discussion is one that includes far more than merely economic factors such as the availability of capital or an increase in gross national product. Technological innovation is seen as perhaps the most basic factor in producing growth. But if an innovation is not economically feasible or justified in terms of the local cost structure (which may include high interest rates because of a shortage of locally generated capital), then it will not produce results. Economic factors are thus vital as providing the *possibility* for self-sustained growth. They may more often provide the *barrier* to it.

But the main precipitant cause, triggering off the growth made potential by technological innovations in societies which, like Vunamami, are relatively affluent and not agriculturally involuted (Geertz 1963) is, I maintain, one of organization. By this term I mean much more than merely economic entrepreneurship. True, individuals must be free to take risks and exploit economic opportunities as

119

they see them, but this is a minor aspect of what is needed. A society attempting to grow by individual entrepreneurs acting alone would not get far. Growth requires that individuals must be able to invent organizational forms, or to adapt them creatively, both to get production going efficiently and to provide the supporting institutions ensuring that contracts are kept, that information can be communicated, and that training can take place. In a word, growth requires political development.

On the broad level this may well be a matter of the consolidation of small, quasi-autonomous political units into larger wholes – a process which, when viewed from the village level of Vunamami, appears to offer possibilities into the distant future. Consolidation of an already unified nation-state could imply the involvement of a greater number of people in the policy decisions of that society, by means of an improvement in the administrative structure. In either case political activity provides the improved security and communications that are required for economic development. It is also vital in providing the spur of leadership, the opportunities for mobility, and the managers to cope with organizing economic production.

On the village level, by contrast, the implications of organizational change appear dramatically in the tables given in chapters 3 and 4 of the proportions of manpower employed in various activities. Under the pre-1875 non-expanding economy, 70 percent of people's time was spent in production and distribution, 10 percent in sickness, and 20 percent in "organizational" activity. (I have included 2 percent of the trading category as being *tabu* trading and hence a political organizational activity.) Slight increases in political activity followed each consolidation, but since productive activities also subsequently increased, there was not much cumulative change. The major changes have come since the 1940's as more people have gone into paid labour, until the time expenditure is now 52 percent in production and distribution, 6 percent in sickness, and 42 percent in other activities, Most of these other activities have not been work for European primary producers, but work within the village as providers of administrative services. Self-sustained growth will mean the continuance of this trend. What "development" means for the village is the provision of the services of education, justice, communications, entertainment, religion, and family life on a steadily increasing scale, and by individuals who are paid to specialize in providing those services more efficiently than before. This has meant an increase in the proportion of incomes paid in taxation – directly to the Council, indirectly to the Central Administration, and in the form of church collections and offerings and *nidok* contributions to the *tubuan*. I have estimated annual *tubuan* contributions (Salisbury 1966) as 35 percent of *tabu* incomes. I estimate the "taxes" paid in cash as about the same proportion of cash receipts.

But those who provide services in turn buy food and housing from the primary producers. Incomes have risen all around, so that after-tax incomes may well be no less than they were ten years earlier, while the services received have increased many times. The proportion of non-primary producers that can be supported (hence also the level of services that primary producers can expect) clearly depends on the level of productivity of primary production. Yet the availability of employment outside primary production has helped directly in raising the efficiency of that production. Though the absolute size of the primary productive labour force has not declined, the availability of a variety of jobs has meant a highly mobile labour force, and much switching from less rewarding forms of primary production to those giving a higher return per man-day. Thus the increase in service personnel within the society has had the multiplier effect of raising the incomes of primary producers while also improving the efficiency of production.

In short, at the local level, the process of economic development can be seen as involving both technological improvement and the desire by the people to provide increased services for themselves. Only with technological improvement can a larger proportion of the people be "freed from the productive process." Only if there is a positive pressure for more services, however, will that liberation occur. Only if there is full employment will the service providers not be seen as exploiting the "producers." Only if the people are prepared and able to provide those services for themselves will there be a cumulative increase in the flow of benefits from those services. The people of Vunamami can look back with nostalgia to the days when the *tubuan* was a *matanitu kai ra tarai* – when the people provided the services of government for themselves. They can appropriately feel that their traditions are worth preserving because they strengthen them in their adoption of sustained economic change. They appreciate the interdependence of political consolidation and economic development.

Notes

1.   This article presents descriptive material in support of the present characterization of Melanesian leadership, and reconciles the practical despotism commonly found with the universal democratic ideology which is most commonly described and analysed. The article is based on Tolai experience but uses Highland materials to confirm the picture. Subsequent studies have tended to confirm the existence of despotism indigenously but at the same time to question whether all directors were despotic.

2.   When, as sometimes happens, a single business is as great as the country in which it is located, the situation is unstable and fraught with suspicions of exploitation. The existence of international corporations that are often larger than the national unit within which they are operating poses one of the most urgent problems of political control in developing countries today.

References

Geertz, C. 1963. *Agricultural Involution*. Berkeley and Los Angeles: University of California Press.

Rogers, E.M. 1962. *The Diffusion of Innovations*. New York: The Free Press.

Plotnicov, L. and H. Befu. 1961/1962. "Types of Corporate Unilineal Descent Groups." *American Anthropologist* 64:313.

Salisbury, R.F. 1964. "Despotism and Australian Administration in the New Guinea Highlands." *American Anthropologist*, Special Issue, 66(2):225-239.

------------1966. "Politics and Shell-Money Finance in New Britain." in M. Swartz and A. Tuden (eds.), *Political Anthropology*. Chicago: Aldine.

122

6.

AN ANTHROPOLOGISTS'S USE OF HISTORICAL METHODS

by

Richard F. Salisbury

Source: Paper presented to the History Seminar,
University of Papua and New Guinea, 7 July 1967.

My forthcoming book, *Vunamami: Economic Transformation in a Traditional Society*, indicates how an unsophisticated anthropologist with interests in economic theory, but dissatisfied with the short-run picture obtained from fieldwork alone, became involved in what has turned out to be a major historical study, taking almost ten years of work. It indicates how the research focused down on the history of a particular village – Vunamami – and why it was felt that the study of such a "worm's eye view" of history could yield a more thorough insight into the processes of economic change and development than is provided by the macro-view obtainable from histories dependent on written records, which are usually written by Europeans.

What this paper will try to do is to evaluate the contributions that can be expected to accrue from the combination of anthropological techniques of interviewing and participant observation, and historical methods of documentary research. I hope it will do more than merely illustrate my lack of knowledge of the latter. But before plunging into specifics, I would like to say something about my understanding of anthropological techniques. These involve nothing mysterious, and few gimmicks, but basically an approach to people that is probably very similar to a historian's approach to documents. It is that whenever someone is talking to you, he is talking good sense, even if you, the listener, do not understand that sense.

On one level there is the question of language. Sense often becomes lost in translation, particularly when apparent synonyms have different connotations – the furore in English-Canadian circles when French-Canadians, who "demandaient qu'on parlait Français," were translated as *demanding* that people speak French in Quebec is an example of this. Hence anthropologists' preference for using vernacular languages where possible and, where that is not possible, their care in always checking whether a meaning is correct. On a second level there is the question of actions making sense in relation to other activities going on at the same time.

An anthropologist faced with a notice saying that "a taboo has been put on coconuts for three months, with a fine of one shilling for infringements," does not dismiss this as irrational superstition, or simply a survival of "old customs." He looks for sense in many directions. In one direction he looks for who proclaimed the taboo, the sources of his authority and the nature of the (usually religious) ideology that connects his authority with coconuts. In another direction he looks for reasons why such a taboo should have been proclaimed at this particular time. In the case I have in mind, it was to ensure that cash would be available from copra production when the annual mission collection was due, although this answer does not explain why this method was adopted, rather than one of saving by small contributions. In yet a third direction he looks for the implication of the taboo: what alternative activities do people undertake? who collects the fines and what does he use them for? what is the effect on people whose businesses depend on a regular flow of coconuts, such as copra driers or trucks? The taboo can well make sense from all these directions.

Yet a third sort of sense involved in an informant's statement, is that it must make sense or be for his personal advantage for him to say what he does. An anthropologist may look simple-minded as he notes down everything that everyone says; but basically he is highly suspicious, and every individual's report is considered as a distortion of the truth in a direction that is advantageous for that individual. Even if numbers of informants agree and "truth" can be established, there is still the question of why they should have told the truth in the first place. More commonly, accounts differ and although the divergences are rarely because of deliberate falsification (though they may be) the different statements cannot be held to "make sense" until the divergences have been explained. None of this may appear strange to historians versed in criticism of textual sources, but it may be novel to think of applying the same technique to everything one hears.

It may also be novel to look at the testimony of most Europeans as being perhaps the furthest divergent from the truth about events that it is possible to get, except in the matter of dates. Most European reports are written by people who do not speak the same language as the people reported about, and who interpret events through a set of preconceived ideas about New Guineans that bear little resemblance to reality. The reports are also aimed at convincing an audience. Patrol reports, for example, will stress either the work that the officer did, berating people about the poor state of their latrines, or how effective he was in that things were much improved over the state of the last patrol and say little about the state of sanitation. Travellers' tales will stress the exotic and the dangerous, to convince the reader what a hero the traveller was, and are entirely untrustworthy on this issue for which they are most often cited.

124

Perhaps the main difference between an anthropologist and an historian is that the latter is merely critical of sources. The former is downright suspicious – unless he has seen things for himself, when he refuses to accept anyone's questioning of his veracity. "Seeing for oneself" is the other main tool in an anthropologist's armoury, and although it may be over-valued it is nonetheless highly valuable. By both seeing, and participating in, events the anthropologist has two checks on the truth of what people tell him. If he has misunderstood their words, the discrepancy with what he sees will be obvious. If he then has to act in response to what other people say and do, and he has not understood the implications of what has been said, or the different interests of various parties, then his actions will be greeted by negative responses. These may vary all the way from polite silence, after a social gaffe, to social ostracism. It is the hard way to learn whether you are right or wrong. As will be indicated below, the technique is equally revealing of other people's attitudes and understandings, and above all it inspires confidence in informants if they know that their listener is also involved in the consequences of their actions.

With that as background let us now consider how an incident might appear looked at from standard historical and the ethnohistorical viewpoints – the murder of Moses on March 28th 1890. I describe it in standard terms as follows. "Neither the [German New Guinea] Compagnie nor Queen Emma expanded [their plantations] entirely peacefully. 'Inland tribes' from Vunamami, Keravi, Bitareberebe and Tingenvadu villages attacked Ralum [Plantation, the base of Queen Emma's enterprise] in March 1890 with success, until a combined force led by [Richard] Parkinson and Judge Schmiele repelled them killing three natives and burning Tingenavudu." (Nachrichten 1890:75; Monatshefte 1890:134)[1] The spelling of place names in the reports has been corrected, and some details omitted. The fact that the war started with the killing of a Filipino plantation overseer when he was clearing the route for a road from Ralum and Malapau plantations, both owned by Queen Emma, is mentioned for example, but to include these details in what seems to be a simple case of local resistance to European expansion would seem unnecessary pedantry.

The case recurred in the records as follows. "One major effort [by the Sacred Heart Mission] to ensure the full conversion of local people was the boarding school. ... Another was the unsuccessful trial defence by the Bishop of the leader of the 1890 uprising. When the leader was executed, his son was adopted by the Mission." (Monatschefte 1892:153,168) Again the record cites the names of the leader, ToRuruk, and of his son TeTenge. One source that also refers to the incident is Mead (1963). I have not cited this, as the reference is obscure, and confused with a later war, though it does mention the destruction of a sacred place (*Marawot*). It is virtually a verbatim account of interviews with Mrs. Parkinson in about 1929, with much interesting detail, but questionable overall accuracy.

In fieldwork I mentioned the name of ToRuruk. People were amazed that I knew the name, and eagerly filled in graphic details of the murder. Everyone knew the name of Moses, and mimed the way in which, when he had been knocked down, ToRuruk killed him by biting his jugular vein. There was often some confusion over the sequence of this and other wars, but everyone knew that one war had been about the destruction of a sacred place (the exact spot near the present site of Butuwin Hospital was known), apparently wilfully and despite requests not to. They also knew that when the war was over ToRuruk had escaped to the bush, and that the Government had decreed that as compensation for the murder of Moses the strip of land along the coast between Ralum and Malapau plantations should be given to Parkinson and Queen Emma. Vunamami and Keravi people were expelled from this land. As the grounds and evidence for the decisions of Judges Hahol and Phillip regarding land ownership in Ralum have been lost, it is not possible to say whether this aspect of the land claim has ever yet been discussed legally. The circumstantiality of the local general knowledge is convincing however.

Parallel with my historical inquiries about ToRuruk occurred a fortunate accident. The people of Vunamami became involved in two land matters relating to the possible purchase of Ravalien (Ralum) Plantation, and contesting the title to the plantation in a case before the Land Titles (Restoration) Commission. This gave me an opportunity for participation, along with observation, and when they asked me to investigate the history of their expulsion from their traditional lands, since I knew the published sources, I gladly agreed. It meant that busy and important men were prepared to sit down clarifying minor historical details. It involved me in hours of mapping and writing reports submitted to the District Office and Director of District Services. It gave point to my studies, a motivation to local people to help, and a control over my own studies which had to be accurate down to the minutest detail possible to meet legal and official objections.

At this point the general comment was made that a 70 year old local man, Alwas ToMatinur, the first Tolai hired as a Government clerk in the 1920s, was the son of ToRuruk's brother, ToInia. He was an excellent informant, and general talk about his father discussed such issues as how ToInia had been an early mission convert; how he had trained as a preacher at Vunamami church; how the land he finally owned, and on which his son was still living (with the permission of his father's matrilineal clan Tetegete), had been given to him by his father; how a member of a third clan had married a local woman of Vunabalbal; how he had been one of two important headmen of his own clan, Vunaibu, in Vunamami village, owning the rights to an ancestral religious *tubuan*; how TaInia had helped give a huge feast (*matamatam*) in honour of his father and the dead of Tetegete clan, contributing 600 fathoms of *tabu* (shell money, worth $600 at today's exchange rates). Alwas finally said, with a smile, "You know it was ToInia who gave ToRuruk away. ToRuruk came out of the bush behind ToInia's garden (a ravine, which would have then been uncultivated, runs nearby) and tried to persuade his wife to come into the bush with him. She told ToInia, and he went for the police." Dates and even sequences were hard to establish, but it proved possible to do so. ToInia had been a relatively young man when his son was born – say 25; Alwas had not been born when Moses had been murdered but was born soon after on the beach land near Vunamami Church; he had been born but was too young to remember the ceremonial *matamatam*; he estimated his own birth at 1892. The firm date of March 28th 1890 for the murder of Moses thus serves to establish a sequence.

But first the question must be asked: was Alwas' evidence biassed in any consistent way? Clearly he was giving information to build a picture of his father as an important man. Exaggeration could well be present, but the specific details of clans involved, of contributions to the *matamatam*, etc. were all confirmed by other individuals. All that would be needed to assess his information would be to take away some of the halo, and to consider whether less favourable interpretations could not put on the same facts. Another bias in Alwas' story was his clear desire to justify his own residence on this piece of land. Young men normally live with their fathers until marriage, but go to land belonging to their own clan when they marry and bring in a complete foreigner of a wife. They certainly leave when the wife starts bearing children of her clan. Not only was Alwas still living on his father's land, but his adult daughter was keeping house for him, now that his wife was dead. Was there something fishy about ToInia getting the land? And if one were really suspicious of the evidence, why did Alwas mention his father's "betrayal" of someone who would be assumed to be a local hero, in the course of praising his father?

Further small pieces of information fit into the puzzle. ToRuruk, as head of Vunaibu clan, had his home at the ancestral land of the clan in a village three miles inland. He was not the full brother of ToInia, but a more distant relative. Tetegete clan, who gave away the land, is one of the two major landholding groups in Vunamami. Giving away land to distant relatives is a traditional way for aspiring leaders to recruit supporters.

The picture that I reconstruct is thus one of ToInia, born about 1866, the son of an important Tetegete man in Vunamami, growing up in a village that enthusiastically adopted Methodism in 1876. In about 1899 he married, and should by rights have gone inland to Vunaibu land, to become an unimportant person under the control of his classificatory "older brother" and clan head, ToRuruk. Instead he compromised and went with his wife to live next to Vunamami Church on mission land to train as a preacher. Alwas was conceived soon after his father's marriage. The murder of Moses happened soon after and also Alwas' birth at the beach. There was clearly no love lost between ToInia and ToRuruk, despite their formal ties. We can infer causes for this – rivalry over power in Vunaibu clan, and an antagonism between a "progressive" mission trainee and the head of a group avenging the desecration of a clan shrine by cannibalism. ToInia's betrayal of ToRuruk was not overtly of him as a clan rival, or as a Tolai patriot, but as a person guilty of a serious offence in native custom and one even more disapproved of by the Methodists – "coveting thy brother's wife." It was no shame for Alwas to reveal such an act: he was demonstrating his father's moral rectitude.

There now comes the rapid acquisition by ToInia of 600 fathoms of *tabu* (still a sizeable fortune) and his gift of it to his father for the ceremony. My suspicious mind would wonder whether the German Government paid a reward, and whether for ToInia to give it away was not a satisfactory disposal of tainted money. The gift of land in Vunamami was highly convenient for him (though expectable in the light of his contribution) as I doubt whether he could now have returned in safety to the inland territory of Vunaibu. He does not seem to have lost political ambitions however. His later purchase of rights to a Vunaibu *tubuan*, his encouragement of distant branches of Vunaibu clan to live on his new land, his education and protection of his son (Alwas was also initiated by his father into the *tubuan* religion about 1920), all are typical of aspiring Tolai politicians, seeking to gain a base of support. They also suggest that ToInia's opposition to ToRuruk was not because of a rooted objection to conservatism or the indigenous way of life, but from a realistic appraisal of what the benefits of Europeanisation were, and a willingness to compromise in going about obtaining them.

What light does such an incident, seen from the worm's eye view, throw on the general historical picture? In the first place there is the question of European land claims, and what the local people thought they had given to Queen Emma and Richard Parkinson at the time of purchase. There seems to have been a peaceful acceptance by local people of their residence at Malapau and Ralum, and even of the construction of the road connecting them. Equally clearly, however, the local people felt that the land on which they themselves lived was their own and not sold. When conflicts arose they were not directly a matter of "pressure on land," but of affronts ("calculated affronts" even?) against native custom. Why should Parkinson, a sensitive observer, have allowed or encouraged the desecration of a *marawot*? Certainly not from ignorance, as local testimony shows. The suspicion would be that only by provoking exaggerated native reactions could he and Queen

Emma force the German Government and New Guinea Compagnie into supporting them, into providing troops and judicial decisions that would confirm their ten-
uous hold on the land, and force natives into accepting it.

But if the case illustrates the lack of a solid block of "Europeans"
(and Bishop Couppe's intervention on behalf of ToRuruk would indicate yet another line of European cleavage), it also illustrates the importance of the lines of cleavage in indigenous society in permitting European expansion. Those most affected by
European penetration – those living in Vunamami village itself – appear to have been
least involved in opposing penetration. Yet their support for the benefits of contact
did not protect them from punishment at the hands of the Europeans who treated
all villagers as a unitary whole. Inland-coastal antagonisms and the differential advantages to the different areas of various types of trade seem to have been of great
importance in the first acceptance of traders (monopolised by the coastals) on the
coast, and in later inland insistence that the coastal monopoly be broken to allow
them the advantages of direct trade with Europeans. The antagonism between "progressive" factions and "resistance" factions have been hinted at in this case, and
could be followed through later Tolai history up to the Raluana incident of 1953, the
Navuneram incident of 1957 and much current controversy over the Tolai Cocoa
Project. But that is not possible, however, if one accepts the usual European myth
of a single cohesive society, with a single "native opinion."

The third hint that this case gives is of the role of individuals in
the indigenous society in producing changes that are too easily assumed to be the
result of European teaching. ToInia, though not the most important such individual
in Vunamami's history, was of considerable significance in inducing Vunamami to
take its current creative response to the possibilities for economic development. This
political progress, and my guess that it was founded on a German Government
reward, obviously smoothed the path of acceptance after the war. His own son's education and work for the Government both as a clerk early in life, and as head of the
local school committee and as a consultant in land law (Smith and Salisbury 1961) in
old age are another such influence. The outstanding Vunamami paramount *luluai*, and
first President of Vunamami Council, Enos Teve, is the son of another Vunaibu
clansman, Levi ToLingling, a close associate of ToInia who was presumably persuaded to settle in Vunamami largely because of ToInia. Their joint business ventures
(and rivalries) of the 1910-1920 period, culminating in the initiations of their sons,
would appear to have been a driving force. Their wealth led to some of the earliest
purchasing of horses and carts by natives and the building of houses with metal
roofs, well before the decline of native incomes in the 1920s and the depression
stopped further expansion.

Finally, let us return to the question of anthropological methods and the historian. Although I have enjoyed working through this case, virtually as in a detective story picking up clues, let me say that I don't feel that arriving at the solution requires the skills of any particular discipline – other than the suspicious mind I mentioned at first, and perhaps long acquaintance with detective stories. Where I feel the anthropologist scores is in the collection of data, or, to pursue the detective story analogy, the recognition of what may be a clue. Any anthropologist would have turned up the gift of land to ToInia by Tetegete clan in the course of a survey of land-holding, and would probably have worked out the anomalies of father-son inheritance in a matrilineal system, and of the father-son residence pattern of Alwas and ToInia.[2] The patterns of relationships both within the Vunaibu clan segment living in Vunamami, and between this segment and the main clan, based inland, would have turned up in a routine genealogical inquiry. Questioning about employment histories would inevitably have discovered Alwas' employment with the District Office of the 1920s. In fieldnotes obtained by Charles Julius, Government anthropologist, from Alwas in 1953(?) is a long note on the customs of *rara na ubu* (the giving of gifts of land to the son of a clan member, when that son has performed services for his father's clan) and *warap* (the making of a large thank offering by a son to his father in return for the food that father gave him during childhood) – topics that might easily come up in any anthropological study of customary exchanges.

In all these examples there is an element that would strike an anthropologist as anomalous because of his training – a particularly telling example perhaps, that no anthropologist could resist obtaining a few more circumstantial details about, to colour his narrative with; or an anomaly as in the matter of father-son inheritance that would require genealogical and circumstantial elucidation. More questions would be asked by any trained anthropologist.

But the advantage does not lie entirely with the anthropologists. I can visualise that the material I have presented could quite easily appear in a Tolai ethnography with this particular case buried in many different sections. Some of it might appear as an example in a discussion of the variability found in matrilineal land inheritance; some as one statistic in a chapter on household composition and the degree to which affinal and filial ties are used to recruit membership of domestic groups, as well as ties of clanship; some as a particular case to illustrate *warap* in the chapter on kinship ties between father and children; and some in the chapter on religion as an example of how *matamatams* are organised. Without the framework of dates given by historical research, without the controls that enabled me to isolate confused verbal reports of different wars, and without a constant forcing of informants to put events in sequences, and to establish relative dating for events by asking such questions as "were you born when ...?" or "was this in German times?", I do not think that the interconnection of these various events could have been established. Half their significance would have been lost by the anthropologist working solely in his own disciplinary framework. In other words, if I had not consciously been trying to be a historian I do not think that I would have obtained half the evidence. I would feel that anthropologists have much to learn from historians.

But I must have my last word as an anthropologist. I feel that historians could collect much valuable data (especially in places like New Guinea) if they looked at some of the drier and apparently irrelevant chapters in anthropological monographs – land tenure, customs, kinship, religion, etc. If they learned from this reading and realised more how these dull background features interconnect with such dramatic things as political leadership or cult movement, historians would be able to sit through and ask provocative questions about the verbal narration of personal reminiscences about pieces of land, or who kinsmen were, or what exchanges were made at ceremonies. It is in the course of such, apparently irrelevant, conversations that important if disconnected material emerges. Unless it is collected, the organising skills of the historiographer cannot be applied. I would also finally add one fairly distinctive, though by no means original anthropological technique that I found proved to be of great value: the keeping of a file of names of past figures, with their approximate dates, villages, clan membership, etc. Using such a file a questioner can easily prod informants about particular times and/or places by asking about specific named individuals. People are always ready to talk about other people. Anthropology has been called "the higher gossip" because it often consists mainly in noting down such comments about other people's behaviour, and in annotating them in the light of the anthropologists' suspicious minds. I would advocate, if I had to, that historians develop the same interests in gossip and suspicions as anthropologists have.

NOTES

1. Salisbury 1970:229. Queen Emma, formerly Emma Coe, was the part-Samoan wife of Thomas Farrell, a trader based at Mioko. Her younger sister was married to Richard Parkinson, a German-English plantation manager.

2. On Alwas' death in 1967 his daughter left this land and it reverted to Vunaibu clan.

REFERENCES

1890. "Monatschefte zur Ehren unserer Lieben Frau vom Heiligsten Herzen Jesu, 1890." *Journal of the Sacred Heart Mission*. Westfalen: Hiltrap and Munster.

"Nachrichten aus Kaiser Wilhelmsland und dem Bisrmarck Archipel, 1885-98." *Organ of the Deutsche Neu-Guinea Compagnie*.

Salisbury, R. F. 1970. *Vunamami: Economic Transformation in a Traditional Society*. Berkeley: University of California Press.

Smith, S.S. and Salisbury, R.F. (eds.). 1961. *Notes on Tolai Land Law and Custom*. Port Moresby: Native Land Commission.

7.

Transactional Politics: Factions and Beyond

by

Richard F. Salisbury

Source: Marilyn Silverman & Richard F. Salisbury (eds.), *A House Divided: Anthropological Studies of Factionalism*. St. John's: Memorial University of Newfoundland (ISER), 1977.

When a theorist first clearly defines a new concept that has emerged vaguely in earlier empirical work, the usual reaction of other theorists is to elaborate the concept, to describe variant sub-types, and to proceed with what Leach (1962) called "butterfly collecting." When Nicholas (1965) defined what distinguished factions as units in political conflict, this process did not occur. No great consideration was given to documenting the variety of factional forms or processes, or to constructing typologies of *factions* on the basis of induction from empirical cases. Such study is still needed, but the decade 1965-1975 has seen the emergence within anthropology of a more general approach to politics that may be called *transactional politics*. This approach is sufficiently productive to permit one to derive hypothetical typologies of factions and factional processes from it, by deduction. The present paper attempts to develop such a typology, to compare it with some empirical data, and to suggest where future research studies could be profitably directed.

Transactional politics is the study of how individuals, within particular institutional systems, exercise political power through transactional behaviour which may be described as the transmission of goods and services by leaders in exchange for acceptance of their power by supporters who grant them authority. Factions, by Nicholas' definition, are *ad hoc* political groupings, linked to a leader in relation to specific conflict issues, that is, in terms of what followers can obtain through the leader's action. They are thus special groupings that emerge in transactional politics, despite the individualistic basis of transactions.

However, this general definition leads us to ask other questions of factions. How do different institutional contexts affect the nature of factions and factionalism? Are there particular institutional environments within which politics tend to take a factional form? How does the wider availability of goods and services affect the strategies of leaders, and the responses to them of potential followers? How does

133

the value of the support of different followers vary, and how does this variation affect the behaviour of leaders? While many other questions also come to mind, these few provide the basis for our abstract analysis of the game of factioning, for a consideration of some variations in it, and for some added understanding of the ethnography of factionalism.

FACTIONS AND CORPORATENESS

All definitions of factions agree that they are political groupings that are not corporate. But this does not mean that the societies within which factions occur are devoid of corporate groups, or that those corporate groups do not affect the factions. I would go so far as to assert that factional groupings always emerge within the framework of a wider "political community" that is corporate – a nation state, a village, a commune, or a tribe – and that although the factions may be composed of leaders and individual supporters, those supporters are commonly members of smaller corporate groupings, such as households. Does the nature of the circumscribing corporate groups (CCG) affect the nature of factons? Does it matter whether the members of factions are single individuals, or representatives of smaller corporations?

Bailey (1969) sees the pursuit of "offices" as the aim of politics. The concept of an office, however, implies that there be some corporate entity which provides resources to the office and whose members recognize the office. In defining what those offices are, and in setting limits on the means that may be used to attain those offices, the CCG provides the parameters within which factional competition occurs. As Bailey and others have noted, however, factionalism is rarely, if ever, normatively prescribed as a means of political action; it emerges as a pragmatically productive "strategy" (Salisbury 1968) that can be described (or what Bailey [1969] would term "a pragmatic rule"), and derived from the parametric conditions of the cultural rules of the CCG. The question to answer is what characteristics of the CCG produce and affect the nature of the emerging factions.

At the same time, it must be recognized that factions are not the only type of competing group which may be engaged in trying to obtain an office for its leaders, and by derivation, benefits for its supporting members. The competing groups may well have a corporate identity. For example, in New Guinea the corporate groups such as clans, landowning lineages, or village groups, who now compete for elected offices in the local councils or national legislature (Bettison, Hughes and van der Veur 1965) are the same groups who competed for prestige, pigs, and valuables in earlier times. "Big man" techniques of gaining support through transactions have continued to be used by leaders within those corporate groups. The New

Guinea groups, which will be returned to later, provide a graphic example of the meshing of factional and corporate group politics, and of changes over time in the balance of one against the other. For the present we should merely note that factions and corporate groups are alternative types of political grouping in supposedly tribal societies.

In peasant societies, particularly in the best reported areas of South Asia (Nicholas 1965; Bailey 1960; Islam 1974; Attwood 1974a; and others), it is often hard to distinguish from the given descriptions whether the politically active group (Islam uses the Bengali term *dal* and Bailey talks of *dolidoli*) is a corporate lineage, or sub-caste group, or an *ad hoc* factional grouping under a leader with a nuclear cluster of members of a corporate group. Characteristics of both types of grouping can be discerned. In studies of Lebanese village factionalism in the 1950s (Ayoub 1955), Christian, Moslem and Druse factions were reported alongside factions recognized as surname groups. The Hatfields and McCoys are legendary in the United States, as the Montagues and Capulets are in Verona. The lineages had clear corporate identities even if their boundaries were not clear. In modern Malta Boissevain (1965) explicitly showed how the competition for offices may be between factions, or between corporate political parties – again with unclear demarcation. Frankenberg (1957), without using the factionalist idiom, showed how manoeuvring for power in a Welsh village involved organized corporate groupings such as football clubs or church groups in some contexts, and non-corporate groupings in others. The question becomes widened. Do characteristics of the CCG similarly affect both corporate and non-corporate competing groupings? Does the nature of the CCG affect the probability of factionalism occurring at all?

A first characteristic of CCGs to be considered is their degree of multifunctionality, since transactional propositions can be derived from this multifunctionality.

Many studies of factionalism are of single villages, as are those of Silverman (1973) and Islam (1969), in which the village is treated as a corporate administrative unit by the bureaucratic structure of the surrounding nation-state; although many types of sub units are recognized by the local people, they are predominantly ignored by the nation-state. The village is also a significant unit for various other activities of a religious, economic, and recreational nature, to mention but a few. Benefits defined as flowing from the nation-state to "the village" predominantly flow through the office of village representative (or council president), whether these benefits relate to subsidies for irrigation, education at government schools, or prestigious offices in religious assemblies. The primary axis of factionalism is therefore the competition between aspirants for the office of village representative to the nation state. Though the same individual may not be the representative in every activity, the faction that has control of the major office is in a position to obtain control of all offices. Since the government recognizes only the village unit, there is no legal way for individuals to obtain access to benefits from government, except through factional competition. Short-circuiting this competition by personal appeals to higher authorities is common, but theoretically illegitimate.

Once in power (and assuming that no parameter changes occur), the faction with control over benefits from the nation-state has the means to retain power indefinitely through transactions. It can distribute patronage to enough individuals to give itself majority support. A majority faction has almost absolute power, subject largely to the readiness of the CCG to intervene. It may be called on to intervene should the majority seek to eliminate its minority (something of which anglophone Quebeckers became aware at the moment when the Prime Minister refused to extend them protection in linguistic matters at the provincial level; yet Canadian Indians had long been aware of how a federal CCG protected them in conflicts with non-Indian neighbours). The minority can also seek CCG intervention should the majority faction become too blatant in its exercise of patronage.

The multifunctional CCG, I argue, tends to produce a dualistic set of opposing sub-groupings – the powerful in-group and the weak out-group – with a relatively permanent in-group or establishment and an opposition out-group which may appear and disappear. Within such a system it also makes a great difference (in theory at least) whether there exist subgroupings that are corporate. Southwold (1968) has analysed in game theory terms what happened with corporate sub-groupings in Uganda before 1901. Division among the in-group of the benefits of winning provided less to each winner if the in-group comprised much more than 50 percent of the population, whereas less goods could be extracted from the losing minority if the minority was a small one. What occurred were coalitions of corporate groupings that exceeded 50 percent of the population by only a small margin, and that tried to placate losers after any confrontation. The visibility and relative fixity of corporate sub-units meant that the margin necessary for insurance against miscalculation could remain small.

In factional recruitment, however, the major threat to the leader of the establishment faction is not from a visible opposition but from the secret seduction of individual supporters within his own faction. Both Bailey and Nicholas (1968) have observed that where a single caste group constitutes a majority in an Indian village, factional competition tends to be entirely between members of that caste group. I would derive this empirical finding from the more general multifunctional corporateness of village units, rather than from demographic composition.

If a rival within a faction can divert a significant portion of the benefits that come from the nation-state to the corporate village to his own subgroup within the main faction, and can also secretly gain the support of the opposition, he may well achieve an overall majority within the village. Once a majority has been achieved on one occasion, power is likely to remain with the new faction, and its leader is likely to switch from the majority faction, even if his immediate supporters constitute a minority of the faction. He can always threaten to rejoin the old majority faction, and is the most likely leader to seduce more supporters from the old majority faction; this no other opposition leader of dissenting supporters can do. He has power over the swing-voters, and this is decisive.

If the above is a valid analysis of how factional politics differ from corporate group coalition politics, it has implications for the size of majority factions in apparently stable factional situations. If the majority faction numbered only 51 per cent, a sub-group leader with only one-thirtieth of the faction behind him could swing the balance by defecting to the opposition. If the major faction were 66.7 per cent of the total active population, then the defection of one quarter of it would be needed to produce a swing. Although security against all rivals is impossible to guarantee, a faction size in the range of 66 percent would be needed to provide a majority leader with an effective compromise of security with manageability.

A second implication of this analysis – one that has been incidentally indicated and implied by the description of dualistic sub groupings – is that when the CCG is multifunctional, there is little possibility for an individual to stand aloof from factional disputes. To do so would mean getting none of the benefits of faction membership; the majority leader is little interested in buying individual votes: a non-supporter of the majority faction would become branded as a "dissenter" and a member of the opposition, willy-nilly. The dominant faction may, in many cases, be the only active faction, with the "dissenters" forming a faction only in the perception of the dominants, and in reality not combining for action nor having a leader. Even so, their potential emergence as a faction, should an appropriate conflict situation develop, is a major factor structuring the behaviour of the dominant faction and its leader. In this sense, everyone is involved in the factional politics of this kind of CCG.

By contrast other types of CCG are illustrated in the works of several contributors to this volume (Schryer 1974; Attwood 1974a; Nagata 1970). The nation-state may provide the only single circumscribing group for all purposes, and for most specific purposes or specific decisions, there may exist a multitude of intermediate groupings, each of which is looked to by different people at the village level for specific decisions. Each specific grouping provides an arena for a distinct factional game. The various games inevitably are interrelated, as both leaders and followers can each bargain independently for support or benefits in one arena in exchange for benefits or support in a different arena. Inevitably there is some tendency for alignments in every arena to parallel the alignments in the arena where the largest volume of benefits is obtainable – the national political level in most cases – but many degrees of freedom exist. Most strikingly the role of the "independent" is necessarily tolerated, and may become critical in such situations. In any one arena no faction necessarily comprises a majority of participants, and decisions may be made by a minority, often depending on the acquiescence (or at least the non-opposition) of a category of "solid citizens" – an undistributed middle.

The presence of an undistributed middle provides a role for two kinds of factional leadership. In one direction a leader who appeals to the moral feelings of uncommitted solid citizens has the opportunity to cast himself in the role of community leader. Bailey (1972) has called this the role of *Tertius Numen*, otherwise known to television viewers as *Mr. Clean*, the fighter of corruption. In another direction, where the undistributed middle has previously been politically inactive, the self-appointed spokesman for grass roots sentiment takes the role which Attwood (1974b) has termed the *group mobilizer*.

The result is an open set of factional games marked by much individual shifting of support, and much wheeling and dealing by leaders active in different areas. Schryer (this vol.) describes such a situation in Mexico where municipios, regions, hamlets, the national PRI party, trade, ranching, and religion provide the different arenas. Oppositions appeared multiple and changing. It is noteworthy that such an open situation also provided the possibility of a united front emerging among competing factional leaders, when non-participants in the factional situation appeared likely to enter the fray the merchants or even the village peasants. Factionalism could lead to class-solidarities among an elite.

Attwood (1974b; also this vol.) indicates what could happen when there is a multitude of CCGs, each with a different function: state, municipal, and regional administrative units, each with an elected political representative, as well as a series of irrigation and sugar factory cooperatives, religious groupings, caste groupings, school groupings, and charismatic (quasi-political) movements. No grouping at any time has exclusive control of a majority of the benefits, and at any one moment any individual has a choice of several factions he can ally himself with (or, indeed, refrain from alliance). Although Attwood (1974b) shows how the situation he observed put power in the hands of supporters (via their mobilizers), this does not mean that such a situation always locates power at the grass-roots level, rather than in the hands of an elite. It does suggest that under these conditions an open market situation occurs, in which authority and benefits are openly exchanged.

Theoretically, in an open market situation, the rate of exchange between support and benefits should reach an equilibrium, if undistorted by monopolistic pressures from either side. In other words, where multiple CCGs exist, each unifunctional, and where monopolistic pressures are minimal, the exchange rate between support and benefits will depend on the balance of supply and demand – on the volume of benefits provided by the CCGs and the number of supporters available (and needed). Leaders will be effectively controlled by their supporters who will receive benefits from the leadership. But these quantitative aspects of factionalism are the concern of our next section; let us return to corporateness.

We have, at the minimum, established two polar types – factions within multifunctional CCGs which approach a predictable pattern of dualistic opposition, and factions within widely embracing CCGs that may be either specialized or distant, and where the opposition between factions and their patterns of recruitment are those of the multiple distributive oppositions found in a market system. Whether there are other relationships with other types of CCGs remains an open question.

CORPORATE GROUPS WITHIN FACTIONS

Though Nicholas defined factions as non-corporate groupings, it is clear that in reality all factions are more than purely *ad hoc* alliances of individuals who have no ties outside the factional relationship. As Mayer (1966) and others indicate most factions have a "core" of individuals who have close multiplex relations with the faction leader (and often among themselves), and around this core the bulk of the supporters constellate. The core is quite often a major segment of a corporate group: a caste group, a lineage, a religious group, and so on. In the local folk model of factions it is common for such groups to be referred to as though the faction actually *was* the corporate group to which its core belongs even though this is not the case. I would venture to suggest that if many of the studies of local politics of the 1940s and 1950s were re-analysed in a modern idiom, it would be found that much of what was analysed as "descent group" politics in Africa could be interpreted equally well as factional politics. Where oppositions are described emically as being "between descent groups," they could often be better analysed etically as being between the factional followings of individual leaders. Evans-Pritchard (1940) indicates for the Nuer, for example, how the "descent group" idiom that is used by local people to describe political oppositions masks a much more complex process in which local headmen or "bulls" recruit followings. By contrast, in the study of New

139

Guinea politics, the recruitment of followings by individual "big men" has often been emphasized (see for example, Sahlins 1964) without adequate recognition being given to the degree of corporateness within the groupings which they then lead (cf. Salisbury 1964).

In accordance with our initial definition, we concern ourselves in transactional politics with the non-corporate groupings – the factions. But, as indicated, the relationship of factions to corporate political pressure groups is of major concern. Let us look at the advantages and disadvantages of the two types of grouping, for both the leader and the followers. For the leader a corporate following gives him defined obligations towards his followers, but an assurance of free rein and unqualified support in negotiations outside the corporate group (provided, that is, he can live up to his internal obligations). A following that has been recruited transactionally may give the leader less general and more easily fulfilled obligations to his followers, but it also means that his freedom to commit those followers in a conflictual situation outside the faction is unpredictable. For the supporters the immediate transactional benefits may be high, and the immediate cost of obligations to support may appear low; but there is always the possibility that if the leader succeeds, he may desert his erstwhile supporters, whereas if he fails, nothing will accrue to the supporters in any case. In New Guinea the successful leader gets advantages of both kinds. Traditional (Salisbury 1964; Strathern 1971:223ff) and modern "big men" (Finney, 1973; Salisbury 1970) who are successful in their external negotiations can exert almost despotic power over members of their support group. It tends to appear as a corporate unit. For the supporter, again, the demands of the leader are known and the rewards from a successful leader predictable (and high if he lives up to his obligations). The relationship of leader to followers is likely to be strong enough to persist should there be one or two examples of failure, by one side or the other, to live up to defined obligations.

Both leader-follower relations also contrast with the pattern described by Banfield (1958) for Montegrano in Southern Italy, and called by him "amoral familism." One may doubt the empirical validity of Banfield's description (cf. S. Silverman 1968), but his abstract model may be analysed regardless. It is of a situation where each family unit is so suspicious of any other party exploiting them, should they join to form a faction or enterprise of any kind, that no larger groupings ever cohere. The result is that none of the benefits from wide-scale collaboration ever are produced, and everybody suffers.

In the three-fold contrast of no groupings/*ad hoc* groupings/corporate groupings, factions appear as the middle term – a compromise between the predictable benefits to be obtained from wider-scale collaboration and the unpredictable costs and dangers of exploitation by other parties should long-term relationships develop.

We would expect to find empirically, in any situation of transactional politics, a fluctuating balance. To the extent that major additional benefits accrue from organized group activities, the entropy of interpersonal suspicions will be overcome and groupings will persist; as leaders see external benefits regularly obtainable by entrepreneurial action on the part of their faction, they will try to incorporate their support group to stabilize it, and to make predictable the claims of the followers for a share in the benefits; supporters will also attempt to stabilize and incorporate a group which gives them important benefits in an attempt to control the leader. Against this centripetal tendency are centrifugal forces leading to either no groups, or to *ad hoc* groupings only. These forces include both overall quantitative factors (i.e., no benefits resulting from combined action, or benefits received which are lower than those obtained otherwise) and internal conflict factors (i.e., dissatisfaction by either leaders or supporters with what they receive from the other party, making them suspect exploitation).

Many variations are possible within this three-category dimension of corporateness of factions. It is clear that a wider study would amplify the range, and would test the value of these theoretical predictions.

THE RESOURCE PARAMETER

This parameter – the nature and quantity of resources which are allocated as a result of factional competition – is one where change can be easily seen. Silverman's study of Guyana (1973), and Attwood's (1974a) study of Maharashtra both sought to show how factional struggles changed when the resources available for allocation by political means also changed. Empirically, of course, the nature of CCGs (most commonly, the degree of involvement in local affairs of the nation-state, colonial administration, or large business enterprises) has also changed in any local area studied. It is only analytically, or through the construction of models, that one can separate the effect of resource change from that of a changing political structure. In the sections on corporate groupings we left implicit the assumption that resource availability does not change; in the present section we make explicit that our model construction has to be understood in terms of the unchangeable nature of the CCG.

To characterize leader-follower attitudes to resources and positively desired benefits, I would reverse an old saying: "Enough is enough, but enough is too little." A continuation of the same amount of benefits is recognized as satisfactory, but always leaves the lingering suspicion that through change, a larger amount of benefits could be obtained. (Parenthetically the original saying "enough is enough, and enough is too much" applies to negatively valued acts, so that for positively valued resources the apparently reversed expression actually has the same meaning). In other words, in real human society the degree of satisfaction is likely to depend more on *the rate of change of benefits received*, than on the *absolute volume* of benefits. We can theoretically envisage four main types of changing rates of benefits: rising, falling, stable, or oscillating volumes of benefits. We could further subdivide each of these types in terms of how long they have been offered, of whether they follow a different pattern, and of whether people anticipate the continuation of these benefits. More generally I would subsume all these latter considerations under the heading of how predictable the current pattern is. And as soon as one talks of predictability, one must clearly include the degree to which the action of the predictor can affect the likelihood of the prediction coming true. There are infinite variations in the rate of change and of predictability of resources available for distribution through factional competition, and each variation could affect factionalism distinctively.

Within such a range one can, however, make some theoretical hypotheses. Easiest are the hypotheses having to do with predictability and stability – conditions which would generally be expected to promote a long-term stability of distribution according to standard terms of exchange. That is, under stable and rising conditions of resource availability, distribution tends to be through corporate groups, within which further distribution tends to be standardized by permanent relationships between leaders and followers. *A priori*, one would expect factionalism to emerge either when an unpredictable increase occurred in distributable benefits and competition ensued over who would receive the benefits, or when unpredictable decreases in distributable benefits made some people band together to ensure that they did not suffer. Oscillation, or unstable variation in rates of increase, presents situations where no *a priori* hypotheses seem immediately evident.

The empirical evidence does contain several findings that can be fitted within this general framework. Silverman (1973) reports a period of factional peace (or, alternatively, a time when aspirant competitors found it better to support a single leader and to emphasize village corporateness) at a time when resources for distribution through the corporate village were rapidly increasing. Attwood (1974a) also reports that at a time when increases in income from sugar were being created by efficient management of the sugar factory, rather than by manipulations of quotas and the like, factional strife did not occur in that arena.

On the other hand although steady increases in available resources may have made factionalism irrelevant in one arena in Attwood's study, it did not eliminate faction in all arenas. Given a situation of multiple CCGs, the switch from factionalism to stable allocation as a means of distributing benefits within one CCG has little effect on other CCGs. The overall impression given by many studies in which there has been a major increase in the volume of resources available to the local community through political channels is that factionalism (together with other processes of transactional politics such as patronage, coalitions, and others) *expands* its scope proportionately with their resources. Even if the corporateness of the main CCG is stabilized, factionalism becomes an important process for benefit allocation *between* subgroupings and on issues of a more personal kind, during a time of expansion.

These two divergent empirical findings are reconcilable if one assumes that a *long-term* increase of resources allocated by a CCG will decrease the incidence of major internal conflicts (until the increase slows and competition emerges); however, short-term increases requiring distribution by smaller sub-groups provoke the emergence of factionalism. The factional sub-groups become functionally specialized, and then further encourage the emergence of multiple-opposition "open market" factionalism.

Factional behaviour within situations of oscillating or declining availability of resources for transactional political distribution is less commonly described. Yet it is likely that this is the state of resources in the traditional, apparently stagnant societies which Siegel and Beals (1960) considered as showing "pervasive factionalism." Whereas they saw pervasive factionalism as the reason for the communities not combining for progressive improvement, the present analysis would suggest that causation went in the opposite direction. It is true that the existence of factionalism in the Siegel and Beals cases meant that the new resources introduced by change agents went to one faction only, and still further polarized existing splits. But a longer term view would see these newly introduced resources as just another phase in an oscillating pattern – of resources available at one moment but likely to be unpredictably few a little later. Each infusion of resources and each withdrawal over a long period created a succession of conflict situations, as to who was to benefit and who to be discriminated against. Yet the situations were not predictable or similar enough for the emergence of institutionalized relationships and rules. This (though without supporting empirical evidence) I would interpret as a common situation in traditional societies with pervasive factionalism.

This comment underlines the need to consider the resource situation as it is perceived by the local people, and not merely as viewed ethically by outsiders. Change agents are seen as indicative of a new era by outsiders, but until the input of resources from a change agent has exceeded all previous inputs and until it has lasted longer than any previous increase, the change agent will be seen by local people as just another unpredictable oscillation. He will be followed, people assume, by a predictable oscillation downwards, so that everyone will strive for his own short-term gains in sharing the new inputs. The expected result would be a sharing out among the established powerful faction and a blunting of change, or, if the change agent tried to benefit the "dissenters," a rejection of his work by the in-group who sabotage his work.

But if this oscillating or declining pattern of change in resources has been less explicitly related to types of factionalism, there is all the more need for closer analysis of new cases, along with others of the infinite variety of potential patterns.

INTERNAL RESOURCE AVAILABILITY

Empirically one must note that factions are always reported as involving the grouping of people with heterogeneous resources – minimally, the different resources of leadership abilities and physical strength. One might postulate that unless there is heterogeneity of resources there is no reason for a grouping to emerge, and no basis for any transaction between the participants. In practice the resources that are most commonly discussed as provided by followers are the potential for physical support in a fight, emotional support by presence at a time of strain, or electoral support through a vote; and as provided by leaders, the contacts with high-status outsiders which can lead to an inflow of benefits to the local community. In short, transactional politics emerge mainly in a context of stratification, although the stratification may involve local people versus party members or *cadres* with external contacts just as much as peasants versus landowners. Factions rely for their internal solidarity on exchangeable resources; they rely for their emergence on the existence of situations of conflict wherein a single winner can result, and wherein his success depends on the size of his support group.

Though this may be the simplest type of factional situation and one that can be seen as a model, even this model is far from a simple one. Outside contacts differ in quality as well as quantity. Even the value of individuals in a one-person-one-vote situation differs because some will advertise their vote and others will not, some will turn up, and others may be unreliable.

More complex, but theoretically more challenging, is the situation where a variety of resources exist *within* a community which could potentially be grouped together to produce a sum greater than the parts – where, say, construction skills could be combined with local finance and with established contacts with outside religious bodies to build and staff local schools. In such circumstances the efficacy of a faction in a conflict situation does not depend on numbers alone, but on the effectiveness and appropriateness of selective recruitment for the particular question at issue. On the one hand this condition theoretically makes for less permanent factions, since each issue ideally demands a different factional composition; it opens matters up for greater bargaining by different individuals who see their position as more or less critical in particular conflicts, and thus should tend to produce more "open-market" factionalism. On the other hand it tends to concentrate power in the hands of those with the scarcest but most generally relevant resource – the entrepreneurial ability to organize other people. In terms of Pareto's circulation of elites, this is a time for foxes.

The introduction of universal secret-ballot suffrage by a nation-state is one change that, as many studies show, produces a most dramatic restructuring of factional struggles which earlier were confined to an elite, or were simply dualistic. It reduces to a minimum the differences between individual supporters as resources in the struggle for the main CCG offices, at the same time as it increases the importance of external links which an office-holder develops. But then complexity (in all the cases reported) reasserts itself. Differential resources held by individuals (especially such resources as literacy, accounting skills, access to information, or organizational ability) become more significant. As suggested the composing of factions (and factional slates) to achieve a balance of different internal resources becomes a very important skill. It presages the role of the party organizer, if factions incorporate as parties. Uneven internal resource distribution, in short, is a condition for factions to exist, as well as something which factions perpetuate by their nature.

What happens if all resources are equalized in a socialist system? If our earlier analysis is correct, factions initially disappear. If previous owners of resources – middle peasants, for example – attempt to gain support from a section of the proletariat, they find this impossible in a situation where class consciousness has been fully aroused. Schryer (1974), Attwood (1974a) and Islam (1973) all give examples of initial egalitarian euphoria and freedom from factions when earlier class or ethnic privileges were abolished. But in none of these cases did a fully egalitarian system emerge. If previous differences based on private property did not reassert themselves in their previous form, the existence of a nation-state itself produced differences in access to the benefits provided by the nation-state. Factions supported brokers who promised access to these benefits, and competition between factions reemerged in practice, if unrecognized in ideology. Behavioural studies are needed of the way conflicts over the allocation of external inputs of resources into socialist communities are resolved. Do official, institutional ways always cope? Or, as Frank (1958) found when examining the way Russian managers coped with the problem of

145

maintaining their positions (and support from their workers) in the face of irreconcilable demands and persistent shortages, are officially unsanctioned entrepreneurial techniques utilized? To complete the range of studies of variations in internal resource availability, we also need studies of perfect equality.

The Ethnography of Factions

The preceding sections have considered only two main dimensions of variation in the social and resource environment, but in them, I have tried to indicate how variations in the forms of factionalism may be seen as dependent on these variations. The same analysis has implied that a dynamic process is involved: that changes in the social and resource environment produce changes in the factions themselves as a result of differential individual reactions to those changes.

A variety of characteristics of factions have been described. Although these have been analysed as though they were dependent variables, in other frameworks of analysis, they could constitute the major foci of study or the independent variables, and a major task could have been to set up typologies of factions. Though this paper does not take that approach, its attempt to show how factionalism can take many varied forms leads one to suggest that more detailed ethnography is needed, documenting variation in factionalism as well as its common elements.

Knowledge of the number of factions involved is clearly critical to an understanding of the tactics used by factionalists. Yet it is easy to accept crude folk models which report merely "X's group, and Y's group," but difficult to get at the reality of how people actually align themselves, and of whether (particularly in the past) there were issues which inspired other groupings to form. Both folk-models and actual behaviour need description, for both affect the decisions people make.

So too is the factional situation critically different if community members are able to ignore factional disputes and not align themselves if they do not wish to do so. What proportion of the community is involved in the factionalism? And for what reasons do they involve themselves and others abstain? Again these are data that are sometimes difficult to collect, especially when all attention is focussed on the actors who are upstage centre.

The issues of conflict are perhaps the simplest data to record as these are public – though the availability of written records to stimulate the memory of participants, who wish to remember the past as harmonious, is desirable. The details are likely to be unclear and selectively remembered by both winners and losers. Furthermore, the transactions which accompanied the conflict are, for the most

146

part, not public (indeed, they may well be officially illegal). Even if one can find out who supported the faction leader, that is who composed factions (since this may be a matter of public record), the material goods or services flowing the other way are usually not recorded at all. Promises or expectations of goods and services, which are likely to have been the bases of recruiting support, are even less commonly recorded. Most likely they become public knowledge only when the promises are not fulfilled, or the expectations thwarted.

The degree of corporateness of a faction is critical in the present analysis. Again it is something that is hard to document, for no grouping in any context is ever fully corporate in relation to the actions of all its members all of the time. What one sees are attempts by both leaders and followers to claim lasting relationships with a wider framework (within which their transactional behaviours are embedded) and the recognition of (or refusal to recognize) these claims by other parties.

In this sense "corporateness" is one possibility in a dimension of permanence and predictability. To speak of permanence and predictability we ideally need to know how many people remained in the same faction, and how many left it (the latter is difficult data to obtain); whether remaining or leaving was what was expected, and how often surprises happened. How do people obtain the information on which they make predictions about the behaviours of others in a factional situation?

Even this brief review of a few dimensions of ethnographic variation of factions is enough to indicate the possibilities for greater precision, and to show relationships that even the best ethnographies to date have rarely produced. One is led to wonder how the ethnographer can ever hope to do a thorough factional study, especially in a society other than his own, or one which demands that the ethnographer describe the culture as well as the factions.

TACTICS AND RULES

I have, deliberately, given only the briefest mention of tactics and rules in regard to factions. I have suggested that for factionalism (and not violence) to occur as a process, the circumscribing corporate group must set certain limits. It must define what is possible and what is not possible for factionalists. It may also set rules for the operation of corporate groups, which, if followed by a faction, give it claim to treatment as a corporate unit. The desirability of setting up one's political interest group or faction as a party is clear in the Canadian context, for example, for parties have parliamentary privileges which independents do not have. To academics the acquisition by a faction of a title of "Institute," "Programme," or "Centre" is the example which springs to mind of the way CCG rules relevant to corporate groups affect factional behaviour.

But it is only at these levels that I feel that the concept of rules applies to the factional process. In factions we are studying strategies of behaviour – perhaps not in pure form, for all individuals are influenced by rules obtaining in other domains where they have interests – but at least it is the strategic aspect that is the focus of study.

Strategies imply both constant reassessment of tactics and change in response to changes in the perceived situation. Perceptions of situations are conditioned in part by pre-existing structures of perception, and in part by empirical behaviour. What we can study most clearly in studying transactional politics (and particularly factions) is one way in which individuals cope, within a defined structure of perceptions, with changes in the availability of resources or in the behaviour of others, by altering their tactics, and less frequently, their strategies. Corporate groups, parties, nation-states, and cultural rules provide the elements of fixity, predictability, permanence – the continuity of structures; at the point at which these emerge, we have indeed gone beyond factions. But in our study we may have clarified major issues in the analysis of where political variation ends and where political change occurs. The behavioural study of variation in factionalism has barely begun.

REFERENCES

Attwood, D.W. 1974a. Political Entrepreneurs and Economic Development: Two Villages and a Taluka in Western India. Ph.D. Dissertation. Montreal: McGill University.

------------1974b. "Patrons and Mobilizers: Political Entrepreneurs in an Agrarian State." *Journal of Anthropological Research* 30(4):225-41.

------------1977. "Factions and Class Conflict in Rural West India." in Silverman, Marilyn and Richard F. Salisbury (eds.), *A House Divided: Anthropological Studies of Factionalism*. St John's: Memorial University of Newfoundland (ISER).

Ayoub, V. 1955. Political Structure of a Middle East Community. Ph.D. Dissertation. Cambridge, Mass.: Harvard University.

Bailey, F.G. 1960. *Tribe, Caste, and Nation*. Manchester: Manchester University Press.

------------1969. *Strategems and Spoils*. New York: Schocken Books.

------------1972. *Tertius Gaudens aut Tertius Numen*. Burg Wartenstein Symposium, No. 55.

Bailey, F.G. and Ralph W. Nicholas. 1968. "Introduction to Part Four." in Swartz, M. J. (ed.), *Local Level Politics*. Chicago: Aldine.

Banfield, E.C. 1958. *The Moral Basis of a Backward Society*. Glencoe, Ill.: The Free Press.

Bettison, D.G., Colin A. Hughes and Paul W. Van Der Veur (eds.). 1965. *The Papua New Guinea Elections, 1964*. Canberra: Australian National University.

Boissevain, J. 1965. *Saints and Fireworks: Religion and Politics in Rural Malta*. London: Athlone.

Evans-Pritchard, E.E. 1940. "The Nuer of Southern Sudan." in Fortes, M. and E.E. Evans-Pritchard (eds.), *African Political Systems*. London: Oxford University Press.

Finney, B.R. 1973. *Big Men and Business*. Honolulu: University of Hawaii Press.

Frank, A.G. 1958. "Goal Ambiguity and Conflicting Standards." *Human Organization* 17:8-13.

Frankenberg, R. 1957. *Village on the Border*. London: Cohen and West.

Islam, A.K.M.A. 1969. Conflict and Cohesion in an East Pakistan Village. Ph.D. Dissertation. Montreal: McGill University.

------------1973. "Bangladesh in Transition: Reformation and Accommodation." *Southasian Series Occasional Paper* no. 21. Michigan University Press: Asian Studies Center.

------------1974. *A Bangladesh Village: Conflict and Cohesion- An Anthropological Study of Politics*. Cambridge, Mass.: Schenkman.

Leach, E. 1962. *Rethinking Anthropology*. London: Athlone Press.

Mayer, A.C. 1966. "The Significance of Quasi-Groups in the Study of Complex Societies." in M. Banton (ed.), *The Social Anthropology of Complex Societies*. ASA Monograph 4. London: Tavistock.

Nagata, Shuichi. 1970. *Modern Transformations of Moenkopi Pueblo*. Urbana: University of Illinois Press.

Nicholas, Ralph W. 1965. "Factions: A Comparative Analysis." in Banton, M. (ed.), *Political Systems and the Distribution of Power*. ASA Monograph 2. London: Tavistock.

Sahlins, M.D. 1964. "Rich Man, Poor Man, Big Man, Chief." *Comparative Studies in Society and History* 5: 285-303.

Salisbury, R.F. 1964. "Despotism and Australian Administration in the New Guinea Highlands." *American Anthropologist* 4:225-39.

------------1968. "Formal Analysis in Anthropological Economics. The Rossel Island Case." in Buchler, I. and H. G. Nutini (eds.), *Game Theory and the Behavioural Sciences*. Pittsburgh: Pittsburgh University Press.

------------1970. *Vunamami: Economic Transformation in a Traditional Society*. Berkeley: University of California Press.

Schryer, Frans J. 1974. Social Conflict in a Mexican Peasant Community. Ph. D. Dissertation. Montreal: McGill University.

------------1977. "Village Factionalism and Patronage in a Rural Municipio of Mexico." in Silverman, Marilyn and Richard F. Salisbury (eds.), *A House Divided: Anthropological Studies of Factionalism.* St. John's: Memorial University of Newfoundland (ISER).

Siegel, Bernard J. and Alan R. Beals. 1960. "Pervasive Factionalism." *American Anthropologist* 62:394-417.

Silverman, Marilyn. 1973. Resource Change and Village Factionalism in an East Indian Community, Guyana. Ph.D. Dissertation. Montreal: McGill University.

Silverman, S. 1968. "Agricultural Organization, Social Structure and Values in Italy." *American Anthropologist* 70:1.

Southwold, M. 1968. "A Games Model of African Tribal Politics." in Buchler, I. and H. G. Nutini (eds.), *Game Theory and the Behavioural Sciences.* Pittsburgh: Pittsburgh University Press.

Strathern, A. J. 1971. *The Rope of Moka.* Cambridge: Cambridge University Press.

IV

ANTHROPOLOGICAL ECONOMICS

by

Henry J. Rutz

A number of years ago I attended a dinner for the Fellows of the National Humanities Institute at the University of Chicago. The speaker that evening was Philip Rieff, then Benjamin Franklin Professor at the University of Pennsylvania and author of *Fellow Teachers*. Rieff had spent his long and distinguished career interpreting Freud as a master of modernism. His main point was that master teachers need good disciples. Richard Salisbury was a master teacher who attracted dozens of graduate students to anthropology at McGill University, myself among them. As a younger member of a loose coalition of anthropologists who were rethinking social anthropology, among them Raymond Firth (1951, 1954), Edmund Leach (1961) and Fredrik Barth (1966), Salisbury attempted to move the comparative study of social structures and their functioning toward an accommodation with social action and what, today, we would call cultural practices. The problematic relationship between normative structure and social action was everywhere in the air. Firth (1951) had already designated the proposed new perspective as the study of "social organization." By this, he meant a methodology that would capture the way in which persons and groups constructed their own social reality and acted on it to maintain or alter social structure. The emphasis shifted from the functional maintenance of structure to questions about how action became structured, i.e., the process of structuration. The study of social organization was the study of the variable responses of social actors to their recognition of normative constraint, subject to the availability of resources and their allocation among alternative individual and social ends. The oversocialized view of human collective behaviour as fundamentally moral took a back seat to a view of human social behaviour as strategy, situational logic and interested transaction. Salisbury spent his own long and distinguished career developing a methodology for the study of social organization in such diverse subject areas as politics, economics, and development and public policy. As his professional reputation grew, he attracted students from many parts of North America who went on to make their own contributions to these fields, among them the authors of essays appearing in this volume.

What made Richard Salisbury a master teacher was his ability to teach his students a common methodology underlying diverse subject matter, and to inspire them to do the kind of fieldwork that was necessary for supporting new knowledge claims. The muse for his own ethnography was a passion for the detailed observation required of all good fieldwork.

SOME CONTRIBUTIONS TO ANTHROPOLOGICAL ECONOMICS

It was a short step from social organization conceived as action-oriented strategy and transaction to a new sub-discipline of anthropological economics. With the publication of *From Stone to Steel* (1962) Salisbury arguably was the leader of a group of anthropologists who believed that at least some of the principles which were refined in a long tradition of liberal economic thought in the west were applicable, with modification, to an understanding of a large body of information which field workers had collected on comparative exchange systems. His contributions to an anthropological economics form the largest part of his corpus of writings. The selections from his corpus which appear in this section are based primarily on his methodological contributions as one of the seminal thinkers in anthropological economics. Together, these essays reveal the power of Salisbury to formulate an unambiguous research programme that encompassed not only his own research, but the research of an entire generation of young scholars. Each highlights a particular aspect of that unity and has been chosen to convey the spirit of the contemporary intellectual scene in which Salisbury was writing. Several were chosen because they have become less accessible to a new generation of readers. Over the past several decades, I have returned time and again to these writings to clarify and deepen my own understanding of anthropological economics.

"Anthropology and Economics" (1968; Chapter IV.8 in this volume) strikes a middle ground in a polemical debate between the view that economic behaviour must be understood from the perspective of its embeddedness in social structures and their functioning as opposed to the perspective offered by models of social organization. The debate between self-styled substantivists vs. formalists had become polarised and heated when Salisbury stepped into the fray. His article appeared as the last chapter in LeClair and Schneider's *Economic Anthropology* (1968), the first volume to systematically review all the issues that went into the debate to that point. LeClair and Schneider recounted in their preface how "we were wrestling with an effort at summation, closure and prognostication for economic anthropology when we heard Richard Salisbury read the initial version of Reading 30 at the Annual Meetings of the American Anthropological Association in Pittsburgh in 1966. In this, Salisbury had already done very effectively what we were trying to do and so before the day was out we sought and received permission to incorporate his paper in our reader." As a personal note, I had just completed my baccalaureate degree in 1966 by writing an honour's thesis for Schneider, who corresponded with me later that year about the volume, mentioning in passing that I might want to work with

Salisbury at McGill. I had read *From Stone to Steel*, which by then had been favourably received on both sides of the Atlantic, but at that time I had no awareness that I would soon come under the spell of the master teacher. Some years after, when I had already completed my graduate degree at McGill, Schneider founded the Society for Economic Anthropology and was elected its first president, succeeded by Salisbury.

"Formal Analysis in Anthropological Economics: The Rossel Island Case" (1968; Chapter IV.9, this volume) should be seen as an exemplar of programmatic statements which appeared later in "Anthropology and Economics." In this earlier paper, Salisbury already was thinking about ways in which to formalize and model aspects of exchange that took into account power and social hierarchy. The paper was delivered at the Conference on Applications of the Theory of Games in the Behavioral Sciences, held at McGill University in the summer of 1966, with Salisbury in charge of local arrangements. It appeared in Buchler and Nutini's 1969 volume on *Game Theory in the Behavioral Sciences*. With the exception of Barth's modelling of Swat Pathan pakhtun lineage alliances (1959) and Davenport's modelling of Jamaican fishing strategies as zero-sum games (1960), this conference and volume stand out as the only collective effort by anthropologists to use game theory as an analogy for understanding vast amounts of fieldwork data on conflict, negotiation, coalition formation, alliance-building, networking and other processes of group formation based on strategy and transactional behaviour. The focus of the conference was on the rules for playing games, not game rules *per se*. The participants felt that anthropologists had dwelled too long and hard on the cultural framework of rules to the exclusion of how people strategized, manipulated and manoeuvred for advantage within the framework of rules, sometimes changing the cultural framework in the process.

Salisbury's contribution was to use analogies from game theory to clarify and make more explicit the relationship between models and ethnographic data. He exemplified an approach later made programmatic in "Anthropology and Economics" by undertaking a re-analysis of the Rossel Island exchange system. The choice was intentional, because this case had already been used to support competing claims in the substantivist verus formalist debate of the 1960s. In retrospect, the whole debate was about whether the focus of research would be on regulatory agencies or constrained choice. The answer, of course, was both, and Salisbury said so in everything he published.

"Non-equilibrium Models in New Guinea Ecology" (1975; Chapter IV.10, this volume) was occasioned by the appearance in the 1960s-70s of the New Ecology, a paradigm for ecological anthropology that drew on population ecology and some of the neo-functionalist assumptions of negative-feedback systems analysis. The central figure in the New Ecology was Roy Rappaport who, in 1968, had published a sufficiently detailed and sophisticated conceptual account of the human eco-system of the Tsembaga Maring in his classic work entitled *Pigs for the Ancestors*. The explicitness of Rappaport's methodology and careful fieldwork afforded Salisbury a further opportunity to contrast overly mechanistic to under-reported actor-oriented approaches to human behaviour. Equally important for this volume is how the article carries forward connections made earlier in *Vunamami* (1970) between formalism, ethnography, and history in improving theories of economic development and cultural change. The re-publication of an article originally published in *Anthropologica* will make more accessible this important contribution to ecological anthropology.

The publication of *Vunamami* in 1970 was the result of work begun as early as 1958 which involved intensive work using several languages in eleven archives and libraries in different parts of the world. During fieldwork, Salisbury recorded oral histories as a means to reconstruct different phases of development as these were perceived at the local level. His most scholarly achievement, *Vunamami* is an ambitious, sometimes daunting, but always insightful account of how the Tolai managed to become the most developed people in their region of the world. Nevertheless, this achievement never received as wide an audience as *From Stone to Steel*, perhaps because of its ambitious scope, its detailed ethnohistory and its organization. Reproducing the "Introduction" to *Vunamami* (Chapter IV.11, this volume) may rekindle interest in this extraordinary work among those who are interested in the intersection of models, history, and ethnography.

An Overview of Salisbury's Contributions to Anthropological Economics

Richard Salisbury enjoyed an international reputation during the 1960s-70s for his contributions to the two distinct but related fields of anthropological economics and the anthropology of development. The first addressed the question, "How can we understand production and exchange in disparate cultures and variable resource environments?" The second addressed the same question from a more historical and global perspective by asking, "Can ethnography contribute to general theories of economic development and cultural change?" His search for theories that would take into account endogenous change at the regional or local level constitutes an indirect critique of overgeneralized claims of national modernization, international dependency and world-system analyses of the day, all of which rely primarily on exogenous factors in theorizing about economic development and on endogenous culture in their theories of underdevelopment.

Salisbury was dismissive of any attempts to caricature cultures as so different from one another that generalizations about their behaviour could be portrayed as difficult, if not impossible. At the same time, he was attentive to those differences between cultures which, if not taken into account, would lead to false inferences about their behaviour. In "Anthropology and Economics" (1968, Chapter IV.8, this volume), Salisbury rejected both substantivism and formalism as these methodologies had been portrayed in the debate over the best way to understand exchange systems in different cultures. He accepted the substantivist position as espoused by Karl Polanyi (1957) and his followers, in particular George Dalton (1961, 1965), that economic exchange in all societies is embedded in social institutions and derives some of its meaning from them. But he rejected their attempt to type whole societies as similar to or different from one another according to whether their exchange systems followed rules of either reciprocity, redistribution or the market. Once the strategy of totalizing one type of exchange was abandoned, it was immediately apparent that every society contained within it different spheres of exchange governed by a wide variety of rules, including market and reciprocal forms of exchange. Salisbury's main complaint was not that substantivism claimed exchange was embedded in institutions, but that it was satisfied to apply, in his words, "... labels from Polanyi's typology, rather than [to do] the detailed investigation of the underlying processes which generate the social types ..."

For Salisbury, the generative processes were those of recognition, strategy, and transaction among social actors who everywhere faced a similar problem of making decisions under constraint. But some formalists erred by universalizing the calculating attributes of individuals derived from a too-narrow idea about economic rationality. In the ends-means calculus of self-interested individual maximizers, there was little room for social obligation, commitment and collective ends that were the common stuff of ethnographic reportage. Salisbury himself had written copiously about such observations in his own work and that of others. The way out was to examine different types of social action, to distinguish rules from strategies, individual decisions from collective decisions, and to separate short-term outcomes from long-term plans. One crucial difference between games and social organization is that the latter contains the possibility that action may be directed toward changing the rules by substitution, renaming, bending them or ignoring them altogether. But generally, Salisbury accepted Firth's own inclination that most social change is the result of an accumulation of incrementally small changes in the same direction over the long run. Quantity, at some threshold, turns into quality. Salisbury returned time and again to the importance of internally complex and differentiated organizations in shaping the long-term strategies of individuals and the part entrepreneurship played in processes of development and social change. By definition, entrepreneurs effect change through new combinations of people, resources and organizational innovation.

In "Anthropology and Economics," Salisbury also touched on the importance of building models of processes and how they generate organizations and institutions. Models were tools that allowed the anthropologist to make educated guesses about what game was being played. Unlike the economist, however, whose models considered a restricted range of assumptions about technology, organization or risk, the kinds of models with which Salisbury was primarily concerned were those that exploited fine-grained ethnographic studies to discover specific historical sequences of economic development and cultural change. He hoped that ultimately the discovery of multiple sequences could be used to re-establish on a firm ethnographic and quantitative basis the formal analysis of social evolution.

In "Formal Analysis in Anthropological Economics" (1968, Chapter IV.9, this volume), Salisbury asked "What is the relationship between analytical constructs and empirical phenomena?" Game theory, he thought, provided the anthropologist with a simple means to advance our understanding of economic behavior in different institutional settings or from one period of structural transformation to another. Game rules are analogous to institutionalized norms, and games proceed with the development of many informal rules that are always open to negotiation by players. Games also generate different degrees of uncertainty about the rules, the players, the plays, the amount of risk and the evaluation of consequences of players' failure to develop winning strategies or make correct decisions. Games also allow for nondiscrete choices in a linked series of moves analogous to actors who have social commitments and relations that endure beyond the game, however defined. Of special interest to anthropologists, he thought, would be non-zero sum games, in which there was an outcome that could make everyone better off.

The problem for the ethnographer was to guess the game, an act of abstraction from the complexity of everyday life. Many different games might be conceptualized using the same ethnographic data, raising questions about possible games that were never realized in history and culture. One of the simple but important points about games is that different strategies are *necessary* to the outcome of the game. Cultural and social differences are a prerequisite for playing the game. Of what, then, should an ethnographic analysis consist? There should be the following: a description of formal rules about which all the players agree; diverse strategy statements, often explicitly formulated as maxims; sufficient information to render the strategies comprehensible (e.g., estimates of the magnitude of risk and degree of uncertainty, quantities of goods and services to be exchanged, resource limits, technology, etc.).

"Formal Analysis in Anthropological Economics" uses the game analogy to guess what the game is with regard to the case of Rossel Island shell money. Armstrong, a neoclassical economist who produced the original data on Rossel Island

(1928), concluded that the different kinds of shells were all convertible, and that all men had a single short-term strategy of maximizing compound interest by converting one kind of shell (with its stipulated value) into another kind of shell. Dalton, incidentally, an acolyte of Polanyi and standard-bearer for the substantivist cause, had earlier re-analysed Armstrong's data to show that the shells were not really money, that they were different in kind, and that transactions were limited within each sphere of exchange according to the norms that governed social relations in each sphere (1965). In other words, there was little, if any, convertibility between spheres. The only reasonable conclusion was that Rossel Island shell money exchange was governed by the moral obligations attendant on structured social relations. Exchange had no other purpose than to function to maintain an existing social order. This analysis satisfied the requirements of a good structural-functional analysis, but it didn't account for the exchange practices of Rossel Islanders.

Salisbury rejected both perspectives, preferring instead to infer a set of diverse strategy statements from inconsistencies in informants' statements, their position in the social structure and their putative interests. He guessed the game to be an attempt to optimize the volume of services that could flow from an exchange of shells. Salisbury accepted Dalton's observation that Armstrong's facts supported an indexing of the shells, different denominations of shells being indexed to specific goods and services, with minimal convertibility from one sphere of exchange to another. From these few elements of a model Salisbury went on to describe the system from the perspective of three different strategies and perspectives on what the system was about. The implication is that the strategies of different groups affected the strategy of each as the game was played over time. Young men, who had to incur barely acceptable levels of debt to play, considered the system to be too rigid. A second group used the system for short-term needs, such as acquiring a pig for an important ceremony. This group viewed the system as a stable one of short-term borrowing and reciprocation. And then there were the entrepreneurs, who possessed a supply of shell money sufficient to control a large share of the flow of goods and services and who used their position to gain political influence. These men tended to see the system as open to opportunities, engaging in the time-honoured practice of representing their own interest as the interest of all. This habit of locating informant statements squarely in the context of their own position of power and interest before using them in an analysis of the whole system is typical of Salisbury's ethnography.

Another characteristic of Salisbury's ethnography is that he was able to squeeze the last drop of analysis from the smallest detail of fieldwork data and then to speculate on what missing information a future fieldworker would expect to find or, alternatively, what variations of the pattern would result from changing conditions. In this case, he goes on to speculate on strategies of collusion that might result in cornering the shell money supply, especially the shells of high denomination which are required to attain political influence. And he also speculated on how a change in any of the parameters might affect strategies that would result in oligopolistic practices.

Salisbury took every occasion to further the application of formal analysis and model-building in anthropology. One of the most important books of the 1960s was *Pigs for the Ancestors* (1967), the most sophisticated study of a human eco-system yet produced by ecological anthropology. In it, Rappaport treated a New Guinea society as an eco-system in which Tsembaga Maring ritual exchange cycles were at the centre of complex functional dynamics that had consequences, through their regulation of cycles of war and peace, for the maintenance of the Tsembaga population in an undegraded environment. Like Salisbury, Rappaport was a tireless field investigator who collected detailed information on enough relationships in different sub-systems to write a monograph that has become a classic because it is an exemplar of a particular methodological orientation within a well-defined field of inquiry.

In effect, Rappaport attempted to show that Tsembaga Maring history amounted to cultural adaptation to an environment in a way that resulted in a stable equilibrium between environmental and cultural processes. Salisbury took sharp exception to this characterization of New Guinea history. In "Non-equilibrium Models in New Guinea Ecology" (1975, Chapter IV.10 this volume), he reiterated his thesis in *Vunamami* that New Guinea history had been a dynamic one, re-stating his arguments for why human eco-systems in general fit non-equilibrium models. In contrast to the assumptions of stability and mechanistic adjustments of whole populations to each other, what he considered to be revisiting functionalist mistakes of the past, Salisbury asserted that the most reasonable assumption was that the Tsembaga Maring system had been slowly expanding against other groups in the region for a long period. Instead of assuming that the present represented a functionally-equilibrated adaptation, by reading history backwards, Salisbury suggested that the best way to do history in the region was to model phases of the system as gradual changes in population, technology and social relations that never were quite adjusted to one another. Drawing on his own detailed ethnographies and theories of the Siane (*From Stone to Steel*) and Tolai (*Vunamami*) exchange systems, Salisbury argued that "a large number of cultural behaviours observed at any one time in a particular society are *not* aimed at adapting populations to current physical environments." He proposed a non-equilibrium model of cultural extrapolation that incorporated active planning by entrepreneurs using organizations as agencies of change. A formal analysis would include "disciplined guesses" about the phases it would have gone through to reach its current, not final, state. The article concludes with a discussion of the value of model-building as a form of disciplined conjecture, calling once again for a view of culture as *relatively* invariant rules that reflected the current state of play under changing circumstances.

Vunamami: Economic Transformation in a Traditional Society (1970) is Salisbury's most complete statement about the methodological approach he laboured to clarify and improve for two decades. His "Introduction" (Chapter IV.11, this volume) is an eloquent summation of all his thoughts about relationships among formal analysis, ethnography and history. "No theory of economic development," he declared, "is adequate if it ignores the calculating abilities, the entrepreneurial tendencies, or the range of individual variation found among traditional farmers." At times, he appears to exaggerate the importance of variability for non-linear theories of development, for example when he asserts that "... every farmer is different, and differences in size of family, in area of land owned, in political aspirations, in technical knowledge, or in energy profoundly affect his farming." These and other statements are not meant as merely celebratory comments on the intrinsic virtue of diversity. On the contrary, the methodological intent is to use the messy diversity collected as a fieldworker to understand the source of dynamism that could aid in constructing a theory of local economic development and cultural change. This was brought home to me time and again when I was doing fieldwork in Fiji from 1968-70. Dick would send long letters exhorting me to collect detailed and quantitative information on decision-making, but to do so for the purpose of aggregation and macro-analysis of diversity within the system that could be used to build models of social and economic change.

I was in the field doing dissertation research when *Vunamami* was published. After I returned to McGill and opened the book, I read about what I had been practising all along. Such is the wizardry of the master teacher. In plain writing, before my eyes, I read that there were three tasks of Salisbury's methodology without knowing it, thinking that I was creating it as I went along. If master teachers need good disciples, they also need to create in their students the illusion of freedom.

This brief overview of Richard Salisbury's contributions to anthropological economics began with a personal anecdote about master teachers and their disciples. To conclude where I began, on a personal note, Richard Salisbury had within him the capacity to inspire, to instill confidence and, by example, to show how to do fieldwork, ethnography and formal analysis. The work of his students is ample evidence of this gift. I had begun my graduate career at the East-West Center in Honolulu in 1966. During that year, I had written Professor Salisbury a letter inquiring whether I might continue my graduate work under him at McGill. After some delay and anticipated disappointment, the mail brought a very short note from him.

He was inquiring as to why I had not yet completed the forms for admission and signed an acceptance agreement for a teaching assistantship.

Shortly after arriving at McGill in the fall of 1967, I went to meet Professor Salisbury for the first time. The purpose was to discuss my doctoral programme. But he seemed unconcerned about such matters and asked instead whether I could speak Dutch! So this is what it would be like, I thought, to be an American in a Canadian university in Quebec having an Englishman as mentor. I needn't have been so dramatic. He had been reading Boeke on dual economy in the Netherlands East Indies and wanted someone to tell him how the original read. Then he announced that after one seminar in the fall and spring, and a tutorial with him, I would take my exams and forthwith go straight to the field. "By the way," he asked, "what is your research problem and where will you do it?" The effect on me was transformative. His confidence transformed me from a classroom student into a field researcher through the magic of words and the man who spoke them. And true to his words, the following autumn I was in his office again to say "goodbye." He expressed some surprise and said that he thought it would be some time before I left for Fiji. And in the same motion, he swivelled around in his chair and rapidly tapped out on an old typewriter a letter that he put in my hand. It said that I was a student in good standing at McGill, that I was doing anthropological research and that the correspondent would be grateful to any person who, on reading this brief introduction of his student, would be of assistance. Signed, Richard F. Salisbury. Like magic.

A liberal reformer in his adopted country of Canada, he remained ever optimistic about the good qualities of others and had an eye on the prospects for bettering their own lives in whatever way they saw fit to do. This optimism was liberally bestowed on his students.

References

Armstrong, W. E., 1928. *Rossel Island*. Cambridge: Cambridge University Press.

Barth, Fredrik. 1959. "Segmentary Opposition and the Theory of Games." *Journal of the Royal Anthropological Institute* 89(1): 5-21.

------------1966. "Models of Social Organization." *Occasional Paper* No. 23. London: Royal Anthropological Institute of Great Britain & Ireland.

Dalton, G., 1961. "Economic Theory and Primitive Society." *American Anthropologist* 63 (1):1-25.

------------1965. "Primitive Money." *American Anthropologist* 67:44-65.

Davenport, William, 1960. "Jamaican Fishing: A Game Theory Analysis." *Papers on Caribbean Anthropology*. New Haven: Yale University Publications in Anthropology No. 58:3-11.

Firth, Raymond. 1951. *Elements of Social Organization*. London: Watts & Co.

------------1954. "Social Organization and Social Change." *Journal of the Royal Anthropological Institute* 84:1-20.

Leach, Edmund. 1960. "The Sinhalese of the Dry Zone of Northern Ceylon." in Murdock, G.P. (ed.), *Social Structure in Southeast Asia*. London: Tavistock:116-26.

------------1961. *Rethinking Anthropology*. London: Athlone.

LeClair, Edward and H.K. Schneider, (eds.), 1968. *Readings in Economic Anthropology*. New York: Holt, Rinehart & Winston.

Polanyi, Karl, 1957. "The Economy as an Instituted Process." in Polanyi, Karl, Conrad M. Arensberg and Harry W. Pearson (eds.), *Trade and Markets in the Early Empires*. New York: Free Press.

Rieff, Philip. 1973. *Fellow Teachers*. First edition. New York: Harper & Row.

Rappaport, Roy. 1967. *Pigs For The Ancestors*. New Haven: Yale University Press.

Salisbury, Richard F. 1962. *From Stone to Steel*. Melbourne: Cambridge University Press.

------------1968. "Anthropology and Economics." in LeClair, Edward and Harold K. Schneider (eds.), *Readings in Economic Anthropology*. New York: Holt, Rinehart & Winston.

------------1969. "Formal Analysis and Anthropological Economics: The Rossel Island Case." in Buchler, Ira R. and Hugo G. Nutini (eds.), *Game Theory in the Behavioral Sciences*. Pittsburgh: University of Pittsburgh Press:75-93.

------------1970. *Vunamami: Economic Transformation in a Traditional Society*. Berkeley: University of California Press.

------------1975. "Non-equilibrium Models in New Guinea Ecology." *Anthropologica* 17:121-147.

8.

Anthropology and Economics

by

Richard F. Salisbury

Source: Otto Von Mering and Leonard Kasdan (eds.),
Anthropology and Neighbouring Disciplines, Pittsburgh: University of Pittsburg Press,
1968. Reprinted in: E. Leclair and H. Schneider (eds.), *Readings in Economic
Anthropology*. New York: Holt, Rinehart & Winston, 1968.

A review of the relations between Anthropology and Economics
is made easier[1] by the existence of an excellent summary of their relationship,
through 1960, written by Joseph Berliner (1962). Since the state of the two disciplines has changed considerably from 1960, a stock-taking of these changes is in
order. For the first principles, the reader is referred to Berliner's work.

Berliner's major analysis showed that all social science data can be
visualized as a matrix with rows representing particular societies and columns standing for such entities as "economy" and "religion." Anthropology has involved mainly the comparison of all cells in a column (i.e., cross-cultural studies of single
institutions) or of all cells in a row (i.e., studies of functional relationships between
institutions of a single society). Berliner showed the strength of Economics, as a discipline, to be the intensity of its study of relationships within the single cell of
"Western economies," and called for much more intra-cell studies of non-Western
economies. The attempt to demonstrate that non-Western economies had the same
institutions as Western economies had doomed earlier economic anthropology to
sterility; Berliner felt that the suggested intra-cell studies might bring about a revital-
ized anthropology.

To anticipate some of the conclusions of this paper, Berliner's
predictions would seem to be borne out by the currently healthy state of economic
anthropology (if economic anthropology was not already more healthy in 1960 than
Berliner knew). Currently the major issue in economic anthropology is not whether
non-Western economies have different substantive economic institutions, for it is
now accepted that they do, but to what extent different formal calculuses of rationality or of "economizing" can be isolated in non-Western conditions. Before consid-

ering the anthropological work that has led to this point of development, let us review some of the last decade's changes in economic thinking.

THE ECONOMIC SIDE

In 1960, Berliner could still generalize plausibly about main trends in economic thinking as comprising Marshallian (or classical) theory, Keynesian theorizing about cyclical changes in national economies, and institutional Economics and economic history. However, by 1966, the unmentioned infant economic fields of 1960 seem to have effected a revolution in Economics. Neo-Keynesian thinking no longer studies regular cyclical fluctuations but focuses on how to induce continued expansion and secular change. Development Economics in 1960 was concerned with transplanting Western Economics to underdeveloped areas, it now studies and generalizes about the form of developing economies in their own right, and theorizes about sequences within the developmental process. "Structural transformation" is now a respectable term in Economics and not merely a use of social-anthropological jargon. Even though economists focus on such readily quantifiable topics as changing patterns of income distribution, and wage differentials between export and internal sectors, they are closely concerned with the same problems as anthropologists who study the breakdown of caste barriers in plural societies. In 1962, Hagen was avant garde in proposing an individual psychological explanation of the emergence of entrepreneurship; in 1966, he is more concerned with how entrepreneurial behavior relates to (or is irrelevant in) the context of economic choice for peasant farmers. Economists, in short, are emerging from their private "Western economies" cell. They are going up and down columns into different societies and along rows into other institutions, and they are increasingly concerned with secular change.

Another, not unrelated trend in Economics has been the study of decision-making at the levels of individuals, business firms and nations, and outside the classical context of supply price demand balancing. Von Neumann's invention of game theory was one initiator of this trend and the use of computers for playing simulated economic "games" has been another stimulus. Linear programming is perhaps the most mathematically advanced branch of this type of study. The effort is not to disprove the "maximizing" assumption of classical economic theory, but to demonstrate how most rationally to maximize specific magnitudes under various conditions of risk, where differing time spans exist or one decision is contingent on other people's decisions. Economics has moved far from the classical *homo oeconomicus* position, based on hypothetical Robinson Crusoes, ridiculed in anthropological literature from Malinowski to Polanyi.

Another closely related and expanding economic field is business administration. For the anthropologist this field is perhaps most accessible through the works of sociologists such as Mason Haire with his studies (1959) on growth of business organizations. Such works enable economists to conceive of alternative total organizations, and to compare the efficiency of overall structures in terms of their ability to respond to particular environmental problems and their eventual outputs. In short, this enables economists to see "organization" and "managerial skills" as factors of production to be measured and considered in general analysis.

THE ANTHROPOLOGICAL SIDE

(i) ETHNO-ECONOMICS

As economists have escaped from their cell, anthropologists have become more focused on the internal analysis of single cells. Starting with Bohannan's study of the Tiv (1955), there have been several studies of the economic categories used in non-Western societies, which are intra-cell studies of single economic systems. My own study of categories used in relatively affluent tribal societies (Salisbury 1962) would serve as another example. Foster's (1964) discussion of the concept of "the limited good" is a major comparative summary of a form of conceptualization that would appear to be prevalent in many societies. This important new sub field may be labelled "ethno-economics" insofar as it aims merely at the description of single economies. As description, it undoubtedly benefits from the refined methodology of the "new ethnography." I would maintain, however, that its major theoretical importance has been the advances it has permitted in the field of formal analysis. I will return to ethno-economics when I deal with formal analysis.

(ii) SUBSTANTIVISM

Achieving greater prominence in the period 1957-1966, the so called substantivist school generalizes about the channels through which goods flow in total economies. This school stems largely from Polanyi's (1957) seminal *Trade and Markets in the Early Empires* which introduced a typology of societies "integrated by reciprocity, redistribution, and market exchanges." Considering the lack of quantitative studies then available, this was a remarkable synthesis. Unfortunately, most of the subsequent work of the school has involved the application of labels from Polanyi's typology, rather than the detailed investigation of the underlying processes which generate the social types Polanyi discussed. The major finding of Bohannan and Dalton's (1962) 800 page compilation of studies of African marketplace trade is that societies where trade is "imbedded" in other institutions and which do not use cash differ from those which form some system of "market exchange."

"Redistributive," as a label, has been applied to societies such as those in Polynesia and West African kingdoms. This use seems indiscriminate in the light of quantitative studies. Nadel's excellent early study of the Nupe economy (1942) shows that only a small portion of the total flow of goods and services is channeled through the king, and even where guilds nominally operate as agents for the king, the degree to which they organize production in terms of private customers is mainly determined by the size of the private market. Village self-sufficiency, trade partnerships, and open market trading are more common. What substantivists have done is to seize upon some rare, but distinctive, features – a court, guilds, tribute payments, and negotiated foreign trade between the court and foreigners – and to use a label based on these features to characterize the total economy.

Polanyi's own posthumous work on Dahomey (1966) does indeed get away from the rigidity of regarding reciprocity, redistribution and market exchange as mutually exclusive and as characterizing entire economies or integrating entire societies. He sees all three principles as operating together, each in a different domain within the single society. Yet, at the same time, he sees the main achievements of the book as the classification of institutions as "primitive" (i.e., found in reciprocative societies), "archaic" (i.e., characteristic of redistributive societies), or "market." Thus, Polanyi goes to great lengths (pp. 141-169) to unravel the difficulties Europeans had in balancing their bookkeeping in the 17th and 18th century slave trade, resulting from empirically fluctuating and varied, but nominally fixed, units used in different areas and times in West Africa. He concludes that West Africa had "archaic money," incompatible with a modern monetary system. Polanyi then isolates the characteristics of "archaic money" in terms of its status building function in the emergence of state systems (p. 192). To an audience that accepts the fact of "trade in equivalencies," mere classification appears sterile. The identification of what caused the changes in exchange rates – such as differences of power balance, numbers of slaves, or availability of manufactures – becomes the interesting problem.

In short, "redistribution" or "archaic economy" may be useful labels for summarizing the way emergent national polities centralize certain services and organize taxation and the production of specialized commodities by infant industries by providing stability in market, raw materials, and labor. But such concepts would appear equally useful for analyzing the actions of newly independent, but fully monetized, nation states. They are not terms that characterize "entire economies" or "modes of integration," nor are they terms which fit economies into a unilineal progression from "primitive" to "archaic" to "market."

The same is true of the concept "reciprocity." Analyses of the actual working of societies crudely labelled as "reciprocative" (Salisbury 1960, Sahlins

1963, 1965) have shown that inter-individual transactions are always unbalanced and involve a continual struggle to obtain as much advantage over an "opponent" as possible, short of breaking off the relationship and establishing new relationships with another partner. Each relationship between a pair implies a series of other relationships by each of them, and the terms of trade between one pair can be understood only against a background of their other relationships. The same generalization could be made about exchanges between partners in a monetary economy. The differences between "reciprocal" and "market" exchanges are not sufficiently clarified by attempts to characterize total systems of which they are parts. Rather, they are better understood through closer analysis of the specific situations, in both monetary and tribal societies, where it is mutually advantageous to use recurrent rather than isolated exchanges, or where imbalances in volumes tendered can be, or must be, tolerated for long periods. Such studies consider "markets" as general economic phenomena, not as the peculiar institution of localized "marketplaces"; the recent proliferation of such studies indicates the decline of the "anti-market mentality" (Cook 1966).

(iii) Specific Institutional Studies

In practice, most descriptive anthropological work has been more specific in its aim. An impressive literature has been emerging regarding the types of exchange and marketing behavior found under different conditions of risk, volume of the total market, relative numbers of buyers and sellers, knowledge of the market, and the power positions of parties to the exchanges. This has been extensively summarized elsewhere (e.g., Belshaw 1965, Salisbury n.d.), and further review of the findings is not needed here. It will suffice to mention, as outstanding examples, Dewey's (1963) full length discussion of *Peasant Marketing in Java*, and of Nash's (1961) analyses of the calculations involved in the marketing of pottery in Chiapas. In terms of the trends in Economics there has been a convergence of interest here, with both disciplines focusing more precisely on how the context of economic choice can influence the nature of the choices actually made.

Spheres of activity other than marketing have not received such close scrutiny. Ethnobotanists and geographers have encouraged anthropologists to record how far considerations of plant varieties, soil types, or micro-climatic variation enter into the calculations of bush-fallow agriculturalists (Conklin 1961). Agricultural economists too have often done studies that could be considered anthropological in the same way. Edwards' (1962) study of why Jamaican small farmers often rejected agricultural officers' advice led him to ask for their evaluations of land types and crop species. Returning later to the area, he found that peasant evaluations, initially at variance with agronomists' orthodoxy, had often become orthodox after research led agronomists to change their minds.

A relatively small number of anthropologists have collected labor input figures for different crops or techniques of cultivation and have investigated the extent to which agriculturalists make choices on this basis. But those few studies- for example, Pospisil (1963b) comparing labor inputs and yields for field and mound cultivation of sweet potatoes in New Guinea, and Nash (1965) comparing them for various crops and techniques in Burma indicate the value of investigating this variable. Such studies also need to be linked to a treatment of how variations in labor demand correlate with different patterns of choice in production – of how, for example, different labor demands affect deep-sea and inshore fishing.

The use of capital, and its accumulation in peasant societies, has been the focus of less analysis than would appear from the publication of Firth and Yamey's (1964) *Capital, Savings and Credit in Peasant Society*. Most of the authors in this volume were social anthropologists who proudly vaunted their ignorance of economic analysis and merely described how different social groupings accumulated cash in particular societies. Little attention was devoted to the use made of such accumulations or to the nature of "capital." Among the exceptions to this general criticism of the 1964 volume was Barth's analysis of the capital needs and flows among South Persian nomads, and of the ways in which needs are related to the arrangements for meeting them. And Firth's own classic study of *Malay Fishermen* (1946) still stands out as an examination of the relation of credit to production.

Again, agricultural economists have contributed to this sub field of study. Besides Edwards' previously cited study, Polly Hill's (1956, 1963) discussion of how Ghanaian cocoa farmers accumulated capital and land, and how different organizational forms were used to facilitate investment at different stages in the growth of the cocoa industry, is outstanding. Many anthropologists in the South Pacific have similar interests. Belshaw's study (1964) of Fiji, studies by the Australian National University's New Guinea Research Unit (e.g., Crocombe and Hogbin 1964), and my own study of the New Britain Tolai (1970) could be cited. The focus in all these is the forms of organization used in capital holding groups.

Entrepreneurship is another aspect of economic process that has been studied. Many descriptive studies of social change have listed the forms of cash-earning businesses that have emerged in formerly subsistence agricultural societies, and have classed all such businessmen as "entrepreneurs." Relatively few (e.g., Hazelhurst 1966) have gone back to theoretical treatments of entrepreneurship, notably to Schumpeter, to consider the various roles focal to the concept. These roles include risk-taking, the middleman bringing together production factors, and the organizational innovator who exploits technological innovations made by others by bringing together new groupings. Yet the study of such roles would seem to be of primary interest to classical anthropological theory. It would seem that consideration of the nature of organizational innovation would be a major area, where new developments within Economics could parallel and fructify developments in formal organization theory and in economic anthropology.

Organization theory regarding both entrepreneurship and capital use constitutes a common thread to the studies above. Organization of production, generally, needs to be given greater consideration. Udy, in 1959, surveyed cross-cultural anthropological evidence on production organization, comparing such activities as "hunting, fishing, collection, animal husbandry, construction, and manufacturing." His conclusion, that technological demands were highly significant up to a certain level of social complexity with a widely varying range of organizational types thereafter, demands closer analysis to explain the residual variance in organizational forms. The ethnographers' laboratory of variant forms and variant social and physical environments should be exploited to provide information on the relative efficiency of particular forms. On the one hand, existing ethnographic descriptions need comparison and analyses in terms of a consistent theoretical viewpoint – Barth (1963) has analyzed a series of field studies in Norway in this way and Sankoff (1965) has begun such work using published sources. On the other hand, more ethnographic studies are needed in which investigators trained in organization theory can ask appropriate questions about organizational efficiency in both traditional and cash activities. Such studies, like Erasmus' (1956) early study of the advantages and disadvantages of work bees and hired labor in Meso-America, should give much greater insight into the process of economic development than do analyses couched in terms of all-or-none "value changes."

(iv) MODEL BUILDING

Anthropological economic studies have not been confined entirely to specific institutions and increasingly detailed studies of relationships between even smaller segments of social and economic activity. Just as input-output economists have interested themselves in constructing models of total economies, seeing the total system as the outcome of the flows and transactions between sectors, so some anthropologists have also begun to visualize entire economies as the resultant effects of flows between particular sectors. Development economists have proposed models of economic change which involve phase sequences. For example, infrastructure development at one phase leads to increased profitability of later industrial investments, and so to mass marketing. So anthropologists (and ethnohistorians)

171

have proposed models of local economic development in terms of phase sequences and have looked for the causative relationship between phases.

The differences between economists' and anthropologists' models have largely been the different range of included phenomena. Economists tend to include such factors as demography, technology, organizational techniques or political controls only as boundary conditions for their models, making such simplistic assumptions as they remain constant, or they increase at steady rates. These assumptions are often disguised. A simple statement that it is "assumed that the marginal product of labor is positive" or that "it may be assumed that in a period of growth there is some organizational slack," implies questionable assumptions about the nature of technology or organization. However, making such assumptions, the economist can clarify the logic of his model and can proceed immediately to quantification.

The anthropologist is more concerned with building relationships between technology, organization or politics, and the economic activities into his models. Thus, Geertz's (1963) model involves technology as a major variable in the interactions of labor-intensive monocrop agriculture in Java with foreign-exchange earning, cash-cropping and multicrop bush-fallow agriculture in outer Indonesia. The model shows the long-term prospect of impoverishing and "peasantizing" the outer islands. In my own model (1962, 1970) organization is the major variable. It shows how in New Guinea surpluses are created by technological change funneled into the creation of more complex political organizations and how such political change permits the organizational change for the establishment of new types of productive activity.

It could be argued such models represent a return to many of the fundamental concerns of anthropology – the problems of social evolution and cultural change. Leslie White pioneered the return to interest in these problems, but his unidimensional scheme relating social development to the availability of energy sources was too simplistic. It may now be hoped that general models of a Leslie White type may become increasingly available. In such models technology levels, communication technology levels, and organizational variables may be given quantitative forms, visualized as forms of entropy (Adams 1960) – in order to consider types of society in terms of evolutionary dimensions.

FORMAL ANALYSIS

Such a Utopian idea would see anthropologists returning closer to the traditional interests of their own discipline. But then, where does the future for a relationship between Anthropology and Economics lie? Here I would return to my earlier analysis of substantivism and of current trends in economic anthropology. As I see it, where the substantivists attempted to classify total economies and came up with static models, more recent workers have tried to see the low level relationships which generate the eventual form of total economies. The models they build inevitably include a dynamic element. Yet to arrive at the relationships occurring at low levels, they have used the tool of economic analysis which substantivists scorned – that is, formal analysis. The formal approach of economists have involved seeing economic magnitudes as the primary data, and by comparing magnitudes, has demonstrated inductively the relationships among numbers of variables, each of them impinging, at a low level, on vast numbers of economic choices. Only when the formal analyses have been undertaken and the variables isolated, have dynamic models of the interplay of multiple variables been constructed.

Ethno-economists may take a short cut. Instead of isolating variables by the mathematical analysis of quantitative data, they may consider the economic concepts given them by informants as close approximations to the operating variables. But they then should consider deductively how the systematic use in the society of such concepts would give rise to overall patterns. They should construct models based on ethno-economic concepts. While it may be untrue to say that goods are absolutely limited in peasant society, it may be useful to consider what would happen if all (or many) members of a society believed that life were a zero-sum game. Game theory (or formal economic theory) could then be used to make predictions about such matters as the size of coalitions found, or the degree of tolerance of income inequalities. Anthropologists have been generally averse to such "as if" deductive theorizing, preferring to "stick to the facts." Exposure to economists and their methods could be invaluable in correcting this bias and in making deductive model-building familiar.

At the same time as ethno-economic description of the principles of choice verbalized by informants is leading to the formulation of ideal or hypothetical models, behavioral analysis must also be progressing. It must determine principles of choice from a consideration of transactions actually occurring and test the fit of hypothetical models against quantitative reality. Here, too, anthropologists have much to learn from working with economists and their tools. In the 1950's, Gluckman argued (1964) that it is better to remain naive about other disciplines, even when intruding on fields which they cover. I do not feel that this is true for anthropology and Economics in the 1960's. Anthropologists should study Economics and vice versa. I do agree with Gluckman that this should be done not to make the anthropologist an economist, but a better anthropologist. Given economic tools, he will improve anthropology. Give an economist the anthropological tools of sensitivity to what people say and of readiness to try to see order in different conceptual systems, and he may improve economics.

NOTES

1.   It would also have been made easier if Nash's textbook (1966) had appeared before rather than after its writing, as the lines of thought in both are parallel. The reader is referred to Nash for a fuller documentation of much descriptive material mentioned below; the present article presents a somewhat more developed stand on the nature of formal analysis and models than Nash might agree with. The author wishes to acknowledge how his thinking has developed in the course of discussions, not only with Nash, but with, among others: C. S. Belshaw, R. Crocombe, A. G. Frank, L. Hazelhurst, L. Kasdan, M. Sahlins and G. Sankoff.

REFERENCES

Adams, R.N. 1960. Energy and Expanding Systems. Paper presented at the American Association for the Advancement of Science Meeting, New York, December 31.

Barth, F. (ed.). 1963. *The Role of the Entrepreneur in Social Change in Northern Norway.* Oslo: Norwegian University Press.

Barth, F. 1964. "Capital, Investment and the Social Structure of a Pastoral Nomad Group in South Persia." in Firth, Raymond and B.S.Yamey (eds.), *Capital, Savings and Credit in Peasant Societies*. London: Allan.

Belshaw, Cyril S. 1964. *Under the Ivi Tree.* Berkeley: University of California Press.

------------1965. *Traditional Exchange and Modern Markets*. Englewood Cliffs: Prentice Hall.

Berliner, Joseph S. 1962. "The feet of the natives are large: an essay on Anthropology by an Economist." *Current Anthropology* 3:47-61.

Bohannan, Paul. 1955. "Some Principles of Exchange and Investment among the Tiv." *American Anthropologist* 57:60-70.

Bohannan, Paul and George Dalton (eds.). 1962. *Markets in Africa*. Evanston, Ill.: Northwestern University Press.

Conklin, Harold C. 1961. "The Study of Shifting Cultivation." *Current Anthropology* 2:207-61.

Cook, Scott. 1966. "The Obsolete 'Anti-Market' Mentality: A Critique of the Substantive Approach to Economic Anthropology." *American Anthropologist* 68:323-345.

Crocombe, R.G. and G.R.Hogbin. 1963. *The ERAP Mechanised Farming Project*. New Guinea Research Bulletin No.1. Canberra: Australian National University.

Dewey, A. 1963. *Peasant Marketing in Java*. New York: Free Press.

Edwards, D. 1961. *An Economic Study of Small Farming in Jamaica*. Jamaica: Institute of Social and Economic Research.

Haire, M. (ed.). 1959. *Modern Organization Theory*. New York: Wiley.

Erasmus, Charles. 1956. "Culture Structure and Process Occurrence and Disappearance of Reciprocal Labor." *Southwestern Journal of Anthropology* 12: 444-469.

Firth, Raymond. 1946. *Malay Fishermen: Their Peasant Economy*. London: Routledge.

Firth, Raymond and B.S.Yamey (eds.). 1964. *Capital, Savings and Credit in Peasant Societies*. London: Allan.

Foster, George M. 1965. "Peasant Society and the Image of Limited Good." *American Anthropologist* 67:293-315.

Geertz, Clifford. 1963. *Agricultural Involution*. Berkeley: University of California Press.

Gluckman, Max (ed.). 1964. *Closed Systems and Open Minds*. Chicago: Aldine.

Hagen, E.E. 1961. "Analytical Models in the Study of Social Systems." *American Journal of Sociology* LXII (Sept.):144-51.

------------1962. *On the Theory of Social Change*. Homewood, Ill.: Dorsey.

Hazelhurst, L.W. 1937 .*Entrepreneurship and the Merchant Castes in a Punjabi City*. Durham: Duke University Press.

Hill, P. 1956. *The Gold Coast Farmer: A Preliminary Survey*. New York: Oxford.

Nadel, S.F. 1942. *A Black Byzantium*. London: Oxford.

Nash, Manning. 1961. "The Social Context of Economic Choice in a Small Society." *Man*: 186-191.

------------1965. *The Golden Road to Modernity*. New York: Harcourt.

------------1966. *Primitive and Peasant Economic Systems*. San Francisco: Chandler Publishing Co.

Polanyi, Karl, C.W.Arensberg and W.H.Pearson (eds.). 1957. *Trade and Market in the Early Empires*. New York: Free Press.

Polanyi, Karl and A. Rotstein. 1966. *Dahomey and the Slave Trade*. Seattle: University of Washington Press.

Pospisil, Leopold. 1963. *The Kapauku Papuan Economy*. New Haven: Yale University Press.

Sahlins, Marshall D. 1963. "On the Sociology of Primitive Exchange." in *The Relevance of Models for Social Anthropology*, pp. 139-227. Association of Social Anthropology Monographs No. 1. London: Tavistock Publications.

Salisbury, R.F. 1960. "Ceremonial Exchange and Political Equilibrium," in *Proceedings of the 5th International Congress of Anthropological and Ethnological Sciences*, Paris: 2:255-260.

------------1962. *From Stone to Steel*. Melbourne: University of Melbourne Press.

------------n.d., "Trade and Markets." in *Encyclopedia of the Social Sciences*.

------------1970. *Vunamami: Economic Transformation in a Traditional Society*. Berkeley: University of California Press.

Sankoff, G. 1965. *The Organizational Factor in the Economic Development of Traditional and Peasant Societies*. M.A. Thesis. Montreal: McGill University.

Udy, Stanley H. 1959. *Organization of Work*. New Haven: HRAF Press.

9.

FORMAL ANALYSIS IN ANTHROPOLOGICAL ECONOMICS:

THE ROSSEL ISLAND CASE

by

Richard F. Salisbury

Source: Chapter 4, in Ira R. Buchler and Hugo G. Nutini (eds.), *Game Theory in the Behavioral Sciences*. Pittsburgh: University of Pittsburgh Press, 1968.

The present study attempts to demonstrate the utility of formal analysis in anthropological economics, by making sense of a body of reported[1] data, which a "substantivist" analysis (Dalton 1965) and a more traditional economic analysis (Barić 1964) discard as inconsistent. Anthropological economics...takes as its aim the demonstration of the logic of choice used for resource allocation – that is, it accepts the aims of economics but, using empirical data of the kind familiar to anthropologists, it studies those sectors of social behavior to which the classical analysis of traditional economics does not apply. It assumes that choices are made logically, even if the logic is not that of maximising immediate returns of material goods by "higgle-haggling," which substantivists appear to view as the only form of rationality. Choices logically designed to produce optimum results over a long term can be expected to differ markedly from choices made on a short-term basis. Where there are different degrees of uncertainty about environmental conditions or about the actions of other persons, different magnitudes of inherent risk, different degrees of seriousness of the consequences of failure, the logical pattern of choice should not coincide with the short-term rational choice. To put these statements in game theory terms, classical economics formally analyzes the consequences that would ensue if everyone employed a maximax strategy of concentrating on the activity giving him the greatest comparative advantage in a non-zero-sum game with a large number of players. Anthropological economics concentrates on other strategies, other payoff matrices, and other game situations. In these terms a formal analysis of nonclassical, non-Euclidean economics is possible (Salisbury 1962b:71). The present paper seeks to show that such analyses are productive.

The game theory approach also clears up much of the confusion that exists in cultural descriptions of other economic systems. When describing a game, one must specify formal rules to which all participants must subscribe or be considered "outside the game." One finds similar economic rules, usually phrased as existential statements such as "there are one hundred cents to a dollar," with which all actors in an economic system agree. On the other hand, in a game there are many alternative strategies that different actors describe as "*the* way to play the game," or to which they ascribe moral qualities, arguing that "everyone *should* play the game in this way." Such strategy statements appear culturally as maxims, such as "A penny saved is a penny earned." The strategy statements can be related to the rules as logical extensions of them, if one makes certain assumptions about the risks involved in the game, about the consequences of failure, or the rewards of winning. But what is immediately apparent, and what would be a source of confusion if one attempted to write a consistent cultural description of Western economics, for example, is that there are alternative strategies and alternative cultural maxims. "Penny wise, pound foolish" is the obverse of Franklin's doctrine of frugality. It is also clear that the alternative strategy-statements are equally logical, under different views of the economic situation. Using different strategies may be equally logical if the true risks are unknown, or when the situation may change from time to time. The stock market exemplifies this clearly. Sellers, who believe stocks will drop, can find buyers only if others believe stocks will rise. Economic behavior thus demonstrates admirably what is coming to be recognized in other areas of cultural behavior (Salisbury 1959, Wallace 1961:29-42), namely, that complete consensus makes interaction impossible and that cultural diversity, within a framework of agreement on a few formal rules, is essential in human society.

Such a position demands that a straightforward ethnographic report on a social system of resource allocation (an economy) should contain a number of formal rules about which all informants are agreed, a series of strategy statements (usually of highly inconsistent natures) often explicitly formulated by numbers of informants as maxims, and enough information about the nature of the game being played to render the different strategies comprehensible. Specifically, information on numbers of players (the population), their different roles, the risks and limiting situations in the society (its ecology and technology), and the quantities of goods and services being allocated are required as a minimum. By these criteria, Armstrong's description of Rossel Island (Armstrong 1928)[2] stands out as a classic of ethnography; its main defect is the ethnographer's attempt to interpret large bodies of data in terms of a single strategy (the taking of interest), which obscures somewhat the view of Rossel Island. Beside it, Malinowski's account of the Trobriands appears as naïve sensational reporting; it cites few figures, obtrudes the author's own feelings about what should be the single strategy governing allocation (reciprocity), and, by not citing the differences in informants' views, makes it difficult to say which views are Malinowski's and which are Trobriand views. Unfortunately, Armstrong treats only one aspect of Rossel Island economics at length – shell money. This has the compensating advantage, however, that it is possible to use the topic as a concise illustration of the nature of anthropological economics and the ethnographic reporting it demands.

The case is also useful in illustrating the methods of the anthropological economist. His basic data are quantitative descriptions of transactions and the series of explanations given by people to justify their behavior. His task is to construct the rules of a game in which players would be expected to behave in the ways observed and to present their explanations of their own behavior as logically derivable from the least number of assumptions about the rules and the conditions of the game. In many cases the classical economic game, and the assumption that every player is trying to maximize his short-term material gains, provides an adequate basis for analyzing the observed behavior. In other cases, as Foster (1965:293) has shown, the assumption that all persons are playing a game in which the rewards are so limited that one man's gain exactly balances another man's loss (i.e., a zero-sum game) is the most parsimonious explanation of observed behavior. In yet others, strategies of minimizing the possibility of loss (minimax strategies) may be seen as underlying observed behavior of apparently cautious, unadventurous types.

It may be empirically untrue that economic life is a zero-sum game, since increases in aggregate yield are possible; it may be that, empirically, conditions are inappropriate for minimax strategies. The investigator must seek to establish what the empirical conditions are. But merely by establishing the apparent logic behind people's actions, he can make predictions about their other actions under the same conditions, and can extrapolate their actions under changed conditions.

In more complex situations the investigator is confronted by individuals apparently using different strategies, or even playing different games, even though each one's behavior is contingent on the behavior of others.[3] This occurs particularly when the true payoff matrix is not widely known or is unknowable, or where people are in different power positions, make different evaluations of long-term security and short-terms gains, or are exposed to different risks. The investigator can then follow the game theorist's technique of following through the implications of long series of interactions (plays) in which players adopt different strategies. If he has also established the objective conditions of risk, payoff, etc., he may later be able to predict the future outcome of series of plays, should those conditions be changed. The Rossel Island material does permit at least a tentative analysis up to this point.

181

ROSSEL ISLAND SHELL MONEY

Rossel, situated at the extreme eastern end of the New Guinea archipelago, is perhaps the remotest of all the islands in the archipelago. On the island small shell discs (*ndap*) are given in exchange for goods or services in most transactions where men are involved, from the purchases of craft goods to weddings. Other shells (*nko*), also used in transactions, are said to be female shells, but these will not be discussed here – largely because Armstrong's information about these shells is quite spotty. The Rossel use of a single term for all male shells indicates that they are considered a single logical set, contrasting with female shells. The set of *ndap* is differentiated into twenty-two named types (1928:61) ranked in an order that Armstrong numbered from 1 (low) to 22 (high). Each type or denomination is appropriate to a particular set of transactions. High denominations, particularly No. 18 and No. 20 are appropriate to only one or two types of transaction (No. 1 8 for weddings or pig purchases, No. 20 for cannibal feasts or purchase of ceremonial canoes); lower denominations are appropriate to a longer series of specific transactions – No. 4, for instance, buys a basket, lime stick, or lime pot (1928:85). The various denominations have a qualitatively different value, although each represents a quantitatively different level of prestige. The relationship between the prestige levels of adjacent denominations of shells is a complex one, which Armstrong tried to analyze in oversimplified terms of "compound interest," as if the difference in value were a matter of the time for which a shell is loaned. The evidence is incomplete but it would seem that in Rossel thought a shell of denomination n is equated with the shell of denomination *n-1* (its *ma*), plus a consecutive series of up to ten lower ranking shells (the *dondap* of the *ma*) (1928:71-73). There are special terms for each member of a consecutive series starting from the principal (*yono*) down to the first (*wo*) (1928:79). Lending and borrowing of *ndap* is common, with the loan of one denomination being returnable by a higher ranking shell, with the rank difference varying roughly with the length of the loan (1928:72-73). Armstrong gives examples of loans of short low-ranking series (e.g., No. 3 plus No. 4, which presumably immediately equate with No. 5) being repaid after a few days by a single higher value (No. 6), and of loans of single high-ranking shells repaid by the same shell plus a series of lower ranking shells (*dondap*) (1928:67). It is also possible to obtain the loan of a shell (*ma*) by depositing the next higher ranking shell as a security (*tyindap*) with the lender; presumably in such a case the return of a shell of the *ma* value, in exchange for the original *tyindap*, eliminates all indebtedness.

Stated in formal terms the complex manipulations of Rossel Island money appear as a game in which the object is to maximize the volume of services received from others in exchange for shells. At any one time, different people want different services. Some individuals possess shells but temporarily do not want services. The system regulates the demand for a complex of goods and services, and the existence of shell money equivalents motivates other individuals to provide those goods and services.

Thus far the formal description relies almost entirely on Rossel Island terminology, clearly stated by Armstrong and about which there is no argument among informants (although Armstrong, from a short stay, could not fully work out the complex relationships of *tyindap*, *ma*, and *dondap* for all denominations and times). Other aspects of the shell money exchanges appeared to Armstrong as unclear, inconsistent, or illogical, and he mentions disagreements among informants as well as disagreements among parties to exchanges. I propose to interpret these obscurities or disagreements as the expression of diverse strategy statements, formulated by informants with different interests to maintain, which Armstrong, given his old-fashioned Malinowskian idea of uniform cultural homogeneity, was unable to include in his explanation. As an ethnographer who has repeatedly listened to such conflicting strategy statements, I respect Armstrong's work all the more because he had the intellectual honesty to admit doubts and confusions. Let us, however, attempt a series of formal analyses of the Rossel Island system and so arrive at the nature of strategy disagreements deductively. We may then return to the empirical evidence, to show the fit between it and the formal analyses.

Armstrong's own formal analysis is that of a classical economist. Although the time and percentage indices are unclear, the Rossel system is a system of compound interest. For the person owning a *ndap* the interest gives him an incentive to lend his shell, and penalizes him with the interest loss, should he hoard it. For the person desiring services the interest constitutes a cost against which he can measure the value of the services at the present moment. It motivates him to provide services to someone else in advance, and so avoid the obligations of debt, or to return the loan as soon as possible. The strength of the incentive/sanction is provided by the interest rate, and Armstrong tries to calculate this, estimating that the expectation is that loans will be repaid in about three weeks.

The analysis has considerable merit. It predicts the high velocity of circulation of *ndap* through loans, and suggests that individuals could make a living by lending at high rates (i.e., forcing speedy repayment) and borrowing at low rates (i.e., delaying repayment of others) (1928:66). It suggests that the individual who has clear owner ship of a shell (whose stock possessed, plus loans due and minus debts owing, is a positive number) has a claim to a constant supply of services from others. Those without shells must constantly supply services at a certain rate; only if they supply a larger number in a given time period can they acquire clear title to shells, and thus accumulate claims to future services from others. Those with claims to services are those who own shells and are chiefs (*limi*); upward mobility is achieved initially by providing services and acquiring shells, but is then dependent on "playing the market." This is a common situation elsewhere in Melanesia (cf. Salisbury 1966).

It is not a very powerful analysis, for it assumes that *ndap* exist in large quantities, and that there is ready convertibility or subdivision of *ndap* into other denominations. It assumes that individuals can switch immediately from being lenders to being debtors, and that each position is simply the reverse of the other. None of these assumptions is entirely true, though the assumptions may be approached in relation to the low-ranking shells and the goods and services which they buy.

Let us consider other assumptions in turn, and the analyses they lead to. Firstly let us take the relative inconvertibility of *ndap*, and the equation of each denomination with a specific set of services. This means that an individual, A, requiring a specific service must seek out not only an individual, B, who is prepared to provide that service, but an individual, C, who can lend him the appropriate denomination shell, and an individual, D, who will accept yet other services from A, and so enable him to repay C. It may sometimes occur that A has the correct denomination himself and a simple purchase occurs, or that B and D turn out to be the same individual and the transaction becomes one of delayed exchange of qualitatively different services. Normally, however, a simple desire for services from others sets in motion a complex series of relationships, involving at least four parties.

On the other hand the position of a shell possessor is relatively simple. He has to seek out only one individual, the man who wishes to borrow his shell; or, having once lent the shell he is simply preoccupied in insuring its return with interest as quickly as possible. The relative inconvertibility of *ndap* complicates his position in that a possessor who envisages becoming in the near future a buyer of the specific services his shell will obtain may wish to hold onto his shell until that time arrives, in order to avoid the complications of being without the shells to obtain the services. This complication would not concern shell possessors who took either a short-run view of matters, and always lent out whatever they had, or a long-run view that shells are in constant circulation so that by lending one obtains a sequence of different services and shells and the eventual return of a shell of the same denomination. If each denomination changes into the next in three weeks, one could expect to have gone through seventeen changes in a year and have one's original shell back plus a No. 17 at that time. More realistically, an individual possessing two or more shells and loaning each one continuously could expect to have any particular denomination pass through his hands two or more times each year.

In short, one would expect to find three discrepant views of the system as a result of the relative inconvertibility of *ndap*. The service-desiring non-possessor would describe it as a burdensome system of debts, putting him at a disadvantage with respect to the wealthy and involving him in needless complications. This aspect is mentioned by Armstrong (1928:67) especially as it applies to young men; the system is seen as inefficient and demanding ten times as much lending as would be required if a more convertible monetary medium were used (1928:65). Dalton (1965:53) particularly stresses this aspect. The careful possessors of a few shells would tend to emphasize the purchasing aspect of the system, and the specific services that can be obtained with each denomination shell – "any commodity or service may be more or less directly priced in terms of them" (1928:59). They would tend to see wealth in terms of concrete possessions. It would be expected that such people would also tend to favor more or less direct exchanges of services and/or shells, buying services when the right shell is at hand, and reciprocating when the exchange partner needs services. Armstrong (1928:88) describes in a puzzled footnote an apparent tendency for reciprocity to occur in pig sales. The third group of shell possessors includes both those who have only immediate gain in mind and those who have many shells and long-run perspectives. Their tendency would be to see the system as an open one, which rapidly circulates goods and services, and which provides frequent feasts and ceremonials as loans are repaid and new obligations incurred. This group would emphasize that it is a generous system, in which each man seeks aggressively to lend valuables as soon as they come into his possession, and in which one's well-being depends not on the number of shells he owns but on the number that pass through his hands. Again Armstrong cites (1928:74) the desire to touch *ndap* as they pass by, but interprets this only as "evidently a witnessing of the transaction."

The rigidities of the system as a whole appear much less acute to individuals who possess large numbers of *ndap*. To a Rossel Islander these rigidities are more or less serious, depending on the numbers of *ndap* of different values a man holds, on the size of the population (and the likelihood of any one individual holding a shell of any particular denomination), and on the frequency of transactions involving particular denominations. Theoretically, one could assign hypothetical values to each of these factors and, by substituting them in a computer simulation of the Rossel Island exchanges, predict what strategies would be most successful under different conditions. This is impracticable for present purposes, but Armstrong does give some of the parameter values for 1920-21, and these may be used in a single substitution. The effects of population increase, the introduction of European consumer goods, or the production of new shell currency might then be predicted as departures from the 1920-21 state.

Rossel Island's population in 1920 was 1,415, including 406 adult males, who lived in 145 "villages" (1928:230), 116 of which are mapped by Armstrong as forming two rings around a rectangular island, half of the villages fronting on the coast, and the other half backed by the central mountains. The island perimeter is about sixty miles. The villages are evenly scattered approximately a mile apart along the coast and on the inland ring, but the two rings are more than a mile apart. Armstrong obtained figures for the number of *ndap* of different denominations as follows (1928:62-63): 7 x No. 22, 10 x No. 21, 10 x No. 20, 10 x No. 19, 20 x No. 18, 7 x No. 17, 7 x No. 16, 10 x No. 15, 30 x No. 14, 30-40 x No. 13, and larger numbers of all lower denominations; No. 4 was "by far the commonest," with at least 200. He estimated a grand total of less than a thousand *ndap* altogether. The average adult male owned, therefore, slightly over two *ndap*, but only seven *ndap* were present in the average village.

Armstrong does not cite frequencies of transactions, but the population figures would indicate about fourteen marriages and twenty-eight funerals each year, assuming a stable population and a life expectancy of about sixty years. Each No. 18 shell would thus be needed roughly once every year and a half for a wedding; the number of times each would be needed for the purchase of a pig at a feast could vary widely, as the production of pigs increased or decreased, but considerations of the size of pigs and the meat-eating capacity of Melanesians suggest that five uses per annum was a ceiling, and probably one or two uses was usual. Cannibal feasts, construction of large houses, or the sale of gardens, each requiring a higher value *ndap* as *yono* but an No. 18 as part of the series, probably occurred highly infrequently so that higher denomination shells were virtually immobile, and a few No. 18's were involved as dondap in payments of higher denomination shells.

The denominations between No. 17 and No. 14 appear to have circulated mainly as *dondap*, when higher denominations were the *yono ndap*, principally at pig feasts. This would have involved slightly higher rates of circulation for No. 17 and No. 14 than No. 18, since they were fewer in number. For the lower denominations it is impossible to calculate frequencies of use as, for example, No. 13 could be used to compensate for three months of work; No. 13 was also the *yono ndap* for small canoe purchases (1928:86). All others figured as members of *dondap* series *and* as *yono ndap*, and so were probably in virtually constant circulation.

Let us now consider the circulation mechanisms of shells of which less than thirty five were in circulation, and of those with over thirty-five in circulation. An individual wishing to borrow one of the scarce denominations could not expect to find one available in his own village or the three neighboring ones – on the average there would be one for every five villages. He would have to expect to travel to distant villages to obtain the loan or would have to wait until a shell was paid into his immediate neighborhood and then petition the possessor for a loan. Even if the network of relationships described by Armstrong (1928:31-37) and implied by the virilocality of residence and nonlocalized matrilineal clan system of the island would have spread contacts over wide areas, these factors would not have vitiated the need for travel beyond the local political unit to obtain the loan of scarce shells.

Rather than to travel at random to obtain shells, it would be more practical for prospective borrowers to follow the peregrinations of particular shells and to wait until a shell reached an individual with whom the borrower had a preexisting relationship. The borrower could then immediately ask for a loan. Armstrong discusses the fact that all coins above No. 12 rank are individually named (1928:62). Such names would play an important part in enabling people to follow shell movements. Shell movements would not only be traced, they would be anticipated. Preexisting relationships would be cultivated with those individuals who were adjudged likely to be shell-recipients in the future. Stated the other way around, individuals likely to be shell-recipients would be the objects of cultivation by individuals in search of future loans. To establish a reputation of being a likely shell-recipient would be a major aim of a person seeking power. Such a person would try to establish a fiction (which other people would deny) that he was entitled by right to control shells. Armstrong (1928:60, 68) makes several rather vague comments linking possession of such shells with chiefship and the ownership of large canoes. Chiefs (*limi*) are presumably, if Rossel is similar to virtually every other area of Melanesia, men of ability who possess a minimum of inherited advantages, and who have achieved their positions by politicking and financial manipulations. In such a context it is reasonable to expect an investigator to report a variety of imprecise statements, such as "Chiefs are wealthy men," and "Wealthy men are chiefs by right," as well as statements complaining of the arrogance of wealthy upstarts. This would seem to be the situation Armstrong reports.

Yet the claims of chiefs to outright ownership have other consequences. Let us consider a hypothetical situation in which all twenty No. 18 shells are in the hands of individuals who have no debts to others; individuals, in other words, who can claim an unclouded title, or one held by right. Let us call these twenty men chiefs. A nonchief, X, wishing to obtain a wife for his son, or to buy a pig, would have to incur a debt toward one of the chiefs. To repay the debt he would have to approach another chief and also collect a series of *dondap* shells of low denominations. Otherwise, he would have to obtain the loan of a No. 19 of which there are only ten in circulation. Clearly, in view of the discrepancy in numbers of No. 18 and No. 19 shells alone, there would be a tendency for loans of No. 18 to be repaid by a return of the No. 18 and *dondap*, rather than by the higher denomination. Let us consider only the implications of direct payment of No. 18 shells, and further borrowing from one of the chiefs. Having first borrowed from chief A, individual X would remain permanently indebted, borrowing from chief B to repay chief A, and from C to repay B. Each time he would have to add low value shells as *dondap*. To liquidate the debt he would either have to marry off a daughter or sell a pig, or (less likely) manipulate loans until he could himself claim clear title to a No. 18.

The twenty chiefs themselves would have a vested interest in keeping the shells circulating among themselves alone, thereby increasing the probability that shells received by nonchiefs in ceremonial payments would be returned to their keeping to circulate in the ring. To the extent that a chief had other lower denominations in his possession he would also be able to let debtors pyramid their debts until they were obligated to the extent of a No. 18. At that point the chief would be assured that the debtor would continue to pay him interest, and that if the debtor ever obtained a No. 18 from a sale or a wedding, that shell would come straight back to him also. Limitations on the giving of pig feasts by nonchiefs would also tend to minimize leakage of No. 18 shells (cf. 1928:88, cited above) to nonchiefs. The leaks could never be entirely stopped – even the hypothetical model cited above implies that there should be twenty-one chiefs for twenty shells, with the twenty-first receiving the shell in the transaction that starts the circulation. The existence of social mobility testifies to the possibility of newcomers entering the ring of chiefs. Yet the members of the ring, by collusion, could buttress their own positions. They could assume the aura of legitimacy referred to above and control access to power.

Some of the conditions under which collusion is likely can be specified. The shell denomination concerned would have to be in short supply to permit oligopoly control to be obtained. It would have to be a denomination in periodic demand by most individuals in the system (women and pigs are universal desirables among Melanesian males). The possibility of the ring being broken by access of nonchiefs to higher denomination *ndap* would be reduced by a sharp discrepancy between the numbers of the monopolized denomination shell and of the next higher denomination. At the same time, the efficiency of the ring would be increased to the extent that pyramiding of debt could also be used to make nonchiefs owe the appropriate shells. Nonchiefs could also be better persuaded to accept the manipulations of such a ring if, in theory at least, they had the possibility open to them of pyramiding their own loans up to the crucial denomination, and thus of entering the ring themselves. On all these grounds the No. 18 shell would meet the formal criteria for oligopoly control.

The ethnography also indicates the corollaries of such a control: the infrequency of circulation of values higher than No. 18, the payment of debts of

No. 18 by the same value plus either work or additional small shells, and the apparent generosity (1928:67) with which chiefs lend out No. 18 shells to promising young men at virtually no interest, presumably as an investment designed to involve the young man as a political supporter as he gains skills in financial manipulation. The chiefs would also expect a different attitude toward shells of the crucial value and above from that expressed toward shells below this value, even though it would be ideologically important for chiefs to insist that the shells all form part of a single system, governed by the same formal cultural rules. Armstrong expresses exactly this situation thus (1928:68):

> Nos. 18 to 22 seem to be in a somewhat different position from the lower values ... My informants did, however, state that the same principles operate with these: that a No. 17 becomes a No. 18, a No. 18 a No. 19 and so on- in just the same way as with the lower values. Yet, as ... in the example given ... a No. 18 can be borrowed for a short time without the debt increasing ... Nos. 18 to 22 are peculiar in one other respect. They have a certain sacred character. No. 18, as it passes from person to person, is handled with great apparent reverence, and a crouching attitude is maintained ... Probably Nos. 17 and below have a sacredness and prestige proportional to their position in the series, but I am inclined to think that there may be a real gap, in this respect, between Nos. 17 and 18.

I would submit that all these ethnographic peculiarities (and their obscurity) can be predicted as the effects of a game coalition between people calling themselves chiefs, seeking to maximize rationally their long-term gains by manipulating the formal rules to suit their particular strategy.

CHANGES IN THE SYSTEM

The analysis of the operation of the Rossel Island system at one time period with only one set of numerical parameters makes it clear that changes in those parameters could make for dramatic changes in the operation of the system without any change taking place in the formal cultural rules. Population changes (assuming a virtually constant stock of *ndap*) would alter the ratio of shells to adult

189

males and would alter the denomination at which inter-village borrowing and the naming of individual shells becomes important. It would alter the rate of transactions and up to a certain point would increase the dependency of nonchiefs upon chiefs for the use of No. 18. Chiefs would keep larger followings. But increased velocity of circulation of No. 18 would also would also increase the likelihood of leakage of shells to nonchiefs, and at a certain point the closed state of the ring would be expected to break down. With it would go changes in the uses of and attitudes toward higher denomination shells.

Changes in the availability of goods and services would also affect the system. The lower values, up to about value No. 4, would seem to have been so widely distributed and readily exchanged as to have the characteristics of multipurpose, divisible coins. With more services and goods available, the money supply would have to increase proportionately, and in due course a system of simple relationships between coins would be expected to emerge as the rate of transactions reached a crucial level. In practical terms, I would predict that No. 4 may have become equivalent to a shilling, and in time replaced by it, with other low denominations becoming equivalent to fractions of a shilling, and perhaps remaining in use as small change.

The possibility of the emergence of oligopolies at levels other than No. 18 should also be considered. The decrease in the numbers of shells between denominations No. 14 and No. 15 would make this a possible locus for an oligopoly to develop, but the universal desirability of European axes (costing No. 11) might indicate a lower value for such control. At this point, however, the nature of the supply of axes – presumably through European monopolistic traders, or through Rossel Islanders earning money by work on plantations or gold mines – would tend to make oligopoly by chiefs unlikely. It might be predicted that, with trade stores and Australian money replacing *ndap* in transactions up to those of denomination No. 11, the circulation of all higher values might begin to resemble that described by Armstrong for values above No. 18. Interest in the form of cash would accompany reciprocal exchanges, loans and repayments, and the complexities of the earlier Rossel system of equivalents would be lost.

Formal Analysis vs. Substantive Analysis

It must still be demonstrated that a formal analysis is indeed more powerful than a substantive analysis in explaining more empirical facts from fewer assumptions.

Barić (1964) gives a sympathetic exposition of Armstrong's ethnography but concentrates on the relationship of the system to productive investment, by which she means the accumulation of larger quantities of nets, land, canoes, etc. (1964:48). Her conclusion is that the shell money system was virtually a zero sum game, as relatively few transactions were aimed at investing, and "despite great activity in the economic sphere, aggregate capital is largely maintained at the same level, although individuals may become wealthy." She virtually ignores Armstrong's abundant evidence that new goods such as saucepans and steel axes had already been included in the system by 1920, and that circulation rates of high denomination *ndap* had changed shortly before 1920. It may be granted that the technological level of Rossel Island meant that relatively little increase was possible in the use of material capital goods to produce additional foodstuffs – the availability of abundant sago and fish would seem to have made additional food production unnecessary – but it would seem that great variations were possible in the volume of services produced. What the shell money system permitted was the accumulation of command over services by chiefs and nonchiefs alike; entrepreneurs, it would seem, were constantly trying to increase the volume of services they commanded, and may well have been progressively increasing the aggregate volume of services available in the society as a whole. The apparent stagnation of Rossel Island in terms of volume of material goods available should, from the dynamic picture suggested by formal analysis, suggest that something (presumably technology) was "positively stopping" (*contra* Barić 1964:49) growth in this particular direction.

Barić (ibid.) does deal with the relationship between shell money and power, but interprets the two as separate.

> There were several routes to prestige and power. The sheer accumulation of liquid capital was one way: ... Reckless expenditure could purchase prestige by financing activities in the form of feasts or the purchase of ceremonial canoes. The ceremonial canoes were the capstone of the edifice of wealth. They were the monopoly of the chiefs, in effect, since those who could get them ... became chiefs.

Attempts at accumulation of shells were the strategies of the unprogressive middle levels of society. Expenditure that may have seemed reckless to Barić can be explained in terms of the purchase of command over services of particular types. Ceremonial canoes, purchaseable only by No. 20 *ndap*, at a time when circulation of values over No. 18 was minimal, could only be obtained by a limited few – those who could dispose of cannibal victims, big houses, or land – any of which would obtain No. 20 shells for them. Barić, in each case, is forced to distort the ethnography. More generally she forces herself into a static interpretation of Armstrong's data by myopically considering "economics" as dealing only with goods and not with services. The description of feasts, marriage payments, and payments for the services of prostitutes (*ptyilibi*) bulks large in Armstrong's work but is virtually ignored.

Dalton's analysis of the data tries to show that "Rossel Island economy is not integrated by market exchange" and that "if all the *ndap* shell transactions ... were abolished, subsistence livelihood of Rossel Islanders would remain unimpaired" (1965:55). Theoretically, Dalton (cf. Belshaw 1954, Salisbury 1962a) tries to revive the dead issue of the nature of primitive money in terms of substantivism (Cook 1966). Dalton's analysis must be evaluated in the light of the fact that it almost invariably does not explain the ethnography as Armstrong's informants related it, but denies the accuracy of Armstrong's data.

Thus Dalton says (1965:54): "There are ... faults in Armstrong's analysis. ... He ... regards all transactions as commercial purchases." And (1965:57): "It is about as useful to describe a pig feast on Rossel as buying a pig with a No. 18 *ndap* as [it is to describe a Western marriage in terms of buying the ring]. To do so one must ignore the folk view of the event." In fact, Armstrong states (1928:59): "Any commodity or service may be more or less directly priced in terms of [*ndap* shells]." And (1928:88): "A pig feast is known as *bwame bwobe* [pig-buy] ... One man, A, [makes] insulting remarks about the pig of another man, B; whereupon B retorts by suggesting that A buy the pig." The "folk view" is clearly one of purchase. Certain fish are subject to buying and selling with No. 11 shells "even from an own brother" (1928:86). Marriage too is clearly viewed as the purchase of services for a No. 18 shell, though not as a purchase of the person of the bride. This emerges clearly from a comparison of marriage with the purchase by a group of men of the services of a *ptybili*, also with a No. 18 shell. The latter transaction involves no additional handing over of a series of lower denomination *ndap* to the clan of the *ptybili*, such as is involved in the marriage ritual, although otherwise the rituals are similar (1928:97). The owners of a *ptybili's* sexual services receive payments from other men who utilize her services temporarily, and each co-owner receives a No. 18 *ndap* from the eventual husband of the group *ptybili* when she settles down with a single individual. By contrast, the ritual for *ptybili* purchase does nothing to allocate rights over the children she produces; these rights are purchased in the marriage ritual by the subsidiary payments to the bride's clan relatives. Armstrong's informants were vague and even contradictory in their statements about the rarity with which *ptybili* produce children, about the advantages any of her children may possess by having several fathers, and about the wide dispersment of relationship terms for *ptybili* children.

Dalton also criticizes Armstrong for treating *ndap* as twenty-two types within a single logical set and for adopting a numbering system that suggests a uniform relation between each category. He concludes: (Dalton 1965:55-56)

> What is clear, however, is that shells below No. 18 are not convertible into shells 18-22 by borrowing and repayment. One cannot start with a No. 1 or 17, and by lending work it up to a No. 18-22 ... Convertibility via borrowing and repaying ... most certainly breaks down between Nos. 17 and 18. I suspect between Nos. 10 and 11 as well ... It is very clear that the entire series is not linked ... because the uses to which the shells 18-22 are put are of an entirely different order from the uses of lower shells ... Without exception Nos. 18-22 enter noncommercial transactions exclusively.

The ethnography has already been cited which directly contradicts each of these statements. Informants directly state that the relation between No. 17 and No. 18 is the same as that between Nos. 18 and 19, and can in theory be interchangeable in terms of borrowing and repaying. The series is clearly linked, though the small numbers and special uses of all shells from about No. 12 upwards means that there is a steady and progressive change in attitudes of individuals to shells. In the folk view, all transactions involving shells are exchanges of them for goods and services, which denotes commerce. What is true (and Armstrong devotes several pages [1928:81-84] to analyzing the components of collective purchase in a pig feast, and components of kinship) is that the number of additional noncommercial relationships involved is much larger for a high-denomination than for a low-denomination transaction.

Dalton also feels that Armstrong's comments on the sacred nature of high-denomination shells mean that "Nos. 18-22 are obviously treasure items." This, Dalton feels, justifies his contradicting the ethnographic evidence that *ndap* is a unitary set. It is clear that Dalton has never seen the display of ten $100,000 bills in a Las Vegas gambling saloon. Ethnographically they could be described by a paraphrasing of Armstrong (1928:68): "They have a certain sacred character; [such bills are viewed] with great apparent reverence, and a [gasping and pointing] attitude is

193

maintained ... [They] are almost always kept enclosed and are not supposed [to be taken out of their case] to see the light of day." In Las Vegas, people make pilgrimages to view the $1,000,000 in bills; the shrine is lavishly decorated, and temple watchmen, armed with guns, see that nonsacred commoners do not come into dangerously close contact with the sacred objects. There is no question but that the ten pieces of paper could, in theory, be converted into an equivalent number of, say, ten-cent cigars. Formal analysis and an understanding of game theory explains why they are not converted.

What the formal analysis enables one to demonstrate is that despite the rigidities imposed on Rossel Island's economy by its small size, its simple technology, and the difficulties of balancing supply and demand for goods and services within a single island, all aspects of life – from the purchase of fish or baskets to the obtaining of unskilled labor for a month, the specialized services of a *ptybili* or legal rights to children – are to some extent regulated within one single system of exchange. The system motivates individuals to supply services to catch fish or to breed pigs. It rewards those who are adept financial entrepreneurs. It "increases the necessity for doubling for doubling and redoubling social links" (Barić 1964:39) in a sparsely populated land. And it provides the basis for political loyalty to about twenty chiefs. It is a flexible system, though formal analysis suggests that this flexibility is not unlimited without a change in the formal rules. All this is accomplished by the circulation of less than a thousand chips of shell, which Armstrong (1928:64) felt in "the native point of view" were most nearly equated with units of time: "e.g. a wife could be said to cost a year, a basket of taro a week, and so on." For all that Rossel Island does not meet the specifications of the "perfect market" of classical economics, I feel it has been demonstrated that whatever island-wide integration there was in 1920, was almost entirely an effect of market exchange.

NOTES

1. This analysis has been progressively refined in the light of questions by students in Pacific ethnography courses since 1957. I wish to acknowledge this help, but to accept full responsibility for errors remaining.

2. Armstrong's volume is cited hereafter merely as (1928).

3. Dr. A. Rapoport pointed out in discussion that it is only where contingency of expectations is involved that game theory becomes a more powerful analytical tool than probability theory or linear programming. Unfortunately the pure theorist, advancing the mathematical precision of analysis, needs to be able to specify or control the payoff matrix before predicting the results of the game. The task of the empirical or applied worker is to work back from results to the payoff matrix, and he is thus merely the user of theoretical findings, not the advancer of theory.

REFERENCES

Armstrong, W. E. 1928. *Rossel Island*. Cambridge: Cambridge University Press.

Barić, L. 1964. "Some Aspects of Credit, Saving and Investment in a 'Non-Monetary' Economy (Rossel Island)." in Firth, R. and B. S. Yamey (eds.), *Capital Saving and Credit in Peasant Societies*. London: Allen & Unwin.

Belshaw, C. S. 1954. *Changing Melanesia*. London: Oxford University Press.

Cook, S. 1966. "The Obsolete Anti-Market Mentality." *American Anthropologist* 68:323-45.

Dalton, G. 1965. "Primitive Money." *American Anthropologist* 67:44-65.

Foster, G.M. 1965. "Peasant Society and the Image of the Limited Good." *American Anthropologist* 67:293-315.

Salisbury, R. F. 1959. Joking Relations and Ritual Ambiguity. Paper presented at American Anthropological Assoc. Meetings, Mexico City, December 1959.

------------1962a. *From Stone to Steel*. Cambridge and Melbourne: University Presses.

------------1962b. "Comment on 'The Feet of the Natives Are Large' by J. S. Berliner." *Current Anthropology* 3:70-71.

------------1966. "Politics and Shell-Money Finance in New Britain." in Tuden, A., V. Turner and H. Swartz (eds.), *Political Anthropology*. Chicago: Aldine.

Wallace, A.F.C. 1961. *Culture and Personality*. New York: Random House.

10.

Non-Equilibrium Models in New Guinea Ecology:

Possibilities of Cultural Extrapolation[1]

by

Richard F. Salisbury

Source: *Anthropologica* 17(2), 1975

Résumé

Beaucoup d'analyses anthropologiques qui se disent écologiques, sont vraiment du fonctionalisme pur; elles assument gratuitement une relation équilibrée entre facteurs culturels et milieu physique, se basant sur l'étude d'un seul moment historique, et sans démontrer aucune histoire de feedback ou d'adaptation à long terme. Une analyse des fêtes de porc des hauteurs de Nouvelle Guinée et du développement de la population Tolai de Nouvelle Bretagne depuis sa première colonisation aux environs de 1200 (A.D.) illustre la possibilité de construire une famille de modèles écologiques qui n'assument pas l'équilibre. On assume en premier lieu une population humaine en croissance continuelle, qui n'est pas limitée absolument par le milieu, et qui possède des règles culturelles relativement fixes. Même avec des règles constantes on en observerait diverses réalisations dans le comportement selon la densité de la population, la disponibilité de terre, etc. Parmi les Tolai, aucune réalisation équilibrée "adaptée au milieu" n'est survenue, pendant sept cents ans. On considère qu'il faut un séjour d'au moins trois cents ans dans un milieu stable et limitant, pour produire une "adaptation." On ne trouve cette stabilité que très rarement. L'analyse écologique culturelle ne devrait pas viser à l'analyse d'adaptations culturelles à des milieux fixes, mais plutôt à l'analyse des façons de réaliser des configurations culturelles stables dans des milieux changeants et changeables.

The ecosystem models most commonly used to organise the data obtained from traditional subsistence-based societies have been equilibrium models. This has been particularly true for New Guinea, where one of the most sophisticated such analyses – that of Rappaport (1968) has been a paradigm. Unfortunately, despite their sophisticated techniques for the collection of data, such studies have relied on data from only relatively short time periods. The multitude of variables measured for any one society have not been fully demonstrated to be causally related, but most have rather been *assumed* to be functionally related. Much "ecology" has actually been a modern neo-functionalism, explaining why traditional society was unchanging and/or "adapted to its environment."

The present paper begins to develop a family of models, in which equilibrium is *not* assumed, and which seem relevant to New Guinea reality. Human populations are generally assumed to be continuously but slowly expanding, over very long periods, within a physical environment that is not generally restrictive. Technological modifications of productive techniques, and modifications of social relationships within and between populations, are seen as related to progressive increases in population density. But the relationship is not a Malthusian one of negative feedback, where overpopulation causes famine and population reduction, but rather the positive feedback mechanism of new techniques and relationships being seen as more productive with greater population density. The models are time-related phase models, not necessarily valid for infinite extrapolation. The family of models also assumes that a large number of cultural behaviours observed at any one time in a particular society are *not* aimed at adapting the population to the current physical environment. The aim of these behaviours, and much of their content, is derived from a long cultural tradition which current generations try to replicate; *qualitatively* the cultural tradition may change slowly. But the extent to which any population does tangibly recreate the tradition is highly variable, with the availability of resources, technology, or relationships dramatically influencing *quantitatively* the population's success with that culture. The maintenance of cultural continuity is indeed the major parameter for each model.

The effect of the technological change from stone axes to steel (Salisbury 1957, 1962; Sharp 1952) exemplifies this assumption. In about ten years, and without the introduction of pacification or colonial control, most measurable aspects of New Guinea highland societies were drastically altered. The single change in the amount of time spent in subsistence activities altered the balance of political power, the involvement of social groups in religious ceremonial, the balance of relations between the sexes, the distances travelled for trading, and a hundred and one other features. All listable features of "traditional culture" were retained in the repertory, and very few features added, so that studies made five years after technological change appeared entirely "traditional." Yet the "florescence" actually observed was quantitatively extremely unlike the drabness of life ten years earlier. Yet many fieldworkers, without a historical or economic sense, have interpreted their descriptions of steel-using times as though they corresponded with life in stone-using times. This has had no disadvantages for qualitative studies of symbolism, myth, child-training, etc., and the cultural continuity through cargo-cults, colonialism, and copper-mining is striking. But for more quantitative studies of politics, economics or of ecology the assumption of "traditionality" is questionable. At the very least it makes extremely suspect any studies of "long-term balanced adaptation to a physical environment." Not only is "balance" something that must be proved, not assumed, the idea of "adaptation" as "arrival at a relationship, through mutual negative feedback" is something that is extremely unlikely to occur within a ten year period.

RAPPAPORT'S ECOLOGICAL MODEL

Specifically Rappaport's (1968) analysis of Mareng pig feasts as an ecological mechanism, whereby religion automatically regulated crises of over-population by humans and pigs, suffers from all these difficulties. In the first place its figures on productivity were all obtained five years after pacification and twenty years after the first advent of steel axes; they say little about the state of crop production, pig populations and consumption even ten years earlier. Secondly, and this comment will be explicated later, the figures were all collected in villages which were in the last year of preparation for a pig feast. Thirdly, "there is reason to believe that Mareng occupation of the Simbai valley is relatively recent ... within the last 200 years" (Rappaport 1968: 36). With a population of 200 people now occupying 1,060 cleared acres in a total area of 2,033 acres it would seem unlikely that a "balance" has yet been reached between population and land, but rather that a continuous, if uneven, process of expansion averaging five acres per annum has been in progress over 200 years and still is occurring. Fourthly, the extreme intricacy in detail of the "adjustment" to the local environment of the Mareng analysed by Rappaport raises the twin questions of why other New Guinea Highland groups in different environments also have similar pig feasts, and of how the Mareng, within two hundred years, could have worked out by trial and error such a fine adjustment.

And finally (for the present argument) the literature on other New Guinea Highland societies where pig feasts are celebrated indicates that the population dynamics of pigs, which Rappaport takes as "natural" or inherent in pigs and something to which humans adapt, are, in fact, the result of deliberate planning by pig breeders. Pig feasts, and the crises which trigger the final slaughters are all matters of deliberate long-range planning. My own Siane data of 1952-53, for example, were collected mainly in a village that had had a pig feast two months before my arrival. During that year many pig owners explained to me their problems in ensuring that the two or three pigs which they had left after the slaughter would multiply for the next planned pig feast; any unexpected ceremonial demand for a pig during the first year can have disastrous consequences for planning. At the same time I was puzzled as to why farrows that I knew to have been of nine or ten piglets at birth were uniformly three young pigs when later censused; the answer is, of course, that although pig population must be made to grow exponentially to provide for a massive slaughter, it is only in the final generation before a killing that the exponential rate can be raised from a rate of doubling each year to quadrupling in the penultimate year; for the final year before a ceremony no piglets at all are bred but in early years the survival of piglets is consciously manipulated to increase slowly (Salisbury 1962:93). It is this final year that Rappaport witnessed – a year for which the Mareng had deliberately planned years in advance, knowing that the huge pig population would create huge demands on garden production of sweet potatoes to keep them fed until slaughter, and knowing what demands and problems to plan for. He would have obtained very different data on planning if he had studied a year later. Thus it may be noted that during my year among the Siane I saw no sweet potatoes at all being fed to pigs in villages which had recently celebrated pig feasts; foraging in fallowing gardens provided sufficient for all pigs. The crises, human and porcine, which Rappaport saw the pig feasts as being a ritual adaptation to, are best seen as the predictable working out of breeding programmes, planned to produce crises. Pig Feasts are causes, not effects, and I am sure Mareng would explain this to any anthropologist who asked, in just the way Siane do. In support of that argument I would cite the fact that the Siane, on religious grounds, gave up Pig Feasts in 1959; in 1966 they decided to reinstitute Pig Feasts "in order to make pigs grow big again" – something pigs had ceased to do when breeding and killing were being planned in terms of maintaining a constant size population. It is the deliberate planning for pig feasts that results in a greater total output of pork than would result from other human planning strategies.

CULTURAL EXTRAPOLATION MODELS

The family of non-equilibrium models that this New Guinea Highland experience directly suggests is that of cultural extrapolation – the analyst assumes that cultural rules as formulated explicitly by informants are followed in practice as far as they can be, and he projects empirical consequences until his projection indicates that constraints emerge. For pig feasts these rules would be those described for pig breeding, and for planning for competitive feasting at intervals. The major data given by Rappaport would then be interpretable as the attempt by Mareng breeders/feast-givers to follow the rules as far as possible, consistent with resource availability.

The long-term ecological model would then be one of Mareng initially moving into a "new" environment of primary forest, at low population density, giving small feasts using largely feral pigs; of gradual change in the human and pig population densities, in importance of domestication, in the frequency and size of pig feasts and in the associated political activities, as more primary forest was converted into arable bush-fallow land – with the dynamic being the entrepreneurial drive of the New Guinean pig-feaster; such progressive development of pig-feasting might endure for two or three hundred years, before limits to land productivity would necessitate a change in "the culture" away from competitive pig-breeding. Pig-breeding would not be an "adaptation" to a static environment, but the definer of a dynamic self-modifying culture. The culture, would, for a long time, adapt the environment so as to meet its own ends, but only after a very long time would the environment become selective against the culture, and then only *against* a critical feature of the culture – pig-breeding.

      Historical data are not yet available to specify such a definitive model for New Guinea Highland pig-breeding and feasting. Yet the archaeological picture of underlying continuity of populations, dramatic local changes with changing technologies of drainage and fencing, composting and changing crops, of taro, pueraria, and (two hundred years ago) of sweet potato (and recently of Irish potatoes) suggest that such a model may be constructed. The work of Brookfield (1968), Watson (1965) and White (1970) appears to lead in this direction, confounded, it is true, by arguments about whether changes were "revolutionary" or not. As it is, the present suggestions for Highland models remain speculative .

CULTURAL EXTRAPOLATION BY PHASES – THE TOLAI

      By contrast, recent work among the coastal Tolai people of New Britain (Salisbury 1970, 1973; Specht 1966) gives a fairly firm time horizon of between 700 and 1,000 years, for the expansion of a small population of around 100 within a defined geographical area, to a size of about 50,000 people in the same geographical terrain. The exercise of trying to interpret the "ethnographic present" of 1883 (Parkinson 1887) and 1961 (Salisbury 1970) as the working out of cultural rules derived from an earlier less densely populated period (with recent modifications of technology or social relationships), and of then iterating the process to arrive back at the founding 100 – although it may be empirically erroneous – is instructive about the nature of a particular model of cultural extrapolation.

      In the first place there have been many attempts to show how the "traditional ethnographic present" Tolai were in an equilibrium functional relationship with their environment of rich volcanic soils surrounding the harbour of Rabaul (e.g. Salisbury 1970, Epstein 1969, Bürger 1913). These attempts will be discussed as they highlight how the equilibrium is questionable. Since 1870 – the time of first European contact – there has been a rapid population growth from 20,000 to 50,000 in a hundred years, though pressure on land resources first surfaced only in the 1920's and became acute after World War II. Since 1950 land has been acquired in "foreign" areas, although at a rate less than proportionate to population growth. In 1961, the time of my first study, the Tolai still produced enough food locally to support their entire population. They themselves did not eat all they produced as they sold for cash large quantities of root crops and vegetables, for European residents in town, and for the feeding of immigrant workers in town and on European plantations; these sales balanced Tolai purchases of canned proteins (corned beef and fish) and storable carbohydrates (rice, sugar, biscuits). Less than a quarter of Tolai land was used for subsistence crops in 1961, however, the vast bulk being planted to cocoa and coconuts as cash crops. Local pressure on land was pressure to obtain higher cash incomes, aggravated by the alienation of about one third of their 1870 land for use by European plantations. It was not a matter of population density exceeding *subsistence* carrying capacity of the land.

In 1950 Tolais owned about 500 square miles of land, giving an average population density of less than 80 per square mile, but local densities of over 400 per square mile. If as much as a quarter of the land is under subsistence crops, the carrying capacity under subsistence agriculture of the fertile Tolai land would appear to be between 320 and 1,600 per square mile. By contrast, in 1870 the average density was below 30 per square mile, and no local group exceeded 150. Pressure for land can hardly be invoked as a Malthusian cause for a stable situation in 1870.

Nevertheless at this time, late ages of marriage, high bride-prices, small families due to spaced pregnancies, and considerable bachelorhood among non-wealthy men suggest that population growth was actually very slow, if not zero. An equilibrium theorist might argue that population was then spaced, at a level below one fourth of what would "fill" this ecological niche, by the endemic feuding, with cannibalism between groups of neighbouring hamlets which limited normal travel to a range of four or five miles. Contrasting with this local dispersion were several area-wide activities – ceremonials, held periodically in individual hamlets, to which people came from a wide area, and at which shell money was distributed (Salisbury 1965), local markets, for trade in the specialties of ecologically different but neighbouring villages; and long distance voyaging to obtain shells for manufacture into currency. But the extrapolationist would realise that although the feuding may have *acted* to limit population growth, it can hardly have been *introduced* because people valued low population growth; twenty years of Pax Germanica stopped warfare, lowered bride-prices, produced a lower age of marriage, and produced a 3% per annum population growth that was continuous thereafter except for the crises of an eruption in 1937 and occupation by 120,000 Japanese in World War II. A pre-existing cultural-valuation for ritual and shell money political entrepreneurship which had previously been checked by feuding and cannibalism, then worked itself out in ways which had marked consequences for population growth and man-land relationships.

But even the 1870 pattern of endemic entrepreneurial expansion constrained by feuding and cannibalism showed evidences of not being stable but of having changed during the preceding hundred years. Richard Parkinson (1887, 1907) suggested that the Tolai themselves were recent arrivals in the area from New Ireland, and his suggestions were widely adopted by other German writers. His strongest evidence, however (Bürger 1913:12) was of the importation of particular *tubuan* rituals from New Ireland or New Hanover less than a hundred years earlier. Whether this was the first importation of the rituals, or whether it involved the addition of a set of new variants to pre-existing local rituals is uncertain; my own evidence and collections of myths (e.g. Meier 1909) suggest the latter. Another field in which the 1870's evidenced recent change was that of overseas voyaging to find shell money. This appears as an infrequent and highly dangerous activity in the first ethnographies (Parkinson 1887, Powell 1884) but within twenty years (Kleintitschen 1906) had developed into regular annual exoduses using established over-night villages en route with major portions of villages temporarily absent. My own calculations of the rate of manufacture of new shell money suggest that at a period somewhat before 1780 enough shell could have been produced from Tolai beaches without the need for overseas voyaging, and that production since 1780 accounts for more than is now in circulation. The 1870 situation must be seen as the delayed result of dynamic forces already present in 1780.

Finally there is historical evidence that volcanic activity has produced changes in the environment. In 1878 islands emerged from the sea in Rabaul Harbour after an eruption of the local volcano; in 1937 two cones grew on opposite sides of the harbour, one from nothing to one thousand feet, and the other (Matupit cone) spewed out ash and mud over a wide area. The island of Matupit at the foot of the cone was reported in 1878 to have risen above the water only a few generations previously (Brown 1908) and this report is confirmed by Epstein's genealogical inquiries (1969). He reports myths of first settlement going back only a few generations, and a pattern of conflict over land rights almost unique among Tolai, but resembling what was ascribed by Burger (1913:17-18) to the effects of pioneer individualism on newly cultivated land. 1780 may well have been a volcanic eruption period.

The ardent equilibrium ecologist might then wish to go back beyond 1780 in his search for a stable equilibrium and might try and recreate the preceding, less populous society, without developed *tubuan* rituals or elaborate shell money, and probably without the internal political differentiation that both contribute to. Would it have had cannibalism? Probably not. Inter-village cannibalism would seem likely to have been part of a phenomenon of increasing political differentiation, whereby big men made use of population density and "sold" "troublemaking" supporters to big men of nearby groups in a pattern of elite collusion to buttress their own powers. Any "balance" would have had to exist in a very much simpler society than existed in 1870. And such a "balance" would probably not have had feuding and cannibalism to maintain it; it would have existed at a time of potential population expansion with much available land, before the advent of feuding and cannibalism as control mechanisms. In short, having started in a search for an equilibrium, one would have had to go back to before 1780, to a time when populations were much smaller, and when there would have been no apparent ecological constraint on expansion, and when "balance" would have been unlikely. At the same time one would have suggested how phases might have succeeded one another in a growth model.

There is local evidence for relatively static, non-dynamic agricultural populations in the region. In the ethnographic present the neighbouring people to the Melanesian-speaking Tolai are the non-Melanesian Baining. They had, before recent village consolidations, populations densities below one per square mile, and cultivated swidden patches in primary forest, rather than the long-fallow rotation of areas of secondary forest and grassland used in the Highlands and to some extent by the Tolai. It is hard to envisage a sharper cultural boundary than that between the Tolai and the Baining, and one which, before recent modifications, was more closely tied to the ecological boundary of the volcanic soils used by the Tolai.[2] Elsewhere in New Britain, in the other islands of the Bismark Archipelago, and in the Solomons, other enclaves of Melanesian speakers dot the coastline, while bordering sparsely populated areas are inhabited by non-Melanesian speakers. On linguistic (Goodenough 1961) and archaeological (White 1970) grounds the dispersal of a Melanesian-speaking stock, and the arrival of people using Lapita-type pottery on many of the islands has been placed about 3,500 years ago. Could it be that the emergence of an equilibrium between a static non-Melanesian agricultural population and a dynamic immigrant Tolai population had still not been established after 3,500 years of boundary interaction, sporadic warfare, and occasional trade for feathers, stone clubs, obsidian etc.?

The time-horizon is actually much shorter in the Tolai case. At a conference at Santa Cruz in 1971 on the Bismarck Archipelago the role of periodic catastrophes or unique events in the cultural evolution of small scattered populations such as the Baining was considered. In the Tolai area the periodic volcanic eruptions provide just such catastrophes. Specht's (1966) excavations of the island of Watom, just off the Tolai coast, indicate that the early bringers of Lapita-ware to the area, were in fact overwhelmed by a massive eruption that dumped ten feet of pumice on the island, twenty miles from the centre of the Rabaul crater. This eruption must have been of the same order as that which disrupted Krakatoa, blasting away completely the east side of an earlier crater about eight miles in diameter, and leaving deposits over a hundred feet thick near the crater edge. While a firm date has not been established for this cataclysm, J.M. Specht informs me that it must have been somewhat before 1250 A.D. and could have been several hundred years earlier. I shall use the figure of 1200 for convenience. Tolai occupation of the area now covered by the volcanic soils must date from after the eruption, which rendered the whole area sterile. It could have begun as early as 30 years after the eruption, if one is to judge by the first clearing of forest and planting of gardens on "new" land created by the 1937 emergence of Mt. Kalamanagunan. By 1971 these were under way. On the other hand a longer interval may have been necessary in the 13th century as the new cone of 1937 was not too far distant from reservoirs of seeds brought by winds or birds; the 1200 eruption must have desolated an area of up to 1,000 square miles.

With this background I was intrigued during fieldwork in 1971[3] to be insistently told myths of the first peopling of the area by Tolai, which I had not previously heard. Though they do not mention any volcanic eruption, they make no mention of a previous local population being present, and they are uncannily consistent with the picture of a steady intrusion of a new population into a vacant ecological niche created by a volcanic eruption. The places cited as the first and second settlements – the second occurring when the first split over a trivial conflict – were respectively at the east and west ends of the boundary between the pumice deposits and the non-volcanic soils. These would have been the first areas to become habitable after the eruption, offering an ecotone with the neighbouring primary forest (occupied presumably by Baining people) as the pumice weathered and vegetational colonisation occurred. No settlement was made on any intervening coastal site – presumably because that land was still sterile. The second settlement, the home site for all western Tolai, unfortunately proved disease-infested – it is low-lying and virulently mosquito-ridden even today – and the myth narrates sequences of moves by some groups inland along the ecotone of the forest-pumice boundary, and sequences of moves by other groups gradually north into the pumice area. The legendary original home site of the western Tolai was in fact unoccupied at the time of German takeover in 1883. The occupation of Matupit island in central Rabaul Harbour was narrated as a most recent stage of direct movement northward. The movement eastward around the forest boundary was rapidly completed, by a linking up with eastern Tolai groups who maintain no myth of a western origin. For both eastern and western groups subsequent movements are reported as mainly northward, towards the coast, but east-west ties are common and no sharp "border" can be demarcated between east and west.

This myth provides a base for extrapolation forwards to meet the extrapolation backward from ethnographic data. We have a picture of a single settlement in the eastern Tolai coast some time around 1200, of two boatloads of settlers (say 50 people). Our first assumption is of constant population expansion. Initially the period of doubling may have been every fifty years. The original settlement probably fissioned into two, of fifty each, about fifty years later, and one half migrated westward about 1250 and settled in vacant newly cultivable land. Disease and periodic moving may then be considered to have slowed the population increase but, assuming for simplicity a constant rate, the southern boundary of Tolai territory would probably have been demarcated, and groups of fifty first settlers located on all Tolai parishes by about 1450. The total population would have been 1,600, and the population density about three persons per square mile. Expansion to a population of 12,800 would then have taken until 1600 A.D. and would have involved the internal expansion within their own territories of these small kin groups to yield a density of 20 per square mile. Slowing population expansion thereafter with the next doubling taking up to 200 years, and stability thereafter would have gone along with progressive increase in political differentiation, in the power of descent groups and the development of feuding and ritual. Such an assumed development accounts for most available ethnographic facts.

Put in more general terms the Tolai "model," is one of a population colonising a vacant niche. In the first phase of expansion by doubling every 50 years, fission and the definition of boundaries and territories were crucial. Internal expansion and occupation of a defined niche then proceeded at probably a slightly reduced rate for a long period depending on local soil fertility and ease of transport. The density-linked control mechanism braking population growth would then seem to have been brought about by increasing internal political differentiation, produced as higher population density gave opportunities for political entrepreneurs.

DISCUSSION

This scenario sounds plausible, but lacks proof. Its strongest support is the way in which it takes features which equilibrium models proved unable to incorporate, and builds them into a consistent picture, through the use of two assumptions: 1) that a human population will double in fifty years, unless constraints operate to prevent this, and 2) that cultural rules, reported in the present, have usually had a long existence but many form part of very different sets of actualized social behaviours as resource availability varies.

It also suggests particular phenomena that could be studied archaeologically or by comparative ethnology. In the first place it suggests how small populations having sea transportation can establish themselves in small particularly fertile, coastal niches, and within a relatively short space of time can, through simple demographic expansion, appear dominant over a wide area, where nearby sparse, moving, swidden populations face more severe restraints. The Tolai today form one of the largest single language groups in New Guinea and their educational level has enabled them to become dominant in the national bureaucracy of independent Papua-New Guinea. It is hard to realise from the present situation that they were only two boatloads of settlers 700 years ago.

The model also suggests a long time-horizon for processes of adaptation and equilibration. The phase of establishment and definition of territorial boundaries may require hundreds of years. Internal expansion within boundaries may also last further centuries before active expansion outside the cultural boundaries takes place. The fertility of Tolai soil and the size of the area they initially marked out are, indeed, exceptional, so that their extremely long internal expansion phase is probably unique. Until the nineteenth century it had possibly involved an abnormally long period of no external conflicts. Nonetheless lack of competition between coastal Melanesian speakers and interior speakers of non-Melanesian languages is reported elsewhere also. Intermittent trading relations for special products in an ample and permissive land environment was the normal rule and the reported Tolai raiding of coastal Baining groups for slaves in the 1870's may well have been a recent development.

None of this is to argue that volcanic eruptions have been the major factor in the establishment of Melanesian-speaking groups throughout New Guinea. It is merely to argue that eruptions provide the most dramatic examples of completely new and vacant ecological niches of considerable productivity being created, and permitting local expansion. Changes in coastlines, minor climatic shifts in rain shadow areas, introductions of new plants and many other features could have comparable though less dramatic effects, while the periodic extinction of local sparsely populated groups by stochastic processes would also explain the creation of vacant areas.

A third use of a model such as this is an aid to thought. Although the Tolai example is derived largely from induction, the thought processes that have gone into it are analysable. Most important is the explicit use of the assumption that "cultural rules" (Salisbury 1968; Bailey 1969) obtained in ethnological description from informants' statements are a highly stable aspect of social behaviour. Such "cultural rules" should be contrasted with the realisation of those rules in actual behaviour and the *strategy statements* (Salisbury 1968) [or *pragmatic rules* (Bailey 1969)] used to summarize appropriate behaviour, which vary according to the quantitative parameters of the environment. Leach's (1961) demonstration of this contrast for Ceylon is a classic study. Among the environmental parameters, land availability, population density, productivity of technology, and the state of the natural environment are highly important. When the social anthropologist quantitatively records social behaviour at one particular time and in one place, he is not describing a balanced adaptation to a specific environment, but one specific realisation of the cultural rules, by particular people who modify their behaviour to cope with particular parametric constraints of time and place.

Critical in constructing such models is the isolation of what are relatively invariant rules, and what are significant parameters. The intellectual process of modelling and model manipulation enables one to try out many alternative possibilities, but one starts empirically. In ethnographic fieldwork one can deliberately look at, say, a land-rich village and at a land-poor village within a group that asserts its cultural unity (cf. Goldschmidt et al. 1965), to see what "cultural rules" are asserted in both areas, and what specific environmental differences condition the behavioural differences found in the two localities. One can look at different cultural groups with a single cultural rule in common; one can compare sub-groupings of a cultural group and how they act when a range of environmental parameters is varied.

But the primary parameter that any archaeologist or culture historian should always hypothetically vary as a first step is population density. He should ask how a society with the current cultural rules would have operated with a population half its size, and a quarter its size. Depending on assumptions of population increase rates these scenarios would represent 50,100, 200 or 400 years ago. Lesser political or economic complexity would be indicated on general grounds, but existing cultural rules would also suggest many specifics such as whether settlements would have been nucleated or dispersed, whether descent groups would have been large and solidary, or constantly fragmenting into local segments.

In the Tolai case, for example, the twin current rules of matrilineal land tenure (Salisbury 1970:68-71) – that "clan land" is inherited by the sister's son, whereas a man may pass "family land," which he has cleared from forest or otherwise acquired personally, to any person he determines (usually his own children) – clearly have different implications whether "new" land is available or not for conversion into "family land," and these implications further affect the degree of solidarity of matrilineal descent groups, the proliferation of new sub-groupings and their later consolidation into new corporate matrilineages. In fact in the perspective of a society that has land available at its frontier, the rules make better sense than they do now. If one envisages an early period of whole territories of forest, each of three or four square miles, inhabited by single viri-avunculocal matrilineal groups of less than 50 persons it would be expected that these could expand internally several times with little fission over centuries. Even above these population densities, fission of matrilineal groups by male children leaving their natal household, yet clearing new sites for dwelling within the territory owned by their father's clan could have been a common practice, producing internal differentiation. It is widely reported for other matrilineal societies. Eventual institutionalization of such new groupings in their separate clearings as local sub-clans of exogamous major clans is what is stated by modern Tolai beliefs about sub-clan origin sites (*madapai*). The relatively stable period of Tolai internal expansion could be visualised as crystallising an organization of each "village" territory as comprising two or four resident sub-clans, each a section of different non-localized clans. At this point moiety exogamy (a firm current cultural rule) would have modified itself to being consistent with the present predominant village endogamy, where earlier it would have required village exogamy. With further population increase village endogamy could have led to less frequent inter-locality relations, more power in the hands of authoritarian big men who could control local marriages and could prevent further clan fission. The scene would then have been set for the proliferation of shell money exchanges among big men, for inter-village feuding and cannibalism and for the social life of the mid-nineteenth century. The basic cultural rules of matrilineal land tenures can be seen as implying vastly different social arrangements under different quantitative conditions of population density.

This process of projecting backward is, in some ways, an exact opposite of the process of functionalist equilibrium analysis. In the latter type of analysis one may indeed consider what would happen if parameters were to change (usually by growth) from what they are at present, but only to argue that such change is currently being prevented by some homeostatic mechanism, or else the society would not be the way it now is. Cultural extrapolation tries to see if the present is intelligible as growth from a past, without assuming that any mechanism producing homeostatis has necessarily come into play.

It involves taking a long time perspective. If behaviours exist which do now counteract expansion – limits on the primary forest land available for initial clearing, for example – they must be considered. But not as features that the society *adapted* to in the past. They may constitute the limits beyond which a society cannot in future expand, given existing cultural rules: but the reaching of those limits may take a hundred or more years even with the most rapid expansion. Generally it seems likely that at any one time more societies are in phases of expansion lasting several centuries, than are in states of dynamic equilibrium, mediated by feedback mechanisms, with their environment. Europe, South and Southeast Asia, Africa south of the Sahara, and central America have all been involved in rapid social and technological change for the past fifteen hundred years; during those fifteen hundred years it is the rare exception to find a period lasting over 300 years in which there has been "stability."

Periods of apparent stability, such as the European middle ages, have seen massive depopulations through epidemic disease, but these depopulations, though they may be seen as an epidemiological reaction to greater population density, have not been periods of "balanced feedback," but rather as catastrophic statistical accidents in a growth curve.

A final point, that this use of a growth model for understanding Tolai society brings out, is the need at some point to incorporate cultural innovation into the model. Although many of the rules of present-day culture (such as the land-tenure concepts listed earlier) can be easily visualised in the context of a different stage of population growth, others cannot. Some present-day rules may be innovated strategy statements, that have only recently become accepted as cultural rules. Some of these changes may be historically documented; others may be indicated by model manipulation.

For example, the current extravagance in the use of shell money among the Tolai, I find incongruent with a population smaller than 10,000 in the area, though complex shell-money systems such as that of Rossel Island (Salisbury 1968) *can* exist with population densities of less than 2 persons per square mile, and using a total of only a few thousand shells. An early simpler system of shell money perhaps dating from original Tolai settlement, could easily be visualized as subject to local elaboration and innovation (with political connotations) as exchanges became more frequent.

This suggestion (and similar suggestions about the relative recency of cannibalism, and of *tubuan* ceremonials), I have earlier derived more directly from historical and oral evidence. But using a cultural extrapolation model as a tool for hypothetical analysis, I maintain, would have thrown up the same elements as anomalous ones, given earlier periods of lower population. To phrase this another way, any extrapolation backwards should always consider successively eliminating one of the current cultural rules from each calculation, hypothesizing it as having been an innovation of the time period under consideration. A whole family of alternative reconstructions would thus be possible as different rules were successively considered as innovations; the most probable reconstructions would serve as guides in the search for hard evidence of specific innovations, either archaeologically or through literary or oral history. Using a model, however, permits the search to become explicit and reasoned.

210

CONCLUSION

As this paper developed, I have steadily realised how close many of its formulations come to those expounded by Kroeber (1943) in his *Configurations of Culture Growth*. It also sees societies with cultural rules, elaborating and playing with those rules, and applying them to varying environmental settings to provide varied realisations of the culture over centuries of time. Like Kroeber it sees the dynamic in this cultural variation as being individual inventiveness in modifying rules to fit personal circumstances. Culture, in short, does not itself adapt to environments but is the means through which *individuals* adapt to their environment which, they as individuals and in the short term, take as "given." Culture develops, elaborates, or stagnates in a process of individual cultural innovation. The vast majority of innovations, like minor genetic mutations, are unrelated to survival, either by individuals or by culture. But the richness in number of innovations occurring (the complexity of a culture and the variability of possible individual behaviours within it) does lead to a greater possibility that *some* survival-related behaviours will occur and will be selected for. Selective pressure when it eventually develops, can then most rapidly favour particular mutations if a previous period of affluent cultural expansion has permitted increasing variability.

But the conclusion is also that "adaptation" of whole cultures to environments (either as a static state, or as a feedback process) occurs only rarely. A state of "balance" may have existed among some hunting groups, living in the same slowly changing environments for thousands of years. But the two hundred or more years needed for the selective elimination of maladaptive cultural traits in a constant environment, that would appear needed to produce a state of adaptive balance, is a rare phenomenon in the world of agricultural societies. Even then the elimination of whole societies would seem most common; not a specific selection against the maladaptive feature itself but a collapse of all features of the culture. People rarely learn the lesson of what is maladaptive. The alleged crisis in Rome because of lead-poisoning from the plumbing, would be an example of an unselective elimination of a whole society, which did not solve the problem itself; a better adaptation did not occur as a result of the catastrophe. Crises of over-population may, as Geertz (1963) has shown, unselectively eliminate highly efficient technological systems in favour of a much more intensive "involuted" agriculture which produces a greater total output, but at a much higher cost. Again, the catastrophe is unlikely to produce a balance between people and environment.[4]

Cultural ecology should be looking, not for examples of stable adaptations to stable environments, but for the processes whereby unstable societies with relatively stable cultures cope flexibly with environmental change.

Notes

1. Fieldwork among both the Siane and the Tolai has been conducted at various times with the support of the Australian National University, the University of California, the U.S.P.H.S. grant MH-4912, McGill University, the Canada Council, and H.H., the Administrator of Papua New Guinea. For discussions leading up to the present paper I would like to thank Ann Chowning, Ward Goodenough, Jim Specht, Peter White, John Terrell, Dale ToPin, Tirupia, ToMange and Titai. The paper itself was first presented at the Smithsonian Conference on Biogeographical Models, May 1974.

2. The physical anthropological boundary is not so clear; Tolai and Baining appear phenotypically to be more similar than Tolai are to other Melanesian speakers from Bougainville or Papua; the latter appear more similar to neighbouring non-Melanesian speakers than to other Melanesians.

3. This fieldwork was as a consultant investigating causes of dispute among the Tolai, one of which was a resettlement project, involving the site listed in the myth. Details of the myth, particularly local place names, are given in Salisbury (1973): the present article explores the significance of the myth and modifies some of the figures hypothesized earlier.

4. Contrary to Boserup's (1965) view that innovation occurs in response to population pressure, my position is clearly that innovation occurs much more frequently within cultural systems that have not reached a tight limit within a particular environment. It is, however, in affluent societies where multiple alternatives have already become available, that increasing population pressure can then lead to the selective elimination of technologies that are maladaptative under those conditions, and thus to the institutionalisation of changed technologies.

REFERENCES

Bailey, F. G. 1969. *Stratagems and Spoils.* New York: Schocken.

Boserup, E. 1965. *The Conditions of Agricultural Growth.* Chicago: Aldine.

Brookfield, H. C. and J. P. White. 1968. "Revolution or Evolution in the Prehistory of the New Guinea Highlands." *Ethnology,* 7: 43-52.

Brown, G. 1908. *George Brown D.D.* London: Hodder & Stoughton.

Bürger, F. 1913. *Die Küsten und Bergvölker der Gazelle Halbinsel.* Stuttgart: Strecker und Schröder.

Epstein, A. L. 1969. *Matupit.* London: C. Hurst.

Geertz, C. 1963. *Agricultural Involution.* Berkeley: University of California Press.

Goldschmidt et al. 1965. "Variation and Adaptability of Culture, a Symposium." *American Anthropologist,* 67: 400-447.

Golson, J. 1966. "Archaeological Prospects in Melanesia." in Yawata, I. and Y. H. Sinoto (eds.), *Prehistoric Culture in Oceania.* Honolulu: B.P. Bishop Museum.

Goodenough, W. H. 1961. "Migration Implied by Relations of New Britain Dialects to Central Pacific Languages." *Journal of the Polynesian Society,* 72: 78-100.

Kleintitschen, A. 1906. *Die Kütenbewohner der Gazelle Halbinsel.* Hiltrup: Herz Jesu Missionshaus.

Kroeber, A. L. 1943. *Configuration of Culture Growth.* Berkeley. University of California.

Leach, E. R. 1961. *Pul Eliya.* Cambridge: University Press.

Meier, J. 1909. *Mythen und Erzählungen der Küstenbewohner der Gazelle halbinsel.* Vol. l. Vienna: Anthropos Bibliotek.

Parkinson, R. 1887. *Im Bismarck Archipel.* Leipzig: F.A. Brockhaus.

------------1907. *Dreissig Jahre in der Südsee.* Stuttgart: Strecker und Schröder.

213

Powell, W. 1884. *Wanderings in a Wild Country*. London: Sampson Low.

Rappaport, R. A. 1968. *Pigs for the Ancestors*. New Haven: Yale University.

Salisbury, R. F. 1957. Economic Change among the Siane Tribes of the New Guinea Highlands. Ph. D. thesis. Canberra: Australian National University.

------------1962. *From Stone to Steel*. Melbourne and Cambridge: University Press.

------------1966. "Politics and Shell-money Finance in Britain." in Swartz, M. and A. Tuden (eds.), *Political Anthropology*. Chicago: Aldine.

------------1968. "Formal Analysis in Anthropological Economics; The Rossel Island Case." in Buchler, I. and H. G. Nutini (eds.), *Game Theory and the Behavioral Sciences*. Pittsburgh: University Press.

------------1970 *Vunamami: Economic Transformation in a Traditional Society*. Berkeley: University of California Press.

------------1973. "The Origins of the Tolai People." *Journal of the Papua New Guinea Society*, 8: 79-84.

Sharp, R. L. 1952. "Steel Axes for Stone-Age Australians." *Human Organization*, 11: 17-22.

Watson, J. B. 1965. "The Significance of a Recent Ecological Change in the Central Highlands of New Guinea." *Journal of the Polynesian Society*, 74: 438-450.

White, J. P. 1970. "New Guinea: The First Phase of Oceanic Settlement." in Green, R. and M. Kelly (eds.), *Studies in Oceanic Culture History*. Honolulu: B.P. Bishop Museum.

11.

INTRODUCTION – *VUNAMAMI:*

ECONOMIC TRANSFORMATION IN A TRADITIONAL SOCIETY

by

Richard F. Salisbury

Source: *Vunamami: Economic Transformation in a Traditional Society.*
Berkeley: University of California Press, 1970. pp. 1-16.

Can the non-industrial countries achieve sustained economic development using their own resources alone? This book's answer is "Yes, given adequate resources, and given the right social changes during development." The answer is based on a detailed study of ninety years of development in a small society in New Guinea. A succession of technological changes, each one associated with a political change, has led the society to the threshold of sustained development – a net capital investment of from 10 to 23 percent of income, almost 100 percent literacy, and rapidly rising incomes. Although much of the study does describe the economics and history of the society, the focus is on the nature of the internal political changes, which, it is argued, have been the crucial factors, turning pre existing conditions conducive to development, and available technological knowledge, into the reality of development.

The focus on internal factors producing growth does not deny the importance of external factors – overseas finance, technical know-how, and advice and personnel to create an infrastructure of social services. Technological knowledge indeed is fundamental to growth, but the other factors only facilitate it, though the assumption is often made that they are the causes for it. They are the factors most often stressed by economic advisers and planners from overseas – largely because they are the factors that can be most easily contributed from overseas. Yet too many people in the developing countries themselves – administrators and expatriates in particular – tend to make the jump to assuming that they are the *only* important factors. What is needed internally, such people argue, is to remove barriers which prevent the external inputs from being effective – local disincentives to saving, political instability discouraging foreign investment, low levels of skill or productivity in labour, rigid social barriers which discourage efficiency, or corruption which diverts investment into private gains. For such people the volume of external aid is of first importance with the readiness of the recipients to learn how to use it "properly" a second need.

Such a formulation presents a gloomy prospect to the people of low-income countries. Rich countries are increasing their per capita income faster, both absolutely and proportionately, than the poor countries. Aid would need to increase beyond any contemplated present level if it were to counteract this process. Nor does income from imports promise to increase greatly. Prices for exports from low-income countries have declined, virtually as productivity has increased, while the prices of machinery from high-income countries have risen. At the same time repayment and interest due for loans already incurred take an increasing amount of earnings. Further borrowing and further debts seem to indicate a future of bondage. Since most low-income countries have high birth rates, it is as much as many of them can do to sustain present per capita incomes. Self-help, though desired by many, seems to offer little; it means reducing barriers, but not providing positive growth.

This pessimistic view, the present study argues, is not necessarily justified. On the one hand, pessimism is based on a false view that "traditional society" was inherently unchanging and economically stagnant. The speed of change in societies before they were contacted by literary cultures is hard to document, even in New Guinea, where Europeans were making first contacts in the interior even into the 1950's. Yet it is clear that crops like tobacco and sweet potatoes had spread rapidly across the country well before Europeans arrived (Riesenfeld 1951, Watson 1965), dramatically altering the economies of many areas. Cult movements were endemic long before European contact (Salisbury 1958), and groups prided themselves on their cultural borrowings from elsewhere (Mead 1938). What was seen by the first European explorers was not "age-old traditions persisting for centuries," but the current versions of rapidly changing sets of behaviours. If the adoption of manioc in Africa (Jones 1959) and the American adoption of the horse (Ewers 1955) are guides, similar rapid changes within traditional non-industrial societies were common in other parts of the world too. Unreasoning conservatism was not characteristic of "traditional society." Experimentation was (and is) constant, but it is necessarily on a small scale when a crop failure can mean starvation. Innovations must be clearly successful before they are widely accepted, yet once they are widely accepted the outside observer without historical records has difficulty in realizing that they have not always been part of the local scene.

Nor are traditional societies internally homogeneous. True, almost every adult male may be a farmer, and so a village appears homogeneous to an external and superficial observer. Yet every farmer is different, and the differences in the size of his family, in area of land owned, in political aspirations, in technical knowledge, or in energy profoundly affect his farming. Each subsistence farmer's running of his farm is much more significantly different from every other farmer's than is the running of different machines by operatives in a factory. The farmer must make highly complex decisions: he must, in a subsistence society, visualize how much land must be planted to feed his household until the next-harvest-but-one is ready; he must make allowances for contingencies of weather, or social needs like weddings or funerals throughout that period; he must evaluate crop possibilities in terms of land types available to him; if he practices bush fallow, he must think of how the cultivating of a particular piece of land now will affect his children twenty years hence; he must plan his work so that the necessary weeding of one crop does not coincide with the time needed for planting a second or harvesting a third; he must think ahead to how he can get additional labour over and above that of his household for major tasks like fencing or harvesting; he must anticipate capital needs by months or years so that scarce imported requirements are on hand when needed; to accumulate pigs for a wedding feast he must begin breeding years ahead. Even if all farmers had the same level of technical knowledge, their plans would be expected to differ, as their labour and land resources, as their consumption needs, and as the risks they are willing to run also differ. In fact vast differences in technical knowledge abound. Much technical knowledge is embodied in rules which, to the city dweller, seem part of an immutable cultural heritage, known to everyone – everyone knows you make hay when the sun shines. But much of the total corpus of knowledge in a village is not known to everyone, nor is it universally available. Particular lineages own particular varieties of seed yam; different families swear by different herbs to be used for blessing gardens; good fishing and hunting sites are jealously kept secrets; fathers pass on knowledge of soil types to their sons alone, in the course of cultivating familial land. No theory of economic development is adequate if it ignores the calculating abilities, the entrepreneurial tendencies, or the range of individual variation found among traditional farmers.

The false view of "traditional society" as necessarily conservative, unchanging, and homogeneous has indeed been fostered by many anthropologists even as they have gone beyond the point of view of the superficial outside observer. In trying to show the wealth of knowledge, the cultural richness, and the intricate interconnectedness of activities in other societies they have often generalized their descriptions of diversity and talked about uniform "cultures," organized bodies of "rules of behaviour" verbalized by informants, or "norms" abstracted from the observation of diverse behaviour. They analyse the rules as being logically consistent, so that any other behaviour is seen as deviant or illogical. They treat the "rules" not as statistical central tendencies or technical precepts but as moral norms, enforced by social control mechanisms and conformed to by everyone but deviants. The compelling force of "tradition" is assumed, when the "rules" may often be little more

217

than practical suggestions which leave the choice of actual behaviour open to the individual. Other tasks than haying may take precedence even in sunshine.

A different picture emerges, however, when field anthropologists initially assume that the behaviour they observe is the result of a choice by the actor among other alternatives.[1] The assumption is supported, since actors can always, when properly questioned, give coherent reasons *in their own terms* for their behaviour. In their own terms they can outline the calculations that they made in choosing. Three main tasks confront the economic anthropologist who has data of this kind. He must first properly translate the terms that the informants use to describe their economic calculations, and must never assume that the terms have exactly the same connotations as those used in the intellectual discipline of economics. But he must be aware that his translation is being made for people versed in the terminology of "economics" and so must relate the two terminologies. His second task is to relate local economical terminology to its background in the local society and culture – to show, for example, how different categories of land or land tenure are associated with different types of social grouping, or with different religious concepts. His third task is to record in quantitative terms the decisions that people make, and to determine how the decisions are in fact related to the various decision criteria listed earlier. The economic anthropologist expects the final answer to be that the decisions are "rational" given the uncertainties involved, the variable resources of different farmers, or the extremely high costs of alternative courses of action. They may turn out, unexpectedly, to be empirically "irrational" and the reasons for irrationality must be sought.

Much of the present study, particularly in the second part, is a documentation of the economic calculations, the economic terminology, the social background, and the quantitative implications of such calculations among a group of Tolai villagers in New Britain. No argument is explicitly made against anthropologists or economists who assume that people living in "traditional societies" are "bound by custom" or are "inherently conservative." An exposition of the facts is enough to show the falsity of the assumptions on which such theories are based. The reader should bear in mind during the exposition of Tolai economic concepts, with which each chapter starts, that the aim is to demonstrate quantitatively how these concepts underlie the decisions that are made. This demonstration is, I feel, the main contribution of the study to economic anthropology.

But if simple societies show such diversity and such internal rationality, how can the present study be reconciled with studies of economic development such as those of Rostow (1960), Hagen (1961), and McClelland (1961), in which a stagnant, unchanging, traditional society forms an integral part of the theory? Before concluding that the theories themselves are incorrect, one must examine several alternatives. It may well be that the sort of society called "traditional" by such theorists is a stereotype, based on stagnant agricultural societies of Latin America and South and East Asia (usually of "peasant" type), which is inapplicable to the sub-sistence-based societies found in the Pacific, Africa, or North America. If this is true, and I shall later discuss evidence supporting this answer, then the present study should be viewed as complementing theories about stagnant traditional societies with one analysing the development process in "dynamic traditional societies."

The second alternative is that such theorists have postulated stag-nant unchanging society in the pre-change situation merely in order to construct a hypothetical model, and not with the intention of generalizing about real societies. With this single assumption about the internal conditions of a society, the way is open for discussing only inputs into the system from outside and for relating changes in the total system only to those exogenous forces. But such a procedure deals only with exogenous forces; it assumes that endogenous forces are either negligible, or are randomly related to the exogenous forces and so cancel out in a study of the latter. Again, the present work, in discussing mainly endogenous developmental forces, complements studies dealing only with exogenous development. But at the same time it should be noted that to the extent that the presence of developmental forces with-in traditional societies facilitates or reinforces the working of exogenous forces, to that extent the amount of variation apparently explained by theories of the latter type must be reduced by the amount due to interaction between endogenous and exogenous forces.

Finally, theorists may have assumed that "traditional societies" are stagnant simply because they were working from faulty primary descriptions. The present study suggests that for historical materials, as well as for old-style anthropo-logical reports, this may very likely be true. Reports of a small-scale society written by external observers, knowing the society for only a short period, will describe it as unchanging during that period. The reports tend to be of topics that interest the out-side observer – the way of life of plantation owners for the tourist attracted to gra-cious living, the administration of law and order for the government official. Histories are usually compiled from just such written accounts. The historian reads each observer's report, and can place it in terms of the history of the country from which the observer came; he can place it in terms of the innovations of expatriates reported by earlier observers. The results inevitably focuses on the way in which for-eigners, or events in the outside world, bring local change out of stagnation. An equally intensive study of local (oral) sources is needed to place the events in a local historical sequence of dynamic events.

Historians are not unaware of the biases of their sources. A modern social historian, by cross-checking differing accounts, by critically appraising the influence of differing viewpoints on the testimony of missionaries, traders, government officials, or visiting travellers, and by compiling statistics, can often disprove the accuracy of particular documents. He can give a plausible approximation of the truth. But he still gives a version in which the local people – "the natives" – appear as puppets, moved by the action of foreigners, or, where the observer could see no reasons for what the locals did, as "irrational savages swayed by impulse, emotion, and tradition."

Part One is an attempt to review the history of the Tolai people of Vunamami village as it might be written by a social historian with access only to written records.[2] To some extent its purpose is that of illustrating how different would be a history written by the people themselves, as attempted in Part Two. But it also highlights the merits of such a historian's account. Such an account is easily understood by the foreigner – he knows about the voyages of discovery, missionaries, traders, and colonial administrators, and can gradually be introduced to the exotica of New Britain. One can more easily remember a sequence of local events if they are presented within a wider chronology of German imperial expansion, the First World War, the Depression, and the Second World War. And most important, on particular topics – the dating of events in absolute chronology, the identities of Europeans, and to a lesser extent statistical magnitudes-written accounts are reliable where local memories definitely are not.

The value of having compiled a documentary history became evident when collecting oral materials. Nearly every event that a foreign observer reported was remembered by local people (at second hand for most events before 1890), who would describe it with great circumstantial detail. Names mentioned briefly in written reports stimulated long discourses on where they lived, or what their clan was, and/or what events had occurred in their lives. This kind of detail (along with ethnographic information) indicated that in almost every case the foreign observer had misunderstood what the local people were doing, had misinterpreted the effects of his own actions, and was unaware of the local circumstances surrounding the events he observed. But though each event could be put into a local context, it would have been very hard to construct even a relative chronology for events that were not considered to have even a casual connection, and no suggestion of the complex motives of foreigners could be reconstructed from local accounts. Foreigners' descriptions here complemented local narrative.

Thus in the history of Part One, development appears to be entirely exogenous, as many theories of development assume it to be. The remainder of the book reconstructs the fuller history obtained by taking both the foreign "bird's-eye view" of documents and the local "worm's-eye view" of oral accounts. It shows how, although the bird's eye history may describe real events, it consistently misinterprets them. It omits almost all mention of development by self-help, of local people selectively utilizing knowledge made available to them and incorporating it into their own economic planning, of local people organizing themselves *against* foreigners as much as because of them, and following the creative leadership of their own big men. By contrast, the balanced history is one in which continuity is evident, where at all times the local people can be seen as trying to make rational choices in situations of great novelty, and in the face of tremendous ignorance of the long-term consequences of their actions.

Understanding the past in this way presupposes that one also understands the indigenous economic concepts, by an anthropological analysis of the kind already described. With minor exceptions, these economic *concepts* of the Vunamami people do not appear to have changed since the 1880's, when the first ethnologies of the area were written by Parkinson (1887) and Danks (1887). Marketing ideas of equivalence, and categories of payments for labour, or of title to land changed very little between the 1880's and the 1960's. But the decisions that individuals made at various times have changed dramatically as the types of goods entering the market changed, as populations rose and fell, as alternative demands for labour arose, and as new crops altered the balance of agriculture.

The plan of the second part of the book reflects the interplay between ethnohistory and economic anthropology. Each chapter considers a different aspect of the economic life of Vunamami village. It presents the relevant Tolai economic concepts first, and then relates those concepts to the situation as it was when Europeans first arrived in the area. It traces how in that particular aspect of economic life events succeeded one another until the present – specifically until 1961, but more generally until the period from about 1958 to 1963 for which detailed observations were available. Each chapter concludes by analysing the relevant economic activities of Vunamami, as they were observed during the ethnographic "present," as the results both of history and of local economic decisions.

As outlined thus far, the book is merely an analytical description of one history of successful economic development, dependent for its novelty on a combination of the methods of the oral historian and of the economic anthropologist concerned with formal microanalysis. Both of these techniques, it is maintained, give insights that are not available to workers relying on written history, on macroeconomic analysis, or on descriptions utilizing only the concepts of the discipline of economics. Part Three shifts focus and tries to relate this pattern of successful economic development to the political events that accompanied each economic change, both empirically and in theoretical terms. Chapter 9 pulls together references to the most important economic innovators, and by tracing their life histories indicates how their innovations fitted within their political careers, and within the options of choice open to them at different ages. Chapter 10 sees their political innovations as changes within a total political *system*. It shows the interconnections between the changing political system and the institutionalization of economic innovations. The whole is presented as a formal model of development, in which progressively greater political consolidation is the dynamic force.[3]

Models of development based on micro-analysis of small societies are not common in the literature (see Hill 1966). The present model is most clearly derived from a model advanced earlier (Salisbury 1957, 1962a) to explain the effect of technological improvement in inducing social change. It was based on a study of the consequences of introducing steel axes into a prosperous Highland New Guinea society, the Siane, some twelve years before the area was brought under Australian administrative control. Briefly, the new tools at first produced no increase in production, for diet was (and is) adequate, and consumer goods were few; their efficiency meant that less time was used to produce the same amount of needed goods. The time set free was used for politicking, ceremonials, legal disputes, and fighting. Individuals who proved effective in this lively period consolidated control of larger groupings than had previously had a unified control. Australian administrators confirmed them in their new-found positions when they took over administrative control in 1945. They also found a ready supply of young underemployed men eager to earn the ceremonial valuables which the politicians had used to successfully in the previous decade. Indentured migrant labour was avidly adopted and consumer luxuries became widespread. Only in 1953 did increased capital investment occur with the building of roads and airstrips and the planting of coffee under the leadership of the big men. These new capital investments promised to yield sufficient income locally to supply the consumption demands which had by then arisen. All seemed set for the beginning of a new cycle of change, based on a new crop-processing technology.

The types of consumer demands found at different times were seen as the major indices of the phases in the cycle – demands for power-yielding valuables immediately after a labour-saving innovation; demands for consumer luxuries by many aspiring people after political consolidation; demands for capital goods and for mass consumption of what had formerly been "luxuries" in the final stage. The major dynamic forces of the model, however, were seen as the perfect elasticity of political activity by big men in the early phase: following Parkinson's law, it expands to fill whatever time is available for it. In the next phase came emulation of the leaders by the population at large, and an increased tolerance for individualism after political consolidation spread the demand for luxuries. In the final phase of capital investment (and possibly new innovation) two forces were active: economies of scale or organizational efficiency facilitated production, and affluence permitted the establishment of new inventions.

Although this micro-model could be applied to several other small case studies (e.g., Kwakiutl, Maori, Tiv, Chagga, Hawaii, Nupe, Lapps),[4] it clearly did not apply to others (Fiji, Truk, Samoa, Australian Aborigines, Mundurucu, Tzintzuntzan, Ojibwa). One important difference seemed to be that it applied in societies where significant political decisions were still taken at the local level; it did not apply when local decision-making was in the hands of outsiders such as traders, officials, or non-local bureaucrats. Banfield (1958) and Foster (1965) also see political apathy in villages as typical of town-dominated peasant societies.

A second limitation of the model is implied by the lack of increase in production following increased productivity (see Nash 1965). This would occur only if existing demand for food and subsistence requisites were already met – in other words, in a relatively affluent society. Overpopulation, pressure on land, or food shortage would mean that productivity increases would result directly in increased production; no time would be set free for political consolidation, organizational innovation, and the development of new consumer demands. It is to just such areas of south and southwest Asia, Latin America, and southern Europe, where land shortage and overpopulation are problems and where the solution appears to be to absorb the unemployed population by urbanization and industrialization, that most specialists in development have paid attention. In such countries wage levels are already low because of such unemployment, and labour-saving techniques depress wage levels further. In countries with available land, where wage rates are high (in real if not in money terms), so the model would maintain, technological innovation can provide for growth without any decline in wage levels. Labour needs to be absorbed in *either* manufacturing *or* service occupations at the same rate as it is freed from agricultural production; consumer demand must increase to absorb new manufactures or services. High wage rates make this possible, again provided that they are not used to purchase imports alone. Parallel explorations on the macro-model level of the significance for development of gains in agricultural productivity have been conducted by an increasing number of economists in recent years – by Boserup (1965) in Denmark, Colin Clark (1964) in England, Fisk in Australia, and by several workers in Latin America. The present study was designed to contribute further to this field, by improving the anthropological micro-model of the Siane.

Several considerations were involved in the design of the study. An area was sought showing the same end result of successful economic and social

223

development with indigenous political involvement, but where development had continued for a much longer period. A larger historical study and an analysis of its phases would show first how general was the succession of phases isolated for the Siane, and second whether the process described was a single unique process – the emergence of a society from subsistence agriculture – or a cyclical repetitive process. In so far as only the end results of successful development were used as a criterion for selecting the new case, other similarities between it and the Siane would tend to be confirmed as related to successful development.

Personal knowledge of New Guinea[5] and a perusal of non-specialist journals suggested that the Tolai people of the Gazelle Peninsula of New Britain, who surrounded the town of Rabaul, fitted the first condition, of successful economic development combined with strengthened indigenous political organization. United Nations mission reports talked of "rapid progress" resulting from "communal enthusiasm" as "the local people set to with a will" (U.N. 1954). Newspapers cited successful "village councils" embracing thousands of individuals each, and receiving bank loans of over £50,000 to operate large-scale cocoa fermenteries. Independence of expatriate control was indicated by an anti-administration demonstration in one "village of a thousand persons in 1953, during which the District Commissioner was hit on the head." Settler reports characterized the Tolais as "obstinate," "overeducated and cheeky," and "hard to get along with." A survey of readily available literature confirmed the suitability of the Tolai for study and led to the formulation of a detailed research proposal (Salisbury 1959) for a Tolai study.[6]

Documentary research in 1960 and 1961 (Salisbury 1962b) corrected many of the historical errors of this research proposal, and indicated clearly that the Tolai had indeed gone through several sequences of economic and social change, each one resembling the Siane sequence. One cycle had followed the introduction by traders in the 1870's of a market for surplus coconuts. Another had followed the deliberate planting by Tolai of coconuts for the market beginning in the 1890's. A third had begun with the introduction of hot-air copra driers in the late 1930's, but had not been completed until after the Second World War, and a fourth had involved the development of cocoa growing and mechanized processing in the late 1950's. Unfortunately, because contacts had gradually spread, documents did not enable each cycle to be clearly distinguished over the whole of the Tolai area. Villages near the coast had gone through all the cycles in succession, building their political organization as they went. Inland villages, which began later, had skipped phases, adopting several innovations simultaneously, and had developed less political unity.

The confirmation of the general hypothesis of the study thus opened the way to a more specific investigation in the field, in which it was hoped to develop the model -- the way in which pre-existing local political organization con-tributed to economic development, or, to phrase it more dramatically, the way in which "tradition" ensured successful change. Not only were all the economic data obtained in the Siane study to be collected – on land ownership, land usage, yields, labour inputs, consumption, cash incomes, capital ownership, investments, and cere-monial expenditure – but the changing political structure needed to be reconstruct-ed, and the history of each technological innovation correlated with it. For both purposes a file was kept on every Tolai individual mentioned by name in any docu-ment, listing his village or area, his probable birthdate, his significant actions, and the date to which the reference applied. This file of about two hundred names of indi-viduals important in all Tolai areas before 1939, and the dates of their activity, proved invaluable in later investigations of oral history, although it did not in itself contain sufficient information for statistical treatment.

It also served to focus interest on four villages, all of which had gone through all four cycles of technological and social change, and all of which had long and full historical records – Matupit, Nodup, Raluana, and Vunamami (called Kinigunan in many early records). Each could have served for detailed study, and the final decision to study Vunamami was not taken until arrival in the field. Three fac-tors were decisive: reports of the 1950's that Vunamami was the most progressive of all village councils, having independently built its own post-primary school; the arrival of Dr. A.L. Epstein to study Matupit, which had developed into a peri-urban satellite of Rabaul; and a meeting in Port Moresby with Vin ToBaining, M.L.C., the president of Vunamami Council.

Vunamami, it is true, is an exceptional "village," not only for New Guinea as a whole but among the Tolai. It was one of the first four villages in New Guinea contacted by missionaries and traders in the early 1870's, and the first European plantation was established on its borders in 1883 by the famous "Queen Emma" Forsayth, and Richard Parkinson. The German administrative centre for the area – Herbertshöhe, or Kokopo as it is now called – was also next door, until 1910. The most extensive alienation of land in all New Guinea occurred in Vunamami and the surrounding villages, and when the administrative capital moved across the bay to the modern town of Rabaul, Kokopo remained as a main centre of plantation and social life in the Territory of New Guinea. Under Australian administration Vunamami had dynamic local leaders between the late 1930's and the 1950's. It most quickly espoused Local Government (or Village) Councils when these were first offi-cially established in 1950, and Vunamami Council, as the most progressive council in New Guinea, was awarded a mace by the Commonwealth Bank, and a presidential chair by the Sydney Town Council. Its president was elected to represent the New Guinea Islands constituency in the first Legislative Council elections of 1961.[7]

The village itself, the focus of the council to which it had given its name, included some five hundred persons in 1961. It was then a rich village, though by no means the richest in the Tolai area, with an average income per family of £150 and almost complete subsistence from local sources. Housing varied all the way from dwellings constructed entirely of native materials to three-bedroom houses of the Australian suburban type. The Council operated its own electric generator, though no private houses were wired to it, and it had its own medical aid posts, wells, laundry facilities, schools, brickmaking machinery, and a cocoa fermentery. The local Methodist church, with its own ordained Tolai minister, was attended by most of the population every Sunday in spotless, white, ironed clothes. Ninety-nine percent of the population was literate.

But though this aggregate of characteristics is unique, and makes Vunamami the most advanced village in New Guinea, there is no single characteristic that could not be parallelled in many other places in New Guinea and elsewhere in the Pacific. Council activity on a similar scale and with similar local enthusiasm is common in the Highlands; similar thoroughgoing involvement in cash cropping, while retaining a subsistence agriculture, prevails throughout Polynesia. Similar histories of enthusiastic adoption of Christianity in the nineteenth century, and of the emergence of locally run churches with universal church attendance and high literacy rates could again be cited throughout Polynesia and in much of Papua. Problems of land alienation and the co-existence of plantations and small farmers occur throughout the Pacific, and in New Guinea are acute around Madang and on Bougainville. Vunamami, in short, combines features from many histories of development; the lessons to be learned from it could be of considerably wider generality.

At the same time a caveat should be entered; the history of Vunamami is not representative of every Tolai area, nor has the development of all Tolai areas been the same. Separate studies of Matupit (a peri-urban satellite village of Rabaul in which "traditional" features were at a minimum) by A.L. Epstein, and of Rapitok (the most distant, and most land-rich Tolai village, but also one of the least organized villages politically) by T.S. Epstein, were conducted independently while the present study was in progress. No effort is made here to analyse the differences and similarities among the three areas, or to relate them to their different histories of relations with Europeans; such a comparison would require another book. But the reader should be warned in advance against assuming that the findings of any one of these studies can, without modification, be applied to any other Tolai area. As this entire study will show, the pattern of economic development and change in any one village is very much a function of its own internal social changes and their timing, and of the way in which economic choices appear in a given micro-situation.

One should not expect contiguity and subordination to the same external administering authority to produce identical results.

NOTES

1.   Within the terminology current in economic anthropology in 1965, I clearly espouse what has been called a "formalist position." I do not see any "controversy" between my position and what has been called the "substantivist position." It is merely a matter of substantivists having used antiquated field data, which ignored the role of individual rational choice in non-Western economies. Given these inadequate data, "substantivists" have made important contributions describing the institutional framework of choice. It is on the basis of such knowledge that more modern formalistic, quantitative studies are possible.

2.   Research for this part of the study was conducted between 1958 and April 1961 with support from the University of California Committee on Research, the U.S.P.H.S. (Grant No. M-4427), and the University of California Institute of International Studies. Current newspapers were reviewed, and all issues of the *Pacific Island Monthly* (which began in 1931). Libraries in the United States (particularly that at Harvard) were consulted for German colonial publications; the library of the Sacred Heart Mission (M.S.C.) in Münster, Westfalen, was searched, together with the Richard Parkinson collection and colonial materials at the Museum für Völkerkunde in Hamburg; in Australia the Methodist Overseas Mission collection at the Mitchell Library was made available to me, as were the archives of the Department of Territories in Canberra. The only major source not consulted, owing to lack of permission, was the German official archives in Potsdam. I should like to express my gratitude for permission to view the other records, and to cite manuscript sources in the case of the Methodist Overseas Mission and the Australian Department of Territories. Neither, of course, should be considered responsible for any views expressed in this study. Mr. Klaus Koch and Mrs. Helgi Osterreich assisted with the analysis of documentary materials. An early version of this analysis was published as Salisbury (1962b).

3.   It is interesting that macro-studies of national economic development have found (Moore 1966:36) that the single event that consistently has been followed by dramatic economic development, despite expected empirical difficulties, has been the granting of independence, or the emergence of a régime based on popular support. Though the present study only parallels the macro-study finding and cannot claim to deal with a national unit, it is hoped that the processes it analyses may be usefully applied for the understanding of the processes occurring at the national level.

4.   Some of these cases were analysed by myself (Salisbury 1962a); others were analysed by Leighton Hazlehurst, Helen Kreider Henderson, Allan Hoben, Stephen Holtzman, Grover Krantz, Henry Lewis, Leonard Plotnicov, and Zenon Pohorecky in seminar papers.

5.   I should like to thank Dr. K. E. Read for first interesting me in the area in 1954, when he himself was planning a Tolai study. Mr. Ralph Craib rekindled my interest in 1958.

6.   This hasty and often seriously erroneous document is closely parallelled by T.S. Epstein (1963). She adopts the same division into phases, though she sees the difference between them as being ones of, first, agricultural investment, second, consumption, next investment trial in secondary processing, and finally tertiary investment. Unfortunately my later research showed that the history I then cited was highly inaccurate, and the phases I then proposed are inappropriate. Salisbury (1962b) presents a better, though still inexact, survey of the early period, based on original research. In view of its historical inaccuracy, no further historical use will be made of Epstein's publication, based as it is on unreliable secondary or even tertiary sources.

7.   In the elections of 1964 he failed to secure re-election, owing to a divided constituency, when Vunamami was separated from other Tolai areas and grouped with a large majority of non-Tolai-speaking people. One of the latter secured election.

REFERENCES

Banfield, E.B. 1958. *The Moral Basis of a Backward Society*. Glencoe, Ill.: The Free Press.

Boserup, E. 1965. *The Conditions of Agricultural Growth*. Chicago: Aldine.

Clark, Colin and M. Haswell. 1964. *The Economics of Subsistence Agriculture*. London: Macmillan.

Danks, B. 1887. "On the Shell Money of New Britain." *Journal of the Anthropological Institute* 17:305-17.

Epstein, T.S. 1963. "European Contact and Tolai Economic Development: A Schema of Economic Growth." *Economic Development and Cultural Change* 11:289-307.

Ewers, J.C. 1955. *The Horse in Blackfoot Indian Culture*. Bureau of American Ethnology, Bulletin 159. Washington: Smithsonian Institution.

Foster, G.M. 1965. "Peasant Society and the Image of the Limited Good." *American Anthropologist* 67:293-315.

Hagen, E.E. 1961. *On the Theory of Social Change*. Homewood, Ill.: The Dorsey Press.

Hill, P. 1966. "A Plea for Indigenous Economics: The West African Example." *Economic Development and Cultural Change* 15:10-20.

Jones, W.O. 1959. *Manioc in Africa*. Stanford: University of California Press.

McClelland, D.C. 1961. *The Achieving Society*. Princeton, N.J.: D. Van Nostrand.

Mead, M. 1938. *The Mountain Arapesh: A Improving Culture*. Anthropological Papers of the American Museum of Natural History, Vol. 36.

Moore, W.E. 1966. *The Impact of Industry*. Englewood Cliffs, N.J.: Prentice-Hall.

Nash, M. 1965. "Review of *From Stone to Steel*, by R.F. Salisbury." *Pacific Affairs* 38:105.

Parkinson, R. 1887. *Im Bismarck-Archipel*. Leipzig: F.A. Brockhaus.

Riesenfeld, A. 1951. "Tobacco in New Guinea." *Journal of the Royal Anthropological Institute* 81:69.

Rostow, W.W. 1960. *The Stages of Economic Growth*. Cambridge: The University Press.

Salisbury, R.F. 1957. *Economic Change Among the Siane Tribes of the New Guinea Highlands*. Doctoral Dissertation. Canberra: Australian National University.

-----------1958. "An 'Indigenous' New Guinea Cult." *Kroeber Anthropological Papers* 8:67-78.

-----------1959. "Social Factors in New Guinea Economic Development." in *Proposal for an Institute of International Studies Submitted to the Ford Foundation*. Berkeley: University of California Press.

------------1962a. *From Stone to Steel*. Melbourne and Cambridge: The University Presses.

------------1962b. "Early Stages of Economic Development in New Guinea." *Journal of the Polynesian Society* 71:328-339.

United Nations. 1954. *Report to the Trusteeship Council of a Mission to Visit the Territory of New Guinea.*

Watson, J.B. 1965. "From Hunting to Horticulture in the New Guinea Highlands." *Ethnology* 4:295-309.

V

APPLYING KNOWLEDGE:

ANTHROPOLOGICAL PRAXIS AND PUBLIC POLICY[1]

by

Harvey A. Feit and Colin H. Scott

In the midst of an academic world that has become increasingly specialized, increasingly sceptical of claims to sound knowledge and wisdom, and increasingly ambiguous about the role of scholarship in the wider world, Richard Salisbury stands out. He believed in the value of an intellectually rigorous point of view, a commitment to what he thought was right and a passionate activism in the service of other people and peoples. He said repeatedly that knowledge was for use and that informed decisions were better than uninformed ones.

Salisbury was among the few anthropologists who were as well known for their applied work as for their theorizing. His exploration of the links between intellectual and applied concerns reached a depth rarely seen in contemporary anthropology. His most widely-known applied research, on the socio-economic implications of the James Bay Hydro-electric Project in Quebec, forms the main focus of this section. In fact, the history of how he began the research in James Bay, outlined below, could easily provide the grist for one of his own analyses of the potentials and constraints of entrepreneurship and power in New Guinea big-men politics.

In elaborating and testing ideas from economic development theory and organizational analysis through applied research in both these parts of the world, Salisbury emphasized several analytical themes: the need for decentralized development; the possibilities of economic development through the service sector; and the institutional pre-conditions for common interests and actions in emerging regional societies within larger nation states.

His arguments for decentralization were based both on pragmatism and on a commitment to justice for local peoples. He argued that effective negotiations between development agencies and local peoples were essential to both. Thus, Dick often addressed audiences of government policy-makers, regional and Indigenous leaders, business people and the public. In these formulations, he elaborated the arguments of many of the growing Indigenous rights and self-governance

233

movements around the world. But he carried these arguments to development agencies and corporations, with conclusions drawn from cross-cultural, social science research. He thus showed that research was equally critical for local peoples and macro-institutions. In the process, he decisively contributed to the early development of the new partnership relationships that are emerging between anthropologist practitioners and local peoples.

PRINCIPLED ENTREPRENEURSHIP AND NEGOTIATED INTERVENTIONS

Salisbury's earliest and best known books, *From Stone to Steel* (1962) and *Vunamami* (1970) not only addressed debates in anthropological economics and the economics of development, they also were laden with practical implications for development as practised by government and international agencies.[2] His first specifically applied research resulted from a request in July 1971 from the administrator of Papua New Guinea to accept an appointment as an anthropological consultant to investigate and report on an increasingly violent four-year dispute among Tolai factions and the government over new, local governing institutions which were being proposed in the context of the move towards national independence. With Tolai support for his mission, Salisbury conducted a month of discussions and research with the various factions in August 1971. He reported after that he had attempted to lessen the tensions by increasing each group's awareness of the reasons for the positions adopted by the others as well as by increasing their awareness of alternative means for resolving the conflicts (1971). His later reflections on the general lessons which he drew from this experience in the Gazelle Peninsula (1976a) are reprinted here as Chapter V.13.

At about the same time as the work in Papua New Guinea, Dick took his first initiatives to do applied research in northern Quebec. One of us (Feit) recalls being invited by Dick to accompany him in May or June of 1971 to a meeting at which the first Quebec Minister of the Environment introduced himself and his portfolio to researchers at McGill University, and invited them to tell him about what research they were doing which might be relevant to his mandate. The James Bay Hydro-electric complex had just been announced in April, and the project would take place on the lands of the James Bay Cree. It was in this area that most of the earlier research by the McGill Programme in the Anthropology of Development (PAD) had been conducted. Dick had taken on the Directorship of the Programme in 1969, after Norman Chance left McGill.

Dick, in the audience, asked whether the Minister knew what the social impacts of the hydro-electric project at James Bay might be[3] and "What do you intend to do about them?"[4] He then noted that researchers from McGill had been doing social research on development processes in the region since the mid-1960s, including studies of land use and social change. The minister was visibly interested, saying frankly that, so far, the government knew virtually nothing of the social and environmental impacts but that it needed to remedy the gap. He then turned to an assistant, finger pointing vaguely in Dick's direction, with an evident instruction for the aide to find out who it was who had asked the question. In a matter of weeks, correspondence and an invitation to become involved in social impact research had arrived from the government and from the James Bay Development Corporation (JBDC), which was then the lead Crown agency for regional development. Salisbury later noted that he thought the Minister had been pressured to act because of protests by the Cree, environmentalists and student supporters (1982c:264).

During the same period, Dick initiated discussions of research possibilities with several Cree band chiefs, with leaders of the provincial Indians of Quebec Association (IQA), with Cree post-secondary students in Montreal – all of whom were becoming part of an emerging Cree, regional-wide leadership – and with the lawyers working for the IQA and Cree. The emerging Cree leadership had announced strong opposition to the hydro-electric project (Feit, 1985); and Dick advised the Cree that studies should be commissioned and carried out by the Cree. He also said that he would like and prefer to work for them. He argued in favour of them undertaking research, claiming that it would provide additional information for opposition as well as clear foundations for decisions and Cree planning. He was initially dismissed by provincial Indian political leaders, and told by young Cree leaders that it was impossible for them to think of doing research in their present circumstances, as Cree communities had no regional political organization or decision-making structure at the time, and no funding (Salisbury 1983b).

Dick continued discussions into the fall, and Cree and provincial Indian leaderships eventually adopted the view that "although they would not endorse anything having to do with the [Hydro-electric] Project, [they] would prefer that we do the study than that it not be done, especially if they would be informed" of the results (Salisbury1983b). With growing support from Cree leaders, Salisbury responded to the invitation of the government corporations to do "social impact studies" and to make recommendations.

But it took several months of negotiations with the JBDC, and some mobilization of public pressure on Dick's part, to reach an acceptable agreement for the research. The sticking points were his insistence that the initial results be fully provided to the Cree as part of consulting them on their views and that the final results be made public immediately – procedures which the JBDC did not initially accept. He refused to undertake the work without full disclosures.[5] For him, the research plan and the report were not simply pieces of research for the JBDC; they were direct interventions by the researchers in communicating information about the development and social conditions to the affected peoples. Dick thus envisaged a consultative process that would be truly two-way and which would facilitate the development of new Cree structures for possible future discussions and ensuing negotiations with central governments.

To get his conditions accepted, Salisbury had to enhance the pressure for social impact studies. In September 1971, when he returned from the Gazelle Peninsula project, the Quebec Minister of the Environment asked him to join the Federal-Provincial Task Force on James Bay. The Task Force was formed in response to pressures for environmental impact assessments; and it was mandated to survey and synthesize quickly, for the government, existing knowledge on the James Bay region and the potential impacts of the hydro-electric developments.[6] The final report of this Task Force, submitted just a few months later, concluded that there was "only one ecological impact of potentially alarming proportions and significance," namely, the impact on the Cree (Federal-Provincial Task Force on James Bay 1971:50). Its recommendations were that intensive studies should be initiated on the impact of the project "on the native population of the territory;" and that such "programs ... provide full and open discussion with representatives of the native community on the planning of the regional development" (ibid.1971:2-3). These recommendations had resulted from Salisbury's input (Salisbury 1983b).

The Report, circulated within government circles before its public release, had the impact which Salisbury intended. A contract was signed by the JBDC and McGill University on 21 December 1971, the day after the Task Force Report was made public. The contract made a single concession to the Corporation: that the specific list of recommendations which would be presented by the researchers in their final report would remain confidential for a period of three years. This was, in Dick's view, a token concession because, as he indicated in his introduction to the final and public report in August 1972, the "recommendations, we feel, spring quite readily from our analysis" (Salisbury1972a:15).

MAKING THE CASE FOR DECENTRALIZATION AND AUTONOMY

Dick's commitment to sharing information was not only politically wise and morally sound, it was central to the analytical position he adopted as an anthropologist and to the development of new directions in the theory and practice of anthropology. It flowed from his early defence of formal economic analysis, and his subsequent call for an ethno-economics (e.g., 1968), both of which contributed to the reviving interest in actor-oriented models and to the emergent appreciation of the centrality of local knowledge and praxis to the analysis of broader histories and processes.

This personal and professional commitment to participatory decision-making was linked by Dick to practical reasons for its acceptance by corporate, government and other "macro-system" planners. When emphasizing to them the need for increased consideration of social factors, local implications and the knowledge of local people, he attributed the repeated failure of many development plans to insufficient attention to precisely these issues (Salisbury 1972a:5). In his report to the government, he said that the value of the research would be "nil" if the Cree were not present on planning bodies.

Part of Dick's strategy was to address those who were affected by development plans as well as those who consciously saw themselves as planners. Vis-a-vis the Cree, he deftly and, in our view, accurately summarized their position: that they had no choice but to oppose the proposed project but that they could be willing to discuss the future of the region as full participants in planning bodies. He thus addressed and treated them as potential decision-makers. In so doing, however, he emphasized the need for them to take up their own planning more actively, and he urged them to become researchers themselves. He predicted that there was likely to be a crisis in Cree society within a few years: as the large cohorts of youth entered adulthood, not all would be able to pursue careers in subsistence hunting. He argued that the hydro-electric project was one of the options that they should consider in planning a response to the potential crisis. He thus wrote his report from the assumption that the project would proceed; but he also assumed that it was not an "irrevocable unchangeable scheme" (Salisbury 1972a:14) and, therefore, that the Cree could have an effective role in its planning.

Some readers of the 1972 Report to the JBDC were not comfortable with making such projections, or with making them public. Dick argued that models were not about inevitabilities; that he was not predicting a future outcome but trying to make it possible to effect outcomes. Models, he argued, were useful for changing the world; and failure to anticipate and consider possible outcomes reduced the chances of changing what would happen. He also argued that it was wrong of some experts and researchers to "exclude 'people' from the ranks of policy-makers" (Salisbury 1978a:88). Indeed, he repeatedly emphasized the possibilities of local control and effective participation in wider planning arenas because he saw decentralization as contributing to relative autonomy and self-governance of local peoples.

In practice, Dick constantly balanced commitments with a strong sense of pragmatism as well as a vision. In the James Bay debates, he was one of the earliest professionals, if not the first, to advise the Cree that they should challenge the hydro-electric project on the basis of their Aboriginal legal rights to the territory on which it was to be built. He presented his case to both Cree leaders and their legal advisors in his early discussions with them in 1971. But the lawyers were reluctant at that time – considering it politically impossible – to argue on the basis of Aboriginal legal rights to land (Salisbury 1983b;1986b).[7] However, the advice which Dick gave coincided with views being expressed by a number of Cree; and this option was initiated in court action in the spring of 1972, although the case was not pressed forward to hearings until late in that year, after renewed efforts to establish effective negotiations failed. Indeed, it was on the basis of the plausibility of Aboriginal land rights that the Cree won the first Cree court victory, in late 1973, which finally forced the province into serious negotiations with them.

RESEARCHING IMPACTS, HAVING AN IMPACT

The report, *Development and James Bay*, was prepared in the five months between January and June 1972 by Dick and three young co-researchers, Fernand G. Filion, Farida Rawji and Donald Stewart (Salisbury 1972a). The earlier delays in signing a contract resulted in a winter research schedule which meant that no new fieldwork was undertaken as part of the project because Cree hunters were in isolated bush camps. However, unpublished data were gathered from official statistical sources and from other researchers in order to examine regional conditions and patterns of change. As well, consultations with Cree students at McGill, and with Cree who were resident in Montreal, went on continually during the research, both individually and through a series of weekly university working seminars. The seminars, taken for credit by some graduate students, provided a forum for informal and middle-level discussions both among those involved directly (Cree youth and JBDC officials) and those academics, media people and social activists involved in the ongoing public debates and protests which the hydro-electric project had sparked.[8] The first draft of the main chapters, completed by June, was presented to the Cree for consultations and inputs. This provided the occasion to report on existing development plans and data to the emerging Cree leadership, and to invite them to respond to the JBDC data and research findings. The results of this consultation were incorporated into a final chapter; and the full report was circulated in September to the JBDC and the public.

The Introduction to the official report, *Development and James Bay* (Salisbury 1972a), included in this volume as Chapter V.12, set forth a clear view of a practical social science and the problems inherent in such consulting. This report was read extensively by specialists and policy-makers working in northern Quebec and Canada;[9] but because this was primarily a study for the planning stage of a particular project, it was not very widely circulated beyond those with regional interests.

Nevertheless, this Introduction affords an overview of Salisbury's ideas about applied research, just at the moment when he was beginning to undertake extended work of this type.

The full Report included some forty recommendations; and Dick later commented that he was pleased that three-quarters of them had eventually been adopted (1988a:243; see Chapter V.16, this volume). Some of these recommendations, because they involved a full turn-around in government planners' policies, were particularly important to Cree and the corporations. The recommendations included new initiatives for local involvement in the planning process and regional governance, recognition of the need to support the subsistence sector, recognition of a local role in plans for developing service industries (as well as relocating and isolating construction camps and staging areas away from Indigenous settlements), and creating a local priority for on-the-job training programmes. The practical consequences of the adoption of these recommendations for the development of Cree society have been significant.

While Cree leaders were also arguing most of these issues, it seems clear that formulating these issues in planners' terms and documenting what was known from other parts of the world were critical for the adoption of the policies and programmes. Dick's position as an independent researcher also gave him the opportunity to meet, explain and press for his recommendations with corporate and government officials, outside the increasingly confrontational context of government-Cree relations.

For the Cree leadership, the report elaborated the issues that Salisbury had raised earlier with them, emphasizing the consequences of demographic growth, the vital but limited potential for the growth of subsistence hunting activities, the need to upgrade job skills in the population, the role the hydro-electric project could play in training and enhancing skills levels, the need to evolve region-wide planning, and the crucial importance of political rights and of building an effective organization for social and economic development.

Dick's own assessments of the effectiveness of his report were generally positive, but qualified. Looking back three years later, he wrote in 1975:

> I am convinced that even [with] the inadequacy
> of previous research, the empirical irrelevance
> of much existing theory, and the haste and lack
> of sophistication of our early emergency
> efforts, our predictions were vastly superior to

239

> those that anyone else was making at the time,
> using "common sense." (Salisbury 1978a:86-7).

In the final chapter of the report itself, in which he reviewed the consultations with Cree leaders in June of 1972, he had been more uncertain. There he reaffirmed his conviction that there was a need for "enlightened planning going beyond mere traditionalism if dependent status is to be avoided" and if negotiations among the Cree, the corporation and government were to proceed. However, although he noted some emergent beginnings, he did not see many concrete instances. He concluded the report by noting that it was probably "somewhat in advance of its time," that "the questions it answers are not yet being asked" and that the extensive communication efforts "have been largely ineffective" (Salisbury 1972a:174-5).

But the report was not without consequence; and it changed the very conditions under which it had been conducted. During the discussions with the Cree leaders, Dick was invited to undertake field research for them in the three communities most directly affected by development. This second research project was urgently undertaken in August 1972, before hunters went to their bush camps; and the report was submitted in September, in time to be used by the Cree in their unsuccessful efforts to get effective negotiations underway with Quebec before the courts started hearings on the legal proceedings initiated by the Cree as a last means to get effective participation and recognition. This report, *Not by Bread Alone: Subsistence Activities of the James Bay Cree*, was written with three students, Jacqueline Hyman, Kenneth Hyman and Nathan Elberg (Salisbury, 1972b).[10] The report – edited, introduced and concluded by Dick – documented the subsistence economies and the cash incomes of the affected communities. It confirmed the importance of subsistence production and activities to local economy, diet and health. It also warned of the potential pauperization of the Cree if the hydro-electric development led to reductions in game harvests and a need for increased importation of foodstuffs paid for with the limited cash that families had.

Reflecting on the reports three years later, in 1975, Dick commented that more had been accomplished by and with Crees in ensuing negotiations than had been the case in his initial June, 1972 assessment (quoted above). The Crees'

> primary reason for interest in the data was
> based upon a desire to oppose the project more
> effectively ... and, at least initially, [they] had no
> interest in our analyses of other problems they
> would face if the project did not go through, or
> in the sections dealing with ways in which

industrial development could be utilized to produce benefits for local society.

... As negotiations between the Cree and the James Bay Development Corporation developed between 1972 and 1975, so the questions became important: how to produce long-term benefits; and what social advantages had to be guaranteed in any agreement which involved damages to subsistence economy, or to local social autonomy? Our report was eventually well used – but in ways chosen by the Cree (1978a:87-8).

Looked at from the present, Dick's desire for more effective political and economic negotiations between local groups and governments has now become a commonplace feature of the various initiatives for Aboriginal self-government being explored across Canada, and by Indigenous peoples and regional societies around the world. His works are among the finest examplars, in both scholarly and policy-oriented publications, which argue that local knowledge, participation and a sense of real autonomy are key components of the planning and development processes and of legal claims. His formulations of these issues contributed to and enhanced a direction in applied research which has since then been greatly extended. Analytical and methodological approaches, such as participatory models and increasing local control over research, have been much elaborated. At the same time, there has been extensive acknowledgment that Salisbury's James Bay studies were the early models for participatory applied research.[11]

REFLECTING ON THE ROLE OF THE ANTHROPOLOGIST

Shortly after completing the initial James Bay studies, Dick wrote generally about his vision of the emerging and potential role of anthropologists, drawing on the experiences in both Canada and New Guinea. The paper, which is included in this volume as Chapter V.13, was circulated for the International Congress of Anthropological and Ethnological Sciences meetings held in Chicago in August/September 1973 (Salisbury 1976a).

The direction of his argument is well conveyed in his title, "The Anthropologist as Societal Ombudsman." In the paper, Dick developed his case that the anthropologist should ideally not take sides but should be impartial. It is important to note, however, that such neutrality did not mean, in his view, that the results of their work would be neutral. His position acknowledged the imbalances of power that kept local people from effective participation in regional and national decision-making and that limited access to information was one of the roots of that inequality (1976a:263). He thus envisaged that if the applied anthropologist effectively communicated information, the result would not be neutral with respect to power, but would enhance the position of the relatively powerless groups.[12]

He presented a range of arguments in favour of impartiality, the core ones being set out in this paper. Here, as elsewhere, he also implied that the anthropologist committed to working only with local people runs the constant risk of preempting the local group's own representations (see 1978a:88, 89). One other reason such intervention was inappropriate, he argued, was that it jeopardizes effective resolution of the disputes. To succeed, the conflicting parties must make their own choices in negotiations, they must negotiate compromises they can live with and they must identify the outcome as one of their own making.

Dick was careful to explain that certain key conditions were essential for the emergence of impartial ombudsman roles in society. These included a "relatively enlightened central bureaucracy" and local people having confidence in an "outsider appointed and paid by an official organization." As he later noted, events were always changing rapidly, and there was growing uncertainty about how frequently such conditions could be met.

Salisbury's defence of the value of impartial and independent advice was partly a response to the increasingly adversarial views expressed in development conflicts. These adversarial stances, partly although not solely the result of the "legalization" of conflicts, were occurring not only in James Bay but more widely in relation to Aboriginal, minority and local issues throughout the United States and Canada. In Canada, the first modern Supreme Court recognition of the continuing existence of Aboriginal legal rights was handed down in the Nishga ruling in 1973, in time to influence the James Bay Cree's court challenge of the hydro-electric project. An important consequence of that ruling was a much wider use of the courts as an alternative route to gaining recognition of Aboriginal interests in conflict situations, over and above the earlier choices of negotiation and political action.

The legalization of the processes quickly changed the context of social action and applied social science, in ways that left less opportunity for research which was not seen as simply committed to "our side" or the other "side." Salisbury had anticipated and was concerned about this development. In an unpublished presentation to a national social science conference in Ottawa in 1975, Dick expressed the unsatisfactory choices with which social scientists were now faced: the "stereotype of all researchers as useless, or even hostile, is changing, as researchers are being divided into 'good researchers' on our side, and 'bad guys' who are not working for us" (1975:9).

How quickly things had changed was clear at a 1975 Social Science Federation of Canada conference on evaluating change. His paper was cited by the editors of the conference proceedings as the only contribution which actually referred to the role of the scientist in evaluating change or to methodologies for evaluating change (Nelson and Gray, 1978:157). Most of the discussion at the conference, according to Salisbury, focussed on "necessary changes in political and legal processes" (1978b:159). Given his differences with the other participants, Salisbury was invited to prepare a short postscript to the conference proceedings. In it, he said he would not change what he had said, but he acknowledged that:

> I would agree, in short, with all the panelists that attention must be paid to the legal and organizational problems of getting effective action to prevent catastrophes and to implement benefits. It may well be that the most immediate, highest payoffs may be derived from attending to these problems. This unanimity makes it all the more important for at least one paper to stress the actions that the social scientist can take, qua scientist (1978b:160).

By 1981 Salisbury was not speaking of social ombudsmen, but of the role of experts in social negotiations (1982c). In this context, he compared the ability of social researchers to contribute to solutions acceptable to both parties to what he saw as the more limited ability of judges and court proceedings to facilitate solutions satisfactory to each party (1982c:258-9).

On strategy, Salisbury's position was clear: "confrontation doesn't get you anywhere" – words heard more than once as we (Scott) discussed current events in Indian politics. His approach was transactional: that each party be able to formulate its position in the best possible knowledge of the perceptions and expectations of others and that, out of such transactions, the structure of future relationships could be influenced for the better (1976b, 1977; 1979a). This, he felt, could result in development without jeopardy to the autonomy of any party to the process. He expected that people could be convinced to take the interests of others into account, in their own long-term interest. For example, local agreement is often essential for facilitating the stability needed by national and international agencies and corporations making large-scale investment decisions. Of the James Bay case, he wrote:

> The challenge to the anthropologist was one of showing what were the different payoffs to different sub-groups, of a solution that was acceptable to all. Some parties may not have obtained the maximum that they might have obtained from a purely self-centred strategy, but that would have been at the expense of other sub-groups and, we would argue, also to their own long-term disadvantage, as they would have alienated the parties whom they would have "oppressed." Over the long term there would have been major strife in the area (1984c:15).

To show how all parties could benefit from a non-antagonistic transaction of their own interests in relation to others – this was the professional as well as the ethical standard that Salisbury preferred. His discussion thus raised the fundamental issues that two decades later still pervade considerations of the role of anthropology in a post-colonial world, where power is widely acknowledged and the foundations of knowledge are plural, and explicitly moral, but where many anthropologists still struggle to find a self-image, and a role, that can be mutually empowering for those with whom they work and for themselves.

The Public Figure: Other Contexts, Other Texts

From the early 1970s on, Dick was involved in an increasingly wide range of applied research, consulting, media contacts and public presentations in addition to his scholarly publications, teaching, university administration and other professional activities. This extraordinary range of activities expressed his convictions about the relevance and obligations of social scientists. Indeed, over the course of a few years, he became a public figure in Canada and beyond, often sought out for his advice and views on a broad spectrum of topics by governments, Indigenous groups, media and public associations. This applied research not only took him the breadth of Canada but also, in the mid-1980s, back to New Guinea. As a public figure however, Dick was not only active or known for his work with Aboriginal peoples. He also, for example, published on Quebec universities as a member of the provincial *Commission d'Enquête sur les Universités Québécoises* 1977-79 (1978c; 1979c) and he was a Board member of the Canadian Human Rights Foundation from 1980 (1982e).

244

An example of his contributions as a public figure is a dinner address he delivered in 1979 to the Eighth National Northern Development Conference, meeting in Edmonton, Alberta (1979b), and reprinted here as Chapter V.14. Attended by several dozen oil company and mining executives, senior government ministers and bureaucrats, and a handful of Indigenous spokespersons, his paper ("The North as a Developing Nation") offered them rich and provocative conceptual fare. It is an exceptionally succinct and clear interpretation of the lessons that he drew from what was known about third world development, and of the implications of those experiences for the future of development in the northern regions of North America. But it is also an example of the ways in which Dick used scholarly findings, and his own personal vision, to address businessmen and government officials about how some of their interests overlapped and needed to be co-ordinated with local interests. His moral rationality, simultaneously addressed to the different sectors of decision-makers involved in development, became a hallmark of his public communications.

THEORY AND PRACTICE

The relationship between the application of knowledge and the advancement of basic knowledge was the central focus of Dick's vision of anthropology. His 1979 paper, "Application and Theory in Canadian Anthropology: The James Bay Agreement," which is included here as Chapter V.15, reviewed the key, applied research that he and his students had done during the 1970s in James Bay in order to show how applied research and theoretical developments were linked. Indeed, it was a recurrent theme in his publications that anthropologists could not ignore theory when doing applied research, just as it was his view that they could not ignore applications when developing theory. In the above-mentioned 1979 paper, he showed the dialectical relationship between economic and transactional theories and the applied research he was doing.

In another article, when describing how to build predictive models based on existing social science findings, Dick argued that original research formulations had to be re-worked. This was because earlier findings usually revealed cases of "[c]ircular arguments, non-causal relations masked as causal ones by loose wording, or correlations which, in reality, are merely attempts to construct 'types' for inclusion in a typology" (1978a:89-90). Thus, to "recast the analysis of existing findings, into a form suitable for use, with a specific set of social data, may lead to theoretical advance in and of itself" (1978a:90). In addition, "[c]onstant use of theory to make predictions ... lead to much more objective testing of theory, with many more theories being rejected. As a result, theory would develop more rigorously" (1978a:91). As he concluded in an unpublished report: "[T]he theorist who does not involve himself in pol-

245

icy research is depriving himself of invaluable stimulation" (1975:12). The paper included in this volume provides his most extended defence of these views.

THE 1980s – A TIME OF COMPARISON AND ASSESSMENT

After a decade of concentrated work in Northern Canada, Dick went back to Oceania where, during a six-month sabbatical at the University of Papua New Guinea (UPNG) in 1983-84, he set out to do comparative research on how well provinces were using local governments to deliver services. He made contacts with a number of provincial premiers and established a research agenda which included work in New Britain, Siane and Bougainville. While he was at UPNG, the University wanted someone to take part in assessing the social impacts of the Luluai hydroelectric proposals in Bougainville. Dick volunteered; and he used participatory research models very similar to those he had developed in James Bay a decade earlier (1984f;1984g). Salisbury was also drawn into a UPNG project team that was investigating rumours of "uncontacted tribes" in the Schrader Mountains. The Miyamiya group "indeed had never previously been patrolled ... [and] I have some unforgettable and almost unique experiences, that shed dramatic light on what 'delivering services' means" (Salisbury 1984d;1984e;1984g). Despite such a very full sabbatical, Dick did get to compare developments in several provinces, and he prepared a synthesizing report on "Decentralization and Local Government in Papua New Guinea" (1987; 1984g).

It was Salisbury's intention to bring this phase of the PNG research to completion during a sabbatical projected for 1991, upon finishing his term as Dean of Arts at McGill. The sabbatical was also to enable him to complete a major theoretical book on development, bringing together the lessons learned from his longitudinal research in both New Guinea and northern Canada. Also in progress was a volume on economic anthropology that he was editing, to deal with parallel issues. The long-term plans for synthesizing his New Guinea and Canadian research findings were cut short. Nevertheless, he did complete several syntheses of the James Bay findings.

Dick said that he became aware of "the great need for a brief descriptive study of the Cree experience" which would be accessible to a wider audience than anthropologists, after he presented a Canadian "case study" at a United Nations University symposium on "Development Alternatives" at Ste. Marguerite, Quebec in 1980 (1982d:1-2). *A Homeland for the Cree: Regional Development in James Bay 1971-1981* (1986a), his last book, was the fulfilment of that need. Alongside the book, he published a series of papers on theoretical aspects of the analysis, in particular: "Formulating the Common Interest: The Role of Structures in Cree Development" (1982a); *"Le Québec: microcosme du monde ou monde en soi?"*

(1984a); his "Introduction" to his co-edited volume on *Affluence and Cultural Survival* (1984b); and the 1988 paper reprinted here as Chapter V.16. In this latter paper, "Economics of Development Through Services: Findings of the McGill Programme Among the Cree (1988a), Dick moved from analysing the processes to exploring the outcomes. In so doing, he provided a synthetic survey of the lessons for development anthropology uncovered by a decade and a half of modelling and testing in applied settings.[13]

These publications were facilitated by new social impact research, commissioned by the James Bay Energy Corporation in March 1982, to assess the next phase of the hydro-electric development which was to built on the lands of the southern Cree villages.[14] In the summer of 1982, Dick and five field workers collected data, on a tight schedule, and completed a report before the end of that year. For despite regional-level approval by Cree community leaders, individual communities restricted the fieldwork time to about three weeks in each village because of the extensive Cree-initiated research which was underway at the time. Interestingly, such Cree-initiated research was an objective which Salisbury had highlighted for the Cree a decade earlier. The result was that the Salisbury team had to depend in part on data from organizational files and from recent research which had been done for other purposes (1982b:12-16).[15] Nevertheless, this research provided comparative data for the monograph on the decade of rapid change in the James Bay region since his initial impact studies.

The resulting book, *A Homeland for the Cree* (Salisbury 1986a), parallelled the recognition in anthropology more generally that there were no peoples isolated from national systems. It also foreshadowed the more recent critique of radical separations between local and global social institutions by exploring the recent transformations of local systems. Indeed, Salisbury thought that "the existing literature on most northern Canadian communities pays little attention to the realities of life in the 1980s – it persists in viewing them as collections of people leading 'traditional' lives, though administered by white officials in a quasi-colonial state" (1982d:3). He thus objected both to the analytical models of the social systems and to the locus of social agency on which they focussed. He argued that what had happened among the Cree was that the majority of administrators were now Cree and that local political decisions were being made by Cree. "The relevant 'system' still includes politicians and bureaucrats in Quebec or Ottawa, but the involvement of the Cree in the total system is complete up to, and beyond, the regional level. ... 'Village life' ... is no longer the significant 'system'; the Cree region is the most significant system" (1982d:3-4).

Salisbury thus saw the implementation of the James Bay and Northern Quebec Agreement (JBNQA) of 1975 as a major experiment in decentralized regional development (Salisbury 1983a, in this volume as Chapter VI.18). Local people were in charge of providing services to their communities, maintaining the conditions for land-based production and creating a productive modern sector. Direct negotiation by native political organizations precipitated the native corporate entities and bureaucratic arrangements needed for the task as well as for developing the necessary skills. The required financial and advisory support flowed as compensation and as legal commitments undertaken by external businesses and governments (Salisbury 1979a).

His evaluation was that the JBNQA was in fact a success in many important respects. While he was disturbed that social and ecological impacts tended to get inadequate consideration before hydro development decisions were taken on purely technical or financial grounds, the JBNQA did show, he felt, that the social costs and benefits of development could be balanced via negotiation (1979a). Thus, positive changes in Cree society had been brought about by the development of corporate regional Cree bodies or "structures" that served as vehicles for shaping a "common interest" out of the crisis of hydro-electric development. The existence of such structures permitted action to be taken, court cases to be initiated, research to be conducted, communities to be consulted and a consensus to be expressed to outsiders. In due course, a variety of corporate arrangements emerged that were seen both as "legitimate" Cree entities and as effective in administering the rights and benefits secured in negotiations (Salisbury 1982a).

In the Preface to *A Homeland for the Cree*, Dick argued that changes to Cree society between 1971 and 1981 were an "emergent outgrowth from their preexisting society and culture" (1986a:vii) and that the development of a regional Cree society was a process in which Cree had acted as architects and not merely reacted to external forces. Factors both internal and external had made this possible: the willingness of Quebec and Canadian governments to decentralize governmental powers to a region; the Cree consciousness of regional unity provoked by the crisis of hydro-electric development; the availability of local personnel to operate emergent structures; a regime of services and transfers that made possible the maintenance of a viable local subsistence economy, as well as growth in administration and services; and predictability of resources and programmes enunciated in legal, implementable terms enshrined in the JBNQA.

Dick believed that anthropologists had helped to put local native people on a more equal footing with government bureaucracy and industry in negotiating development. To an important degree, he also felt that Cree had come to share his research values, noting their express appreciation of complete and honest research as essential to sound decision-making – even if the findings were sometimes initially unpalatable (1986a). So far as we are aware, Salisbury never wavered in his optimism for reasonable and decent outcomes among parties who, despite conflicting goals or inaccurate stereotypes of each other, were generally well-meaning. Thus, both the integrity of Salisbury's approach, and its pragmatic value, have remained extremely persuasive. It was the kind of world he wanted; and it was, therefore, life as he himself transacted it.

Notes

1. The authors have been aided in the preparation of this paper by Mary E. Salisbury and Marilyn Silverman. The authors, however, are solely responsible for the contents. Preparation of this paper was funded in part by grants from the Social Sciences and Humanities Research Council of Canada (SSHRC) to Feit (nos. 410-93-0505, 410-96-0946, 410-99-1208) and to Scott et. al. (no 83-91-0035). A few passages in this article have appeared before in papers presented by the authors in a memorial to Dick Salisbury in Culture 10(1).

2. From his earliest fieldwork, Salisbury had been involved in the kind of ad hoc practical policy-influencing initiatives that field workers are commonly asked to engage in by their host communities. During his Tolai fieldwork in 1960, for example, he was asked by people at Vunamami village to investigate the history of the expulsion of a village group from land to which they now claimed rights in a dispute before the Land Titles (Restoration) Commission. The results of this work are included as Chapter III. 6 in this volume.

3. Feit was one of the PAD researchers, and he was writing up his dissertation on Cree hunting economy at the time. Salisbury, his supervisor, urged him to speak up at the meeting, but when he declined, Salisbury spoke.

4. We put the second of these questions in quotation marks because, twenty-five years later, Feit remembers the exact words.

5. For a discussion of the principles, see his comments in 1978a, pages 88-9.

6. With the exception of its two co-ordinators and Salisbury, the Task-Force was comprised entirely of staff from provincial and federal government departments.

7. It is important to recall that, at this time, there had not been any judicial recognition of the contemporary survival of aboriginal rights within Canada.

8. The documentation centre which was assembled at PAD also became a focus of work and meetings among diverse individuals.

9. For example, the report was a key source document for one of the first books published in Quebec on the project and the Cree (Jay-Rayon 1973); and extracts from the French version of the report were included in an appendix to this book.

10.   Jacqueline Hyman, who had done a summer of M.A. fieldwork on 1989 in Fort George (now relocated to Chisasibi), and her husband, Kenneth Hyman, co-ordinated the local research staff in Fort George during the three week field research period while Nathan Elberg co-ordinated the questionnaire interviewing by splitting his time between Paint Hills (now Wemindji) (10 days) and Eastmain (one week).

11.   See for example Ryan and Robinson (1990) and Waldrum (1993).

12.   Hedican (1995:55-73) situates Salisbury's position within the broader debate over the merits of neutral mediation versus advocacy in social research.

13.   The article is the most complete summary of the findings reported more fully in his book on James Bay.

14.   Hydro-Quebec later chose to try to develop the northern-most phase of the proposed development, on the Great Whale River, before going ahead with the southern project. A concerted international campaign by the James Bay Cree and allies within the environmental movement, in the context of worsening economic conditions and reduced demand for electricity, resulted in an indefinite postponement of the future phases of hydro-electric development in the James Bay region. However, the projects have not been permanently abandoned.

15.   It was with much sorrow that Dick did not get the opportunity to undertake extended fieldwork in the James Bay region, constantly working as he did on schedules restricted by various constraints. He did however make shorter trips, and he was in continual contact with Cree leaders, administrators and students who lived in Montreal or who visited the city regularly.

References

Federal-Provincial Task Force on James Bay, 1971. *A Preliminary Study of the Environmental Impacts of the James Bay Development Project, Quebec.*

Feit, Harvey A. 1985. "Legitimation and Autonomy in James Bay Cree Responses to Hydro-electric Development." in Dyck, Noel (ed.), *Indigenous Peoples and the Nation State: Fourth World Politics in Canada, Australia, and Norway.* St. John's: Memorial University of Newfoundland (ISER) :27-66.

Hedican, Edward J., 1995. *Applied Anthropology in Canada: Understanding Aboriginal Issues.* Toronto: University of Toronto Press.

Jay-Rayon, Jean-Claude, 1973. *Le dossier Baie James.* Montreal: Leméac.

Nelson, J.G. and C.A. Gray. 1978. "Introduction [to Postscripts]." in Nelson, J.G. and C.A. Gray (eds.), *Evaluating Change.* Ottawa: Social Science Federation of Canada:157.

Ryan, Joan and Michael P. Robinson. 1990. "Implementing Participatory Action Research in the Canadian North: A Case Study of the Gwich'in Language and Cultural Project." *Culture* 10(2): 57-71.

Salisbury, Richard F. 1962. *From Stone to Steel: Economic Consequences of a Technological Change in New Guinea.* Melbourne, Australia and Cambridge, U.K.: Melbourne and Cambridge University Presses.

------------1968. "Anthropology and Economics." in LeClair, E. and H. Schneider (eds.), *Readings in Economic Anthropology.* New York: Holt, Rinehart and Winston:477-485.

------------1970. *Vunamami: Economic Transformation in a Traditional Society.* Berkeley, California and Sydney, Australia: University of California Press, and Angus & Robertson.

------------1971. *The Problems of the Gazelle Peninsula, August 1971.* Port Moresby: The Government Printer. 59 pp.

-----------1972a. *Development and James Bay: Social Implications of the Hydro-electric Proposals* (with F.G. Filion, F. Rawji and D. Stewart). Report to the James Bay Development Corporation. (Also in French).

-----------1972b. *Not by Bread Alone: Subsistence Activities of the James Bay Cree* (with N. Elberg, J. Hyman, and K. Hyman). Report to the Indians of Quebec Association.

-----------1975. "Policy Regarding Native Peoples, An Academic Social Scientist's Perspective." McGill University, Programme in the Anthropology of Development. *Brief Communication Series* No. 37. 12 pp. (Paper prepared for the National Social Science Conference, Ottawa, November 20-22, 1975).

-----------1976a. "The Anthropologist as Societal Ombudsman." in Pitt, David C. (ed.), *Development from Below*. The Hague: Mouton. pp. 255-265.

-----------1976b. "Transactions or Transactors: An Economic Anthropologist's View." in Kapferer, Bruce (ed.), *Transaction and Meaning*. Philadelphia: Ishi Press:41-59.

-----------1977. "A Prism of Perceptions: The James Bay Hydro-electric Project." in Wallman, Sandra (ed.), *Perceptions of Development*. Cambridge: Cambridge University Press:172-190.

-----------1978a. "Evaluating Social Change." in Nelson, J.G. and C.A. Gray (eds.), *Evaluating Change*. Ottawa: Social Science Federation of Canada:70-92.

-----------1978b. "Postscript: Evaluating Social Change." in Nelson, J.G. and C.A. Gray (eds.), *Evaluating Change*. Ottawa: Social Science Federation of Canada:159-160.

-----------1978c. *Document de Consultation, Commission d'Etude sur les Universités du Québec* (with P. Anger, et al.). Québec: Ministère de l'Education.

-----------1979a. "Application and Theory in Canadian Anthropology: The James Bay Agreement." *Transactions of the Royal Society of Canada* Series IV, 17:229-241.

-----------1979b. "The North as a Developing Nation." in *Proceedings: Eighth National Northern Development Conference* (November 14-16, 1979, Edmonton). N.p.: Northwest Territories, Department of Information:73-78.

-----------1979c. *Commission d'Etude sur les Universités, Rapport du comité de co-ordination, mai 1979* (with P. Anger et al.). Québec: Editeur officiel du Québec.

------------1982a. "Formulating the Common Interest: The Role of Structures in Cree Development." in Merrill, R. and D. Willner (eds.), *Conflict and the Common Good*. Williamsburg, Va.: Studies in Third World Studies, No. 24:135-150.

------------1982b. *Amenagement hydroélectric des rivières Nottaway - Broadback - Rupert: Etude des retombées sociales at économiques sur les communautés autochtones du territoire NDR.* Montreal: ssDcc, Inc. (Rapport pour la Société d'énergie de la Baie James).

------------1982c. *"Le Rôle de l'expert dans la négociation sociale: leçons de la Baie James."* in Mayer-Renaud, Micheline and Alberte Le Doyen (eds.), *L'intervention Sociale.* Montreal: Editions coopératives Albert Saint Martin (Actes du colloque de l'Association canadienne des sociologues et anthropologues de langue française):257-66.

------------1982d. Killam Foundation Fellowship Report, Richard F. Salisbury. Unpublished Typescript.

------------1982e. "Native Rights, Cultural Rights and the Charter." in Canadian Human Rights Foundation Working Papers, Colloquium Report, February 18.

------------1983a. "Les défis et contraintes de l'anthropologie du développement - Entrevue avec Richard F. Salisbury." *Recherches amérindiennes au Québec* 13(1):55-6.

------------1983b. Personal communication: Unpublished letter, R.F.S. to H. Feit, 28 August 1983.

------------1984a. *"Le Québec: microcosme du monde ou monde en soi?"* in G.-H. Lévesque, G. Rocher, J. Henripin, R. Salisbury, M.-A. Tremblay, D. Szabo, J.-P. Wallot, P. Bernard et C.-E. Depocas (eds.), *Continuité et rupture; les sciences sociales au Québec.* Montreal, Presse de l'Université de Montréal:245-255.

------------1984b. "Affluence and Cultural Survival: An Introduction." in R.F. Salisbury and Elisabeth Tooker (eds.), *Affluence and Cultural Survival.* Washington: Proceedings, American Ethnological Society, Spring Meetings, 1981:1-11.

------------1984c. "An Abstract of the 1983 Plenary Address: The Challenge of Consulting." *SAAC [Society of Applied Anthropology in Canada] Newsletter*, 3(1):13-15.

-----------1984d. *Ethnographic Notes on the Miyamiya People*. Waigani: University of Papua New Guinea (University of Papua New Guinea Schrader Mountains Project Report No. 1).

-----------1984e. *Language Work on Pinai*. Waigani: University of Papua New Guinea (University of Papua New Guinea Schrader Mountains Project Report No. 3).

-----------1984f. *Laluai Hydroelectric Project, Prefeasability Study, Social Impact Report*. Port Moresby. (Report for the Laluai Trust and Beca, Gure, Pty [Papua New Guinea] Appendix B).

-----------1984g. Personal communication: Unpublished Letter R.F.S. to D.L. Oliver, 8 November 1984.

-----------1986a. *A Homeland for the Cree: Regional Development in James Bay, 1971-1981*. Montreal: McGill-Queens' University Press

-----------1986b. Personal communication: Unpublished letter, R.F.S. to H.A. Feit, 26 June 1986

-----------1987 [1984]. *Decentralisation and Local Government in Papua New Guinea*. Montreal: McGill University, Centre for Developing Area Studies, paper series. (Report to the Governments of Simbu, West Highlands, East New Britain, and the North Solomons Provinces, and to the Federal Department of Provincial Affairs, Papua New Guinea).

-----------1988a. "The Economics of Development Through Services: Findings of the McGill Programme Among the Cree." in J.W. Bennett (ed.), *The Anthropology of Development*. Lanham, Maryland: University Press of America (Society for Economic Anthropology Monographs No. 5):239-56.

-----------1988b. "Anthropology, Applied." in James H. Marsh (ed.), *The Canadian Encyclopedia*. Second Edition. Edmonton: Hurtig Publishers. Vol. 1:83.

Waldrum, James B. 1993. "Some Limits to Advocacy Anthropology in the Native Canadian Context." in Noel Dyck and J.B. Waldrum (eds.), *Anthropology, Public Policy and Native Peoples in Canada*. Montreal: McGill-Queen's Press:293-310.

12.

THE NATURE OF THE PRESENT STUDY

by

Richard F. Salisbury

Source: *Development and James Bay: Socio-Economic Implications of the Hydro-electric Project.*
A Report Prepared under contract for the James Bay Development Corporation.
Montreal: McGill University, Programme in the Anthropology of Development,
1972.

The James Bay Development Project has become a major contro-
versy within Quebec, and indeed within Canada generally. The present study is not
intended to take sides in this controversy; it aims to present facts, and by making
inferences from these facts to present some of the likely outcomes of particular
actions which might be taken in the development of the region. These outcomes are
of many kinds, some favourable and some unfavourable to the Indians of the James
Bay region. It is hoped that by spelling out in advance — three and eight years in
advance — what these outcomes might be, it may prove possible to avoid more of
the unfavourable outcomes and to increase the number of favourable outcomes. It
is hoped too, that a study completed in five months, as this one was, may be in time
to have an effect on the planning process in a way that a fuller, more academic study
might not. We hope that academic readers may excuse shortcomings due to haste,
and will realise that a more academic study could have been an ineffective one.

THE CONTROVERSY

Not taking sides in a controversy pleases neither side, and this
report will run that risk. But it would be foolish not to outline the nature of the controversy and to run the risk of being treated as naive. Basically the Quebec National
Assembly approved Bill 50 in May 1971 and set up the James Bay Development
Corporation to satisfy the power needs of the Province as a whole, to provide jobs
for Quebecers throughout the Province, and hopefully also to make a profit from
sales of electricity not initially needed by the Province. The vast scope of the project and the obvious impact it would have on the north of Quebec suggested that the
entire region be formed into a single district for planning and administration by the
Corporation. The only major feasibility studies at the time the project was announced
were engineering and financial ones. The major arguments made before June 1972 in

favour of the project remain technical, in terms of the electricity needs of Quebec, and economic, in terms of the employment and industrial needs of the Province (although the latter have obvious political implications).

The major opposition to the project has come from four main groups, the Cree Indians of the area affected, their supporters (white and Indian) in other areas, ecologists, and people who feel that the proposed development and job creation is illusory and proposed only for political purposes. The Cree Indians feel that the area affected belongs to them. They were not consulted before the decision was taken to begin the project, and they feel that the project would destroy their livelihood and way of life, bound up as it is with hunting and the wildlife of the region. They see no middle ground between their desires, to preserve their Indianness and to develop only in directions which they themselves choose, and the project, which threatens them by its size and seeming inevitability. All they can do is to oppose it, categorically and uncompromisingly. Their supporters accept this Indian position unquestioningly and are even more categorical in their opposition.

The ecologists, shocked at the size of the project, and, despite the warning examples of the Aswan and Peace River dams, at the lack of any preliminary ecological research in the area, have unanimously demanded a delay in implementing the project until adequate ecological research has been undertaken. Those less ready to await scientific research have made their own conclusions. They have discounted the Federal-Provincial ecological Task Force's finding in November 1971 that the ecological damages appeared unlikely to be more than local, but have adopted enthusiastically the finding that the local damage would have major consequences for the Indians of the area. They demand the abandonment of the project.

The political opponents of the project have many bases for disagreement, but only one will be mentioned here. They question whether the power is needed for Quebec, and whether it will generate employment in Quebec. They fear that the power will be sold elsewhere, and that no lasting benefits will be generated in the Province, which will export its resources cheaply to benefit people living elsewhere, notably in the United States. Again they tend to oppose the project categorically, without a close examination of its relationship to Provincial or local needs. To them, and to those political supporters of the Project who give especially superficial consideration to the details of the Project, we can say little.

THE PRESENT STUDY

The concern of the present study is to present facts and to explore their implications. The facts involve both information about the James Bay area and findings from studies of other areas. They will be presented in a non-polemical way, and not as supportive of, or in response to, any of the positions sketched above. Many of the facts presented will, it is true, be relevant to the arguments made by others. It is left to the protagonists of particular positions to use the data as they see fit. Nonetheless a brief review of the set of assumptions on which the study is based and their relationship to the positions taken by the various groups may be appropriate at this point to obviate misunderstandings in the exposition of our findings.

In the first place an assumption made by the research team is that knowledge is for use, and that decisions informed by knowledge are better than uninformed decisions. Equally, however, in a participatory democracy such as exists in Quebec and Canada, all persons affected by a decision should be involved in the making of the decision. This requires that information be available to all parties equally. We are happy that the James Bay Development Corporation agrees with this position, and has agreed that all findings should immediately be made available to the Indians of the area and to the wider Quebec public. It means, we hope, that this document can be part of the compilation of facts that will be needed by all participants in joint planning for the development of the region.

In relation to the James Bay Corporation the present study assumes that it is concerned to make well-informed decisions in good faith which are in the best interests of the people of the James Bay Region and of the Province as a whole. But we are aware that the fullest and clearest information available to the Corporation is technical information on James Bay geology and water supplies, and on the Provincial electricity situation, together with information about finance. It is supplemented by information from the Quebec Government about the Province at large. Any decision-maker tends to be more influenced by "hard" information, so that we have deliberately stressed this kind of information about the effects of the project on the people of the region and about the feelings of those people so that there is some balance in the information going into the Corporation decisions. We trust that in this way social factors and local opinion will gain greater recognition in the formulation of decisions, and that these will not be taken on purely technical or political grounds.

We are also aware how reassuring it is to a decision-maker to make plans to cover every eventuality, and to formulate them in detail before commencing operations. When delays or difficulties emerge there is then a tendency to make every effort to stick to the original plan, and to consider the delays as mistakes by specific people or agencies. It may well be, however, that the difficulties are due to factors unforeseen in the original planning, which the first people to become aware of are the people on the spot. It is our experience in developing countries that the failure of many development plans is not through "obstructionism" or "traditional conservatism" of local people, but because planners failed to take into account knowledge that was available to people on the spot in constructing their plans. They also failed to recognise local problems and to adapt plans to ongoing experience. We, therefore stress, wherever possible, the need for flexible planning, adaptable to local circumstances, and in particular planning that is receptive to feedback from the local people who have the best local information. In particular it is our experience that maximum feedback occurs where people feel that they can influence decisions, and so we emphasise meaningful involvement in decision-making by the local people. If our study can be said to be guided by a philosophy it is that decision-making should be ideally in the hands of the people affected by the decision, but in practice be decentralised to as low a level in any organisation as is possible.

In relation to the Cree Indian position, the present study assumes they will continue their existing public position vis-a-vis the project as a whole of categorical opposition, but will also continue their negotiations regarding territorial and other legal rights. The present report does not deal with the issue of land rights and nothing in it should be construed as a reflection on that issue, which is viewed as *sub judice*. But regardless of the resolution of those claims, be it entirely in favour of the Indian case, or be it less favourable, the present report aims at throwing light on factors which must enter into any discussion of the future of the area — namely the long-term prospects for a continuation of the existing pre-1971 economy and social organization of the area.

Put in the bluntest terms, even if there is no power project, there is likely to be a crisis in Indian society in about five years. The increase of Indian population, its changing demographic composition, its increasing demands for manufactured goods and the services associated with southern Canadian society, will be confronted by the relatively limited potential for expansion of the hunting economy which is now harvesting game at almost capacity. The number of people supported by a hunting economy will remain roughly stable, and unless jobs can be found in the north for the large number of educated young adult Cree who will then be reaching age 20, most young people will be leaving the north for the big Canadian cities. This pattern is well-known from the experience of Indian communities throughout North America. It is hoped that the present report, by outlining the problems inherent in the present situation, may enable the Cree themselves to plan, and to take measures to avoid the crises that this report indicates.

Hydro-electric development is certainly one of the many options that should be considered by the Cree. But even if Cree Indians decide not to support hydro-electric projects, the sections of the present report dealing with the *implications* of hydro-electric development for the area should also be worth consideration for they point to problems and possible solutions to those problems that will emerge with *any* change in the economic base of the region — problems of increasing urbanism, of increasing desires for wage-work, of creating a school system geared to Indian needs, of increasing contact with outsiders.

In saying this another assumption is made, namely, that the Cree will be able to influence the pattern of development in the north, and will be able to choose in a meaningful way what is to be their own future. At the moment they appear to have no choice other than to accept, or to vainly oppose, the decisions made by the Corporation under the powers delegated to it by the National Assembly. Unless a Cree voice can make itself felt in the planning body for the region, no Cree is likely to regard development of the area as taking into account *his* wishes. Participatory democracy will not exist and the present situation of polarised opposition to any project is likely to continue. The value of a report such as the present, which aims to set the scene for discussions of long-term regional planning, is likely to be nil unless a Cree voice is present in the planning body.

In relation to non-Cree supporters of the Cree position the study makes no direct comment. It does however document the reality of many aspects of present-day Cree life and attitudes which differ markedly from the perception of them held by many white Canadians or urbanized Indians.

The Cree are neither living as they did before 1670 nor have they lost most major aspects of their culture. They have accepted, over centuries of limited contact with whites, tools, methods of travel, health services, education, wage employment, food and many other features of Eurocanadian life, and they have so far been able to incorporate them into their own distinctive life-style. In this respect they differ markedly from the many Indian groups who now have to fight hard to preserve their remaining Indian identity.

The Cree want yet other items of Eurocanadian culture, but they want them on their own terms. They do not want to be forced to accept changes that would destroy their life-style, but they are not unthinking conservatives. They do not want to be treated as museum specimens to be preserved for display, but they wish to be respected people who can plan and make their own choices. They oppose the project insofar as it shows them no respect, forces them to accept what they have had no chance of considering, and forces them to give up features of their life which they regard as vital. Material benefits from the project — mainly employment to date — have not been rejected so outrightly. Future relations with the project, if Indian claims to land and to consultation in planning are accepted, are likely to take place on an equally pragmatic basis. It is hoped that this study may assist the Cree in evaluating the costs and benefits of particular aspects of development. In this way it may be useful in their pragmatic approach, if it does not speak to the more dogmatic views of their supporters.

To the ecologists the present study says little. Many issues have been already raised by the 1971 Federal-Provincial Task Force (Ecology Report 1971). This report assumes that their general findings of few major ecological changes likely, but severe local ones in flooded areas, especially for the Indians, is a valid "best estimate." It assumes that further research will be continued to test that proposition and to permit any ecological damage to be rapidly corrected.

But the present study does go further, documenting the nature of the severe effect of flooding on the Indian economy and way of life, especially if there were flooding in the southern areas where hunting is more important. Critical here is the beaver, which, although not the major source of cash (now that wage labour and social welfare benefits exist) remains a major source of subsistence food and the anchor of the hunting way of life. It provides an assured supply of food even when other sources fail, and a regular cash income, that covers at least the expenses of outfitting a winter in the bush. Without it, or at least in areas where beavers would cease to be common, a hunting economy would cease. While flooding might undoubtedly cause lesser effects on other wildlife — moose, caribou, geese, etc. — the effect on any of them would likely be less than critical. The present study thus confirms the relatively more serious effects that flooding would have in the south as against in the north. But at the same time it points out the need to minimise the damage to migratory fish of dams on the Fort George and Kaniapiskau Rivers, although figures are not available to fully document this.

As has been said in relation to the more political arguments against the project the present study also has little to say. It has taken as its bases for projections the figures and data supplied by earlier studies prepared for the James Bay Development Corporation, together with data from government departments in Quebec and Ottawa, and from anthropological studies. While none of these sources is likely to be 100% accurate, and discrepancies exist within the various sources used, the possible errors are pointed out in this study.

262

Most significant for present purposes, however, is the fact that whatever errors exist in the data, they are not likely to be errors that would *all* be in favour, or *all* be against any particular interpretation and so of political significance. They would tend overall to cancel one another out. To take two examples, the figures cited on employment projections for dam construction, though they may be incorrect, cannot be dismissed as systematically high or low. They were compiled as part of an estimate of the total cost of the project, and if any bias existed it would most likely be that the cost would be conservatively estimated, and so that the employment figures would be *lower* than what might eventuate. If they were politically influenced it might be inferred that they would indicate that *more* jobs would be created. This would, however, mean that costs would then be higher than necessary. The net effect of these two pressures is thus likely to be that the figures are in fact the best estimate possible.

A second example would be the figures for game animals trapped in the James Bay area, provided by the Quebec Department of Tourism, Fish and Game. Independently gathered figures (Feit 1972, Tanner 1971) suggest that these figures slightly underestimate actual catches, since they are based on furs sold, and there are exchanges of furs between individual trappers previous to sales, so that records of sales do not precisely reflect who did the trapping. Nonetheless, these errors are of little overall significance. A slightly higher actual beaver catch at the moment might mean that current food and cash incomes were really slightly higher than indicated in the report. On the other hand, if more animals were being caught than the figures indicate, then the potentialities for future catch increases up to the capacity of the land are that much smaller. If the present picture is not quite rosy enough, then the picture of the future is not quite black enough. In other words, the bias is not a systematic one. The figures were not collected to prove any particular case, and thus the case which emerges from them is inherent in the facts, and not politically motivated.

PROBLEMS IN THE STUDY

The present study, unfortunately, has few precedents in the field of anthropology. Anthropology as a scientific discipline has usually involved *post hoc* analysis of events which have already occurred, and has usually been content to point out what went wrong in past events, or to hope that a happy present would continue. It has rarely tried to see one event as causing another in such a way as to permit a prediction of the future when once a few critical facts are known.

To attempt prediction we have tried to borrow techniques and designs for study from the fields of cost-benefit analysis, and regional planning in economics, together with more everyday projection techniques from demography. We have reviewed a wide literature in educational and urban anthropology, and on northern Canada and Alaska, to find propositions that were capable for reformulation in positive, predictional terms. We have become ever more aware as we have continued, how sketchy is the state of our knowledge, how simple it would be (given funds and time) to conduct a hundred and one studies that would improve the accuracy of these projections we now make. Even obtaining official statistics for many fields has not proved possible within the time available to us, although we are also dubious as to whether the appropriate statistics always exist.

This leads to our greatest caveat, a caveat that applies to all economic planning projections, that the projections are always based on assumptions. The study attempts to make clear what those assumptions are with each projection — for example in population projections these are that the 1970 fertility rate for Indian women will continue for the next decade, as will the average mortality rate for 1960-70, and that there will be no loss of individuals from band records. The assumptions may turn out to be factually incorrect, and so the projections may turn out to be not factually correct. The point is that by making the assumptions it is possible to examine hypothetical future effects, and if an individual does not like the future that he sees — for example, if he doesn't like the population increase we predict — he can act to make the assumptions incorrect. He could, for example, act to decrease fertility rates even further through family planning, or to increase migration rates by subsidising emigration. The fact that we make an assumption does not mean that we think, in any way, that the things we assume *ought* to take place. We usually try to make several purely arbitrary assumptions (e.g. on the proportion of the labour force that would want to work on dam construction) so that we can examine which assumption leads to the most desirable conclusion. We hope that the reader will be clear at all points what the basis is for our saying such and such an event is likely to occur; it is a statement of probability, based on facts which are stated, and on assumptions which are stated. It is what is most likely to occur, if the facts are the way we say and the assumptions eventuate. In many cases, it should be clear, we make predictions to alert planners about undesirable consequences, and so to encourage them to alter the course of events.

The generality of some of our figures, and the inaccuracies many of them contain, are probably not such serious defects if the foregoing remarks about prediction are heeded. The study demands that it be challenged, that its findings not be taken for granted, but be taken as a starting point for debate. This debate should encourage the collection of more precise and accurate data, and we look forward to continuing in that task. But the debate needs to be structured. The relevance of facts to the argument needs to be stressed. In attempting prediction we feel we are showing the relevance of particular facts to arguments — thus the nature of adolescent aspirations may have been studied in relation to the formative influence of different types of schools (Sindell 1969), but the present context makes those facts highly relevant to discussions of the employment market among the Indians. The facts we now use, dating from 1968, may be inaccurate, but our use of them in predicting 1975 employment patterns still gives the best available estimate for 1975, and hopefully will encourage the collection of newer data which would provide better estimates. The newer data become relevant, however, in the context of the argument we develop.

Within these general limitations let us then sketch the major outlines of the study. We take four major topics, each in a separate section — population, economy (subdivided into hunting and wage employment), education, and urbanism. For each topic we attempt to survey the current state of affairs in the James Bay region, treating the Indian sector and the white, Eurocanadian sector separately. We are much briefer in dealing with the latter sector for we feel that many of the activities and social structure of that population is well-known to other Canadians. Its development is the subject of studies by other agencies. Our study includes it as it is impossible to obtain a balanced view of the development of the region without considering the white population. We hope that our discussion of it is at least adequate, to indicate the extent to which Indian development in the region is affected by what happens in the white sector.

For each section we then follow with a set of predictions. We attempt to predict what would likely happen if there were no James Bay project, but only a continuation of pre-1971 activities and trends — population growth, hunting and trapping, mining, a forest industry, and some tourism, etc. We then consider what the prediction would be should the James Bay project go ahead, in an attempt to assess the extent to which it would supply benefits (positive or negative), not as compared with current conditions, but as compared with what might otherwise happen in 1980. Fortunately the "James Bay Project" is not an irrevocable unchangeable scheme, and within the global assumption that a project will occur, we can examine alternative assumptions to assess which parts of the project yield the most benefits. We deal only lightly with the possibility that the project will involve the diversion and major flooding of the Broadback-Nottaway and Rupert River drainage basin, since it seems that the November 1971 Task Force Report on Ecology recommendation against proceeding with this part of the project has been heeded in the May 1972 decisions about the Project. For most of the study we assume that actual construction will be limited to the Fort George (La Grande) River, and nearby rivers. But our discussion is of the whole region affected by Bill 50. We also deal with alternative patterns of Indian involvement in the project — minimum involvement in wage labour, and maximum involvement — in an effort to stress what the effect of the two patterns would be by 1982.

In terms of both urbanism and education we rapidly exhaust the possibilities of prediction using firm assumptions, and we are forced to consider the alternative choices open during the coming period from a different standpoint. We look at possible social arrangements that might, from our projections, be envisaged for 1982 (or a date post 1980, when major construction was over), and look back at the sort of decisions that would have had to be made earlier to arrive at those conclusions. Most dramatically, for educational planning, taking a possible target for what might be a desirable distribution of employment within Indian society for 1982 enables one to consider what are the options open in the near future. It enables one to consider the evidence for and against each option.

Recommendations, we feel, spring quite readily from our analysis. While as individuals we are capable of making recommendations, we feel strongly that the people affected by the project should have the first chance to see our analysis. Undoubtedly, they have divergent interests and goals; it is in the light of those goals that they should decide what they want to do; having presented our analysis and heard what the goals are, any recommendations should then involve merely an interpretation of the findings of the analysis.

REFERENCES

Feit, Harvey. 1972. Waswanipi Realities and Adaptations: Resource Management and Cognitive Structure. Ph.D. Thesis (1979). Montreal: McGill University.

Tanner, Adrian. 1971. *"Existe-t-il des Territoires de Chasse? La baie James des Amérindiennes."* Recherches Amérindiennes au Québec 1 (4-5):69-83.

Sindell, Peter S. 1969. "How Going Away to School Changes Children." *Reports of the Findings on Education, McGill-Cree Project.* Mimeo.

13.

THE ANTHROPOLOGIST AS SOCIETAL OMBUDSMAN

by

Richard F. Salisbury

Source: David Pitt (ed.), *Development from Below.* The Hague: Mouton 1976.

Since April 1971 my colleagues and I, of the McGill Programme in the Anthropology of Development, have been involved in two projects of what may be called applied anthropology, one in New Guinea and one in northern Canada. Both, it is felt, imply a somewhat new conception of the role of the anthropologist as an intermediary in trouble situations between central agencies and local groups. A report on the two projects and an analysis of the conditions under which this role emerges is timely.

THE PROJECTS

The substantive findings of both projects have already been published as *Problems of the Gazelle Peninsula of New Britain* (Salisbury 1971) and *Development and James Bay* (Salisbury et. al. 1972) so that the nature of each can be summarized here very briefly. In New Guinea a dispute between two factions in the most politically sophisticated and wealthiest language group, the Tolai, had escalated over the previous four years into violence. The issue, as then phrased, was between a "nationalist" faction favoring the development of local government within the framework of ordinances set up for the whole of Papua New Guinea and a "separatist" faction demanding idiosyncratic institutions for the Tolai. Attempts by the central government of Papua New Guinea and by educated Tolai residents elsewhere had failed to obtain agreement between the factions. The attempts of the government to enforce ordinances and maintain services (e.g. keeping roads open) had involved tacit support of the "nationalists" and had exacerbated the polarization.

In July 1971, presumably feeling that most avenues had been tried and that trying an anthropologist might help and could not make things worse, the administrator of Papua New Guinea asked if I would act as a consultant to investigate the situation and, if so, under what conditions. Although the role of consultant for governments is an established one, this role in its usual form was impossible for an anthropologist aware of the strong feelings among the Tolai and knowing that any

269

solution imposed from outside would be no solution. At the same time it would have been an abdication of responsibility to Tolai friends *not* to try to assist them in solving their difficulties, and it would have been a confession of intellectual bankruptcy *not* to stick by the diagnosis of Tolai problems in political development given in my earlier study (Salisbury 1970) which anticipated all the issues of 1971.

The problem was to specify conditions that would make a new role possible. Briefly, the conditions then asked for were the publication of any findings, and agreement by all parties to my conducting an investigation. As far as was practically feasible, given the formal requirement that my report be first submitted to His Honour the Administrator, and given the condition that "the parties" could be approached only informally, the conditions were agreed to. Research was conducted from August 1 to August 31, 1971, at which time a final report was submitted.

In the northern Canadian project the announcement was made in April, 1971, by the premier of Quebec that a 6,000,000,000 dollar hydroelectric scheme would be inaugurated involving damming the major rivers flowing into James Bay and inundating about a third of the hunting territories of various Cree Indian bands, with whom members of our program had been working for six years. We protested that such a decision had been taken without adequate investigation of the social and ecological impacts of the project on the area and without any consultation with the local people. We were asked, in reply, what social research should have been done, and whether we would do it. We indicated the research needed but said we would do it only if the Indians agreed to our doing so and had full access to our findings.

An understanding was soon reached with the Indians of Quebec Association, including provisions that workers from the program would undertake *field* projects only after these had been specifically approved by the Association and only if no Indian group wished to conduct them itself. It took longer before the statutorily-established James Bay Development Corporation accepted the desirability of public access of findings, but once convinced, they actively (and financially) supported our reporting back of the findings to the Indians of Quebec Association and to the Cree Indians.

The study was begun in January, 1972; a report based almost exclusively on published materials and on-going unpublished research by members of the program (and here I must acknowledge the work of Harvey Feit, Jacqueline Hyman, Ignatius LaRusic, and Peter Sindell) was completed in June; feedback of results to Indian groups (and some fieldwork commissioned by the Indians of

270

Quebec Association) lasted into August: and a final report was submitted in September.

Lest it be thought that I am claiming that anthropologists can *solve* problems, I would hasten to add that the issues in both areas are still, in late 1972, involved in intense controversy. But what has happened in both areas has been that a central planning agency (the central government and the Development Corporation) has become much more sensitive to the issues as they appear to the local people and has changed its policies following the reports. On the other side, and here I speak with much less confidence and optimism, many local people have realized the complexity of issues and the possibility of obtaining what they wish through a variety of courses of action of which they had not previously been aware. What is occurring, in short, is that local people are bargaining and negotiating on their own behalf, and on terms closer to equality, with central agencies which had previously appeared distant and all-powerful.

In such a situation the potential contributions of an anthropologist are twofold. The first is to translate and make intelligible to people with a particular perspective the viewpoint of a different group — to phrase locally significant issues in terms understandable to policy makers and to explain to local people the ways in which planners and administrative bureaucracies go about their work. The second is to use the accumulated knowledge of the discipline to suggest possible courses of action *to both sides* — be it how to overcome organizational problems in small businesses or how to avoid the problems of hinterland denudation by large northern settlements. I stress *to both sides*, for I am convinced that when an anthropologist commits himself to one side only, he nullifies many of the benefits that his professional training could give to that side. He is not able to retain any confidence from the other side and so is unlikely to make an accurate analysis of that side's point of view, while any analysis he makes of his own side's point of view is unlikely to carry weight with the other side.

More generally, a major finding of anthropology over the last twenty years has been that to understand and to change any social situation requires a knowledge not only of the internal dynamics of the situation but also of the nature of the macrosystem which provides parameters for the situation. An anthropologist who confines himself to attempting change only one aspect — the macrosystem *or* the microsystem — is ignoring this finding, at his peril.

Field Research Methods

In both studies traditional procedures for nonapplied anthropological research were adopted and found suitable. First, basic sources of data were reviewed to suggest problems requiring detailed investigation and analysis. Second, introductions were made with officials concerned with the area. Third, relationships were established with significant individuals at the local level. Fourth, open activity as a participant-observer, data collector, and analyst established an awareness of the anthropologist and his distinctive role. Finally, the data were analyzed and immediate feedback provided to informants at all levels. Reviewing these stages and the modifications required may serve to clarify the problems involved with the societal ombudsman role.

If we consider the stage of specifying the problems requiring detailed investigation, three observations can be made. First, speed was essential if either of the studies was to have an impact on a situation that was in rapid flux. Meeting this demand was possible only because the investigators had previous experience in the areas and had remained in touch, and so could cut the time needed for the first stage down to a minimum. The availability of investigators at short notice was fortunate but could not always be relied upon to be the case, even though training of workers has been more systematic and concise studies of limited periods have been stressed in our training program.

Second, in neither case did basic descriptive materials need to be collected since previous studies had been done. And third, theoretical work on similar problems in other areas provided a series of possible interpretations of the situations which were neither those assumed by central planners nor those believed in by local people. Caribbean studies of the role of "separatist" groupings in wider region politics provided insights into the New Guinea situation: studies of Eskimo population growth and migration to cities provided a different point of view on the impact of northern industrial development from that held by individuals believing that the major impact of dams was an ecological one.

The three observations hang together. If anthropology is to find applied value in this way, there is a need to maintain a continuing flow of descriptive anthropological studies of communities everywhere. Only a few will be of significance for advancing theory, though basic theory is vital. A majority would serve to provide information needed *within* the communities to help them operate and to provide the base for specialist studies, should these be needed in crises. A constant supply of researchers would then be available to communities to call upon in times of crisis. While these could be specialists, located in universities or institutes but keeping up links with regions in which they have worked, it seems simpler and ultimately more desirable for local people with training to find employment conducting research in their own communities. The foreign anthropologist studying an exotic community may well become a thing of the past when the techniques and findings of anthropology are learned and applied by researchers to their own societies.

The second stage of establishing relationships at the central official level involved for the ombudsman dramatically different procedures from those of the traditional anthropological study. Since he had been invited by senior officials, neither "permission" nor access to information was a problem. The problem, from an anthropological viewpoint, was how to treat senior officials as informants, in order to build up a realistic picture of the structure of officialdom and its policies that could be communicated to local people. The realistic picture in both the cases considered is not that of a monolithic, intransigent, and insensitive hierarchy, but rather that of a set of well-meaning individuals pursuing many conflicting ends, believing in a number of objectively inaccurate stereotypes, but trying to be consistent within a framework of "the law" and "the regular channels." Describing such a picture would make comprehensible to local people the seeming stupidities of planners, while also permitting local people to see the means by which their own wishes can be obtained from planners. But to do so without giving the impression that one agrees with what the planners have said, and without betraying the confidence of any individual informant within officialdom is difficult. If one does not practice the same tact and confidentiality in discussions with officials that one exercises in interviews with other informants, one cannot expect to play a useful role.

The other danger of being officially briefed and sponsored is, of course, that one's impartiality is suspect to nonofficials. I know of no way of overcoming suspicion, which I take to be an entirely justified reaction, other than behaving completely openly. The openness must start from the very first, when the possibility of such work is first broached, and must not be left exclusively to official press releases. Press reports before I arrived in New Guinea emphasized my status as a "government expert" and seriously jeopardized my work; direct contacts with all parties and an avoidance of the press avoided many difficulties in Canada. Publication of final results, however, is a vital part of openness, though not the whole story. The ombudsman must be consistent in maintaining openness on all sides. A government official must know that you are going to talk to an opposition politician from the local area and that you will not necessarily actively uphold the government position: a village radical must know that you have an appointment with the district commissioner tomorrow morning. Both must know that not only will you respect what they tell you in confidence and not identify them in any way that would bring them harm but also that the content of what they say will be treated as public information.

Confidentiality of private information is one thing, but the *open transmittal* of information when informants want it transmitted, and in a form that is understandable to the recipient, is crucial to the ombudsman role. Traditional analyses of this role have emphasized that the ombudsman communicates complaints from individuals to officials while having authority over some officials; the obverse is also true: the ombudsman must convey information about official policies and structures to the individual citizen.

Even though openness is necessary to overcome suspicion, it does not by itself create confidence. Anthropologists have a long way to go to engender confidence among officials, as Cochrane (1971), an administrative official in the Solomon Islands, has forcefully argued. This confidence can only come if anthropologists use as much care in their analysis of officialdom and in their relationships with individual officials as they do in the analysis of any other culture. It is less widely admitted that anthropologists often do not have the confidence of local people. But, with individual exceptions, in New Guinea and among American Indians anthropologists are viewed as useless seekers after exotica, unable to help local people over issues that they feel are significant, or offering help but then leaving the community when the going becomes difficult.

The articulation of local concerns in a language understandable by officialdom is thus one major way of gaining trust; a second way is the accurate and informed analysis of official policy and procedures. It requires, I maintain, a professional ethic of scientific impartiality and openness, which this paper attempts to spell out. Even so, one must recognize that suspicion exists and is normal; to try to overcome it by deceit is both unethical and self-defeating. If openness does not overcome it, then there is no answer but to discontinue the work and to publicly state the reasons why.

The third phase — introduction to locally important people — and the fourth phase — data collection — have been discussed to some extent in the previous section. In brief, the anthropological ombudsman must behave no differently in relation to officialdom from the way he behaves in relation to community members. Local opinion, voiced by local leaders, has as much significance for him but is also liable to exactly the same degree of distortion and selective perception as the views of officials. Not only the same degree of interest and attention but also the same degree of considered scepticism must be paid to local views. The stance of neither agreeing with nor opposing an informant, but of wishing to understand exactly what his opinions or policies are, is, in my experience, the ideal field approach to obtaining a precise statement of those views. It is not merely an interviewing technique but a consistent practice of what one can state explicitly, namely that the anthropologist will express publicly but anonymously the view of the informant even if the anthropologist does not himself agree with them.

The first corollary of this approach is that those sections of any report spelling out local views must be made available to local people for comment and correction before the report appears in final form. In New Guinea I was fortunate that, with the permission of the administrator and thanks to the ability of a skilled Tolai radio interviewer, I was able to present such a preview in Tolai over the local radio station to an audience of an estimated 60 percent of the population. Feedback was rapid and positive.

A second corollary is that one must clearly indicate that the anthropologist ombudsman is in no sense a replacement for "regular channels" of local expression of opinion. Local politicians are, by definition, the spokesmen for their communities and the individuals most concerned to explain to local people (in positive or negative terms) the impact of central policies on local communities. The anthropological ombudsman can only stress that he may have certain abilities enabling him to make those local views intelligible to central officials, and certain knowledge of channels, not available to local politicians, that can supplement direct action by them. Any final settlement of problems must eventually be made through negotiation by local politicians, and the anthropological ombudsman must diligently work to avoid preempting their role. Preempting it would weaken the local community in the long run and result in conflict with those politicians, at a time when providing them with information about their constituencies and about officialdom would make them more effective.

But what one can provide for local people is more than simply information about channels of communication in centralized bureaucracies. A range of generalized findings exists about development — processes of urbanization, business organizational structures, political mobilization and decentralization, manpower training and brain drains, cultural identity and education, industrialism and dependency and many more topics — about which people at large (and here I would generalize even to developed countries) know little. What is generally current "knowledge" is often stereotyped and inaccurate and leads at the local level to the adoption of courses of action typified by the well-known *kago* cults in New Guinea. Though these may seem exceptional and bizarre to outsiders, twenty years of experience of *kago*-thinking has brought home to me the point most dramatically made by Peter Lawrence (1964), that they are a self-consistent and logical reaction, given certain

275

premises about the role of ancestral spirits, to what New Guineans have observed of "development" over the past fifty years. The reactions of people to social change in other areas, based on equally unprovable assumptions, would seem equally bizarre to those who do not share their particular assumptions. More accurate comparative knowledge of the development process is vitally needed.

The anthropologist, as a professional specializing in knowledge about these findings, has an obligation to make them available to people at large and not merely to officials in central bureaucracies. In discussions with local people about their own opinions, this obligation can be easily fulfilled and knowledge communicated by phrasing one's considered scepticism of their opinions in terms such as, "But have you considered what happened in Area X, where they did Y?" In such an indirect way one can introduce ideas to people without advocating them oneself. One encourages an informant to clarify his own position to the listener and to himself by showing that a number of alternative positions exist beside his own and that of his antagonist. If, in so doing, the informant sees advantages in the third position, it is a matter of his own choice if he takes it up. He has not been forced into it by the anthropologists. The anthropologist is only an information source, not an advocate of a particular policy. As an ombudsman he is a catalyst in a situation where the actors are the local people themselves in interaction with central officials and planners.

CONCLUSIONS

It is clear that the ombudsman role for the anthropologist can exist only under certain circumstances. I take it as axiomatic in the world of today that in all areas the need exists for increased communication between central bureaucracies and smaller, relatively powerless local or grass-roots groupings, and that the relative powerlessness of those groupings depends in large part on their lack of access to information. The need for ombudsmen is universal, but the emergence of ombudsmen implies more. In the first place, there must be relatively enlightened central bureaucracy. It must accept that local views may differ from its own, may be justified, and should be listened to, but that it is not omniscient and can only profit by obtaining clearer expressions of local problems to which it must then respond. It must also be ready to explain its own policies and procedures to the general public and must be willing to trust information intermediaries with discretionary powers to reveal information. Such an ideology of "participatory democracy" is not universal, and the projects reported here may have been possible only because of the enlightened nature of officialdom in the two countries.

In the second place, the emergence of an ombudsman role implies that ordinary people of a particular locality place confidence in an outsider appointed and paid by an official organization and trusted by that organization. The experience of national officialdom in many villages of the world makes this condition a rarity on the world scene. Priests, doctors, and lawyers fill some of the specifications, but rarely all of them, since local trust in them often varies inversely with their involvement in national organizations while official trust varies inversely with their community involvement. In any case, their technical preparation does not equip them for the dual role. By contrast, the anthropologist is specifically trained to shift perspectives and to evoke personal trust in small communities while retaining professional status in the wider society. They are often the first nongovernmental professionals that villagers get to know well.

The third necessary condition for the emergence of the ombudsman role is that it be possible to diagnose the nature of the disjuncture between central official planning and local practice and *to do something about it* other than forcing local practice to change. Many disciplines can provide experts who can diagnose how official plans could be improved from a central viewpoint, or how local practice should be changed. Something is very commonly done following official reports of such "experts," but often without remedying the disjuncture. Anthropologists by their training have been habituated to diagnosing what is wrong from the viewpoint of villagers, but then getting nothing done about it because they are unable to communicate their diagnosis to national planners.

Anthropology as a discipline needs to develop its theory of how local level changes can produce national level consequences, and must develop in its practitioners the ability to talk to national planners in their own language. If they succeed, more of their recommendations will be acted upon by planners (at least, if one assumes the same level of good-will among planners in different societies). Whether or not the information and general theory communicated by anthropologists is seen as useful by local people is even more crucial. For that to happen it has to be good advice, and it has to be acted upon. As I have indicated, our own efforts are still being weighed in the balance of experience.

In short, anthropologists with some additional training seem excellently situated to fill the role of societal ombudsman, should such a role emerge. The societal ombudsman is needed when apparently insoluble problems emerge in local societies as a result of central policies and plans. It involves an investigative role, accepted by the central bureaucracy to the extent that the investigator has status and is given cooperation by all officials, but outside the "regular channels" of the bureaucracy.. The role must be accepted by all parties to the situation. It must be primarily a role of open communicator of information, in a form that respects individual privacy and confidentiality, and this flow of information must be both upwards and downwards. As an interpreter of foreign cultures the anthropologist should be able to communicate to officials about small societies by speaking an "official" language. In practice he often cannot, as he speaks a language special to anthropologists. But if the anthropologist is prepared to approach official bureaucracies with the same aims of understanding a "foreign" language and culture, he will do a better job. If at the same time, he has technical knowledge of the processes of developmental change, he could phrase the aims of planners in terms comprehensible to local people, while also suggesting to the local people ways of achieving their wishes which they did not previously realize.

By this means he can remain the professional anthropologist, dispassionately evaluating information, conducting research, and communicating the findings of his own research and of the discipline *to both sides*. By acting as an information broker he can be a catalyst for solving problems whose solution is achieved by negotiations between local groups and officialdom. Although his contribution of knowledge aids both sides, his major usefulness is to the relatively less knowledgeable local groups, who can then use his knowledge to bargain with officialdom on a relatively equal basis. Anthropologists can, sometimes, be useful to their subjects.

REFERENCES

Cochrane, G. 1971. "The case for fieldwork by officials." *Man* 6:279-284.

Lawrence, P. 1964. *Road Belong Cargo*. Manchester: Manchester University Press.

Salisbury, R. F. 1970. *Vunamami: Economic Transformation in a Traditional Society*. Berkeley: University of California Press.

------------1971. *Problems of the Gazelle Peninsula of New Britain*. Port Moresby: Government Printer.

Salisbury, R. F., F. G. Filion, F. Rawji and D. Stewart. 1972. *Development and James Bay*. Montreal: McGill Programme in the Anthropology of Development.

14.

THE NORTH AS A DEVELOPING NATION

by

Richard F. Salisbury

Source: Proceedings of the 8th National Northern Development Conference. Edmonton: Department of Information, Government of the Northwest Territories, 1979.

The theme for this Conference is "At the Turning Point." If we look at the history of the Developing World — the Third World as many of us refer to it — for the last forty years, one major event stands out as the turning point for each developing nation — the achieving of political independence. What I want to do tonight is to look at what that turning point has meant for the nations of the Third World, what happened before independence and what is currently happening, and to see what lessons their experience has for Canada as the north approaches its political turning point, that will be marked by the culmination of Mr. Drury's mission, by decisions on the future political status of the Northwest Territories, and by the resolution of the Inuit and Dene land claims.

The parallel between the north and the Third World is for me so clear that I hope I may be excused in presenting it in terms of personal experience. I began my field research into Third World Development in 1952 in Papua New Guinea. A comfortable scheduled airline flight from metropolitan Sydney to the administrative centre of Port Moresby brought me to a town where office-work was the main industry, where most senior positions were occupied by non-residents while contact with the native people in town was very restricted for someone staying at the hotel. Once outside the capital I hitched a ride on a cargo DC-3 to the area of my study, to be welcomed at the airstrip by virtually the total white population — the local administrator, the missionary, the trading company representative, and the airline rep. During my year living in a village three days walk out from the airstrip (a jeep road was levelled manually during that year) I experienced all the frustrations of there being no "infrastructure," no stores, no regular mail, no roads, no one to repair broken typewriters unless you filed your own pieces of metal to replace what wore out, and learned why you have to have a patient attitude to schedules if you are to exist without ulcers. In a stunning contrast I also visited as a player on the Highlands football team, a gold mine, Bulolo Gold Dredge (I didn't then know it was a Vancouver company). The luxury of running water, of efficient transport, of production run by the clock, of the immense capital equipment of the (then still operating) dredges, and of the plywood manufacturing equipment they were installing — things that are taken for granted in our own industrial society — suddenly appeared as foreign implants that didn't fit in with local society, to one who had become acclimatized to the Third World.

My first fieldwork in the Canadian North, in Fort George, Quebec in 1972 also involved taking a cargo DC-3 up from Val d'Or, where we had spent the previous day flying from Montreal on Air Canada and talking with DINA officials. The people at Fort George airstrip were from the same groups as in PNG. We had the same problems over non-existent infra-structure, and the same need for a stoical acceptance of the non-appearance of flights out and to remoter settlements. The same contrasts were clear when the high-technology activity of the James Bay Energy Corporation were encountered; the same segregation of the economy into two sectors, the local, subsistence based economy involving a majority of low-paid native people using a low technology, and the externally oriented, high technology, affluent economy mainly involving whites. Not only the economy appeared a segregated one, but so did the government. White officials in Val d'Or talked easily of planning and administering the area, but were much more numerous than either the providers of social services in the local settlements, or the Band Council officers who were the only native people involved in Government.

I am sure that everyone who has been north will recognize the general themes of these descriptions, although depending on one's field of action one person may see only a limited section of the global picture. You may be involved in efficient high-technology industry, and deplore the local hunting economy, and the people in it who persist in working when convenient to "Indian time." You may be a government official and see the problems of extending social services over sparsely populated areas, annoyed (or at least a little disappointed) that local people do not welcome very enthusiastically all the "improvements" you are bringing, and that the wealthy industrial developers are in too much of a hurry and demand results tomorrow when restricted government budgets mean results cannot be expected for years. Or you may live in a small settlement, may experience the problems that local people have with their shortage of capital, their low salaries, and their vulnerability both to policy decisions made far away in Ottawa or Yellowknife, and to the immense resources of companies. The views and frustrations of each group have their basis in reality; no one view is the "correct" view, while the others are "wrong"; all three views of the empirical situation have to be borne in mind if we hope that in the future there will be real development in the north.

My sketch of the elements of under-development in a Third World country is taken from a period well before independence. In fact Papua New Guinea did not become independent until 1975. But the sketch provides a basis for spelling out what the Third World expected would be the result of independence. First and foremost was the idea that if political decisions were made in the territory, by residents of the territory, then one would ensure that the decisions that were made were to benefit local people and not to advance the interests of the colonial power, or of the industrial and trading firms that usually had head offices in the metropolitan country. Allied with this was usually the idea that the improvement of social services in the country had been too slow under the colonial government, and had not used local resources in locally appropriate ways. This would be changed as local people staffed the public service, and became responsive to the needs and demands of the general public in ways that expatriates could not be. Insofar as the economic effects of independence were considered there was the expectation of surges in local employment, and in the promotion of local people to their rightful level of skill to replace non-nationals who would speedily be "phased-out"; there was an expectation that a national government would stand up to foreign companies, preventing them from exploiting the local economy, and at the same time would encourage local entrepreneurs to make products for the local economy which foreign companies would not manufacture locally, as they had their own manufacturing plants in the metropolitan country. In that way it was thought the new country would develop its own industry to meet its own internal market, and in so doing it would change the class structure of the country. Instead of an aristocracy of 2% of whites, an incipient middle class of 10% of office workers and semi-skilled personnel in industry, and an overwhelming majority involved in farming for subsistence and export production, local people would rise above the middle class and large numbers of poor agriculturalists would obtain jobs in industry and administration.

If one makes adjustments for the fact that the North hunts, rather than farms, for its subsistence, the expectations I have listed match those of Northern groups such as the Dene Nation.

This rosy anticipatory picture is not what has actually happened in the Third World. In many ways the Third World feels that not much has changed in the last forty years which saw independence, as is witnessed in the recent North-South debates of the UNCTAD conference in Manila. Per capita GNP in the Third World is growing more slowly than in developed countries. For all that Third World Governments are staffed predominantly by local people, there is doubt as to whether they make the right decisions for the interests of their citizens, either because they are pressured by developed countries, or by multinational corporations, or because they represent only a segment of their countries. Efficiency in the delivery of serv-

283

ices is not usually their strong point. The upsurge in employment has benefited an elite whose lifestyle now resembles the colonial officials they replaced, but there has also been an immense migration of former agriculturalists to the towns that were the old administrative centres, and the large numbers of the immigrants have not found salaried jobs. The result is the transformation of towns by new areas of under-serviced squatting settlements, where many people have no jobs, but "hustle" for a living, where about half the population with regular employment is employed by the government, and where capital intensive industry is expanding only slowly, is not providing the expected employment, and is still largely foreign-owned. The low income countries see themselves as remaining poor, as never overcoming the technological gulf that separates the farmers from large-scale industry. Much of the rhetoric of current UN, UNCTAD and North-South debates is concerned to place blame for why the high expectations of pre-independence days have not been realised – usually trying to place it on the wealthy countries of the OECD, or "the capitalist system."

My own conclusions are that many of the expectations were false and unrealistic in the first place, while a major factor in creating the present situation has been the policies of over-emphasis on industrialisation and urbanisation that many Third World countries have themselves pursued, instead of pursuing policies of building up the productivity and prosperity of their primary sectors at a matching rate, to provide a viable base and infra-structure for the towns and local manufacturers. If I may anticipate my final conclusion somewhat, I hope that Northern development may profit from the experience of the Third World and that a decentralised Northern government may adopt policies of balance and partnership in industrial and subsistence production, that can enable local residents to benefit from improvements in the social infra-structure that would then ensue.

But to return to the nature of Third World development. Why, if in many ways the Third World has not dramatically changed its relationship to the industrial world over the past thirty years, do I take independence as a turning point? One world-wide survey of changes in GNP in Third World countries tried to correlate them with a variety of factors. Clearly for individual countries specific events (like, for Papua New Guinea, the opening of a multi-million dollar copper mine on Bougainville, or the boom in coffee prices after the Brazil frost) make for great changes up and down, but among the factors that were more general the only one that consistently preceded a jump in the long-term rate of increase of GNP was the achievement of independence.

Realistically what did independence do? I would isolate three major effects, that were included in the expectations. Firstly that the personnel of government in the country was rapidly "localised." Secondly that foreign businesses now had to negotiate with the local government regarding the terms on which the businesses could operate — conditions of employment, royalties on oil or minerals extracted, the import of capital and the export of profits, etc. — and thirdly, that major investments were made in building the trappings of a nation state — parliament buildings, sports complexes, airports, universities, etc. The expansionist potential of all these changes is apparent. The increase in the incomes of the local public service provides for a major increase in consumer demands, both for imported goods and for local products. The commitment of local governments to industrialise and to increase export earnings coupled with the potential for local sales or the availability of local resources or manpower means that foreign industries and governments were eager to invest, and to agree on terms for that investment. The direct government investments created additional local employment, particularly in construction, and the imports needed for such construction were usually supplied freely, either as a gift from the former colonial government, or as a low-interest loan from another government wishing to gain favour. Local euphoria over independence further encouraged expansionist attitudes, especially as the major beneficiaries of the new jobs were the relatively well educated segment of society living near the capital cities where government investments were made.

The long-term disillusionment of the Third World can, however, be traced to the potentially negative aspects of these same changes. High salaries for local public servants, employment in the public service constituting a patronage benefit usable by governments to reward supporters, and a concentration of such servants in large cities, all combine to make possible the growth of a major rift between the very well-off pro-government elite in the urban areas, and a dissatisfied rural population. The latter has profited little from independence and sees its main avenues for increasing wealth as migration to towns to share in the wealth and the amenities that exist there. The elite and the bureaucracy, without long traditions of efficiency or public service, in many countries have found difficulty in providing the services that the public demands. Their affluence (coupled with accusations of corruption and inefficiency) makes a dramatic contrast with the poverty conditions of rural immigrants to town. The consumer demands of such an elite tend towards foreign travel, Mercedes cars, Scotch whisky, and other expensive international items that drain the foreign currency earnings of generally poor Third World countries.

The agreements negotiated with foreign industries to persuade them to invest in Third World countries have proved to have major drawbacks. Branch-plant installations erected to jump tariff boundaries have often remained uncompetitive internationally, and have been kept operating by the parent company only as long as tax holidays or other Government subsidies have kept them profitable for the foreign owners. Agreements on royalty payments that appeared magnanimous in the 1950's or 1960's (i.e. when compared to practices current at the time), appear very one-sided in the light of modern standards, or when a mining royalty based on a percentage of profits (rather than on tonnage of ore shipped) yields nothing in a year of international recession. Investments that apparently would earn large amounts of foreign exchange, like tourist hotels, have often turned out to require continued imports of foreign goods and services that leave little money in the country itself. If the investments are made on the basis of foreign loans, the interest on the loans may prove higher than the input into the local economy, and is due in foreign currency. If the investment is made by the local loans or Government subsidy to the hotel firm, the retention of control by a foreign firm is questioned.

The history of the last twenty years shows a continuing modification of the terms of these agreements between Third World governments and foreign firms, as those governments have tried to encourage the technology transfer and flow of foreign investment that are needed for industrialization, while minimizing the potentially negative effects of the agreements on the development of local society. Turnkey projects, manufacturing locally under licence, joint ventures (with or without local majority control), initial tax holidays, limitations on the repatriation of local earnings, provisions for local training of staff and limitations on employment of non-local personnel, specified use of locally made components or resources, or of targets for degrees of local resource-processing, the turning over of facilities like roads, ports or power plants to local control after a fixed period, all form items in the repertoire of negotiation that both companies and governments are aware of. As the trained Arab negotiators have shown, the balance of advantage in negotiations is not necessarily in the hands of foreign companies. Nor, as is also shown by the position of the oil companies six years after the creation of OPEC, does the welfare of the Third World bargainers necessarily exclude the companies doing well also.

I don't see any end to this continuing negotiation of terms between local governments and foreign investors to ensure some balance between the returns to the foreigners and the benefits to the local society. No single fixed position can remain adapted to the rapid changes of technology and resources in the modern world. What is important for both government planning and for industrial investment is that there be clear and predictable conditions for defined future periods. As industry has increasingly come to recognise, predictability is best assured by a local government, and especially by one that has wide local support. I remember vividly in 1967 explaining how local views on land rights, liquor licencing, and language use did not conform to the officially prescribed Australian regulations, to the Vice-President of Conzinc Riotinto Australia, when he was planning his company's future Bougainville Copper operations in terms of Australian mining law and practice. His reply, that Bougainville Copper had to plan in terms of operating peacefully for fifty years in independent Papua New Guinea, and so was concerned to conform to local views and to strengthen the emerging independent Government, brought this home strikingly to me. An "enlightened" company policy has here paid off for both the company and PNG. But his remark also made me wonder why his company had, until then, not obtained good advice on what local views were – something that struck me even more forcefully when we conducted the social impact assessment of the James Bay Project in 1971-2. The Berger report (1977) has brought the same point home to all Canadians: the oil companies could have saved themselves millions if Arctic Gas had listened to local views earlier and not merely tried to change local views.

The potential negative effects of showcase national projects like athletics stadiums, national airlines, or steel plants are the distortions of priorities away from more productive but less prominent investments in such infrastructure items as education or pure water supplies. They may provide outward symbols of development, but then either demand that undue portions of the national product goes to maintain them for the benefit of a minority – the air-conditioning may be working in the national capital while oil is not available for transporting food or operating tractors – or they may be under-used if other aspects of society remain backward – if no local people become pilots or aircraft mechanics, and the economy does not grow to support an airline, for example.

To sum up, the three major immediate consequences of independence, that potentially could lead to prosperity in Third World countries, in fact contain within themselves also the potential for destroying that prosperity, for restricting any prosperity to a small elite, and for channelling local development to particular areas or projects in such a way as to counteract effective development within in the country.

Can one use this knowledge to anticipate what might follow a settlement of land claims and a decision on the future political status of the Canadian North? I hope so (and this meeting encourages me that there is an interest in such knowledge).

First I would say that localisation of the public service – and by that I do not mean just in Yellowknife, or Frobisher, but in the delivery of services of all kinds in remote settlements – will constitute one of the most difficult, but also the most far-reaching of all changes that will occur. The present unavailability of local people trained to fill positions as they are currently defined by public service regulations will require dramatic interim steps to be taken, in providing training, in modifying regulations, but also in modifying the structures so that the service-providing agencies are seen to be local and not agencies of a distant, southern, government. Our 1974 study of attitudes in the Mackenzie District (Salisbury et al. 1974), and our 1979 evaluation of the changes following the James Bay Agreement (LaRusic et al. 1979; Salisbury et al. 1979) have shown that continuation and expansion of services in local settlements (as in the Third World) is the first goal of the population. There will continue to be a need for some non-local personnel, particularly for specialties, but the way in which the service-providing agencies adapt themselves to localisation is critical. Not only will localisation demand long-term planning of manpower and of training facilities, it must involve consideration of how to avoid creating the elite status of white-collar workers in the Third World (though Arctic suburbias for bureaucrats already exist, unfortunately), and the accelerated flow of people to the better-serviced centres, even if there are only limited employment opportunities there. Language policies (Inuktitut the official language?), and the need to service non-natives as well as the native people in the North make this a complex issue.

The construction of the trappings of a national government — parliament buildings in Frobisher, say — is unfortunately likely to follow the Third World pattern. That is, the gift of the Federal Government is likely to be frozen in the southern mould of Provincial and Federal works. Can the capital works involved in setting up a new political organization not be utilized to stimulate the local economy, local education, local services? Must they all be in Yellowknife? Could one start with a decentralised structure, rather than having to impose decentralisation after the investments have been made in centralised facilities?

But perhaps the most important area is that of the relations between the future governments of the North, and the industries, investors and technologists whose co-operation is essential if the service economy of the North is to expand its economic base beyond that provided by the subsistence economy. Such an expansion does demand some industrial technology, and in the North that is clearly going to mean a few large localised projects rather than dispersed small enterprises, and a level of investment that the North itself could never provide alone. These projects, like their counterparts in the Third World, are going to require relatively small numbers of highly trained workers and not the large numbers of workers required in nineteenth century industrialism. In short, even if "localisation" places numbers of native northerners in the work force of these projects and avoids the racial problems created by the predominance of skilled expatriate workers in the Third World colonial industries, the same long-term problems appear likely to emerge in the North as have occurred in the Third World when it opted at independence for industrialisation and urbanisation at all costs. We listed these earlier as the weakening of the existing food-producing economy, the attraction of people to a few large centres, even when employment is not really available there for all, and the growing split between the wealthy with employment in high paying industry or government and the under-employed poor.

There are signs that in the North these possibilities are gaining recognition. Belatedly there is a recognition of the importance of the food-producing economy in the North. In James Bay our researches in 1972, the testimony at the 1973 hearings, and major research into harvesting between 1975 and 1978 all confirm that about 60% of the food of the region comes from harvesting wildlife. The COPE and ITC Use and Occupancy studies indicate even greater productivity in the Inuit areas. The Berger hearings established a somewhat lower but still great importance for hunting in the Mackenzie River region. The threats to this economy are not merely those of ecological damage from industrial technology, but, in my opinion more significantly, the decline in the provision of an infrastructure for it at the same time as huge sums are invested in providing services for an industrial economy. Bush radio communications and bush winter roads are allowed to decline both relatively and even absolutely, while television reception and road sealing in urban areas receive millions of dollars of investment. Any northern government must thus consider how best it can utilise the investment fund that will be generated by large projects. Some will be needed to offset the ecological effects that are inevitable, even if reduced to a minimum, and some will certainly have to be used to create the services essential for the projects themselves. But a proportionate amount should be allocated to the provision of services for the dispersed food-production system of the whole region. That system can be improved and strengthened, no doubt, but it is vital to preserve. This is the lesson that the Third World itself has realised fully only in the decade of the 1970's, after the food crises of the late 1960's. The means of strengthening it are not yet adequately known, but hopefully Canadian research can remain in the forefront in this belatedly recognised field.

Improving the food-producing system and decentralising services could both assist with the other problem recognised in the Third World, the growth of internal inequality, of affluence amidst poverty and of high-paid employment amidst unemployment. But it is precisely in its negotiations with the affluent developers that a Third World country has the most leverage to ensure that these disparities do not emerge or are muted by government redistribution of wealth or of employment. The repertoire of potential elements that can be negotiated has already been cited, and needs to be available to Northern governments. Yet what the Berger (1977) and Lysyk (1977) inquiries established in everybody's minds is that at present the constitutional position is that it is Ottawa that does the negotiating or decision-making. Although Ottawa nominally is looking out for the interests of the North, it has conflicts of interest in that it also looks out for the interests of the South. Northerners have little confidence that they are adequately represented in Ottawa decisions; the attention paid to Judge Berger's presentation of their case only underlines the need for more of the same effective advocacy.

The Third World experience does not argue that a local government always negotiates the appropriate or best terms for the local society, but rather that such governments are more likely to cause local people to feel that their interests have an advocate. The more such governments act internally to distribute wealth and employment, and to eradicate disparities, the more likely it is also that the governments will have popular support. The more support they have, the more likely they are to be stable. In the Third World the lesson that has been (again belatedly) learned by foreign corporations and governments is that stable popular local governments are more likely than colonial governments to provide the stability and assurance that make major investments worthwhile in the long-run. Negotiation can establish whether the terms of investment are liveable with. Though immediate advantages might be negotiable with colonial governments, or with unstable, unpopular local governments, the long-term unpredictability is intolerable.

In Northern terms, major southern Canadian companies considering investment in the North should welcome the emergence of political bodies representing exclusively Northern interests. The sooner such bodies are recognised, are constituted in such a way as to make them representative, and are vested with effective authority, the sooner it is that major northern projects are likely to be negotiated with terms that will be appropriate to the 1980's and 1990's rather than with terms that reflect the 1960's.

But, one argument runs, does not the Third World example augur poorly for the North? Do not Third World governments present a sorry picture of incompetent bureaucracies, of sectional internal fights, of minority dictatorships of both right and left, and of general instability? Are there are not signs of similar problems in the North? Are the emerging northern political bodies demonstrating administrative efficiency, a sense of united common purposes, a tolerance of views that diverge from those of a few educated leaders and their coterie of non-elected and often imported advisers, and clear and consistent long-term policies? As a non-Westerner in Edmonton politeness forbids me to ask whether those same attributes appear in Alberta or BC politics, but as a Canadian and a Quebecker surveying the last decade I would certainly not say that we ourselves have finally solved the problems that Third World countries face. They are recurrent problems everywhere. If we look for failures to solve them, we are certain to find some examples of failure — of planes not on time, or snow not cleared on our street yet cleared immediately where a politician lives. We rarely note the smoothly running, universally supported actions of a government — the planes running, and the snow-ploughs available.

No. New governments do face problems that established ones do not. Established procedures, and a plentiful supply of well-trained administrators make good administration easier (though not inevitable); but both procedures and administrators improve most quickly when they are on-the-job, and a new administration learns quickest when it has to do things itself, to make its own decisions, to run its own affairs, and to take the consequences for wrong decisions. Having to make important decisions does bring out in the open divergences of opinion, but these existed previously and were merely hidden when decisions were not being made. As long as only very few people have had experience of administering a government, that minority will make decisions, and will seek advice from a small group of other experienced people (that may include outsiders). In themselves minority decisions are not necessarily harmful. The dangers come later, of those decisions not being modified if they turn out to be wrong, of the views of more people not being sought out, of not bringing new people into the system to gain experience, and to contribute their own special skills.

These are all improvements in effectiveness and democracy that can come only with time and effective practice. Until the North has its own effective representative government(s), attempting to provide real solutions to northern problems, and having the power to do so (and here I mean a control over natural resource use the provinces have), harsh criticism of existing political bodies is unfair. And the period of "learning-on-the-job" is not going to be brief either. It will need a willingness by outsiders not to look exclusively for the faults of the new administration, but to give due respect to its achievements.

Paradoxically it is during this period of "learning-on-the-job" that the major resource companies have the most to gain from negotiating fairly and sympathetically with the emerging political groups. In the short run a company might gain advantageous terms in a contract negotiated with an inexperienced government, but to do so means that local people learn only that the company is ruthless. The government is less likely to become a stable one if it cannot demonstrate its effectiveness to its own constituents. Negotiating in and of itself — provided it is seen as being "for real" — is the most effective way for an emerging political body to gain political experience and public support. This, at least is one conclusion of the assessment, by researchers from our group, of the emergence and effectiveness of administrative structures among the James Bay Cree. Though the James Bay and Northern Quebec Agreement is the document that spells out the structures, the critical determinants of the form they now take derive from the period of negotiations and the credibility these gave to the negotiators and their supporting staff, as much as from the Quebec governmental structures and development corporations into which they mesh (LaRusic et al. 1979).

The new administrations, rightly since they will be local administrations, will have to seek to protect and strengthen the existing subsistence economy. They will have to seek to employ (and to train) larger numbers of local peoples. They will have to try not only to maintain existing levels of services, like hospitals or schools, but to make improvements over what the current Ottawa or Yellowknife administrations already provide. They will be brought up sharply against the reality of the size of transfer payments from the South that are needed to maintain those services, and the need to spend money effectively and efficiently. Support for these goals and these commitments will be the price that any northern government is going to demand from resource developers for the yields they obtain from operating in the North. (And here I do not exclude the Federal Government from having a role both as developer, and as potential payer of the bills.) A clear calculation of how much can be afforded, given the future benefits, will be much easier to make if the logic of Northern demands is clearly expressed by Northern governments, and if the non-Northern developers sympathise with the pressures on any responsible Northern government.

In summary, I think that we are at a turning point in Northern Development. I think that the experience of the Third World with the consequences of independence is highly relevant to understanding what that turning point involves. Before the event local people are unrealistically optimistic, and outsiders are unrealistically pessimistic. The event itself is often something of a let-down. But it need not be if we recognise in advance the potential of the transition. On the part of the local people it demands a rapid and serious involvement in the tasks of building up infrastructures of services, and particularly in the training of manpower to provide those services, and of politicians and administrators who can respond to the real needs and wishes of local people. On the part of outsiders it demands an equally major shift in attitude, towards one of recognising the local administration as legitimate, as here to stay, as representing the interests of local people, and, as such, being subject to local pressures. Given that attitudinal frame the outsiders can make realistic judgements of how to relate to the local administration, that will be valid for the future. It is living in the past that is dangerous. The North, like the Third World, has a future that can be for better or for worse, depending on how the self-government transition is effected. Let us profit by experience and make it for better in the North.

292

REFERENCES

Berger, Thomas R. 1977. *Northern Frontier - Northern Homeland: The Report of the Mackenzie Valley Pipeline Inquiry.* Volume 1. Toronto: James Lorimer & Company.

LaRusic, Ignatius E. et al. 1979. *Negotiating a Way of Life: Initial Cree Experience with the Administrative Structure Arising from the James Bay Agreement.* Montreal: ssDcc, Inc.

Lysyk, Kenneth M. et al. 1977. *Alaska Highway Pipeline Inquiry.* Ottawa: Minister of Supply and Services Canada.

Salisbury, R.F., Nathan Elberg and Robert H. Schneider. 1974. *Development? Attitudes to Development among the Native Peoples of the Mackenzie District.* Monograph 7. Montreal: McGill University Programme in the Anthropology of Development.

Salisbury, R.F., Taylor Brelsford, Louis Goldberg and Susan Marshall. 1979. *Training and Jobs among the James Bay Cree.* Brief Communications Series, No. 44. Montreal: McGill University Programme in the Anthropology of Development.

15.

APPLICATION AND THEORY IN CANADIAN ANTHROPOLOGY:

THE JAMES BAY AGREEMENT

by

Richard F. Salisbury

Source: *Transactions of the Royal Society of Canada*, Series IV, Volume XVII, 1979.

The major theme of this paper is how within Canadian anthropology both theory and application have advanced alternately in a dialectic mutual stimulation. It will argue that the present high international status accorded to Canadian applied anthropology can be related to its strong emphasis on theory (at least in the fields of economic and transactional anthropology), and to the mutual trust that has developed in Canada between researchers and policy-makers. It uses as its main example the McGill University Programme in the Anthropology of Development (PAD), but links this example to wider trends.

Before 1960 the application of anthropology in Canada followed a pattern common elsewhere – anthropologists were used to alleviate problems caused by administrations which took too little account of cultural differences. The theoretical strengths of anthropology at that time were the rigorous description of supposedly stable societies and cultures, and the typologies deriving from those descriptions. In the 1960s the analysis of social process and cultural change that had begun in the 1950s began to offer theoretical formulations that could be used with increasing confidence to predict future social states. Hawthorn and Belshaw's (1958) survey of the Indians of British Columbia is a landmark, as the first Canadian applied study using this theoretical sophistication. But the overall history of Canadian anthropology in this era (and earlier) has been documented elsewhere (Freedman 1976), and will not be presented further here. Instead this case study of the McGill PAD links specific theoretical advances in (a) economic and (b) transactional anthropology and our ongoing study of regional development in the James Bay area of Quebec.

Economic Anthropology

Where pre-1960 studies saw non-Western economies as culture- or tradition-bound, and were satisfied to classify them as traditional, archaic, feudal, pre-capitalist, etc., the early sixties recognized how individuals and groups are everywhere economic decision-makers. The constraints on choice in societies studied by anthropologists may be unfamiliar to Western scholars - the need to balance social gains and losses over a·lifetime in a closely knit community, for example — as may be the commodities produced or exchanged (particularly social services or prestige). But inductive study by anthropologists of how real decisions in non-Western groups reflect these unusual constraints and commodities has an aim similar to that of Herbert A. Simon in economics — producing a realistic theory of decisions that is not bound to Western conditions.

In northern Quebec in PAD research among the James Bay Cree, LaRusic (1968) had investigated Cree decisions regarding involvement in wage labour and in 1971 Feit (1973) was investigating decisions about hunting, when in April of that year the James Bay Development Project was announced. Basically LaRusic and Feit showed how hunting was highly productive and economically rational where the infra-structure for it existed (available credit, stores selling trapping supplies, transportation to isolated areas, markets for furs, protection from depredation by sport hunters). The move of hunters into wage work in the 1960s reflected a reduction in the infra-structure of the region, not a rejection of the hunting way of life. In their choice of wage jobs the Cree were disadvantaged by policies of white employers and by lack of many needed skills (such as literacy or knowledge of English), but still made highly rational use of the skills they had (from skills of bush living to those of organizing work groups without supervision), within the constraints.

Their theory-oriented findings were sufficient to enable applications to be made — predictions of how Cree Indian society would change over the next fifteen years, in the presence of different kinds of hydro-electric project. Wishing both to warn the Cree of the implications of development, and to influence government decisions regarding the project, we undertook to make those predictions as a contracted but publicly available study of the likely social impacts of the project. The resulting applied study (Salisbury et al. 1972) constructed three scenarios of what might occur if there was (a) no project but a continued decline of hunting infra-structure, (b) a project that did not take Cree interests into account, and (c) a project planned to permit maximal long-range benefits to the Cree. Scenario (c) also spelled out some strategies by which the Cree could best make use of the project for their own purposes. As the Quebec government eventually adopted most of the recommendations leading to scenario (c), we feel our application of theory was practically effective.

But spelling out a practical strategy for the Cree involved moving into an unexplored area of theory – regional development based on a subsistence economy. The Cree already produced 60 per cent of their food supply from local moose, caribou, beaver, geese, and fish (Elberg, Hyman, and Salisbury 1972). Administration of services – schooling, health, housing, etc. – in the 150,000 square mile area already employed numbers of whites, and the predictable expansion of those services in the next fifteen years of rapid population growth could, if conducted by the Cree themselves, employ some 30 per cent of the work force. Employment in operating the hydro project and in the requisite environmental protection and transport systems could, with royalties, seemingly provide the basis for a fully employed society and a viable economy. The strategy assumed that hunting could continue, and that would involve support for the infra-structure of hunting and assurance of Cree rights to hunt. It would also require the Cree *not* involving themselves as unskilled labour during the construction phase of the project, but using the construction phase as a time to catch up, to learn the skills needed for hydro-electric operation, but, more important, to train for managerial tasks in local administration. Planning for future service needs and for manpower training over ten years appeared central if the Cree were to take over their own administration of the region.

The practical advice to the Cree was tentatively formulated in a model of a developing subsistence and service economy (Salisbury 1971, 1973) but the testing of this speculative model could not be carried out empirically without a case for study. Happily the negotiations between the Cree and the Quebec government provided such a case. The James Bay and Northern Quebec Agreement of 1975, as is spelled out below, has as themes the strengthening of the native subsistence sector, the transfer to the Cree of the administration of local services (under the aegis of provincial service ministries), and the provision of financial and advisory support (as compensation and as legal commitments) to create a productive modern sector. These elements emerged from hard bargaining between the Cree and Quebec. The former, advised by Harvey Feit and Allan Penn of the PAD among others, argued more strongly for their aboriginal land and hunting rights, and against building the project or surrendering sovereignty to Quebec. The latter, principally through negotiators John Ciaccia and Gaston Moisan, argued more strongly for Quebec sovereignty and for Quebec service programmes, including an experimental income security programme. The resulting compromise nonetheless now represents an immense experiment in regional development, by the decentralization of services and the strengthening of a subsistence sector. In monitoring this development we are conducting applied studies, but doing so in order to test and document the theoretical model put forward in 1973. Some tentative findings of that test will form the third section of this paper.

Theoretical research in economic anthropology in the 1960s led into applied research in 1971-72, and into applied advising in 1972-75; that applied work has led to formulating theoretical models, the testing of which can only be done through further applied research.

TRANSACTIONAL ANTHROPOLOGY

The other theoretical current that has fed into our work has been the field of transactional analysis. In anthropology this sub-field is associated with the name of Frederik Barth (1966). He showed from observations of Norwegian fishing crews how structures of relationships could be understood better as the outcome of negotiations between categories of person — captains, crewmen, etc. — rather than as sets of role relationships controlled by norms, which had previously been the typical formulation. Canadian anthropologists studying the relationships between whites and native people, such as Dunning (1959) and Vallee (1962), had indeed been moving towards such a formulation but had not stated the general principles clearly. The group at Memorial University led by Robert Paine has since taken this approach much further (Paine et al. 1977), stressing the importance of impression management.

In the early 1970s the PAD researchers, conscious of this Canadian activity, began to use this analytic framework to illuminate their personal involvements with the Cree and the interactions between the Cree negotiators and the Quebec representatives, between the Cree negotiators and their other white advisers, and between the Cree negotiating team and the dispersed and initially poorly informed settlements from which they came. In effect we began to use the new theoretical stance to analyse the process of negotiating a land settlement that we had become involved in for applied reasons. We began to try to offer advice about what the potential consequences were of alternative options for Cree decisions. We began to spell out, not recommendations for what the Cree should do, but what the likely results were, in terms of future relationships, of each of the current courses that appeared open for them to negotiate.

The application of theory has, however, led to the possibility of advancing theory. We can now look at relationships and structures existing in 1979, and trace the negotiations which led to their taking the 1979 form. What has happened during this period is that a relatively unstructured system of relationships among the Cree has rapidly become formally structured. Where before 1970 there

298

were 6,500 people, living in eight small relatively homogeneous hunting communities with few formal authority positions, and an administration by a distant white bureaucratic system as the major link between settlements, there has emerged over a nine-year period a political entity, the Grand Council of the Crees of Quebec, uniting the total widely dispersed population. The Grand Council has an administrative arm, the Cree Regional Authority, with a structure formulated in the James Bay and Northern Quebec Agreement, and operating under the Quebec laws governing municipalities. It has committees, advisory bodies, boards, agencies, corporations, each in relationship to a distinct Quebec government department. Internally the elected or nominated officials of each organism are responsive to their Cree constituencies. A structure has emerged, and has been enshrined in a legal document, but the decisions and negotiations that led to its formulation are still clearly in people's consciousness, and we are tracing these links (Penn, n.d.; LaRusic et al. 1979). The constitution is not the basis of the present structure; it is the precipitate of transactions. Here we hope to contribute to the theory of the relationship between transactions and structures.

And that theory may easily lead to further future applications, for if structures are explicitly recognized as the consequence of negotiation and earlier decision, then the possibility of consciously making current decisions in order to influence future relationship structures in predictable directions must also be recognized.

ASSESSING THE JAMES BAY AGREEMENT

Our foci of interest in anthropological theory led us into particular types of applied activity in relation to the Cree land-claim against the Quebec government — predictive impact studies and the offering of advice about negotiating. The PAD is currently involved in making theoretical advances regarding development and emergent social structure, using again the avenue of applied research. We are conducting evaluations, for interested parties, of the practical effects of the James Bay Agreement using it as an immense social experiment. Three studies, completed or nearing completion, will be discussed in the remainder of this paper: (1) evaluations of the programme designed to assist the subsistence economy — the Income Security Program for Hunters and Trappers, conducted by us for the Quebec Ministry of Social Affairs, and the Department of Indian Affairs, with the collaboration of the Cree Income Security Board; (2) a study of manpower, employment, and training among the Cree — the Cree Human Resources Survey — where we are analysing a questionnaire study conducted in 1977 by the Grand Council of the Crees of Quebec; and (3) an evaluation of changing communication structures within the region, begun by two studies under contract for the Department of Communications in 1974-76. Studies (1) and (2) bear on the model of development by the subsistence economy and full employment in the service sector; studies (2) and (3) bear on the emergence of new social structures.

Before discussing these studies, however, a word must be said about the James Bay Agreement. In constitutional form it surrenders all native claims to aboriginal title over land of northern Quebec, in return for a specification of guaranteed rights in modern law over that same territory, a commitment by the Province of Quebec to provide services to the region (in addition to those which the Government of Canada is committed to provide by the Indian Act), plus financial compensation. It follows the historical pattern of earlier treaties, but with major modifications that, in my view, are precedent-setting. In guaranteeing rights to land in the region it did not simply divide the land into blocks of Indian reserves (or, as in Alaska, lands owned in fee simple by native corporations) and blocks of crown land, and leave the enforcement of any Indian hunting rights on crown land subject to arbitrary curtailment by white settlement or provincial game laws. Instead the Indians' rights were defined as they relate to three major categories of land with Category 1 resembling reserve land, Category 3 resembling crown land, and Category 2 being an intermediate one. Thus Indian rights to Category 3 land were embodied in exclusive rights to certain species, in preference, under provincial game laws, over sports hunters for other species, to participation in the decisions about conservation, hunting quotas, and permits with the Ministry of Fish, Game and Tourism, and to government support for harvesting activities through the Income Security Program. In the provision of services the innovation is the commitment by Quebec to create bodies operated by the native people themselves which must deliver those services in ways to be decided by the native people themselves. Though the bodies, such as the Cree School Board or the Cree Regional Authority, are ultimately within the jurisdiction of Quebec departments (of Education or Municipal Affairs in these two cases), the agreement gives them distinctive powers to act to preserve native culture or society (for example, unlike other school boards in Quebec, the Cree School Board may choose its languages of instruction, and its curriculum in some areas). In short, a formal structure has been set up for the decentralization of decisions regarding services to a regional government, using cultural standards different from those of the majority of the province.

Any evaluation of a programme asks whether it is having the effects it was designed for, but also asks whether unanticipated changes also are occurring. In considering the income Security Program (ISP) we asked first, 'Is it strengthening the hunting economy?' and secondly, 'How does a strengthened subsistence economy mesh with the other aspects of a modern society in the North?' Three reports have appeared (Scott 1977; Scott and Feit 1978; LaRusic 1978). They show that the number of people engaged in full-time harvesting (a word which includes trapping small game for furs, hunting larger animals for meat, and ancillary non-hunting activities, such as those performed by women) has risen by about 50 per cent, when compared with the baseline years 1970-75. The number of hunters has risen less than this figure, as there has been a tendency for more entire families to undertake long-term harvesting, and thus for ancillary workers to spend winters in the bush rather than remain in settlements; more dependents have also accompanied hunters. The total amount of meat harvested had risen by about 20 percent, and provides a surplus over the total consumption of the hunting groups, for exchange with non-hunting settlement dwellers. The volume of furs caught has not increased, however, though fur values have done so.

Critical features of ISP that have produced these effects are the guarantee of a minimum income per beneficiary unit (family) varying with the size of the unit but set at $2,800 for a two-child family; the retention of 60 per cent of all income earned, in addition to the guaranteed minimum, until the total income reaches 2½ times the guaranteed amount; and the provision of a per diem allowance per man-day of harvesting that initially was fixed at $12.00. All these payments are indexed to the cost of living. These features have particularly encouraged whole families to hunt together, and to continue hunting as long as harvesting is moderately productive. A maximum number of man-days of per diem payments is part of ISP according to law, and though this limit has not yet constrained the programme, it could do so in future. The programme has been operated by the Cree Income Security Board, through the local 'tallymen,' who are usually the traditional owners of particular family hunting territories. They keep records of days of hunting and of catches made. The payments are made four times a year, the first three in September, January, and April being on the basis of estimates of hunting in the ensuing period, and the final payment in July being an accounting payment – the difference between the estimates and the reality of time spent harvesting and cash income received. The evidence is clear that hunting can certainly be effectively supported by such a programme, and there is quantitative support for the Cree contention that it is strengthening traditional Cree lifestyles and culture, keeping families together, enabling old people to involve themselves with the children, and educating the coming generation in the ways of the forest.

It is having other effects also. The advance payments have obviated the need for external credit sources such as the Hudson Bay Company for 'staking' trappers, who can now plan more deliberately. The major portion – over 50 per cent of cash received – has been spent in using a more mechanized technology for hunting. Aircraft for ferrying personnel and supplies to remote camps have been the major cost increase, as a greater number of people have travelled, with more mechanized equipment such as snowmobiles and chain-saws, to remoter areas with plentiful game which it had previously been too costly to reach. Not only is the equipment heavy, it necessitates the flying in of gasoline. And availability of gasoline means that other comforts can be provided in hunting camps, especially for women's tasks; this in turn suggests that camps may become more substantial and more permanently used than in the more nomadic past. Hunting is itself changing.

Previously social assistance and continuing transfer payments such as family allowances had been a major component — up to 40 per cent — of the cash incomes of the area. LaRusic (1978:103) documents a reduction by 69 per cent in social assistance. Yet both he and Scott find no perceptible decline in Cree hunters seeking wage employment during the summer. The 40 per cent tax offset factor under ISP is not a disincentive against engaging in salaried employment at times when hunting is least productive.

The Cree themselves sum matters up by saying, 'Hunting is a job, as much as wage work is; it is right that hunters should be paid.' In our terms, a strong subsistence sector is not incompatible with a cash economy, but may need special arrangements for the meshing of the two. At the moment the outlay by Quebec is quite high — nearly $5,000,000 a year — but the benefits are also high though less easy to quantify: major reductions ($1,700,000) in welfare payments, and in unemployment, over half a million additional pounds of meat ($1,250,000), reduced service needs in settlements, plus improvements in health, education, and family strength from the bush life. Above all the Cree feel that their culture is secure.

Yet we are conscious of inherent tendencies to change. At some point the game productivity of the forest could be over-extended if Cree population continues to expand. Increasing mechanization and less nomadism in hunting would involve further social changes, in camps and in settlements. The role of the tallyman/hunting territory owner has become a more powerful one, and one that can be exercised without necessarily participating in winter hunting. Will this power lead to a change in a traditionally egalitarian society? More dramatically there may well be an increasing distinction between those Cree who live in settlements and those who are full-time hunters.

This leads to our second applied study, that of the Cree Human Resources Survey. The analysis is not yet complete, but a preliminary report (Salisbury, Brelsford, Goldberg, and Marshall 1979) is available. When its findings are compared to the estimates of employment patterns among the Cree workforce in 1972 contained in Salisbury et al. (1972: Tables 11, 12, and 14), the two biggest changes are seen to be the major decline in the number of individuals whose major activity is casual unskilled labour, and an increase in the number of professional or administrative workers. These reflect very largely the employment in harvesting of younger men who had not the financial credit or the hunting skills to make it worth while for them to enter a hunting career before ISP, and who had previously hung around communities in the winters doing odd jobs and seeking casual work, and secondly, the administrative teaching and planning positions that have been created in local government.

These two major tendencies conceal other less spectacular trends. An increase in the number of white collar positions in the settlements has been numerically as great as the expansion in professional positions, though not as great relatively, since there was some employment in this category in 1972. By contrast the number of skilled manual positions has not increased as much as our optimistic scenario hoped in 1972. The James Bay Project has employed only about ten skilled Cree, and has not served as a training ground for skilled workers. Manpower courses in the communities have helped, but have not provided job experience. The plans for accelerated re-housing of communities, and the formation of Cree Construction Inc., are now providing experience for some skilled workers. Unskilled workers show a similar pattern; their absolute number has not increased, nor has the James Bay Project provided employment for more than about 30 full-time workers, and casual work for about 130 others.

The Cree administrators of 1978 are mainly not recent graduates, but include many senior individuals who obtained on-the-job experience during the negotiations leading up to the agreement, plus some others with post-secondary education. In general the recent graduates from the school system have become white collar staff in the settlements. Those who have not been oriented towards white collar work (or to obtaining post-secondary training) have had a choice between hunting, unskilled work, or training for skilled work. Forced unemployment has not been their fate as it was in the 1960's, though more skilled employment within the settlements would be welcome.

The picture is thus one of almost full employment locally, including many in skilled and well-paid positions, and rapidly rising incomes, in cash and kind. It provides a first picture of a society developing on a subsistence and services basis.

It is a picture that poses further questions. There is a gap in incomes between the administrators and professionals and the subsistence hunters. Another cleavage is the residence of administrators (and the white collar workers) in either the settlements or in the urban centre of Val d'Or while hunters are in the bush. The proportions of the various occupational groups are not at all similar to

303

those of either an industrial society or a homogeneous traditional society: the pyramid is very small at the top, thin in the middle levels, but extremely broad at the bottom *if*, and this would not be the case in traditional Cree culture, if one considers the full-time hunters as 'unskilled.' Is a stratification reminiscent of Latin American developing countries emerging? Is there a gulf developing between an elite and the general population? Is such a gulf inevitable as a society becomes more affluent, even for egalitarian subsistence societies?

The third study, on communications in the region, bears on these questions. In 1972 we observed the difficulties Cree negotiators faced in travel and communication in such a sparsely settled region as they tried to keep in touch with their home communities, informing them of what was happening in Montreal, but also learning from the communities what were the local wishes. We ourselves experienced those same difficulties during our studies of 1972. The subsequent road construction by the James Bay Project, the erection of microwave relays to replace the radio-telephone systems in communities near the construction zones, the increase in frequency of scheduled aircraft, and (critical for DOC's interest) the advent of television via ANIK satellite provided the empirical base for a study of the effects of changing communications on social behaviour.

Two reports (Elberg, Salisbury and Visitor 1974; Elberg and Visitor 1977) have appeared. They have shown two main trends. The first is that the technological improvements in communications to date have all increased the effectiveness of links from the individual northern settlements directly towards a variety of head offices farther south in Winnipeg, Ottawa, Montreal, Val d'Or, and Quebec; to date they have tended to make communication *between* settlements less easy, as the low technology facilities used previously have not been maintained, and little attention has been given to the installing of new high technology facilities to service this need. A continuation of this trend would centralize decision-making in the head offices outside the region, and take it out of the region and the hands of the Cree.

The second trend is the failure of attempts to create a regional centre. An outlying settlement wishing to communicate with a head office sees little advantage in routing communications via a regional centre, if it can communicate directly (e.g. by phone or by plane). Only if *all* separate head offices located regional services and decisions in a single place would other communities look to it. Political pressure would be needed for such concerted action to occur. To date the nearest approach to a Cree regional centre has been the town of Val d'Or, outside the Cree area but used because it is the regional centre for the Department of Indian Affairs and has good air services and other urban facilities. It is the site of the offices of the Cree Regional Authority and of the Cree School Board. About half of the

Cree administrators live there with their families, scattered in suburban housing to the west of town. Keeping contacts between them and the dispersed communities remains a problem, as it was when the James Bay Agreement was being negotiated.

But the nature of the problem has changed. In earlier days the organization and staff in settlements were insufficient to guarantee information diffusion within the settlement; nowadays the problem is one of pressures of time on the administrators, of combining meetings held in Montreal, Quebec, or particular settlements, with feeding back information to settlements in a regular way, and with balancing conflicting demands from different settlements. The administrators' sense of pressure is heightened by not living at home in a sympathetic Cree community, and by the dissatisfaction of their wives and children who do not even have the sense of commitment to an important job.

Yet the Cree, like the PAD researchers, recognize the importance, for maintaining a sense of solidarity, of administrators remaining in communication with their constituents and not becoming a distant elite. Our researches show how technological change has so far tended to make that communication more difficult, and to counteract attempts to decentralize decisions and the provision of services. Is the emergence of a stratified elite, concentrating wealth and power in the hands of a small minority, a necessary consequence of technological development? The Cree do not want that to happen and are seeking ways to avoid it, both by modifying technology and by creating social structures. Existing theory does not provide an answer for such questions, and thus a challenge is posed to develop a theory of 'social performance' (Belshaw 1969) and development. Such a theory would both relate social structures to the type of tasks they are called on to perform, and indicate what transactional negotiating processes would generate appropriate structures. We see our researches as contributing to that goal.

ANTHROPOLOGY AND THE USERS

While the evolution of PAD research has so far been discussed in terms of how the adequacy and validity of theory are both tested and furthered by the process of attempting to apply it in the solution of practical applied problems, we have not so far discussed how the research appears to non-academics. The academic judges the research by its contribution to basic knowledge or theory, disdaining the practical contribution; the non-academic user of research tends to judge it by the solutions it does (or does not) provide to pressing problems. If research solves problems, its contribution to knowledge and theory may be an added plus, but if it does not solve problems it merely serves to reinforce the stereotype of 'useless academics.' The problems of anthropological researchers who are interested in esoteric specialties, who pay no attention to real local problems, and who evoke negative reactions to any anthropological research are well known.

We cannot claim to have overcome completely such negative reactions, either among the Cree or among administrators in Quebec and Ottawa. But we have found that both Cree and white administrators, with questions to which they would like answers, recognize that research is needed to obtain these answers. They rarely have the time, the staff, or the resources for research, which rarely gets done. The academic theorist with the resources is rarely asked to do the research. Only someone who has already proved his ability to give answers is likely to be called in to work on problems that the 'user' thinks of as practical, but which have, as I have shown, considerable theoretical interest. It took almost eight years for the PAD to build up a level of confidence in its researchers in both the Cree communities and in white administrators, and even after fifteen years we still have to re-prove continually that our researches are useful. To the extent that we accept the need for research to be of practical value, others accept as legitimate our concern for generalizing broadly from our research. Without such an acceptance both parties suffer practical questions are not solved, and theoretical research is rejected by the general public. The two types of research are not antithetical — at least in those fields in which a valid body of theory is available — but reinforce one another dialectically. It is a happy situation if they can do so, but one that can be developed only if anthropologists pay attention to developing mutual trust between themselves and the potential users of their research.

REFERENCES

Barth, F. 1966. *Models of Social Organisation*. London: Royal Anthropological Institute.

Belshaw, C.S. 1969. *The Conditions of Social Performance*. London: Routledge and Kegan Paul.

Dunning, R.W. 1959. "Ethnic Relations and the Marginal Man in Canada." *Human Organization* 18:117-22.

Elberg, N., J. Hyman, and R.F. Salisbury. 1972. *Not By Bread Alone*. Monograph 5. Montreal: McGill University, Programme in the Anthropology of Development.

Elberg, N., R.F. Salisbury, and B. Visitor. 1974. *End of the Line: Communications in Paint Hills*. Monograph 8. Montreal: McGill University, Programme in the Anthropology of Development.

------------1977. *Off-Centre: Fort George and Regional Communications*. Monograph 10. Montreal: McGill University, Programme in the Anthropology of Development.

Feit, H.A. 1973. "The Ethno-ecology of the Waswanipi Cree." In Cox, B. (ed.), *Cultural Ecology*. Toronto: McClelland & Stewart.

Freedman, J. (ed.). 1976. *The History of Canadian Anthropology*. CES Proceedings no. 3.

Hawthorn, H.B., and C.S. Belshaw. 1958. *The Indians of British Columbia*. Toronto: University of Toronto Press.

LaRusic, I. 1968. "From Hunter to Proletarian." In Chance, N. (ed.), *Developmental Change among the Cree Indians of Quebec*. Ottawa: Department of Regional Economic Expansion.

------------1978. "The Income Security Programme for Cree Hunters and Trappers." Monograph 14. Montreal: McGill University, Programme in the Anthropology of Development.

LaRusic, I. et. al. 1979. *Negotiating a Way of Life*. Montreal: ssDcc Inc. Report DINA.

Paine, R.W. (ed.). 1977. *The White Arctic*. St. John's, Newfoundland: Memorial University of Newfoundland (ISER).

Penn, A. n.d. Structures of Administration in Northern Quebec. Ph.D. thesis in preparation. Montreal: McGill University, Geography Department.

Salisbury, R.F. 1971. "Development through the Service Industries." *Manpower and Unemployment Research* 4: 57-66.

------------1973. The Service Industries and Planning. Paper presented to Symposium on Interdisciplinary Economics, Indiana University.

Salisbury, R.F. et. al. 1972. *Development and James Bay.* Monograph 4. Montreal: McGill University, Programme in the Anthropology of Development.

Salisbury, R.F., T. Brelsford, L. Goldberg, and S. Marshall. 1979. *Training and Jobs among the James Bay Cree.* Monograph 16. Montreal: McGill University, Programme in the Anthropology of Development.

Scott, C.H. 1977. *The Income Security Programme: An Initial Field Report.* Val d'Or: Grand Council of the Crees.

Scott, C.H. and H.A. Feit. 1978. *Income Security for Cree Hunters: Initial Socio-economic Impacts.* Monograph 15. Montreal: McGill University, Programme in the Anthropology of Development.

Vallee, F. 1962. *Kabloona and Eskimo in the Central Keewatin.* NCRC 62-2. Ottawa: Department of Northern Affairs.

16.

THE ECONOMICS OF DEVELOPMENT THROUGH SERVICES:

FINDINGS OF THE MCGILL PROGRAMME AMONG THE CREE

by

Richard F. Salisbury

Source: John W. Bennett (ed.), *Production and Autonomy: Anthropological Studies and Critiques of Development.* Society for Economic Anthropology Monographs, No. 5. Lanham, Md.: University Press of America, 1988.

In high-income countries over half of the labor force works in the service sector, and much smaller proportions work in farming, resource extraction, or manufacturing; development in the Third World always involves a disproportionate increase in service employment. Materialists since the eighteenth century have decried this as "parasitic" on the "real" sources of wealth — farming or industry. This paper suggests, by contrast, that increasing service employment may, under certain circumstances, be a highly effective way of inducing greater productivity in both primary and secondary industries, and thus of achieving the higher living standards and diversified economy that constitute development. In remote or colonial areas where services are planned and staffed by non-local metropolitans, an increase in local service employment is best accomplished by establishing local control of service delivery within the region.

This proposition was suggested by earlier studies in Papua New Guinea (Salisbury 1970, 1971). The present paper reports on a longitudinal study of emerging regional autonomy in service delivery in Northern Canada between 1971 and 1981. During that period the staff and graduate students of the McGill Programme in the Anthropology of Development (PAD) were able to assist and advise the 6,000 Cree of Quebec as they organized and then took over the regional administration of their area.[1] Before 1971 the PAD (Chance 1968, 1969) had studied several of the isolated, colonially administered villages of the region as mining and forestry expanded into the forest in which the Cree continued their hunting existence. Between 1971 and 1975 regional unity emerged in opposition to a major hydro-electric project, and in 1975 the Federal and Provincial Governments signed the James Bay Agreement (JBNQA) with the Cree leaders granting them regional control and finance, in return for accepting governmental sovereignty in general, and

309

the hydro project specifically. A book is in press (Salisbury 1986) analyzing the changes of the decade 1971-1981 (and the involvement of anthropologists in the changes). The present paper focusses on the economic aspects of emerging regional self-government: its benefits of increasing employment and incomes, improved services, and a build-up of infrastructure and demand for primary and secondary industry; also on its costs, to the wider society and to the local area. It argues that creating regional political unity and improving service delivery have had major impacts as a multiplier of local demand and as a builder of the infrastructure needed for diversified economic development.

CREE HISTORY 1964-1983

The growth of modern-style services of education, health, justice, etc. to Cree living in villages long antedates 1971, even if films like *Cree Hunters of Mistassini* (1973) vividly portray the continuity between 1971 lifestyles and pre-1945 hunting patterns. Between 1945 and 1964 there was a steady sedentarization of hunters around the foci of Hudson's Bay Company (HBC) posts, as Canadian government services were officially extended to native people equally with other citizens. Before 1964, however, more than half the Cree had no permanent residence in a village, but hunted in the bush all winter, and lived in tents or teepees during their summer visit to the village/post. By 1964 the building of village housing and the expansion of forestry and mining industries in the south of the Cree region meant that half had a permanent residence (in a village or near a non-Cree settlement) even if 80 percent still hunted in the bush in the winter. By 1971 about 70 percent of the Cree had permanent housing, and the portion living in hunting camps in winter had declined to about 70 percent. Between 1971 and 1983 permanent housing had been built for 100 percent of the Cree population. The proportion spending winters in the bush had dropped to 50 percent by 1975. It rose to almost 60 percent in 1976, and since then the number of winter hunters has stabilized, though the overall increase in Cree population means that winter hunters now form less than 50 percent of the total.

The build-up of services in the villages implicit in sedentarization was, before 1971, both slow and paternalistic. It was provided *for* the Cree, by outsiders. Schools started earlier by the Anglican or Oblate missions were taken over, either by the federal Department of Indian Affairs (DINA) or by the provincial Department of Northern Quebec (DGNQ). Small primary schools and nursing stations were built in the smaller villages. DGNQ built a hospital in Fort George in 1971; in 1972 the former Anglican primary school in Fort George was converted by DINA into a residential high school for the region. Each year DINA built a few more permanent houses in each village. The HBC had converted its trading posts into retail stores before 1964, and had closed the posts of Nemiscau and Waswanipi, but only three Co-operatives had emerged by 1971 to supplement the HBC. Only in the two largest villages of Fort George and Mistassini were there small convenience stores, a restaurant, and a few other local businesses.

Though the eight administrative bands had elective chiefs and councils, until 1971 these were mainly agencies for requesting DINA to provide more services, and for distributing housing and welfare money to individuals within bands. All planning of schools and houses was done at the District Office in the town of Val d'Or. All administrative staff other than band chiefs — the teachers, nurses, and store managers — were non-Cree.

Money had been used increasingly in the villages after 1945, as family and old-age allowances were paid to native people directly. The HBC had increasingly paid for furs in cash, rather than in "credit," though credit accounts were a regular part of its retail business. Salaries from employment had also grown. Casual summer work, unloading supplies for the HBC or in government construction projects, had provided cash to equip winter hunters even before 1945, and the HBC and missions had employed a few Cree as "homeguard" for over a century. Both types of employment were increasing.

Table 1 shows the economic situation of 1971. The subsistence sector produced most of the production, and most people worked in it. Even a conservative valuation of food and housing produced gave a value of twice the value of salaries, even if the sale of furs provided very little cash. Two thirds of the total cash obtained came from salaries, while transfer payments including welfare provided the other third. But overall it is a picture of poverty — of a GNP per capita of only $1150 — even if the Cree did not see themselves as poor.

The wage employment sector gave every indication that the Cree were destined to become a proletariat (LaRusic 1969). In southern villages the proximity of mines and forestry operations meant that temporary unskilled jobs were available, but few permanent skilled jobs. Village employment was mainly janitorial in schools and band offices, with a few positions as store clerks and secretaries. In the bigger villages to which children came as boarding-school pupils, many people worked in dormitories or as foster parents. The very few more skilled jobs were as radio-telephone operators, airline agents, teacher's aides, band managers, and a few entrepreneurs.

Into this slow paternalistic growth of sedentarization and services came the shock of the Premier of Quebec announcing in April 1971 that a hydro-

311

Table 1
Cree Incomes 1971 and 1981

			1971[1]		1981[2]	
			($000)	%	($000)	%
Hunting:	In cash (furs)		300	4	642 [3]	2
	In kind (meat, etc)[7]		3,864	57	5,700 [5]	20
	Income Security		-	-	6,046	21
		Subtotal:	4,164	61	12,388	43
Salaries:	Government, industry and local businesses		1,580 [4]	23	14,891	52
Transfers:	Welfare		683	11	800 [5]	3
	Old Age, Family Allowances		305 [6]	5	600 [5]	2
		Total:	6,732	100	28,679	100

Sources:
1. Salisbury (1972a) Table 8, except as noted.
2. Various Sources; basically Cree Village Profiles, with omissions corrected from other sources, such as LaRusic (1982) ISP Annual Reports, and Salisbury et al (1982).
3. Figure for 1980.
4. In Salisbury (1972a) Table 8. The figure for this item was based on an underestimate for Fort Geroge, as data then were lacking on Fort George salaries. A sum of $600,000 has been added on the basis of Salisbury (1972b).
5. 1981 figures for smaller populations have been extrapolated for the total Cree population, using census data on ages and NHRC (1982) for overall game harvests.
6. No figure was given for Salisbury (1972a). Estimate is based on number of children and aged.
7. The estimates of total Cree harvests of fish and game in Salisbury (1972a) and NHRC (1982) — the latter modified to account for the change in number of hunters between 1978 and 1981 — are multiplied by the average price for meat in Cree village stores, 1971 and 1982.

electric project costing $5.6 billion would be built on Cree lands. Cree felt threatened, but did not know what to do. There were no pan-Cree structures, and band chiefs met only sporadically at meetings of the Indians of Quebec Association (IQA). The IQA agreed to protest on behalf of the Cree, as did various ecology groups and the McGill PAD. Environmental and social impact studies were not "normal procedure" before 1975, but the protests did elicit a governmental ecology review, and a social impact study by the PAD for the James Bay Development Corporation, reporting in October 1972.

A group of Cree — mainly young people who had attended high school together in southern Canada — received a grant from the Arctic Institute of North America to meet formally in Mistassini. But not until May 1972 did the IQA obtain Federal funding to set up a Task Force on Ecological and Social Impacts, under John Spence (biology) and the author (anthropology). Its field study in August 1972 involved outside experts, but also most of the emerging Cree-educated activists.

In both its reports the PAD recommended as follows: 1) that the Cree hunting economy be explicitly supported, as its viability was currently threatened by poor infrastructure, although it could continue to support most of the population, even after reservoir construction, if its infrastructure were improved; 2) that damages to the hunting economy be compensated for; 3) that damage to village life be minimized by isolating construction camps from villages, and by making then removable after use; and 4) that the Cree would be best served in the long run, not by temporary employment as unskilled construction labor, but by using the project as a time to train local people to take over administration of the region, after construction was completed. We spelled out demographic projections of the labor force, and the employment and training policies that could lead to the Cree administering the region. In 1985 those projections proved very close to reality, and over three quarters of the recommendations had come to pass.

However the recommendations were not smoothly accepted. After a month of negotiations over the reports, the Cree and the developers became deadlocked. Injunctions, a court case, appeals of the verdict, and two years of hard bargaining, in which the Quebec negotiator was an ex-deputy minister of Indian Affairs, finally resulted in an Agreement — the James Bay and Northern Quebec Agreement (JBNQA). In it the Cree accepted the project and Government sovereignty; the Government agreed on compensation and on providing support for Cree regional autonomy. But not before opposition to the project had unified and politicized the Cree villages. The Cree had developed a structure, first under the IQA and the Task Force, but finally independently of the IQA as the Grand Council of the Crees of Quebec. It signed an agreement in principle in November 1974, and, after

313

legal haggling and a referendum of all villagers, the JBNQA Agreement in November 1975.

This agreement recognises a Cree Regional Authority (CRA) as administering regional services to Cree villages, and Cree boards for health, social services, schools, environment, housing, economic development and other services. They are staffed by Cree, and have the status of municipalities, and school or other boards under Quebec ministries. Importantly their employees are paid by the Province at standard rates of pay. The GCCQ remains a non-statutory body and the political forum of Creeland; the CRA constitutes its elected administrators. The core of both are the activists of the 1972 research who also negotiated the Agreement.

The territory administered by the CRA is an area surrounding the eight separate villages, comparable to Indian Reserves, but now termed Category 1 lands. The remaining land was transferred to the Province, which recognized Cree rights to hunt over all of it, except towns and hydro-installations. Over almost a quarter (termed Category 2 lands) Cree hunting rights were exclusive, but over the large remainder (Category 3 lands) the Cree accepted that non-Cree could hunt some species (not those of main Cree concern), but only if Cree food needs were satisfied. To make these rights effective the Cree jointly control decisions over sport-hunting quotas, and are taking over outfitting operations in the region. They have monitored hunting catches for five years to establish what Cree food needs are before any flooding by the Project. The Agreement establishes their right to this yield of meat, and includes a special program, the Income Security Programme for Cree Hunters and Trappers (ISP). This provides the funds to outfit winter hunting for food and furs; it has largely eliminated the need for welfare payments (except to people unable to hunt): it is administered by the Cree themselves, within an indexed maximum total payout, who see it as a "salary for hunting work," even if it is technically a transfer payment.

For the diminution of Cree rights through codification, and for permitting development to proceed, the 7,000 Cree were awarded $150 million, half being paid over five years, and half as a royalty payment as hydro generating is installed. Most funds are in non-transferable government securities. Neither principal nor interest can be distributed to individuals. The interest (and some lump sums) may be used for programs, administrative services, and investment. The Finance Board has acted conservatively, but has already set up Cree Constructions, invested in an airline Air Creebec, and speeded up rehousing by "topping up" funding obtained through regular channels. The GCCQ is exploring other investments in businesses to create northern employment, such as tourism, mining, and forestry. It is able to buy the best technical advice, but is not obligated to follow it. Where previously government officials made decisions, the Cree at first used non-Cree consultants (including anthropologists) but a technical staff now exists among the Cree themselves. Even where consultants are still used, Cree decision-makers include Cree who can evaluate the advice that is given.

In short, the twenty years 1964-1984 have seen the steady buildup of modern administrative structures for the region, planning and delivering services to 7,000 people scattered over 150,000 square miles of land. The period 1971-1984 is distinctive as the time when these structures came to be run by the Cree. Constructing (for $15 billion as it turned out) the hydro project had relatively little effect on the villages, for these were off-limits, and few Cree worked in construction. Its main legacy is the super highway cutting through Cree-land from south to north, with branches to each of the four dams. Flooding of 50 hunting territories has hurt three northerly bands. Transmission lines have cut swathes through more southerly forests, but logging for pulp has had more profound effects. Some hunting territories, recently logged, are desolate; some, cut twenty years ago and now reforesting, are producing abundant game, mainly moose. The 1982 depression severely hit lumbering and mining, and cut Cree employment also. Nor has electricity given the Cree a base for industry, as no villages are linked to the high-voltage transmission lines. The development that has indeed come to Cree villages is attributable to the service industries, and to the delivery of services by the Cree themselves.

ECONOMIC ASSESSMENT

(i) THE INTERNAL ECONOMY

Table 1 (Cree Incomes 1971 and 1981) provides a first approximation of the changes in the Cree economy. The figures are, it is true, approximations based on data collected in individual villages at varied dates, projected to give overall figures for the particular years mentioned. The estimates could undoubtedly have been improved had monitoring of the project been funded, but neither Cree nor government liked the idea of research studies in 1973. The figures are thus the best available, but they are consistent with more impressionistic data. They include amounts in dollars for the value of meat and housing produced by hunters, and for transfer payments made to Cree individuals. They omit transfer payments to Cree organizations that are not individuals, Cree income from investments, and the salaries of non-Cree working in villages. The figures do not consider, either, the flows out of the region to southern Canada and the USA — billions of dollars worth of hydroelectricity. These elements will be considered in the next section, the political economy.

Overall the increase in total incomes over the ten-year period is 426 percent. This increase, when adjusted for population increase (25 percent) and cost-of-living increase (186 percent) becomes a change in constant dollar per capita terms of 83 percent over ten years. The Cree have got wealthier at a faster rate than most Canadians or Americans. But in 1971 per capita Cree incomes were just over $1,000; by 1981 per capita incomes were still generally at the poverty level, but per-family incomes (given the larger Cree families) were within the Canadian range, at $14,366. In doing better the Cree have caught up from a point below the poverty level, to a level comparable with that found in many rural communities across Canada.

The source of income by sector — subsistence, salaries, and transfer payments — has changed markedly. Welfare and family allowances have dropped from 16 percent to 5 percent of total income; salaries have increased from 23 percent to 52 percent. The total of the former has increased absolutely but by less than inflation: the latter has increased tenfold. The hunting sector has tripled in product, but declined — from 61 percent to 43 percent — as a proportion of the total product. Wage work is now the major activity of the Cree, surpassing the formerly dominant hunting.

(1) *Hunting*

The decline of the hunting sector is only relative, however, and in part reflects our calculating a dollar value for meat. Thus the volume of meat produced (in pounds) has risen almost as much as population, by 20 percent. But the price of store-bought meat in Creeland has not increased as fast as inflation, largely because transport costs (and store mark-ups) have reduced with the construction of roads. In constant dollars the price of meat has declined, and even the increased production forms a greatly decreased proportion of total income. But including the ISP payments as salaries to hunters (and this is how the Cree define them) brings the total return to hunters to more than double the meat value. Without ISP payments subsistence hunting would not be viable. Almost half the ISP goes to pay for air transport to hunting territories, and for equipment to set up camp and to hunt and trap. One could interpret the figures in Table 1 as meaning that the half spent on equipment is a business expense, and so deduct it from income. But I do not attempt such detailed interpretation of what are approximate figures. I use them merely to indicate that hunting remains a major focus of Cree life; that ISP plays a crucial role in maintaining local food-production, and that the Cree, by deliberately opting for ISP, see it as vital for cultural survival and — not as a handout to those unable to get a wage job — but as a fair return for the most skilled and respected Cree job, that of the productive hunter.

316

The rate of return per hour of hunting labor may indeed have increased between 1971 and 1981. In 1971 a good hunter could have earned much more per hour hunting (even using the cited dollar values for meat) than as unskilled labor in mining or forestry. Certainly this was true for moose-hunting under favorable snow and weather conditions, which can yield $200 per hour; regular trapping of beaver, walking a trapline, and chopping through the ice at beaver lodges, provided a steady return of meat and fur at about twice the unskilled wage rate (and also provided information about other game); periods of unsuccessful hunting, or of fishing and snaring small game, lowered the average return but enabled the hunter to subsist in the bush and to be on the spot when favorable hunting periods occurred. For an unskilled hunter in 1971 it may well have paid to switch to wage labor, and some observers (e.g. LaRusic 1969) felt that such a switch was occurring, and was likely to continue.

By 1981 the technology and the economics of hunting have changed. Snowmobiles, chain saws, and radios have reduced the drudgery of walking traplines, hauling home meat and fuel, and maintaining a home in the bush. The hours of work needed to produce a comparable amount of meat have been reduced, perhaps by as much as a third. The months that hunters now spend in winter camps thus involve more time with their families — leisure in our terms, "investment in family life" in Cree terms. Though hunters cannot earn very high incomes, ISP ensures that all hunters earn a minimum. The minimum without any meat would be well below the earnings of an unskilled wage earner, but a successful hunter is well rewarded, has an incentive to produce meat, and to maintain the highest Cree status of hunter and provider. The less skilled hunter now has a clearer choice of whether to enter a hunting way of life, or the wage economy, without pressures of poverty pushing him ineluctably to the latter. Above all the standard of living (and comfort) of hunters and their families has increased markedly.

The production of meat has not been commercialized. It is still illegal in Quebec to sell wild game, even in cooked form in restaurants. There is however an exchange between hunters and wage-workers; they reciprocate by caring for hunters' children at school, or by purchasing major items like trucks (Scott 1984). Hunting now also leads to cash income through the guiding of white sports fishermen, through summer outfitting camps operated by Cree bands or entrepreneurs. Minor amounts are earned by selling furs and artifacts made while hunting.

In short, hunting remains a vital part of the economy, but not as the engine of change, or the prime mover of Cree development. By maintaining the productivity of the subsistence sector, however, the Cree economy has been able to maintain a high degree of autonomy. As the productivity of labor in subsistence has

317

remained high, local people have been able to *refuse* low-paying wage labor, and to *choose* to enter only skilled occupations paying higher rates (cf. Salisbury 1971). If Cree hunting had become unproductive, Cree would have been forced into unskilled wage labor — the proletarianization foreseen by LaRusic (1969).

(2) *Salaries*

There are fewer problems in interpreting the figures for salary incomes and their tenfold increase. The number of workers has roughly doubled, and the average wage is five times as high, largely because most of the new workers are in skilled or professional jobs. In 1971 the typical worker was a seasonal manual laborer. The number of such workers has changed little since then, but the number in all the more skilled categories has increased many times. Almost a third of the professionals and white-collar workers are now women.

Simply put, the skilled jobs delivering services to villages in 1971 were held by whites. They staffed the schools and the nursing stations; they planned budgets and housing programs; they flew north for a week to repair telephones, install plumbing, or audit stores. Now most of these tasks are performed by local Cree, and Cree staff the offices of regional government, the school board, the health board, etc. Localization is not complete, and differs for each service, with between 5 percent and 50 percent of jobs still held by whites. Total numbers of staff have also risen to bring services up to provincial standards, and Cree policy has been to "deconcentrate" regional offices from the town of Val d'Or to individual villages. The result has been that most salaries paid by governmental agencies (at standard salary rates), to provide the services normal in any rural Canadian community, now go mainly to Cree people in villages.

As will be discussed later, this has not caused commensurate increases in the ongoing cost to the government (apart from inflation). It was expensive to hire non-local teachers, mechanics, and administrators, to provide them with travel and housing subsidies, and "hardship allowances" for going north. An unpublished Hydro-Quebec study of 1973 showed that the current costs of paternalistically administering the Cree region, and excluding any payments made to Cree, were equal to 85 percent of the total cash incomes of all Cree, while capital costs were equal to 40 percent of total Cree income. A great deal is saved by higher-level governments hiring local people, though we have no data on whether the savings were realized, and the number of white staff reduced.

Employing local people also has "multiplier" effects on the local economy. Most transient whites spent little of their salaries in the villages. Housing was supplied, and there was little to buy locally except food. At the end of their northern duty employees took south the "nest eggs" they had saved, and fed them into the urban economies of the south. Our figures show about 90 percent of salaries paid to non-Cree "leaking" out of the community, either as "nest eggs," or buying goods imported into the villages; only 10 percent went to pay the salaries of Cree workers in stores. By contrast Cree salaried workers, receiving the same rate for the job, do not receive "hardship" and housing allowances. They live at home and their salaries are spent on goods and services used in the villages. Though many goods are imported (from heating oil to radios and flour), buying them employs local salespeople, while all services and housing bought locally go to provide employment. Consumer budgets suggest that 60 percent of local salaries "leak" directly from villages to pay for imports, but 40 percent is recirculated. Iterating the process of leakage and recirculation yields an implied multiplier of 1.11 for non-Cree salaries, and 1.67 for Cree salaries. Every $1 million paid as non-Cree salaries in 1971 produced another $111,111 locally; payment of $1 million in Cree salaries in 1981 adds to village income not only the $1,000,000 but also another $666,667 in "multiplier effect."

There are also more manual jobs in villages, matching a big decline in the number of Cree leaving villages to work in mining or forestry. This increase in village employment is through businesses owned either by individuals, or, like Cree Construction, by the GCCQ. Cree Construction contracted for some work for the hydro-project (e.g., clearing trees from land to be flooded) and now builds most of the houses for the housing program. Such companies make it possible for Cree with formal training in skills such as machine operation or plumbing to gain the practical experience needed to obtain skilled employment elsewhere. Without experience there are no outside jobs. Villages with available skilled and semi-skilled workers, and local companies prepared to carry out the work, can now plan for summer projects, and obtain funding for them as can all municipalities in Canada. Summer projects have replaced prospecting and forestry as the source of seasonal wage-work for winter hunters. The infusion of money by the housing program (some of it from compensation funds) has built up the local construction industry, and that in turn has contributed to producing the multiplier effect.

Another contribution to this effect is the greater ease of buying things in villages. All HBC stores have expanded and employ more staff. But in addition every village has one or more "corner stores" (*depanneurs*), one or more restaurants, and (if it has roads) taxi and truck services. Three villages have co-operative stores, and two have banking facilities. Though villagers still use mail-order catalogues, and travel to larger towns for major purchases (including alcohol), most salaries are spent in villages. The interior of many houses approaches those of suburban housing anywhere in North America. As in other suburbias young people complain there is "nothing to do but hang around," but Cree adults focus interests on improving their homes.

By contrast Creeland has so far produced little "industrial" employment. Two village sawmills of the late 1960s proved uncompetitive with imported lumber, even given the protection from high transport costs. One Cree has staked his own mineral find, but development is likely to be jointly with a large firm, and only when the industry recovers from the depression. A few Waswanipi men subcontract for forestry work from large companies; but without the allocation of a quota to supply the Qevillon pulp mill, the Cree have no other market for forestry production. Subcontracting is the simplest expansion of Cree interest, but the GCCQ is studying other options, especially if Cree Construction and local repair needs make sawmills viable.

Tourism is the other possibility for an "industry," and it too is helped by a village base. Most villages now have a "motel," either band-owned, or individually-owned, thanks to a band loan. Outsiders coming on official business — consultants, bank auditors, skilled mechanics — stay at the motel, when in 1971 they would have stayed at the house of a non-Cree. Rates are exorbitant — but charged usually to expenses. Sport fishing camps are being taken over by the Cree, and provide a means of capitalizing on hunting skills. Summer courses in guiding, run by the school board, teach how to cope with tourists, and promise to make the industry viable.

In short the past ten years have seen great increases in Cree prosperity — though no one except other Indians could call them wealthy (NIB 1982). It has involved a great increase in the social services and housing in villages that now conform to a suburban standard. The services have not followed *after* development of an industrial "base," they have preceded it and facilitated its establishment. The critical change has been that local people now supply their own services. Their salaries, fed into the local economy, have led to diversification in employment. The subsistence sector is strong, and exchanges exist between it and the growing service sector. The economy as a whole has become dynamic, providing the basis for sustained, and locally controlled industrial expansion.

(ii) The Political Economy

Who benefits from this increase in Cree wealth? And who pays for it? Many Indian people in Canada believe, as the National Indian Brotherhood (1982) study of the JBNQA, entitled *Practically Millionaires*, suggests, that the Cree sold their land heritage for money, that the money has been appropriated by a wealthy few, and that it will soon disappear leaving poverty and dependency. Critics of the Alaska Native Claims Settlement Act of 1971 say that this is happening in Alaska. Is it happening in Northern Quebec?

Some unequal sharing of the cash benefits indeed appears in our data, but the inequalities are small and do not split Cree society into antagonistic classes. Increases in white-collar and professional jobs provide salaries to educated younger Cree; but the skilled hunters benefit most from Income Security. Everyone now has better housing. Many women have salaried jobs. It has been deliberate policy not to pay Cree administrators at rates comparable to administrators elsewhere in Canada, but at little more than white-collar salaries, though the non-taxable status of salaries paid on Indian reserves makes the lack of marked differentials less significant.

Household budget figures indicate the differences, but also the comparability between salaried and hunting Cree. Hunting families earn, on average, about $1,000 less cash, and must use about $3,000 to generate their hunting income, but they produce food and housing worth some $6,000. The average salary earner has a very small disposable income — the biggest fixed cost being winter house heating with oil — and uses some of it to produce about $1,500 of subsistence in spare-time hunting. The villager with insufficient cash to hunt on weekends, like the hunter who must also heat a village house in winter, is in a very difficult position. By contrast the above-average salary earner and the full-time hunter can live well, as the other living costs in a village are low.

Whether the spectrum of village income levels is creating class divisions between hunters and administrators has been examined by LaRusic et. al. (1979), Brelsford (1983), and Scott (1984). All argue that classes have not emerged, partly because Cree ideology stresses equality and reciprocity, partly because Cree policy reflects that ideology, and partly because all extended Cree families include hunters and salaried workers. Meat and goods, money and services, are exchanged among kin, reducing inequality, and blurring lines of division. In principle Cree assert that class divisions reflect "white-man's materialism" and are not the Cree way.

The second focus of scepticism — that the Cree are spending the money received for their birthright, the land — is also negated by the data. The Cree have not "sold their land." Over almost all their traditional land they maintain hunting rights, which the Agreement enshrines in legal terminology and provides mechanisms to ensure remain undiminished — largely through environmental and conservation regimes run by the Cree. Foregone rights to subsurface minerals and to land involved in hydro-installations have been matched by payment of $150 million, but this is a minor part of the Agreement. Nor is the sum being spent. Most is in non-transferable government bonds, yielding income. Even the income is not distributed but is used, partly for public purposes and programs, but mainly for investment. Overall the assets of the Board of Compensation are increasing, not decreasing.

Cree investment (other than the bonds) aims at strengthening the local economy, in two ways. First is constructing local infrastructure, for example rehousing the villages. With normal Indian Affairs budgets and Central Mortgage and Housing Corporation loans, rehousing villages would have taken twenty years. By advancing compensation money (and later reimbursing the Fund from annual budgets) the job is being completed in five years and is creating a local construction industry. Secondly there is investment in industries already in the region. Thus the Cree are now majority share holders in the airline that serves Creeland, Air Creebec, formerly owned by Austin Airways who now is a minority owner. The success of investment in Cree construction has been described, though one venture, organized to retail tools and building materials, has already closed, with major losses. The Cree are studying ways to invest in forestry and mining, but as indicated, subcontracting and partnership with major companies seem the most feasible. The possibility of partnership has emerged only because of the improved Cree infrastructure, and the larger pool of Cree skills, managment, and finance.

But if Cree have few industries and most employment comes via government funding of social services, is this not a situation of "dependency?" Or of false security, should a changing government cut funding? I argue against this at two levels — the funding is guaranteed, and the funding is not a gift but an exchange.

The guarantee of funding is the 1975 Agreement signed by Canada, Quebec, and the Cree, and enacted into law. The 1983 Canadian Charter entrenches the provisions of such treaties, containing the precedent dating back to 1763 in Canada. Indian people who recognize the sovereignty of Canada receive in return "protection" by Canada. As interpreted, "protection" means the provision of services similar to those given other Canadians, without having to pay taxes on income earned on reserves, for which the Indians permit whites limited access to their land. In the past services have not been comparable with those provided to other Canadians, but as we have seen services are being improved. Though it costs government more to provide services for an individual in the sparsely populated north than it does for an individual in the crowded south, the extra costs of those services are borne by a large population that benefits environmentally, politically, and strategically from Canadian sovereignty over the North. Provision of comparable though expensive service to northerners is part of an entrenched Canadian compact from which all Canadians benefit.

322

The benefits are not just political, however; there is an exchange of economic benefits between the Cree and the south. If the electrical capacity of the existing hydro-project (8 million kilowatts) operated full-time and the power sold at a price of 40 mil per kilowatt hour, it would earn $2.8 billion each year for Hydro-Quebec. Operating costs are small, though interest and amortization of the $15 billion investment may take $2 billion. Against these figures the compensation of $150 million, and the annual payment of $28 million to support services to the Cree seem very small amounts to "rent" the land for the project. Whether the exchange is precisely in balance is debatable, but clearly both sides benefit from the contract. Abrogation of such a contract is unthinkable.

But if the Cree have indeed received material and service benefits, have they lost what is more precious, their Cree "cultural heritage"? Elsewhere (Salisbury 1984) I argue that the Cree, like many small but newly affluent groups, are experiencing a cultural "enhancement," as they amplify some features of their previous culture while losing others. The culture is evolving, in ways that many Cree see as a cultural revival, as they become an ethnic regional government within the nation-state. I shall not repeat that argument here beyond considering how far they have moved in the opposite direction — toward cultural "dependency."

Any increased "dependency" is clearly not the economic dependency of being "a reserve army of labor"; there has been a major decline in the employment of Cree by non-Cree firms, and a period of relatively full employment within villages. The most obvious visible change, as described, is that Cree village lifestyles now approximate "suburban" ones, of involvement in homes and families, of purchase of consumer durables and transportation equipment (snowmobiles, rather than cars however), of television and recorded music, and of central heating by oil for houses. As described, the purchase of goods imported from the rest of Canada absorbs 60 percent of every dollar of local income, even though this percentage has declined markedly from the time when village service providers were transients from the south. The inflow of goods is even more dramatic if one considers the capital investments that have been made over the past ten years, and that have not been considered in our treatment of the ongoing local economy. These have included roads, communications, and electricity supply provided by government, and housing provided jointly by government and villages. There has been a positive encouragement to the Cree to become consumers, as a banking system has begun to develop, and credit has become available to people who now have a steady income. Elberg et. al. (1977) documents the millions of dollars of credit used to buy trucks and television sets in Fort George, when the highway was opened up, and satellite antennae installed. Several years' disposable income was spent in advance of its receipt. So too the use of compensation funds to speed house building has committed the Cree to import immediately the goods involved in that housing, and to pay for what they have bought from their future income.

But if this is "cultural dependency" the Cree are no different from other Canadians who use money to buy goods that they do not manufacture. What has happened is better described as the emergence of the Cree from what Paine (1982) has described as "paternalism," to a situation where they are participating as partners in the national Canadian economy. They indeed consume manufactures made elsewhere, which they pay for with money earned predominantly through the service sector, though they contribute to the national economy also as the landowners of northern Quebec. In 1985 they now make their own consumer choices, in ways they could not do when they were only the recipients of services provided by white administrators, and not the providers of the services themselves. Though the Crees may have abdicated some sense of "independence" in becoming part of the wider Canadian service economy, what they have gained in becoming a regional government within Quebec and Canada is the ability to use the service economy to produce local development.

This is the message that the Cree case provides. The provision of more services, and not more material goods, is the inevitable trend of post-industrial society. In all "developed" societies, over 50 percent of economic activity is in the service sector. If local, and particularly rural, communities are to "develop" and to participate in post-industrial society they need not merely be provided with local services, they need to have local control over those services. It is when they do not have control that "dependency" becomes likely. The Cree indicate how the service economy can indeed be locally controlled, to produce development.

NOTE

1.　For a review of the work of the Programme in the Anthropology of Development, and of its experiences in training for applied (or action) anthropological work, see Salisbury 1978. Clearly the present paper builds on the work of all previous members of the PAD, starting with that of Norman Chance, its first Director. References in this paper are principally to work done by Programme students and to their theses, but no attempt has been made to be comprehensive. Any attempt to spell out the colleagues and Cree who have contributed to this review of fifteen years work would be necessarily incomplete; it is not, perhaps, invidious to pick out a very few whose discussions have been most productive, namely Harvey Feit, Ignatius LaRusic, Colin Scott, Alan Penn, Philip Awashish, Billy Diamond, Abel Kitchen, Peter Gull and Matthew Coon-Come. I am nonetheless grateful to the hundreds of friends and helpers whose names are omitted.

REFERENCES

Brelsford, T. 1983. "Hunters and Workers among the Nemaska Cree." MA thesis. Montreal: McGill University.

Chance N.A. (ed.), 1968. *Conflict and Culture Change*. Ottawa: Canadian Research Centre for Anthropology.

----------1969. *Developmental Change among the Cree Indians of Quebec*. Ottawa: Department of Regional Economic Expansion.

Elberg N., R. Visitor, and R.F. Salisbury. 1977. *Off-Centre: Fort George and the Regional Communications Network of James Bay*. Monograph No. 9. Montreal: McGill University Programme in the Anthropology of Development.

Feit, H.A. 1968. Mistassini Hunters of the Boreal Forest. M.A. thesis. Montreal: McGill University.

----------1979. Waswanipi Realities and Adaptations. Ph.D. thesis. Montreal: McGill University.

LaRusic, I.E. 1968. *The New Auchimau: Patron-client Relations among the Waswanipi Cree*. M.A. thesis. Montreal: McGill University.

------------1969. "From Hunter to Proletarian." In Chance, N. (ed.), *Developmental Change among the Cree Indians of Quebec*, Annex 2:1-59. Ottawa: Department of Regional Economic Expansion.

------------1979. *Negotiating a Way of Life*. Ottawa: Department of Indian and Northern Affairs.

National Indian Brotherhood. 1982. *Practically Millionaires: Report on the James Bay Agreement*. Ottawa: National Indian Brotherhood.

Native Harvesting Research Committee. 1983. *The Wealth of the Land: Wildlife Harvests by the James Bay Cree, 1972-1979*. Quebec City: James Bay Native Harvesting Research Committee.

Paine, R.P.B. 1982. *The White Arctic*. St. John's: Memorial University of Newfoundland (ISER).

Salisbury, R.F. 1970. *Vunamami: Economic Transformation in a Traditional Society*. Berkeley: University of California Press.

------------1971. "Development through the Service Industries." *Manpower and Unemployment Research in Africa* 4:57-66.

------------1972a. *Development and James Bay: Social Implications of the the Proposals for the Hydroelectric Scheme*. Monograph No. 4. Montreal: McGill University Programme in the Anthropology of Development.

------------1972b. *Not By Bread Alone; The Use of Subsistence Resources by the James Bay Cree*. Montreal: Indians of Quebec Association.

------------1978. "Training Applied Anthropologists: The McGill Programme in the Anthropology of Development 1964-1976." In Weaver, S. (ed.), *Applied Anthropology in Canada*, Proceedings of the CES 4:58-78.

------------1984. "Affluence and Cultural Survival." American Ethnological Society Proceedings, Spring 1981. Washington, D.C.

------------1986. *A Homeland for the Cree: Regional Development in James Bay, 1971-1981.* Montreal: McGill-Queens Press.

Scott, C. 1984. "Between 'Original Affluence' and Consumer Affluence: Domestic Production and Guaranteed Income for J Bay Hunters." In Salisbury, R. (ed.), *Affluence and Cultural Survival*:74-86.

VI

Organizing For The Common Good:

Developing Anthropology

by

Colin H. Scott

Richard Salisbury was a man of extraordinary vitality and creativity who achieved a great deal in developing organizational structures to further the work of anthropology and its impact in the wider society. The present chapter is an account of some factors that shaped this contribution: his values and sense of societal mission, his personal style, intellectual positions and strategic insight – always in vigorous dialogue with unfolding historical conditions and opportunities.

An impression that emerged vividly and immediately as I reviewed his organizational work for this chapter was that Dick was more excited by architecture than by building-maintenance. He moved with astonishing energy into one challenge after another throughout his career. He pursued his purposes pragmatically and with dexterous improvisation; indeed, he took for granted the contingent, entrepreneurial quality of human action. Harvey Feit recalls preparing an introduction for Salisbury who was to give the keynote address at the 1983 annual meetings of the Canadian Ethnology Society/Society for Applied Anthropology in Canada:

> It took me six pages of single spaced typing to briefly list his activities. When I tried to find a set of themes around which to synthesize the review of his career, I found his many activities could be organized around three or four topics, and that this enormous diversity had coherence and focus (Feit 1983:2).

Shown an advance version of Feit's portrayal of his professional trajectory, Dick protested: "But you make it look as though I planned it that way!" – a remark that reflected his keen awareness of the limits of grand design, long before such awareness achieved postmodern fashionability.

Yet "coherence and focus" are unmistakably present, and a second impression that readily emerges is that these qualities flowed from defined purposes in which he was unwavering. Personal values, deeply held, entailed social commitments that were relevant in all contexts, with societal amelioration the right function of knowledge. In an interview not long before his death (Abley 1989), Salisbury steered the line of inquiry away from his reputation as a researcher, and his administrative prominence as McGill's Dean of Arts, with the question: 'How does my development affect people in the north?' This simple, grounded standard speaks volumes about the unity of the man and his professional purpose. Organization-building, like the development of self, was in vain if not in the service of people, enhanced communication and social equality. Salisbury showed in practice the value of anthropology to the development of inter-cultural relations in a multi-ethnic, progressively globalizing, society. He "nurtured all the things he touched. He fostered dialogue between the powerful and the powerless as a substitute for the use of power itself" (Aronson 1989:6).

BUILDING ANTHROPOLOGY AT MCGILL

Those of us who were privileged to be his colleagues in the McGill Department of Anthropology knew that he was not just the founder of our Department but also its central pillar and primary illumination. What distinctiveness and distinction we have, as a Department, built around the study of social change and development, we owe largely to Dick's leadership (Aronson 1990:9).

For Salisbury, the university was not only the central institution for scholarly disciplines and the growth of knowledge, it also had to provide vital means for linking that knowledge to societal issues. This required that a programme of active theoretical and applied research be wedded to the university's teaching mission. Moreover, during the expansionary years of the 1960s, the *sine qua non* of a mature university was to include graduate training and research. Undergraduate programmes, meanwhile, performed multiple functions: as means of disseminating knowledge via a liberal arts-educated public, as a stage in developing young scholars and as a means of material support for research and advanced graduate training. From his arrival at McGill in 1962, Salisbury set his sights on creating world-class graduate research and training in anthropology.

(i) FORMATIVE INFLUENCES.

Several circumstances of Salisbury's own training and early professional experience underlay the way that he approached this task. It was a blend of alternative models, pragmatic considerations and previous experiences which shaped his vision of how to develop a programme in anthropology.

His undergraduate and M.A. work in social anthropology at Cambridge, and his doctoral work at the Australian National University, had exposed him to the British conception of the discipline, centred on the empirical study of social structures. But with an undergraduate degree in modern languages and, later, as a significant contributor to the linguistic anthropology of New Guinea, Salisbury was himself never narrowly committed to conventional social anthropology. Moreover, his A.M. at Harvard had not only afforded a view of American four-field anthropology but also had engaged him in multi-disciplinary perspectives on the analysis of social change and development. At Harvard, he had gone through the Peabody Department of Anthropology which held to a Boasian four-field approach and in which his primary influences were Douglas Oliver and Cora DuBois (the latter had strong ties to Berkeley and was important to his later moving there). But he had also spent time in Social Relations at Harvard (headed by Talcott Parsons), where he worked with John and Beatrice Whiting at Palfrey House on their childrearing project and where he met his Canadian wife, Mary Roseborough:

> I was a research assistant in a course that Dick took (Fred Bales' seminar on small group interaction). Dick always said he had married his teacher! ... He did all the courses in Social Relations, took his comprehensive exams at the Peabody, but also did qualifying exams (in social and clinical psychology, social anthropology and sociology) in Social Relations. ... Social Relations was an exciting place, really charged. ... Dick was trying everything out, including mathematical models. ... Mostellar was a mathematician interested in social data, non-parametric statistics, modelling ... (Mary Salisbury, personal communication, 1996).

Intellectual versatility gained through exposure to both four-fields anthropology and multi-disciplinary studies thus became integral to Salisbury's outlook.

Dick was also well aware, from his early work experience, that different conceptions of anthropology could fuel heated academic rivalry. After receiving his PhD at Australian National University, and following a year of teaching at Tufts University, Salisbury took on an Assistant Professorship at the University of

California, Berkeley (1957-62). Berkeley in 1957, like other universities in the United States and Canada, was expanding. David Schneider, one of Dick's Harvard instructors and mentors, had been recruited from Harvard in 1956 to build social anthropology at Berkeley, in a department already strong in cultural anthropology and archaeology. Schneider did his job so well that by 1958 Time magazine had run an article suggesting that the Berkeley anthropology department was the best in the USA (Mary Salisbury, personal communication, 1996). But internal disagreements arose over the direction that Departmental development should take, with certain senior colleagues apparently concerned that the growing influence of social anthropology threatened to undermine their own strength within a "four-fields" perspective. By 1962, Schneider, and most of the young outstanding scholars whom he had recruited, had left Berkeley for other places.

After a year of research in New Guinea in 1961, Salisbury also decided to leave Berkeley for a variety of reasons, both professional and personal. In addition to the disappointing tide of events in the department, Dick was a British subject, and he experienced unwelcome pressure from a senior colleague to acquire United States citizenship. It was the era of Ronald Reagan's governorship in California, and the hard-line Republican tone of the place and times offended Dick's liberal sensibilities. He was also apprehensive about the kind of education that his two sons, who were reaching school age, would receive. A move to Canada emerged as an option.

(ii) Arrival and Early Work at McGill

Salisbury, his wife Mary Roseborough and her brother Howard Roseborough had all studied at Harvard together; and Howard had been hired as a sociologist in McGill's Department of Sociology and Anthropology. Salisbury learned through his brother-in-law of the job opportunities at McGill. The prospect of joining a department that combined anthropology with sociology was congenial because, in the words of one contemporary, "for Dick, the differences between sociology and anthropology were ones of place, not of theory and method" (Roger Krohn, personal communication 1996). Although the anthropologists were a numerical minority in the McGill department, the "Chicago School" orientation of several of the sociologists was compatible both with Salisbury's social anthropology and with the Harvard Social Relations approach which had captured his interest. William Westley, then Head of the Department of Sociology and Anthropology at McGill, recalled:

> I brought Dick to McGill at the suggestion of
> Howard Roseborough ... and he had a reputa-
> tion of being a hotshot anthropologist. He was

a demon for work. If not working, he was so restless that he would do math problems to fill up the time. ... Dick was a conscientious citizen. He sought duty and worked hard; ... he never refused a request that he fill an administrative job and he always did it well. ... I also have the impression that he was intellectually a compassionate man. When he *understood* a problem, he was always willing to help.

In the university context of the 1960s, characterized by rapid expansion and rapid turn-over of personnel, Salisbury was able to pursue his vision of programme development while becoming a leading member of the Department. His early years at McGill, from 1962 to 1965, were, as Bruce Trigger (1997:92) recalled, years of "dramatic growth and change. The number of anthropologists in the department increased from three to six, but Salisbury was the only anthropologist who remained at McGill throughout this period." Among the anthropologists, then, young and recently arrived as he was, Salisbury soon represented their primary continuity. With his own star rising in international anthropology (he had recently published *From Stone to Steel* as well as a series of important articles), Salisbury also possessed intellectual authority. It was soon apparent that he was the leader. In 1966, the year he was promoted to full professor, Salisbury was named Chair of the Department of Sociology and Anthropology, a position he held until 1970.

As already noted, Dick deeply appreciated the intellectual versatility offered by both "four-fields" anthropology and multi-disciplinary studies. At the same time, however, he prioritized those avenues of intra- and inter-disciplinary communication which furthered understandings of contemporary social and cultural change and of development. This objective, he saw, could be achieved without building a full-blown, four-fields anthropology department at McGill. As a pragmatist, moreover, Salisbury concluded that McGill was unlikely to devote sufficient resources to a "four-field" department of the kind under development at the University of Toronto and Université de Montréal. For despite rapid growth in Canadian universities – between the late 1950s and 1970, the number of full-time university teachers in the country increased five-fold and the number of anthropologists ten-fold (Inglis 1982:87) – Salisbury perceived a form of "double jeopardy" that would preclude the growth of a large anthropology department at McGill. Not only did the McGill administration favour physical sciences and the professions over the Arts Faculty, but the Quebec government favoured the growth of francophone universities over anglophone ones.

Anglophone university staffs in Quebec did not expand as fast as in the rest of Canada, because of the Quebec Government policy of starving those universities of funds, to permit the francophone universities to expand and "catch up" (*rattrapage*). ... the policy of concentrating on strengths allowed the production at McGill of 50% of all anglophone anthropology Ph.Ds in Canada during these years, nonetheless (Salisbury 1976:141).

Thus, topically as well as areally, recruitment was best aimed at "building upon strengths" – both within the department and within other departments and faculties at McGill:

Social change and transcultural psychiatry were obvious departmental interests. Throughout the university, in human geography, political science and economics as well as anthropology, there were ongoing involvements in Northern Canada, the Caribbean, West Africa, and South Asia. Anthropology staff recruitment focussed on these areas. For the first area, the nearby Arctic Institute of North America provided library facilities, while a McGill Committee on Northern Research received funds from the Department of Indian Affairs and Northern Development, to encourage graduate training. The founding in 1964 of a Centre for Developing Area Studies led to obtaining funds from Samuel Bronfmann and the Ford Foundation for training in the other areas mentioned, for library build up, and for the maintaining of ongoing collaborative ties with centres in those areas. Further funds for anthropological research training were obtained by participation in the Consortium for Research Training in the Caribbean, jointly with the Université de Montréal, the University of the West Indies, Brandeis and Columbia Universities, and the Research Institute for the

Study of Man [New York]. Norman Chance initiated an ongoing study of the effects of social change on the Cree of northern Quebec ... supported mainly by ARDA funds for rural development. This research formed the nucleus of the Programme in the Anthropology of Development (Salisbury 1976:140-141).

In recruitment and programme development, Salisbury honoured a commitment to social relevance in the Canadian context, while resisting the parochialisation that an exclusive emphasis on Canadian studies would have meant. According to Trigger (1997:91), Dick consciously sought to diversify the areal concentration of McGill anthropological research, reversing, to some extent, a pattern that had developed through the 1950s among an earlier cohort of anthropologists who had been hired into the department:

> Although none of the first anthropologists hired to teach in the department had done research in Canada, during their stay at McGill all of them investigated Canadian topics. Voget studied religious changes at Caughnawaga, and Fried, Yatsushiro, and Cohen became involved in research on the native peoples of the north. Soon after he arrived at McGill, Fried organized a seminar in which researchers from various institutions surveyed the work that had already been done relating to the aboriginal peoples of Quebec and Labrador. ... During his stay at McGill, Garigue initiated major studies of changing French Canadian kinship and community relations.

Trigger related this pattern of research choices to the "exclusive focus on doing research in Canada (ibid:92)" which the majority sociologists in the Department had. In contrast, Mary Salisbury suggested that such choices had been very deliberate – a conscious attempt on the part of Salisbury's predecessors to study Canadian topics which would otherwise have been neglected, particularly among new appointments from the United States, "who tended to be more interested in things U.S. than in Canada" (personal communication 1996). Indeed, Salisbury's own early engagement with the anthropology of James Bay Cree seems to have been motivated, in part, by his sense of the university's responsibility toward domestic issues as well as to the graduate students who had chosen to work in this domain. But he always considered himself, first and foremost, a New Guinea specialist.

If a high-calibre graduate programme focussed on the anthropology of development was Salisbury's primary objective, a pragmatic compromise with the expectations of the North American job market still seemed necessary. Partly to provide students with the four-field competence that was considered essential to produce employable PhDs, Bruce Trigger was hired, in his own words,

> to teach undergraduate archaeology courses and Middle Eastern ethnology, and to prepare students for the comprehensive examination in archaeology, historical linguistics, and physical anthropology that had to be passed, in addition to the comprehensive examination in social anthropology, by all doctoral candidates (Trigger 1997:92).

The hiring of Trigger was, simultaneously, a felicitous move enabling the Department to extend the temporal horizon of its focus on social change and development to the archaeological record. This remains a key element of programme structure to the present day.

Overall, Salisbury's strategy of concentrating on strengths would serve Anthropology at McGill well over the long haul:

> Salisbury's legacy to the department has not been a static formula for doing anthropology but a highly effective mode of adaptation to an institutional environment in which resources have always been limited and generally grudgingly bestowed (Trigger 1997:99).

Salisbury's success in founding the department is testimony to his development skills.

(iii) Establishing Separate Departments of Anthropology and Sociology at McGill

As chair, Salisbury led the Department of Sociology and Anthropology to several new appointments in both fields. But certain new-generation recruits in sociology saw their discipline's mission as more "quantitative" and as less

336

compatible with social anthropology than had the longer-established qualitative sociologists (Roger Krohn and Don von Eschen, personal communications, 1996). At the same time, a more consensual, participatory mode of departmental administration at McGill was emerging – a process that was occurring throughout Canada:

> University departments in Canada were traditionally hierarchical, with authority centralized in a Professor who was also Head. Many social science departments in the 1960s moved toward an American model in which the headship is replaced by a chairmanship which often rotates among department members, and decisions are taken by vote (Inglis 1982:92).

Salisbury's predecessor, Bill Westley, in a personal communication (1996), explained that he had initially navigated this transition. When he was hired in the early 1950s, it was as Head of the Department, in which capacity he could make appointments and sever contracts at his own discretion. Later, Westley's role was refashioned as that of "chairman." Salisbury's term as chair, immediately following Westley, came while the shift toward less hierarchical practices was still in process. These circumstances apparently exacerbated inter-generational opposition and the push for a departmental split. As Don von Eschen (personal communication, 1996) recalled:

> There was some feeling that there was a cadre of friends at the top. There was a sense of a push for democratization in the move to split. Richard Salisbury, Aileen Ross, Howard Roseborough were all democrats, but the way things had always worked at McGill meant a lot of discretionary power for the senior members. On the other hand, there were young, ambitious sociologists who didn't have the training and mental framework for a joint department. So there were two aspects: an inter-generational opposition, and a push by the new sociologists for what was perceived as a "normal," specifically sociological, curriculum.

Student loads seem to have been a further factor motivating a departmental split. As Trigger recalled (personal communication, 1996), anthropology student enrollments did not increase as quickly in relation to their new appointments. The result was that anthropologists had more research time than had the sociologists who had to carry relatively heavy loads of undergraduate service courses.

Salisbury initially opposed separation. Roger Krohn, in a personal communication (1996), recalled that, along with the qualitative sociologists,

> Salisbury was against the split, but not ready to
> fight it right down to the wire. He never quite
> saw the point of division — he was from the
> British system and real differences (between
> sociology and anthropology) were not apparent
> to him. The differences were not ones of theo-
> ry and method, but rather of place.
> Comparative studies should be the essence of
> science, and he didn't feel foreign or distant
> from sociology.

Another colleague and contemporary, Maurice Pinard (personal communication, 1996), speculated that Salisbury eventually agreed to separation because he recognized that more growth could be achieved as two departments than as one. According to Bill Westley, the anthropologists were also pressuring for separate departments. He, as senior sociologist, and Salisbury, as senior anthropologist, together came to the conclusion that separation was necessary:

> We agreed when I was chairman that it was
> mutually enriching to have anthropology and
> sociology in one department. However, eventu-
> ally, under pressure from the other anthropolo-
> gists, we both agreed that if anthropology were
> a separate department, it would be easier to
> fully develop anthropology. So we agreed to a
> separation (personal communication, 1996).

Given the politics of appointments and growth, Salisbury may well have concluded that the sum of the parts would be greater than the whole. If separation was not, for him, a welcome proposition on philosophical grounds, then at least it was a pragmatic response to the budgetary realities of the McGill administration at the time as well as to the aspirations of several junior colleagues.

(iv) Responses to Student Activism

During his chairship, Salisbury earned a reputation for devising pragmatic solutions to crisis – solutions that took democratization further than in many other departments at McGill and fulfilled, at the same time, objectives within his own pedagogical philosophy. Thus, the student activism and uprisings of the late 1960s that crippled faculty-student communication in many units of the university were turned to advantage in anthropology: said Bruce Trigger: "While many departments were torn apart by the students' movement, we sort of co-opted it into our department from the beginning." Against "many of his colleagues (who) were dead set against giving students a say" (Wells 1989), Salisbury advocated the routine involvement of student representatives on key departmental committees – in faculty hiring, granting tenure and setting university regulations. It was a form of governance that the department has maintained to the present.

A key element of graduate student demands of the late 1960s and into the 1970s was greater control and flexibility in the definition of their own programmes of study and research. The Department was able to consent to changes because, on the one hand, the employment imperative of "four-fields" breadth was weakening, with the diversification of intra-disciplinary styles and structures in both Canada and the United States. On the other hand, student demands played into what had been a central tenet of Salisbury's pedagogical strategy from the start – his commitment to training through research. The department thus reshaped its graduate training along lines which allowed more individualized, committee-supervised programmes of research, requiring more concentrated preparation in the theoretical and ethnographic specialties which bore on the topic of the thesis, but abandoning "four-fields" comprehensive requirements. For Salisbury, the Programme in the Anthropology of Development (PAD), which he went on to direct upon completing his term as chair, was to become the primary vehicle for developing a graduate training tradition of "learning by doing."

The Programme in the Anthropology of Development (PAD)

The McGill Programme in the Anthropology of Development is a brilliant example of Salisbury's penchant for building organizations to get things done. The Programme served, at once, as a vehicle for cutting-edge scholarship, for advanced graduate training and for the use of development theory in promoting more equitable social change. It was the hub of Salisbury's professional activity throughout most of his career at McGill; and it was where he maintained his office – walls straining under a ton of well-worn books, theses and reports; surfaces chronically under heaps of paper to be acted upon; his door habitually open to the graduate students

339

who shared adjacent offices. The old building housing the Programme was rather plain and somewhat dilapidated; but it was a familiar, comfortable setting, and action and economy mattered more than appearances.

Under the leadership of its previous director, Norman Chance (who had now left McGill), PAD had assembled a base of expertise on modernization and acculturation in the indigenous north. The 1960s were the early years of Canadian government enthusiasm for a planned approach to "community development" in rural and remote regions of the country. On the initiative of Chance, Salisbury and others, PAD had obtained federal ARDA (Agriculture and Rural Development Act) funds to support the so-called Cree Project which had begun to address "the introduction of the market economy and of government services to a hunting and gathering culture" (Gold and Tremblay 1982:107). Under Salisbury's subsequent direction, PAD confronted the 1970s era of expanding resource-extractive industries, most notably the James Bay Hydro-electric "mega-project." PAD promoted a perspective in which indigenous societies actively navigated their own courses of development, making decisions, formulating strategies and negotiating their positions within wider economic and public policy settings. These were themes stemming from Salisbury's 1970 book, *Vunamami: Economic Transformation in a Traditional Society*, based on a year of research in New Guinea while still at Berkeley.

PAD's engagement at James Bay illustrates Salisbury's talent for seizing the opportune moment and gaining the resources to support systematic research. As Harvey Feit recalled, "the fortunate appearance at McGill in 1971 of the Quebec Minister of Environment, Victor Goldbloom, to discuss the usefulness of university research, set up the opportunity for a discussion of the newly announced James Bay Hydro-electricity scheme, and led to an initial request for applied research on that project" (Feit 1983:2). Over the next several years, the central commitments of PAD would be to undertake the research that would assist the Cree people in coming to terms with the implications of the Hydro project for their lands and their lives, and in evaluating the effectiveness of the regional claims settlement that it precipitated.

PAD's role in transforming the relationship between indigenous peoples and the governments of Quebec and Canada has received wide recognition:

> *Dick et son équipe possèdent un flair politique exceptionnel lorsqu'on prend conscience que la plupart des recommandations issues de leurs travaux ethnographiques ont été adoptées soit directement par les instances gouvernementales blanches ou indirectement par les Cris à la suite de leur mobilisation politique, de*

leur longue marche en vue d'une Entente négociée sur
leurs droits en 1975 et de la mise en pratique des ter-
mes mêmes de cette entente (Tremblay 1990:7).

And, as another account (Gold and Tremblay 1982:118) declared:

> the most significant example of the relation-
> ship of the new anthropology of Quebec with
> the Native peoples of Quebec is the James Bay
> research directed by Richard Salisbury at
> McGill University. The Programme in the
> Anthropology of Development (PAD)
> approach to the Cree combines social anthro-
> pology with an applied approach that has been
> largely acceptable to the James Bay Natives. ...
> The point of entry for the McGill researchers
> stems from the inability of the Cree to assess
> the particular consequences of the new hydro-
> electric development plan for their communi-
> ties and for a hunting and trapping economy
> that they wish to maintain. Such an assessment
> was carried out by PAD anthropologists and by
> others in one of the most useful research pro-
> grammes ever undertaken by the discipline
> within Quebec.

In fact, the work of PAD achieved international prominence,
attracting the interest of colleagues abroad and providing models for parallel strategies in aboriginal policy and development in such far-flung jurisdictions as Alaska,
Australia and the Fenno-Scandinavian countries.

OTHER WORK IN PROGRAMMES AND CENTRES AT MCGILL

"Building upon strengths" called for active collaboration among
colleagues possessing cognate expertise across departments and faculties at McGill.
To this end, Salisbury involved himself in the construction of a number of centres and
programmes at McGill. Indeed, soon after his arrival, Salisbury enthusiastically took
up an invitation to participate in a discussion group of cross-disciplinary colleagues
organized by Eric Wittkower of psychiatry. Mary Salisbury recalled:

They would meet at peoples' houses (men
only!) and someone would take a turn talking
about their work. ... That was a group which
did expand his appreciation of colleagues in
other departments and the interesting work
that they were doing. Dick always believed that
there was so much talent at McGill, and often
colleagues did not know what others were
doing (personal communication, 1996).

Salisbury recognized as a departmental strength the links forged
earlier by Jacob Fried (who was interested in culture and personality) between anthropologists and other participants in McGill's new Programme in Transcultural
Psychiatry. These linkages and interests were carried forward in PAD Cree Project
research by Chance and Wintrob on mental health and attitudes toward development
at James Bay and by Salisbury's active involvement with the recently introduced
Transcultural Psychiatric Research Review. This is an aspect of Dick's interdisciplinary
commitment that is not well known. Yet his obituary in the *Review* by Raymond Prince
recognized his service on its Editorial Board from 1973 until the time of his death and
his contribution as "a steady contributor of abstracts and personal support and
advice." An early paper by Salisbury, Prince recalled, "sparked the most prolonged
and lengthy debate to occur in the pages of the TPRR" (Prince 1990:74).

Salisbury also enlarged the impact and comparative significance of
work at PAD through sustained commitments and contributions to two cross-disciplinary Centres at McGill – the Centre for Developing Area Studies (CDAS) and the
Centre for Northern Studies and Research (CNSR). As an energetic and successful
fund-raiser, Salisbury helped to found CDAS; and from 1975 to 1978 (and again
briefly in 1986), he served as its Director. CDAS had primary commitments to Third
World research through the active involvement of several of Salisbury's colleagues in
the Departments of Political Science, Geography, Economics and Sociology. Major
grants were obtained from the Ford and Bronfmann Foundations, while McGill's
inclusion in the Inter-university Consortium for Research Training in the Caribbean
promoted collaborative research and summer field-schools for graduate training in
Jamaica, Guyana and Belize. With geographer Theo Hills, Salisbury involved graduate students in research on Native peoples and mining towns in Guyana.

At the Centre for Northern Studies and Research (CNSR) – as a
Member of the Executive Committee (from 1973) and Board Chairman (1977-80) –
Salisbury similarly promoted links among colleagues and graduate students in anthro-
pology, geography, education and other departments and faculties with a stake in

research on northern development issues. During these years, despite a disappointing setback (the Arctic Institute yielded to the enticement of Alberta oil money and headed west), the Centre flourished as a lively nexus of research activity in the North.

The cumulative effect of Salisbury's various and extensive commitments to interdisciplinary communication was that he helped to create the synergy of expertise at McGill that has greatly enhanced the strength and profile of the university in the Canadian north and internationally.

BUILDING PROFESSIONAL ANTHROPOLOGY

It would be difficult to name an academic from abroad who became more involved than Salisbury in promoting things Canadian. He used his involvement in scholarly, governmental and private organizations – at local, national and international levels – to develop the funding, structures and visibility required for the growth of research in Canada and to foster training and employment opportunities for graduate students in this country. This is not to discount the importance of his contributions to international scholarly associations. Throughout his career, Salisbury maintained his membership in a range of international professional associations, many of which he served in executive capacities;[1] and these contributions established an international presence and reputation for Canadian anthropology.

A glance at his *curriculum vitae* reveals an interesting pattern in the executive roles which he undertook. Early in his tenure at McGill, in 1965, he followed up his New Guinea involvement on the United States scene as Chair of the Pacific Research Committee of the U.S. National Academy of Science/National Research. There followed a period of about fifteen years during which he focussed his primary efforts on the rapidly-emerging, scholarly organizations in Canada. When he served a term as President of the Northeastern Anthropological Association (1968-69), it was to capitalize on the opportunity to strengthen collegial links between scholars in Quebec and the northeastern United States. He was also President of the Canadian Anthropology and Sociology Association at this time.

Salisbury was a pioneer in developing the Canadian Sociology and Anthropology Society (CSAA) – the first professional association representing the two disciplines in Canada – and its journal. Formerly (since 1957), they had been represented via an Anthropology and Sociology Chapter within the Canadian Political Science Association (CPSA). In 1965, three years after Salisbury had joined the department at McGill, the CSAA was formed: "a motion by William Westley, seconded by Marc-Adélard Tremblay ... 'carried overwhelmingly.'" Salisbury was a member of the provisional CSAA Executive, chaired by Tremblay, that met in Montreal "to

343

draft a constitution, prepare a budget, and begin organization of a first Annual Meeting to be held at the University of Sherbrooke in June 1966" (Jones 1992:27). Salisbury then served on the CSAA Executive Committee (1965-1972) and as CSAA President (1969-70). During this period, the Executive established a Professional Ethics Sub-Committee, created a Panel on the imposition of the War Measures Act and created a Social Policy Sub-Committee – the general tenor of which was that "Canadian anthropologists and sociologists had a responsibility to conduct research on social problems and on matters of social policy" (ibid:31). Additionally, Salisbury served as business manager of the *Canadian Review of Sociology and Anthropology* from 1970 to 1974.

During these years, pressure was developing among anthropologists to establish an association independent of the sociologists. Proponents of division argued that the timing and content of the annual meetings did not respond to the needs and interests of anthropologists and that anthropologists were under-represented in the pages of the *Review*. A separate ethnology association was advocated, one that could possibly federate later on with archaeologists, linguists and physical anthropologists, following the "four-fields" conception of the discipline. Fission was regarded by many as a natural progression, with professorial numbers in the respective disciplines reaching critical masses capable of sustaining independent associations:

> Although relations between anthropologists and sociologists were cordial ... I think that the preference of most members of each discipline was for separate organizations. While social anthropologists and sociologists shared theoretical and research interests, anthropologists in other sub-fields had no more reason to join forces with sociologists than with those of other disciplines. If anthropologists (and sociologists) ended up together organizationally, it was, as in the case of joint departments, a matter of expediency (Jones 1992:39).

Proponents of unity, on the other hand, emphasized the anthropologists' collegial links and commonalties with the sociologists, and advocated that anthropologists' energies be devoted to enlarging their role within the CSAA (Inglis 1982:94).

It might be thought that Salisbury, consistent with principles underwriting his initial resistance to departmental division at McGill, would have been more sympathetic to the unity proponents. He did not perceive inherent differences of theory or method separating anthropologists from sociologists; and it is likely that, given his interdisciplinary and applied commitments, he did not advocate the disciplinary division of things that were continuous in fields of societal action. Be that as it may, Salisbury joined the pro-division anthropologists. An important factor in his decision was a controversy occurring within the CSAA over which Salisbury was to resign from the organisation. It was an issue which had preoccupied the CSAA from its inception – namely, the domination of Canadian anthropology and sociology by "American" models and traditions of scholarship, with a large (and growing) majority of appointments being United States citizens (Inglis 1982; Jones 1992; Darnell 1998). A Canadianization Sub-Committee (1972-74), and a later Task Force on Canadianization (1974-79), advocated a series of progressively more restrictive measures to discourage the hiring of non-Canadians. As devoted as Salisbury was to the joint nurturing of Canadian anthropology and sociology, he viewed exclusionary hiring as decidedly detrimental; and on this issue he resigned from the CSAA (Salisbury 1974).

In short order, Dick was playing a leading role – with Marc Adélard Tremblay, Sally Weaver, Joan Ryan and others – in the 1974 founding of the Canadian Ethnology Society, to which the great majority of colleagues in Canadian social and cultural anthropology (including some who remained CSAA members) would align themselves. The Society, later renamed the Canadian Anthropology Society/Société d'Anthropologie canadienne (CASCA), launched its own journal *Culture* in 1981.

Well on in his career, Salisbury again assumed key executive responsibilities in international association work. He served terms as Vice-President (1979) and President (1980) of the American Ethnological Society (AES) and, through his involvement in organizing the 1981 AES spring meetings, co-edited a timely volume, *Affluence and Cultural Survival*, in which the work of his graduate students at James Bay and in Oceania was included in a broad comparative discussion. Thus, with the new Canadian associations well established, he was again directing his energies to executive work with international associations; and, again, he was at least partly motivated by a desire to strengthen the position of Canadian anthropology and to extend the comparative visibility of McGill's work in development anthropology.

One such international association became one of the most important forums in which Salisbury communicated the lessons learned through the James Bay experience. This was the new Society for Economic Anthropology (SEA). Salisbury was one of a group of nine colleagues contacted by Harold Schneider with the idea of forming a society. A planning meeting was held in 1980 and the inaugural meeting in 1981. Schneider was elected as the first President and Salisbury as Vice-

345

President for 1981-82. Salisbury took on the task of drafting the SEA Constitution and served the Society as its second President in 1982-83, a foundational year of rapid growth. Apparently more energized than exhausted from this spate of commitments, Salisbury also shouldered the formidable task of Programme Chair for the Eleventh International Congress of Anthropological and Ethnological Sciences, hosted at Université Laval and the University of British Columbia in 1983 – a signal contribution to raising the international profile and participation of Canadian anthropology.

At the same time, Salisbury did not turn away from responding to more local needs and opportunities. Under CASCA's aegis, he sought ways to promote the interests of applied anthropology in particular. In 1986, despite a heavy workload, he took on the presidency of the fledgling Society for Applied Anthropology of Canada/Société d'anthropologie appliquée du Canada (SAAC), and did this with great enthusiasm. *"C'était encore pour lui un occasion d'offrir au plus jeunes de notre profession, aux personnes qui ne fréquentent pas habituellement les réunions de sociétés savantes et les colloques disciplinaires une tribune où elles pourraient s'exprimer"* (Tremblay 1990:7).

Through this involvement, as well as more generally, Salisbury sought to redefine applied anthropology "not as what some academic anthropologists do in their spare time, but as what is done by people trained as anthropologists who earn their livelihood by applying their anthropological training" (Salisbury 1983:192; reproduced as Chapter VI.17 in this volume). Indeed, by the 1980s, it was clear that applied anthropology outside academe had become "the growth point of the discipline" (ibid), as many of the social issues demanding applied research could be more competently handled by anthropologists than by other disciplines. There were several impediments, however: lack of formal mechanisms to bring anthropologists and clients together; little awareness among potential clients of what anthropology had to offer; inability of existing models of advanced training to supply many of the skills needed for applied work outside academe; the inferior value attributed to applied work by the reward structure of academe; and the tendency of anthropology in applied domains to be overshadowed by professionals from larger, better-known disciplines.

Through his work with SAAC in the mid-1980's, Salisbury sought to establish a system for professional accreditation for practising anthropologists which, as Marc-Adélard Tremblay noted (1990:8), was viewed by Salisbury not so much as an entry visa to the job market but rather as a procedure for enhancing the reputation and the credibility of anthropology. Salisbury was gratified to observe that a growing number of local and regional Indian and Inuit self-governing institutions, government agencies and private concerns were turning to anthropological consult-

346

ants to assist them in coming to grips with the legal, political and economic challenges and choices of development. The demonstrated importance of PAD's contributions had helped to precipitate this trend.

Salisbury also extended the role and reputation of anthropology through his own consulting company. He was a founding partner and board member of ssDcc (consultants in social science), formed in 1979 and based in Montreal. The company provided opportunities for a number of younger colleagues as well as embracing aboriginal and governmental – anglophone and francophone – partners and clients. At SAAC meetings, Salisbury spoke practically and candidly to young anthropologists about the realities of the consulting world and the adaptations required to engage it successfully.

In other words, Dick saw as integral to the professionalization of anthropology in Canada that its insights and contributions become recognized and appreciated beyond academe. "It was," as Aronson (1989:6) stated, "remarkable to watch Richard Salisbury listening to problems and communicating his ideas equally comfortably and enthusiastically to mining engineers, regional planners, village politicians, or government administrators." The diversity of his applied research (which included work on the structure of mining towns in northern Canada and the Caribbean; coping by patients in mental hospitals; the problems of Québec dairy farmers; and the effects of gas pipelines on northern communities) is testimony not only to untrammelled intellectual range, but to the conviction that anthropology should serve where such service is needed.

FRANCOPHONES AND ANGLOPHONES

Within the Canadian context, Salisbury was particularly appreciated for broadening and enriching communication, in both languages, between English and French scholarly communities. Neither character nor conviction, or linguistic ability, disposed Salisbury to tolerate the "two solitude" isolation of French-speaking from English-speaking university communities in Quebec. He of course participated as a McGill representative on numerous panels and committees requiring bilingual skills; but his contributions went well beyond the prosaic, as attested in a particularly moving tribute by Bariteau (1989):

> *Au Québec, dans sa vie publique, il a incarné les idéaux qui l'enflammaient. Il s'est fait homme de contact et de communication. Pas seulement entre les Cris et le Gouvernement du Québec. Surtout entre les francophones et les anglophones.*

347

Constant dans sa recherche de communication, ce qu'il estimait être au coeur de l'anthropologie, il a poussé l'ouverture au fait français à l'Université McGill et invité les francophones à la réciprocité, ce qui parut alors audacieux, voire téméraire. Il n'a pas moins persévéré dans cette voie, privilégiant d'emblée le risque du renouveau au confort de l'indifférence. Avec le temps, ses propos firent école et il est devenu un leader de la communauté universitaire.

Son ouverture au fait francais l'a conduit à cheminer de près avec l'intelligentsia francophone du Québec. Il s'y est fait de nombreux amis qui ont su apprécier la qualité et la pertinence de son apport dans la lecture de notre réalité. La majorité de ses collègues francophones reconnaissaient en lui plus que le professeur de réputation internationale. Ils appréciaient sa candeur, sa sincérité, son goût du partage et son audace. Il avait leur estime. La vraie. Celle qui vient du coeur.

The degree to which Salisbury integrated himself into Quebec society and the key roles he played among his colleagues in sociology and anthropology, according to one observer, "entitles him to be considered a 'Founding Father' of anthropology in Quebec" (Tremblay 1989:2).

HIS LAST YEARS AT MCGILL

Like many prominent scholars who also have a flair for organizational work, Salisbury strove to contribute to upper-level university administration without abandoning his research. According to some senior insiders at McGill, he could probably have acceded to such positions as Vice-principal Academic or Vice-principal Research but chose, instead, to write *A Homeland for the Cree* (1986) with the aid of a prestigious Killam Foundation fellowship, thus bringing to a conclusion the work that he had sustained through PAD. Upon completing *Homeland*, he accepted, in 1986, the position of Dean of the Faculty of Arts for what would have been the five-year period leading to his retirement. Beyond this, he envisioned a book on development that would have compared his New Guinea and Northern Canadian research – a book that, sadly, was not accomplished before his death in June 1989.

As Dean of Arts, Salisbury worked to increase awareness within the faculty and on the part of the university administration "of the significant accomplishments and special needs of our Faculty, and of the importance of a flourishing Faculty of Arts to a healthy university" (Trigger 1989a). As another colleague recalled:

> Formidable financial constraints made his tenure as Dean difficult, but he found ways to begin expanding the number of full-time staff members, he solved a number of difficult departmental problems, and he encouraged staff and students across the Faculty to renew their faith in the mission and the future of the Faculty. His open door was unusual among senior administrators, and he still found time to recruit new students into anthropological research as he carried out the obligations of the Deanship (Aronson 1989:6).

Salisbury described his own approach as a commitment to hiring and supporting the development, as first rate researchers, of colleagues who could communicate their enthusiasm for knowledge in their teaching and who combined individual talent with a corporate sense of belonging. This corporate sense of commitment to the university, he felt, could best be achieved through open administration.

Dan Aronson's 1990 tribute to Salisbury's style of institutional development borrowed a metaphor from Salisbury's youthful career as a successful amateur boxer:

> Dick always sought to find the openings, take advantage of the right moments, feint and jab, and above all never to back down from challenges. An entrepreneur, he always stepped in to new opportunities, never away from them. Impatient with methodicalness and grand planning, he preferred to win points where he could find them, and to go on to seize new ground rather than rest on the point already won ... [H]e achieved growth in the Faculty of Arts – point by point, a quarter or a half a position at a time – when many of the rest of us were feeling that nothing could be done (Aronson 1990:9).

Salisbury's second year in the Deanship was interrupted by his first bout with the illness that would take his life. A temporary recovery returned him to the fray, with renewed vigour. Within months, however, deteriorating health forced his withdrawal from active administrative duties. To the end of his energies, though, Dick remained interested and engaged in university and professional matters; and he remained accessible to the many colleagues, students and friends for whom he was ever the leader and for whom his absence from the scene was barely imaginable.

NOTES

1.   During his early years at McGill, he was a fellow of the Royal Anthropological Institute and of the American Anthropological Association; and member of the Association of Social Anthropologists of the British Commonwealth, the Society for Economic Anthropology, the Papua New Guinea society, and the Polynesian Society. He was also a member of the Pacific Research Committee of the U.S. National Academy of Sciences (NAS)/National Research Council (NRC), 1965-67, and in 1965 chaired the NAS/NRC Conference on New Guinea Research. Some years later, he served terms as Vice-President (1979) and President (1980) of the American Ethnological Society.

    Salisbury's service to scholarly publishing internationally was of similar prominence. He served for over twenty years on the International Editorial Advisory Board of *Ethnology*, as a member of the Editorial Board of the *Perspectives on Development* Series of Cambridge University Press (1971-77), and as a member of the Editorial Advisory Board of *Reviews in Anthropology* (1973-79).

REFERENCES

Abley, Mark. 1989. "Anthropologist Seeks Communication Between Cultures." *The Gazette*, Montreal, March 12:D-5.

Aronson, Dan. 1989. "Richard F. Salisbury, Dec. 8, 1926 - June 17, 1989." *The McGill Reporter*, 1 September:1,6.

-----------1990. "Richard Salisbury's Style: A Colleague Remembers." *Culture* X(1):8-9.

Bariteau, Claude. 1989. "Homme de passion, de rigeur." *Le Devoir*, 7 Août:10.

Bibeau, Gilles. 1990. "Richard F. Salisbury (1926-1989): la passion de l'application des connaissances." *Culture* X(1):12-14.

Darnell, Regna. 1998. "Toward a History of Canadian Departments of Anthropology: Retrospect, Prospect and Common Cause." *Anthropologica* XL(2):153-168.

Jones, Frank E. 1992. "The Evolution of the CSAA." In Carroll, William K., Linda Christiansen-Ruffman, Raymond F. Currie and Deborah Harrison (eds.), *Fragile Truths: Twenty-five Years of Sociology and Anthropology in Canada*. Ottawa: Carleton University Press:21-41.

Feit, Harvey. 1983. "Richard F. Salisbury: An Anthropologist as Primitive Man." Canadian Ethnology Society/Society for Applied Anthropology in Canada, Spring Meetings, McMaster University: Hamilton (May).

Gold, Gerald L. and Marc Adélard Tremblay. 1982. "After the Quiet Revolution: Quebec Anthropology and the Study of Quebec." *Ethnos* 1982(1-2):103-132.

Inglis, Gordon. 1982. "In Bed with The Elephant: Anthropology in Anglophone Canada." *Ethnos* 1982(1-2):82-102.

Keesing, Roger. 1989. "Crossing Paths." Tribute read at Memorial Symposium, McGill University, September 28.

Prince, Raymond. 1990. "Obituary: Richard Frank Salisbury (1926-1989)." *Transcultural Psychiatric Research Review* 27:73-75.

Salisbury, Richard F. 1974. Letter. Canadian Sociology and Anthropology Association *Bulletin*, No. 35.

------------1976. "Anthropology in Anglophone Quebec." In Ames, M.M. and J. Freedman (eds.), *The History of Canadian Anthropology*. Proceedings No. 3 of the Société Canadienne d'Ethnologie/Canadian Ethnology Society:136-147.

------------1977. "Training Applied Anthropologists — the McGill Programme in the Anthropology of Development 1964-1976." In Weaver, Sally and J. Freedman (eds.), *Applied Anthropology in Canada*. Proceedings No. 4 of the Société Canadienne d'Ethnologie/Canadian Ethnology Society:58-78.

------------1983. "Applied Anthropology in Canada - Problems and Prospects." In Manning, Frank (ed.), *Consciousness and Inquiry: Ethnology and Canadian Realities*. Canadian Ethnology Service Paper No. 89E. Ottawa: National Museum of Man Mercury Series.

Tremblay, Marc Adélard. 1989. "In Memoriam: Richard Frank Salisbury 1926-1989." Remarks at Memorial Service, McGill University Chapel, September 28.

------------1990. "Richard Salisbury et l'anthropologie du développement." *Culture* X(1):5-8.

Trigger, Bruce. 1989a. "Resolution on the Death of Professor Richard Frank Salisbury." Faculty of Arts, McGill University (September).

------------1989b. "In Memoriam: Richard Frank Salisbury." *Proactive* 8(2):2-4.

------------1997. "Loaves and Fishes: Sustaining Anthropology at McGill." *Culture* XVII(1/2):89-100.

Wells, Paul. 1989. "Anthropologist Known for Work with Cree on Hydro Projects." *The Gazette*, 24 September.

17.

APPLIED ANTHROPOLOGY IN CANADA:

PROBLEMS AND PROSPECTS

by

Richard F. Salisbury

Source: Frank Manning (ed.), *Consciousness and Inquiry: Ethnology and Canadian Realities*. National Museum of Man Mercury Series, Canadian Ethnology Service, Paper No. 89E, Ottawa, 1983.

I shall take the unusual step in this paper of defining "applied anthropology," not as what some academic anthropologists do in their spare time, but as what is done by people trained as anthropologists who earn their livelihood by applying their anthropological training. Some academics may do similar things, but clearly the demography of the discipline indicates that "applied anthropology" as I define it is the growth point of the discipline. I look at the problems involved in applying anthropology, outside academe, both to raise consciousness and to illuminate some of the problems that academic anthropology and anthropologists may face.

The paper starts with a discussion of the careers and activities of a sample of thirty-five Canadian "applied anthropologists," and then, on the basis of personal participatory observation of the actions of the thirty-five, it considers their problems. My first thought was to send out a questionnaire to applied anthropologists, but directories omit them — the temporary directory of the SAAC in February 1981 contained only one of my eventual sample of thirty-five. Applied workers tend to find little of value in existing learned societies that cater to academics (cf. Hammond 1980). My solution has been a pragmatic one.

THE SAMPLE

I have selected thirty-five anthropologists whom I have either known personally, have interviewed at meetings, or have participatorily observed, and have based my generalisation on them. The sample is biased. It is weighted in terms of senior colleagues and ex-students; it over-represents Quebec and Francophones; it includes mainly people working with native people or on industrial development, but it includes a few in law, education, immigration and health; it has people from all age groups and from all sections of the country. Of the thirty-five, eleven have PhDs, seventeen have MAs and seven have BAs as their highest anthropological degree, although four of the latter have law degrees. Thirteen work as independent professionals or consultants (including partnership in an incorporated firm), nine work for Government (national or provincial) agencies, three for business firms, and ten for "local groups" (mainly Native groups at provincial or band levels in this sample).

THE ANTHROPOLOGICAL TASKS

None of the anthropologists can be said to be "making decisions" (except for themselves), but nine of the twenty-two who are employed are senior "staff," heading up professional teams and offering policy advice directly to the decision-makers of their organization. Their work includes a large amount of administration.

The other thirteen employees are more directly engaged in the day-to-day tasks of research and writing that would be familiar to an academic. Inevitably, however, they are also engaged in the chores of running local offices, telephoning and negotiating with people in other offices, discussing with them in meetings, and carrying out instructions of their bosses (who rarely are anthropologists).

The self-employed consultants, explicitly engaged in selling expert advice, find themselves operating as businessmen, administering their offices, selling themselves to clients, and often overseeing the execution of programmes that they have suggested (e.g. public education seminars, or the operation of a local data-gathering system).

Clearly the activities of all three groups overlap in many ways. They all involve elements of research, administration, interpersonal communication, and "chores." I shall, however, deal with the three groups as though they were discrete categories of "administrators," "workers" and "consultants," since the interaction between these roles is the main topic of my paper, and it is easier to discuss in discrete terms, before considering how people move from one category to another.

The common enterprise in which all categories are involved is the use of their knowledge and research skills in social analysis of the type used in anthropology, to advise those who are operating enterprises (of business, government or social service) about how to run them better. I shall use the terms "boss" or "client" interchangeably for the enterprise operators, whether these are federal cabinet ministers, mining company presidents, parents in a Home and School Committee, or a local Indian Band. The common problems that all categories face are the lack of awareness by potential clients/bosses of the contribution anthropologists might make, the lack of formally structured mechanisms for bringing clients and anthropologists together regularly, the failure of academic-training to provide the appropriate skills and knowledge for effective professional practice, and the poor understanding by academics of what applied anthropology means.

With the role of boss/client the three applied roles form a system. Boss/clients must share enough of the problems, about which decisions are needed, with either an administrator or a consultant, whom the boss trusts. The administrator/consultant responds by suggesting the information that needs collecting, the sort of review of options possible, the costs, or the past experience that might be provided to help in making the decision. Realistically every administrator/consultant must try to be ahead of the boss/client, anticipating issues, having the outline of a study ready, or having already marshalled available materials. The administrator must then organize workers inside the organization to carry out the work, or may himself become the client who hires an outside consultant. He is responsible for controlling workers and consultants, getting the report in on time, and ensuring that it (and other studies) appear in a form suitable for the boss to make a decision from it.

Where the organisation is small there may be no administrator intervening between boss and worker. The latter may have to advise the boss, and carry out the work needed for the report/study/plan, and, in many cases, act as the Executive Director for the organisation itself, hiring consultants, but also driving the car that gets the boss to the airport in time. The worker has to be jack-of-all-trades in such an organisation.

The administrator relates to one boss, but organises the work of consultants and workers, depending on them for the effectiveness of his advice to the boss. The consultant must have a wide network of clients to hire his/her specialised skills, and this is critically important as potential clients are the administrators or jack-of-all-trade workers for whom the consultant may work. Workers, though employed nominally by bosses (who may be consultants), depend mainly on administrators for their jobs.

Career Patterns

A pattern of careers does appear, though it is changing. Of the twelve applied anthropologists over age 40, five are administrators and six are consultants; eight have PhDs. Most (but not all) had a period of academic employment and moved from there into a senior position. Originally asked to advise a boss/client as a part-time consultant on a single issue, they have either been taken on staff, or have set themselves up as consulting generally on related issues. The few with MAs entered into lower levels of organisation, and have worked their way up to administrator status, jumping from worker to administrator at the moment when they switched from one organisation to another.

For the under-40s there are fewer PhDs (3 out of 23) and many fewer who have had academic employment, other than teaching assistantships or college lecturing. Those who are now administrators (again 3 out of 23) began as workers within the organisation they now administer (or one closely related) and have worked their way up internally. The majority are workers (13 out of 23) — mostly for Indian bands or sub-provincial groups in my sample, although some work for government and some for business. The remaining seven work independently as consultants, and these include all those who have taught in universities or colleges.

Striking is the fluidity of employment among workers and consultants. A number began their professional career doing academic research or in a government agency, in relation to native people. They subsequently decided to work instead for the group with which they had made contact during their earlier work. They tend to be people who completed an MA, or did course work for it. Those workers who did no graduate study in anthropology commonly sought employment directly with a local group; over time they came to realise the desirability of further graduate work in research (a few cases), or in a profession (like law). Although employment in the organisation could potentially be a career, many have switched to consulting, even though the viability of consulting as full-time provision of regular income has so far been confirmed by only a few of the over-40s. In the reverse direction, several who are now consultants have talked to me about the strains of hunting continually for clients, or the advantages of a steady job (as administrator, or as an academic). Consultant firms, in my sample at least, have not yet become large enough to employ numbers of workers regularly, though one anthropologist does administer for a multidisciplinary consulting firm, and another works for such a firm.

PROBLEMS IN THE WORK WORLD

The major single problem for each category is that the label "anthropologist" gives the typical boss/client or administrator few messages about the person's skills. For most bosses an anthropologist is someone who studies bones, sex habits or ancient ruins; for Indian clients an "anthro" is an unhelpful voyeur who asks too many questions, and gives nothing useful in return. If bosses or clients have worked with an applied anthropologist, they remember the person as an individual name rather than as a particular type of professional. It will take a lot of effective individuals, using the label, to overcome these negative stereotypes: in the meanwhile most consultants find it easier to say they work in "development," "social impact assessment," "land claims research," "social animation," "curriculum planning," etc.

Research administrators should indeed know better, but most agencies undertaking social research have administrators trained in other disciplines. In engineering firms they may be specialists in management or labour relations; in urban planning one finds architects or urban geographers; in land claims research lawyers organise the research; educational research tends to ignore culture differences and be administered by psychologists or specialists in curriculum planning. In government and business, generally, the research administrators are economists. They tend to advise bosses that the problem is one that is appropriate for their own discipline, that an economic study, for example, is what is needed and that no one without economic training should be hired.

Anthropologists in their own journals complain about the dangers of ignoring social processes, culture, values and the community in planning social action, but their strictures have little effect if the planning advisers do not read their journals, and continue to be listened to most attentively when they stress dollar costs as "the bottom line," or technical issues like the orthodox street layout, legal arguments, or teachers' union contract clauses. The applied anthropologist not only has to live with this, but has to learn to express what the discipline's culture tells him/her is important in the language used by the administrator. And as one uses the jargon of the administrator it becomes harder to maintain one's identity as an anthropologist — especially as an academic training leads to a simon-pure insistence on the jargon of one's own discipline.

Even administrators with no negative stereotype of anthropologists are still unlikely to employ anthropologists for reasons of the "invisible college." Though being an administrator demands relative openness, and readiness to try out new techniques to solve new problems, the way to find the new solutions is to keep one's ears open. The places one listens are over lunch at pubs and clubs, in airplanes or on golf courses. The sources of gossip are *Financial Post*, *Canadian Public Policy*, *CARC Newsletter*, where few anthropologists appear as authors or as subjects. The topics discussed are often ones discussed earlier in theoretical anthropological journals, but the sources publicly remembered are those of better-known disciplines. Administrators belong to a "college" where few anthropologists penetrate.

When in a research team, the applied anthropologist worker meets similar problems, downplaying anthropology, and stressing general social science knowledge and skills of research. The distinctive anthropological gambit, "this is how they do it among the Bongobongo," is welcome only if accompanied by abilities to interview effectively, compile a population pyramid, or read a computer print-out. In work on an agricultural project one must be ready to learn from agronomists and farmers about agriculture, while constructing questionnaires where folk categories become standard indices of "big farms," gross farm sales in dollars, percentages of acreage under each crop, etc. Theoretical concepts like modernisation or metropolitan dominance have to be expressed in the terms of the dominant discipline. When one is on the defensive about learning the jargon, it is hard to convince one's co-workers that anthropology has something distinctive to offer. It is hard to avoid the situation, in a generally non-anthropological team where one is "a good worker, despite being an anthropologist."

Having to learn other disciplines on the job in team-work situations is possibly easier than the situation of the lone researcher working for a small group. Here the opposite numbers with whom one must interact involve (e.g. for a band communications worker) the Band Council as employers, office staff, Indian Affairs officials, lawyers, local police, CMHC inspectors, CRTC commissioners, outside consultants, printing firms, auditors, etc. Such a worker can easily be so involved in day-to-day action with non social scientists, especially as deadlines and meetings come frequently, as to forget the abstract lessons learned in academe. A training that did not prepare for reality is looked on as an irrelevant one. The identity it gave is an identity to discard.

PROBLEMS WITH ACADEME

These problems are partly the obverse of the work problems. Academics discount the practical problems of their applied colleagues, as they can retreat into the self-contained world of the discipline, where jobs are reserved for anthropologists, where colleagues talk the same language, and where success is measured by one's reputation among colleagues. Although academics praise interdisciplinarity, few practice it, and the prizes go to the specialist, within departments and in the profession.

Though the applied anthropologist is in more need of intellectual support, because of his disciplinary isolation, academics do not provide it. Academics honour mature reflection and publication of theoretical articles; professionals have a flow of new practical problems to solve, that require a stock of potential solutions for trial, adoption if they work and rejection if they fail. If the solutions fail there is nothing to write about, while if they work one is too busy applying them to write journal articles.

For example, the anthropologist charged with predicting and avoiding deleterious effects on a community of importing a male construction work force of 1,000 men, should find answers in a repertoire of studies of boom towns, of camp organization, of social control among workers, or of administering health, education or transport services. Yet these do not exist in the standard literature. Reports, with few exceptions (e.g. Matthiasson 1977 on Fort McMurray, or Knight 1972), remain unpublished. In academe the classic studies, like that of MIT student housing after World War II by Festinger (1950), are still cited. The reports that pass from hand-to-hand informally are not reviewed systematically for their relevance to wider problems. Academics rarely have access to them, and disdain them as "hack jobs." I have elsewhere argued (Salisbury 1979) that a dialogue between practice and basic research is needed, with each side asking questions of, and thereby stimulating the other. I must confess progress in the emergence of dialogue is slow.

Academic training also tends to provide inappropriately for the needs of the applied anthropologist. In the past complaints have been made that the PhD training is inappropriate. I would agree that the PhD thesis is an inappropriate test for an applied researcher, but would disagree that the research training provided, and the pressures towards synthesis and depth are inappropriate. The number of applied anthropologist over-40s with PhDs (and the number of academics who consult part-time) show that the training is not entirely inappropriate. The need to follow up every blind alley of theoretical argument, to footnote prolifically, and to orient one's discussion to academics exclusively, is not the right preparation for writing reports to tight deadlines, and for grabbing the attention of busy but highly intelligent readers. This requires a distillation of the most important issues, concise presentation of evidence, and the relegation of laborious documentation to appendices.

That PhDs are often over-trained is true. Many still expect that with a PhD they are entitled to be called doctor, and to start at a $25,000 salary — even though some PhDs are driving taxi-cabs. The PhD is indeed an expert in a particular topic by the time the degree is awarded, and that topic may not be precisely what a boss or client is concerned with. But I would argue that the training of fieldwork, of experiencing what it means to be ignorant in a culturally different environment, in order to learn about that environment, is an ideal preparation for humility and flexibility by anthropology PhDs.

In my opinion the serious problem with PhD training is its length. The polishing of a research study to make it academically respectable, over two or more years after data collection, too easily shifts the orientation of the enthusiastic student with important ideas away from the ideas (and their application) and into the academic polishing. Some format needs to be devised to enable credit to be given for an original study that has been well designed and executed in data collection, but can be written up to be practically effective, with its data processed for availability rather than exhaustive analysis. A PhD (Applied)?

However it is the MA which, in my sample, provides the major input of recent manpower into applied anthropology. This is influenced by the Quebec weighting of the sample, for there the production of MAs and their employment outside academe began earlier than in anglophone Canada. Eight of the seventeen MA's are francophone. But the careers of the nine anglophone MAs appear to be largely similar, if later in starting. I feel that the trend is a real one.

In many ways the training is looked back upon as having been successful. Everyone got involved in field research; everyone had one or more stimulating teachers who involved him as a research colleague. Perhaps more importantly the peer group of fellow graduate students developed strong bonds, and these bonds now form (with later colleague ties) an extremely important "old boy network" of contacts between people who are now administrators, consultants, workers, or academics.

Yet in conversation there comes out a strong negative feeling towards academic departments and teaching, both among those who have done some work towards a PhD but have gone into limbo, and those who quit cold turkey with an MA As an academic it would be easy to dismiss this antagonism as the attempts by "dropouts" to blame dropping out on "the system," rather than on their own abilities. More charitably an academic could see it as an attempt to give value to work that most academics deprecate — rapid research and writing to deadlines, with practical goals and an emphasis on communication, as against methodical research, polished writing, basic theory, and full documentation. But if academics call practising anthropologists "quick and dirty," they must expect in return to be called "pedants." Name-calling does not help.

362

Underlying the name-calling, however, there is a reality that MA training could be made more effective. Retaining the features of a field project, following training in research methodology and theory, reducing the emphasis on "comprehensive examinations" over wide fields that are relevant primarily for those training to teach anthropology, but increasing the component of supervised practical experience — perhaps with an internship programme as the University of South Florida has pioneered (Kushner 1979) — could well form the basis of an MA (Applied). The problem with such a programme (as I have described, Salisbury 1977) is that running an internship programme and supervising practical experience demands a teaching staff that can maintain contacts with the agencies where students are placed, and can expend time in the supervision. Current university staffing of graduate departments does not permit this intensive commitment.

Paradoxically the highly motivated undergraduate student can often work out the equivalent sort of programme during an undergraduate career, using summer employment between junior and senior years as an internship. If the experience is not satisfactory it was "only a summer job"; if the experience, and the analysis of it in theoretical terms in a variety of final year courses, proves rewarding, the BA graduate may have a research job already lined up on graduation. If the job is not a direct continuation of the summer job, the latter has given a clear picture of where a job is available.

I would, in principle, continue to urge students aiming at practising anthropology, to complete a broad anthropological training as undergraduates, and to spend at least a year in research and training, and perhaps an MA (Applied) degree, to get the best foundation for practice. But I would also strongly advocate a greater involvement of undergraduates in participant observational studies during their courses, which necessarily would involve them (and their teachers) in applying their theory to everyday situations — organisations of medical services, symbolisms of popular music, the economics of parking meters, the politics of the municipality — rather than to exotica. This might lose a few more graduate students to law, town planning, or medicine — but it might give us more anthropologically minded practitioners of those professions, and more readiness to use specialist anthropologists by the professions.

CONCLUSION

Given the demography of the employment market in academe until 1990, and given the number of individuals in the pipeline of training, it is certain that the number seeking to apply their training is going to increase geometrically for several years. My personal experience is that the number of groups —

governments, businesses, and local groups — seeking advice on social issues, which anthropologists are the most competent group to provide, vastly exceeds the number of workers currently able, and in the market, to provide it. There is no valid reason why, for the next ten years, the increase in jobs as anthropologists should not mirror the supply of trainees, only the invalid one, that the training remains that of academic anthropology. Not all trainees will get the best jobs, but the rewards of success will go to the competent, and those who are aware of the professional pressures.

The career patterns of the under-40 applied anthropologists suggest the model for the training of the next generation. The MA is most important, especially if it can lead to doing research work within an organization, which then provides the job-base (or the contacts) for a regular position. For such people the PhD is of questionable value initially; it may even spoil the chances of immediate employment. But it can be of value, to give an edge in promotion to administrative levels, or to give the independent consultant the wider perspective needed (and the reputation) to be in greatest demand.

Three steps appear needed to fill gaps in the training currently provided. At the undergraduate level the student anthropologist needs to be led to look at the world around her, anthropologically — and not merely to look at the exotic world overseas; needs to recognize the skills that an undergraduate training in social sciences provides, and to be prepared to capitalise on them; and needs to learn that applying skills day to day in real work that other people want is the everyday reality of the work world. At the MA level the present training in research and conceptual skills is relevant, but needs to be supplemented by an immersion in a work situation, where guided research can be undertaken. Critical is the performance of all skills, from conceptual study design to submission of a report complete with recommendations for action, though the content of the task need not necessarily be innovative.

But it is at the professional level that the gaps are the least easy to fill. They include the contacts with agencies that need anthropological skills, the establishment of an information network that can make workers aware of colleagues in the field and of new developments as they emerge, and perhaps most importantly, the provision of forums in which expertise relating to professional anthropology — including basic discoveries that have emerged during applied studies — can be communicated among applied anthropologists. Applied anthropology needs a professional organisation that is adapted to their needs — and not merely to the needs of interested academics — since their needs are different. It is to be hoped that the Society for Applied Anthropology in Canada will respond to those needs.

REFERENCES

Festinger, L., S. Schachter, and K. Back. 1950. *Social Pressures in Informal Groups: a Study of Human Factors in Housing*. Stanford: Stanford University Press.

Hammond, P.B. 1980. "Reinventing the AAA." *Anthropology Newsletter* 21 (8):2.

Knight, R.K. 1972. *Work Camps and Single Enterprise Communities in Canada and the United States*. Scarborough: University of Toronto.

Kushner, G. 1979. The University of South Florida Programme in Applied Anthropology. Paper presented at the Sixth Annual Conference, Canadian Ethnology Society, Banff.

Matthiassen, J. 1977. *Resident Perceptions of Quality of Life in Resource Frontier Communities*. University of Manitoba Centre for Settlement Studies, Series 2, No. 2.

Salisbury, R.F. 1977. "Training Applied Anthropologists - the McGill Programme in the Anthropology of Development 1964-1976." In Freedman, J. (ed.), *Applied Anthropology in Canada*. Proceedings No. 4, Canadian Ethnology Society.

------------1979. "Application and Theory in Canadian Anthropology; the James Bay Agreement." *Transactions of the Royal Society of Canada* 17:229-241.

18.

LES DÉFIS ET CONTRAINTES

DE L'ANTHROPOLOGIE DU DÉVELOPPEMENT:

ENTREVUE AVEC RICHARD F. SALISBURY

PROGRAMME DE L'ANTHROPOLOGIE DU DÉVELOPPEMENT.

UNIVERSITÉ MCGILL

Propos recueillis par Claude-Yves Charron

Source: *Recherches amérindiennes au Québec*, Vol. XIII., No. 1. 1983

Recherches amérindiennes au Québec [R.a.Q.]:

> À quoi tient, selon vous, la réputation internationale de vos travaux en
> anthropologie appliquée et en anthropologie du développement d'une
> part, et la méconnaissance ou du moins la distance relative entre vos
> travaux et ceux de la «tradition francophone» d'autre part?

Richard F. Salisbury:

> Peut-être pourrions-nous attribuer la reconnaissance de nos travaux à
> deux types de facteurs: une emphase importante accordée à la théorie (du
> moins dans les domaines de l'économie et de l'anthropologie transaction-
> nelle), ainsi qu'une confiance mutuelle que nous avons progressivement
> établie avec les «policy-makers.» Quant à la distance relative entre anthro-
> pologues francophones et anglophones ici-même au Québec, sans doute
> faudrait-il faire l'historique du développement de nos différents départe-
> ments d'anthropologie afin de vous répondre de façon satisfaisante.
> Disons simplement pour l'instant, qu'il y a effectivement des différences
> culturelles entre nos modes d'approche: je ne saurais, spontanément, com-
> ment les analyser. Cela est encore un mystère pour moi. Peut-être aurions-
> nous pu faire davantage d'efforts, de part et d'autre, pour nous
> rapprocher.

R.a.Q.:

Quels sont, depuis que vous êtes au Québec, depuis bientôt vingt ans donc, vos objets d'étude et d'intervention privilégiés?

R.F. Salisbury:

L'étude du développement en région ou dans des petites communautés; l'étude du processus de prise de décision; l'approche d'énigmes du type «comment permettre à des instances locales de prendre des décisions au sein d'un réseau organisationnel qui tente d'atteindre un nouvel équilibre entre centralisation et décentralisation.» L'étude des différentes instances de décision et de l'appareil bureaucratique, médiateur privilégié entre l'État et les communautés, constitue aujourd'hui un lieu prioritaire d'étude et d'intervention.

R.a.Q.:

Et votre cadre de référence théorique?

R.F. Salisbury:

Le concept central est sans doute celui d'organisation sociale tel que défini par Raymond Firth. À partir de ce type de catégorie, on peut développer un modèle d'économie de subsistance et de service, ce que j'ai tenté de faire jusqu'en 1973 surtout. Les négociations autour de l'entente de la Baie James ont alors représenté une immense expérimentation en termes de développement régional: comment élaborer un compromis permettant une décentralisation des services d'un côté, simultanément à une consolidation de l'économie de subsistance de l'autre, voilà un défi difficile à résoudre. Si l'on adopte, en plus, dans son cadre de référence, les travaux en anthropologie transactionnelle dont ceux de Frederik Barth (1966), les réseaux de relations sont alors envisagés comme les résultants d'un processus de négociations entre différentes catégories d'acteurs, et non plus sous l'angle d'un réseau de rôles contrôlés par des normes. Enfin, outre Firth et Barth, précisons également que nous adoptons aussi la démarche de Belshaw (1961) et son analyse économique des performances sociales. Voilà, trop brièvement esquissés les principaux axes constitutifs de notre cadre de référence théorique en anthropologie du développement.

R.a.Q.:

Vous avez déclaré, au dernier congrès annuel de la Société d'anthropologie appliquée du Canada, que dans les dix prochaines années la plupart des jeunes gradués en anthropologie interviendraient du côté appliqué plutôt qu'académique. À quoi tient une telle prévision?

R.F. Salisbury:

Je ne crois pas qu'il soit possible pour ces jeunes apprentis anthropologues qui arriveront bientôt sur le marché, dans les dix prochaines années de s'installer en retrait et d'élaborer d'élégantes critiques ou dissertations académiques. Le milieu académique est lui-même d'ores et déjà presque saturé. Et dans la période de coupures budgétaires actuelles l'anthropologie ne semble pas une priorité. J'ai conduit une enquête auprès de 35 anthropologues qui travaillent présentement à l'extérieur de l'université, qui gagnent leur vie en appliquant leur formation anthropologique. Dans cet échantillonnage, 11 disposaient d'un Ph.D., 17 d'une maîtrise, et 7 avaient un baccalauréat. Quant à leur emploi, 13 d'entre eux travaillent comme professionnels indépendants ou consultants, 9 pour des agences gouvernementales nationales ou provinciales, 3 pour des milieux d'affaires et 10 pour des groupes locaux autochtones.

On pourrait les regrouper en trois catégories: les administrateurs, les intermédiaires et les consultants. Et, dans le milieu du travail les préjugés qui prévalent à l'égard des anthropologues représentent une contrainte de taille à surmonter: la plupart des employeurs éventuels perçoivent encore aujourd'hui un anthropologue comme celui qui étudie les os, les habitudes sexuelles ou les vieilles ruines; et lorsque l'employeur est un autochtone les préjugés les plus courants et parfois fondés veulent qu'il soit alors une espèce de voyeur qui pose beaucoup trop de questions et qui n'offre rien d'utile en retour. De tels éléments contextuels représentent des contraintes importantes pour le jeune apprenti anthropologue qui voudrait ou voudra intervenir dans le milieu.

Il y a également d'autres contraintes inhérentes à notre discipline, semble-t-il: la recherche fondamentale vs. l'anthropologie appliquée. L'urgence d'un nouveau dialogue s'impose entre ces deux types d'approche, et les jeunes anthropologues vont devoir réaliser autre chose qu'un dialogue de sourds entre ces deux tendances car les milieux académiques, où trop souvent certains se réfugient dans la pure recherche fondamentale, leur seront à toutes fins pratiques fermés. Et l'histoire récente nous prouve que ce type de dialogue n'est pas, lui non plus, facile à réaliser.

L'un des défis majeurs de l'anthropologie du développement pour les apprentis qui choisiront ce lieu d'intervention consistera donc dans l'application de leur cadre de référence théorique à des situations quotidiennes, dans le domaine de l'organisation des services médicaux, de la musique populaire, les politiques municipales, et non plus seulement les milieux exotiques. Parler de développement exige que l'on ne se limite plus simplement aux soit-disant structures du passé des sociétés exotiques. Les domaines d'application sont quotidiens et actuels, au Nord comme au Sud.

Un dernier point si vous le permettez: l'importance du travail sur le terrain est vitale, en anthropologie appliquée et en anthropologie du développement. Car il est essentiel d'apprendre non pas à assumer le rôle d'un voyeur, mais bien d'expérimenter ce que cela signifie de se retrouver ignorant dans un environnement culturel différent du nôtre, d'apprendre à y avoir accès pour ensuite analyser les processus de prise de décision et de centralisation vs. décentralisation des organisations. Cette humilité et cette flexibilité constituent deux composantes majeures du jeune apprenti en anthropologie du développement, deux composantes parfois trop négligées dans certains milieux et discussions académiques.

Ce sont là des exigences fondamentales dont l'actualité dépasse de beaucoup les différences de tradition «francophones» et «anglophones» au Québec. Des exigences qui, dans la conjoncture actuelle, appellent peut-être aussi un rapprochement de ces traditions, de même que la reconnaissance de la pertinence et de l'importance d'une formation dans le secteur de l'anthropologie appliquée. Il serait ridicule de se limiter à former des chômeurs et il serait encore plus ridicule de prétendre que nous n'avons plus besoin, dans notre société à «virages technologiques», d'anthropologues. Je crois que nous en avons besoin plus que jamais, mais que leur profil de carrière ou d'intervention sera dorénavant très différent de ce que nous avons connu jusqu'à maintenant.

R.a.Q.:

Mais que veut dire anthropologie du développement dans un tel contexte?[1]

R.F. Salisbury:

Il s'agit toujours de l'étude du changement social dans les organisations, en prévilégiant les preneurs de décision, la confrontation entre centralisation vs. décentralisation du pouvoir, et en utilisant le type de cadre de référence que j'évoquais tantôt avec ses dimensions économiques, transactionnelles et performatives. Une nuance s'impose, toutefois: outre le folklore, et les structures de parenté, chez les autres, il faudrait peut-être également s'occuper de dossiers d'actualité ailleurs et chez nous aussi, faire le saut de la culture des autres, hier, à l'interculturel, celui d'aujourd'hui et de demain. Peut-être est-ce là l'un des défis majeurs de l'anthropologie du développement.

Note

1. Les discussions concernant la négociation de l'entente de la Baie James abordées lors de l'entrevue ont été retirées de ce texte pour être plus amplement traitées dans la réponse rédigée par M. Salisbury au commentaire de Pierre Trudel (voir plus loin. dans ce même numéro).

Quelques Références Complémentaires.

Barth, F. 1966. *Models of Social Organization.* London: Royal Anthropological Institute.

Belshaw, C. S. 1969. *The Conditions of Social Performance.* London: Routledge and Kegan Paul.

Elberg, Nathan, J. Hyman and R.F. Salisbury. 1972. *Not by Bread Alone.* Monograph No. 5. Montreal: McGill University, Programme in the Anthropology of Development.

Firth R. 1981. "Engagement and Detachment: Reflections on Applying Social Anthropology." *Human Organization* 40 (3):198-199.

Goldthorpe, J.E. 1975. *The Sociology of the Third World: Disparity and Involvement.* Cambridge: Cambridge University Press.

Myrdal, G. 1972. *Asian Drama: An Inquiry into the Poverty of Nations.* New York: Vintage Books.

Salisbury, R.F. 1977. "Training Applied Anthropologists: The McGill Program in the Anthropology of Development." In Freedman, J. (ed.), *Applied Anthropology in Canada.* Société canadienne d'ethnologie.

------------1979. "Application and Theory in Canadian Anthropology: The James Bay Agreement." *Transactions of the Royal Society of Canada* XVII: 229-241.

VII.

RICHARD F. SALISBURY:

A CHRONOLOGICAL BIBLIOGRAPHY

Compiled by

Richard McCutcheon

The following chronological bibliography does not include published book reviews, of which there are many, and it includes only some of the brief commentaries that Salisbury wrote. It does include most, if not all, of Richard Salisbury's limited circulation project reports and working papers. I have attempted to make the bibliography as complete and accurate as possible, but on occasion was unable to verify the exact form of a reference (this was particularly true of "grey" literature). These are marked: [Not Seen]. This bibliography was compiled with the help of Dr. Mary Salisbury, Tara Goetze and contributors to this volume.

1956.   "Unilineal Descent Groups in the New Guinea Highlands." *Man* 56: 2-7.

1956.   "Asymmetrical Marriage Systems." *American Anthropologist* 58: 639-55.

1956.   "The Siane Language of the Eastern Highlands of New Guinea." *Anthropos* 51: 447- 80.

1956.   "Vocabulary of the Siane Language." *Microbibliotheka Anthropos* 24: 1064-66.

1958.   "An 'Indigenous' New Guinea Cult." *Kroeber Anthropological Papers* 18: 67-78.

1959.   "Comment on 'A Trobriand Medusa.'" *Man* 59: 67.

1960.   "Ceremonial Economics and Political Equilibrium." In *Proceedings, 6th International Congress of Anthropological and Ethnological Sciences, Paris* 2: 255-59.

1961.   With Sidney S. Smith. *Notes on Tolai Land Law and Custom* (Lands Commission Report). Port Morseby: Government Publication on Australian Territories. [Not Seen]

1962.   *From Stone to Steel: Economic Consequences of a Technological Change in New Guinea.* London: Cambridge University Press, and Melbourne: Melbourne University Press. 237 pp.

1962.   *Structures of Custodial Care: An Anthropological Study of a State Mental Hospital.* Berkeley: University of California Press. 138 pp.

1962.   "Early Stages of Economic Development in New Guinea." *Journal of the Polynesian Society* 71: 329-39. (Reprinted 1968. In *Peoples and Cultures of the Pacific: An Anthropological Reader*, edited by Andrew P. Vayda, 486-500. Garden City, NY: Published for the American Museum of Natural History, by the Natural History Press).

1962.   "Notes on Bilingualism and Linguistic Change in New Guinea." *Anthropological Linguistics* 4(7): 1-13.

1962.   "Comment on 'The Feet of the Natives are Large.'" *Current Anthropology* 3: 70-1.

1964.   "New Guinea Highland Models and Descent Theory." *Man* 64: 215-19.

1964.   "Despotism and Australian Administration in the New Guinea Highlands." *American Anthropologist* 66(4): 225-39.

1964.   "Changes in Land Use and Tenure among the Siane of the New Guinea Highlands (1952- 1961)." *Pacific Viewpoint* 5(1): 1-10.

1965.   "The Siane of the Eastern Highlands." In *Gods, Ghosts and Men in Melanesia: Some Religions of Australian New Guinea and the New Hebrides*, edited by Peter Lawrence and Mervyn J. Meggitt, 50-77. Melbourne: Oxford University Press.

1966.   "Politics and Shell Money Finance in New Britain." In *Political Anthropology*, edited by Marc J. Schwartz, Arthur Tuden and Victor Turner, 113-28. Chicago: Aldine Press.

1966.   "Possession in the New Guinea Highlands." *Transcultural Psychiatric Research Review* 3: 103-15. Reprinted 1968 in expanded form in *International Journal of Social Psychiatry* 14: 85-94.

1966.   "Structuring Ignorance: The Genesis of a Salt-Myth in New Guinea."
        Anthropologica 8(2): 316-328.

1967.   Editor, with Mary Salisbury. *Behavioral Science Research in New Guinea*.
        Washington, DC: National Academy of Sciences.

1967.   "Economic Research in New Guinea." In *Behavioral Science Research in New
        Guinea*, edited by Richard Salisbury and Mary Salisbury, 106-20. Washington,
        DC: National Academy of Sciences.

1967.   "Trade and Markets." In *International Encyclopaedia of the Social Sciences* 16:
        118- 22. New York: Macmillan and the Free Press.

1967.   "To Niri Buys a House." In *Towards a Theory of Consumer Behaviour*, edited by
        W.T. Tucker, 33-45. New York: Holt, Rinehart and Winston.

1967.   "An Anthropologist's Use of Historical Methods." Unpublished paper presented
        to the History Seminar, University of Papua and New Guinea, 7 July. (Published
        in this volume for the first time.)

1967.   "Pidgin's Respectable History." *New Guinea* 2(2): 44-48.

1968.   "Anthropology and Economics." In *Economic Anthropology: Readings in Theory
        and Analysis*, edited by Edward E. LeClair and Harold K. Schneider, 477-85. New
        York: Holt, Rinehart and Winston. (The original version of this essay appeared
        only in 1970, as "Economics," in *Anthropology and the Behavioral and Health
        Sciences*, edited by Otto Von Mering and Leonard Kasdan, 62-72. Pittsburgh:
        University of Pittsburgh Press. [See Below])

1968.   "Ethnographic Notes on Wapisiana Agriculture." In *Ethnographic Notes on
        Amerindian Agriculture* (McGill Savanna Research Project Series, No. 9), 9-20.
        Montreal: McGill University.

1969.   "Formal Analysis and Anthropological Economics: The Rossel Island Case." In
        Game Theory in the Behavioural Sciences, edited by Ira R. Buchler and Hugo G.
        Nutini, 75- 93. Pittsburgh: University of Pittsburgh Press.

1969.   "Comment on 'Theoretical Issues in Economic Anthropology.'" *Current
        Anthropology* 10: 89.

1969.   "Anthropology." In *1970 Britannica Book of the Year*, 98-102. Chicago: Encyclopaedia Britannica, Inc.

1969.   "Comment on 'Possession in the New Guinea Highlands.'" *Transcultural Psychiatry Research Review and Newsletter* 6: 95-102.

1970.   *Vunamami – Economic Transformation in a Traditional Society*. Berkeley: University of California Press. 389 pp.

1970.   "Economics." In *Anthropology and the Behavioral and Health Sciences*, edited by Otto Von Mering and Leonard Kasdan, 62-72 (Commentaries by George Dalton, Cyril Belshaw and Leonard Kasdan follow, 72-88). Pittsburgh: University of Pittsburgh Press. (Original version of 1968, "Anthropology and Economics." In *Economic Anthropology: Readings in Theory and Analysis*, edited by Edward E. LeClair and Harold K. Schneider. [See Above])

1970.   "Political Consolidation in the New Guinea Highlands." In *Proceedings, 8th International Congress of Anthropological and Ethnological Science, Tokyo, 1968*. 11: 114-16.

1971.   "Economic Anthropology." In *Anthropology Today*, edited by Gerald D. Berreman, et al, 469-79. Delmar, CA: C.R.M. Books.

1971.   "Anthropology." In *1971 Britannica Book of the Year*, 95-96. Chicago: Encyclopaedia Britannica, Inc.

1971.   "Development through the Service Industries." *Manpower and Unemployment Research in Africa* 4: 57-66. [Not Seen]

1971.   *Problems of the Gazelle Peninsula of New Britain, August, 1971*. Port Moresby: Government Printer. 55 pp. [Not Seen]

1972.   With Fernand G. Filion, Farida Rawji and Donald Stewart. *Development and James Bay: Socio-Economic Implications of the Hydro-Electric Project*. (Report prepared for the James Bay Development Corporation. Also in French. Reprinted 1974.) Montreal: McGill University Programme in the Anthropology of Development (Monograph Series, No. 4). 197 pp.

1972.   With Nathan Elberg, Jacqueline Hyman and Kenneth Hyman. *Not by Bread Alone: Use of Subsistence Resources Among the Cree of James Bay* (Report for the James Bay Task Force of the Indians of Quebec Association). Montreal: McGill University Programme in the Anthropology of Development (Monograph Series, No. 5). 141 pp.

1972.   With Mary Salisbury. "The Rural-Oriented Strategy of Urban Adaptation: Siane Migrants in Port Moresby." In *The Anthropology of Urban Environments*, edited by Thomas Weaver and Douglas White, 59-68. Washington, DC: Society for Applied Anthropology (Human Organization Monographs, No. 11). (Reprinted 1977. In *Change and Movement: Readings on Internal Migration in Papua New Guinea*, edited by Ronald J. May, 216-29. Canberra: Papua New Guinea Institute of Applied Social and Economic Research in association with Australian National University Press.)

1973.   "Economic Anthropology." In *Annual Review of Anthropology, 1973*, edited by B. Siegel, 85-94. Palo Alto: Annual Reviews, Inc. (Reprinted 1987 in *Perspectives in Cultural Anthropology*, edited by Herbert Applebaum, 349-59. Albany: State University of New York Press.)

1973.   "The Origins of the Tolai People." *Journal of the Papua New Guinea Society* 8: 79-84.

1974.   With Nathan Elberg and Robert H. Schneider. *Development? Attitudes to Development among the Native Peoples of the Mackenzie District* (Report for the Department of Indian and Northern Affairs, Government of Canada). Montreal: McGill University Programme in the Anthropology of Development (Monograph Series, No. 7.) [Summary published as *Brief Communication Series*, No. 27]. 109 pp.

1975.   "Non-Equilibrium Models in New Guinea Ecology: Possibilities of Cultural Extrapolation." *Anthropologica* N.S. 17(2): 127-47.

1975.   "Models for a Unified Social Science (Review essay: Alfred Kuhn, *The Logic of Social Systems*)." *Science* 187(4173, January 24): 247-48.

1975.   "Comment on 'Image of Limited Good or Expectation of Reciprocity.'" *Current Anthropology* 16: 89.

1975.   "Comment on 'Anthropologist and Policy Making.'" *Human Organization* 34(3): 315.

1975.   "Policy Regarding Native Peoples: An Academic Social Scientist's Perspective."
         (Paper prepared for the National Social Science Conference, Ottawa, November
         20-22. Montreal: McGill University Programme in the Anthropology of
         Development (Brief Communication Series, No. 37). 12 pp.

1976.   "Transactions or Transactors: An Economic Anthropologist's View." In
         *Transaction and Meaning: Directions in the Anthropology of Exchange and
         Symbolic Behavior*, edited by Bruce Kapferer, 41-59. Philadelphia: Institute for
         the Study of Human Issues.

1976.   "The Anthropologist as Societal Ombudsman." In *Development from Below:
         Anthropologists and Development Situations*, edited by David C. Pitt, 255-65.
         The Hague: Mouton. (In 1973 this article was made available prior to the IXth
         International Congress of Anthropological and Ethnological Sciences as "Article
         No. 1212." Chicago: IXth International Congress of Anthropological and
         Ethnological Sciences.)

1976.   "Anthropology in Anglophone Quebec." In *The History of Canadian
         Anthropology* (Proceedings No. 3, Canadian Ethnology Society), edited by Jim
         Freedman, 136-47. Hamilton, Ontario: Canadian Ethnology Society.

1976.   With Nathan Elberg in collaboration with Robert Visitor. *The End of the Line -
         (or the Beginning): Communications in Paint Hills (A Report on Phase 1 of
         Project Anik and Isolation)* (Report for the Department of Communications,
         Government of Canada). Montreal: McGill University Programme in the
         Anthropology of Development (Monograph Series, No. 8). 122 pp.

1977.   Editor, with Marilyn Silverman. *A House Divided? Anthropological Studies of
         Factionalism*. St. John's, Newfoundland: Memorial University of Newfoundland
         Institute of Social and Economic Research (Social and Economic Papers, No. 9).

1977.   With Marilyn Silverman. "An Introduction: Factions and the Dialectic." In *A
         House Divided? Anthropological Studies of Factionalism*, edited by Richard
         Salisbury and Marilyn Silverman, 1-20. St. John's, Newfoundland: Memorial
         University of Newfoundland Institute of Social and Economic Research (Social
         and Economic Papers, No. 9).

1977. "Transactional Politics: Factions and Beyond." In *A House Divided? Anthropological Studies of Factionalism*, edited by Richard Salisbury and Marilyn Silverman, 111-27. St. John's, Newfoundland: Memorial University of Newfoundland Institute of Social and Economic Research (Social and Economic Papers, No. 9).

1977. "Language and Politics of an Elite Group: The Tolai of New Britain." In *Language and Politics*, edited by William O. O'Barr and Jean F. O'Barr, 367-85. The Hague: Mouton.

1977. "A Prism of Perceptions: The James Bay Hydro-Electricity Project." In *Perceptions of Development*, edited by Sandra Wallman, 172-90. Cambridge: Cambridge University Press.

1977. "Training Applied Anthropologists - The McGill Programme in the Anthropology of Development, 1964-1976." In *Applied Anthropology in Canada* (Proceedings No. 4, Canadian Ethnology Society), edited by Jim Freedman, 58-78. Hamilton, Ontario: Canadian Ethnology Society.

1977. "The Berger Report - But is it Social Science?" *Social Sciences in Canada* 5(3): 14-15.

1977. "Foreword." In Nathan Elberg and Robert Visitor, *Off Centre: Fort George and the Regional Communication Network of James Bay* (Report for the Department of Communications, Government of Canada), i-xv. Montreal: McGill University Programme in the Anthropology of Development (Monograph Series, No. 10).

1977. "Foreword." In Conni Kinfoil, *A Survey of Community Attitudes Toward Curriculum Content in the Sand Park School, Fort George*, i-ii. (A report presented to the Cree School Board and the Fort George School Committee.) Montreal: McGill University Programme in the Anthropology of Development (Brief Communications Series, No. 42).

1978. "Evaluating Social Change: An Anthropological View of Impact Studies." In *Evaluating Change: Proceedings of a Symposium Sponsored by SSFC Committee on the Human Environment* (University of Alberta, Edmonton, June 4, 1975), edited by J.G. Nelson and C.A. Gray, 70-92. Ottawa: Social Science Federation of Canada.

1978.   "Postscript: Evaluating Social Change." In *Evaluating Change: Proceedings of a Symposium Sponsored by SSFC Committee on the Human Environment* (University of Alberta, Edmonton, June 4), edited by J.G. Nelson and C.A. Gray, 159-60. Ottawa: Social Science Federation of Canada.

1978.   With Pierre Angers, et autres. *Document de consultation, Commission d'Etude sur les Universités du Québec.* Québec: Ministère de l'Education. [Not Seen]

1978.   "Group Needs in Communications – Canadian Farmers." In *The Future Development of Public Telecommunications in Canada, 1976-1991.* (Project Delta Reports to Department of Communications, Government of Canada.) [Gamma Consulting] [Not Seen]

1979.   With Pierre Angers, et autres. *Commission d'Etude sur les Universités, Comité de co-ordination, Rapport — mai 1979.* Editeur officiel du Québec. 77 pp.

1979.   "Application and Theory in Canadian Anthropology: The James Bay Agreement." *Transactions of the Royal Society of Canada*, Series IV, Volume 17: 229-41.

1979.   "The North as a Developing Nation." In *Proceedings of the 8th National Northern Development Conference Edmonton. November 14-16, 1979*: 72-78. Yellowknife, Northwest Territories: Department of Information.

1979.   Consultant, with Ignatius E. La Rusic, Serge Bouchard, Alan Penn, Taylor Brelsford and Jean-Guy Deschenes. *Negotiating a Way of Life: Initial Cree Experience with the Administrative Structure Arising from the James Bay Agreement* (Report prepared for the Research Division, Policy, Research and Evaluation Group of the Department of Indian and Northern Affairs, Government of Canada). Montreal: ssDcc, Inc. [Also in French.] 178 pp.

1979.   With Taylor Brelsford, Louis Goldberg and Susan Marshall. *Training and Jobs Among the James Bay Cree* (Report for the Cree Regional Authority). Montreal: McGill University Programme in the Anthropology of Development (Brief Communications Series, No. 44). 9 + 15 pp.

1979.   "Foreword." In B. Stephen Strong, *Alaska Pipeline: Social and Economic Impact on Native People* (ESCOM Report, No. AI-01), 1-2. Ottawa: Department of Indian Affairs and Northern Development.

1980.   "Alternative Paradigms of Urbanization? Papua New Guinea." *Reviews in Anthropology* 7: 87-95.

1980.   "The Impacts of James Bay - Ten Years Later." *Engineering Journal* 63(4): 3-6.

1981.   With Ignatius E. LaRusic. *The Future of Ross River: Potential Effects of Road Reconstruction and Mining Development in the Region.* (Report prepared for Northern Roads and Airstrip Division, Department of Indian and Northern Affairs, Government of Canada, September 1981.) Montreal: ssDcc Inc. 32 + 14 pp.

1982.   "Formulating the Common Interest: The Role of Structures in Cree Development." In *Conflict and the Common Good* (Studies in Third World Societies, No. 24), edited by Robert S. Merrill and Dorothy Willner, 135-50. Williamsburg, VA: Studies in Third World Societies.

1982.   "Le rôle de l'expert dans la négociation sociale: leçons de la Baie James." In *L'intervention Sociale* (Actes du colloque de l'Association canadienne des sociologues et anthropologues de langue française, 1981), edited by Micheline Mayer-Renaud et Alberte Le Doyen, 257-66. Montréal: Editions Coopératives Albert Saint Martin.

1982.   *Etude des retombées sociales et économiques sur les communautés aotochtones due territoire NBR (Complexe hydroéléctrique Nottaway - Broadback – Rupert).* With contributions from Alain Bissonette, Marc Champagne, Ignatius LaRusic, Roger McDonnell, Francis Rieger, Catherine Salisbury, and Karen Schafer. (Rapport produit pour la Société d'energie de la Baie James, Direction de l'environnement.) Montreal: ssDcc Inc. 307 pp.

1982.   "Native Rights, Cultural Rights and the Charter." Canadian Human Rights Foundation Working Papers, Colloquium Report, (February 18). [Not Seen]

1983.   "Anthropological Economics and Development Planning." In *Economic Anthropology: Topics and Theory* (Monographs in Economic Anthropology, No. 1), edited by Sutti Ortiz, 399-420. Lanham, MD: University Press of America.

1983.   "Applied Anthropology in Canada - Problems and Prospects." In *Consciousness and Inquiry: Ethnology and Canadian Realities* (Canadian Ethnology Service Paper, No. 89E), edited by Frank Manning, 192-200. [Also in the French version edited by Marc-Adélard Tremblay, *Conscience et enquête: L'ethnologie des réalités canadiennes.*] Ottawa: National Museums of Canada.

1983.   "Les Cris et leurs consultants." *Recherches Amérindiennes au Québec* 13(1): 67-69.

1983.   "Les défis et contraintes de l'Anthropologie du développement: Entrevue avec Richard Salisbury." *Recherches Amérindiennes au Québec* 13(1): 55-56.

1984.   Edited, with Elisabeth Tooker. *Affluence and Cultural Survival (1981 Proceedings of the American Ethnological Society)*. Washington, DC: American Ethnological Society.

1984.   "Affluence and Cultural Survival: An Introduction." In *Affluence and Cultural Survival (1981 Proceedings of The American Ethnological Society)*, edited by Richard Salisbury and Elisabeth Tooker, 1-11. Washington, DC: American Ethnological Society.

1984.   Edited, with Georges-Henri Lévesque, Guy Rocher, Jacques Henripin, Marc-Adélard Tremblahy, Denis Szabo, Jean-Pierre Wallot, Paul Bernard et Claire-Emmanuèle Depocas. *Continuité et Rupture: Les sciences sociales au Québec*. Montreal: Les Presses de l'Université de Montréal.

1984.   "Le Québec: Microcosms du monde ou monde en soi?" In *Continuité et Rupture: Les sciences sociales au Québec*, edited by Georges-Henri Lévesque, et autres, 245-55. Montréal: Les Presses de l'Université de Montréal.

1984.   "An Abstract of the 1983 plenary address: 'The Challenge of Consulting.'" *SAAC (Society of Applied Anthropology in Canada) Newsletter* 3(1): 13-15. [Also appeared as: 1983. "The Challenge of Consulting." (Paper presented to the Society for Applied Anthropology in Canada, May 10, 1983.) Montreal: ssDcc, Inc. 20 pp.]

1984.   *The Miyamiya Group of Peoples, February 16-17, 1984*. Waigani: University of Papua New Guinea. (University of Papua New Guinea Schrader Mountains Project Report No. 1). 19 pp. [Also as "The Miyamiya Group of Peoples 16-17 February 1984," *Research in Melanesia*, 1985: 6-24].

1984.   *Language Work on Pinai, April 28-30, 1984*. Waigani: University of Papua New Guinea. (University of Papua New Guinea Schrader Mountains Project Report No. 3). 7 pp. [Also as "Language Work on Pinai 28-30 April 1984," *Research in Melanesia*, 1985: 28-36].

1984.   *Laluai Hydroelectric Proiect: Prefeasability Study, Social Impact Report* (Report for the Laluai Trust and Beca, Gure, Pty [Papua New Guinea], Appendix B). 21 pp. [Not Seen]

1986.   *A Homeland for the Cree: Regional Development in James Bay, 1971-1981.*
         Montreal: McGill-Queen's University Press. 172 pp.

1986.   "The Case for Dividing the Northwest Territories: A Comment." *Canadian Public
         Policy* 12(3): 513-17. (Reply to Gurston Dacks. 1986. "The Case Against Dividing
         the Northwest Territories." *Canadian Public Policy* 12(1): 202-13.)

1987.   *Decentralisation and Local Government in Papua New Guinea* (Report to the
         Governments of Simbu, West Highlands, East New Britain, and the North
         Solomons Provinces, and to the Federal Department of Provincial Affairs, Papua
         New Guinea, 1984). Montreal: McGill University Centre for Developing Area
         Studies. 22 pp.

1988.   "The Economics of Development through Services: Findings of the McGill
         Programme among the Cree." In *Production and Autonomy: Anthropological
         Studies and Critiques of Development* (Monographs in Economic Anthropology,
         No. 5), edited by John W. Bennett and John R. Bowen, 239-56. Lanham, MD:
         University Press of America.

1988.   "Les sciences sociales au Québec: Réflexions de l'Université McGill." *Sociologie et
         sociétés* 20(1): 164-67.

1988.   "Anthropology, Applied." In *The Canadian Encyclopedia, Second Edition*, edited
         by James H. Marsh, Volume 1: 83. Edmonton: Hurtig Publishers.

1989   "Discours d'ouverture: La relance de Stendhal." *Stendhal Club*, Grenoble, France.
         No. 118: 93-95. [Not Seen]

VIII

The Contributors

Harvey Feit (Ph.D. McGill, 1979), F.R.S.C.

Professor of Anthropology, McMaster University (Hamilton, Ontario, Canada)

Dr. Feit's research focuses on environmental representations, practices and power in conflicts over conservation and resource development. He has done field research among the James Bay Cree, environmental movements and environmental organizations in the United States and Europe.

He was North American editor of *The Cambridge Encyclopaedia of Hunters and Gatherers* (1999), and his publications include "Hunting, Nature and Metaphor: Political and Discursive Strategies in James Bay Cree Resistance and Autonomy" (in John A. Grim (ed.), *Indigenous Traditions and Ecology*. Cambridge: Harvard University Press, 2001); and "The Construction of Algonquian Hunting Territories: Private Property as Moral Lesson, Policy Advocacy and Ethnographic Error" (in G.W. Stocking Jr. (ed.), *Colonial Situations*, Madison: Wisconsin, 1991). With Mario Blaser he is an editor of *In the Way of Development: Indigenous Peoples, Civil Society and the Environment*, forthcoming with Zed Books. Feit has worked extensively as an applied researcher with indigenous peoples across Canada, and he was a senior advisor to the James Bay Cree during the negotiation and initial implementation of the James Bay and Northern Quebec Agreement in the 1970s. He has served as President of the Canadian Anthropology Society (CASCA), he chaired the Committee which founded the Indigenous Studies Program at McMaster University, and he is a fellow of the Royal Society of Canada.

Henry J. Rutz (Ph.D. McGill, 1973)

Professor of Anthropology, Hamilton College (Clinton, New York, U.S.A.)

Professor Rutz's research and writing on political economy and culture span over three decades. Beginning with problems of economic development and cultural change in rural Fijian villages, his work shifted to problems of Fijian nationalism, urbanism, and the emergence of middle class culture. His most recent research is on the effects of economic globalization on middle class education and culture in Istanbul, Turkey.

Recent publications include an edited volume on *The Politics of Time* (American Anthropological Association, 1992) and a co-edited volume on *The Social Economy of Consumption*, 1989). Recent articles include "Capitalizing on Culture: Moral Ironies in Urban Fiji" (*Comparative Studies in Society and History* 29, 1987); "Occupying the Headwaters of Tradition: Rhetorical Strategies of Nation-making in Fiji" (in Robert J. Foster (ed.), *Nation-Making: Emergent Identities in Postcolonial Melanesia*, University of Michigan Press, 1995); "The Rise and Demise of Islamic Religious Schools: Discourses of Belonging and Denial in the Construction of Turkish Civil Society and Culture" (*Political and Legal Anthropology Law Review* 22, 1999; and "Cultural Preservation" (*Almanac of Global Issues*, 2002).

Colin H. SCOTT (Ph.D. McGill, 1983)

Associate Professor of Anthropology, McGill University (Montreal, Quebec, Canada).

Professor Scott's research focuses on indigenous knowledge, land and sea tenure, indigenous rights actions, and regional development among James Bay Cree of northern Quebec and Torres Strait Islanders in Northern Queensland.

He recently edited *Aboriginal Autonomy and Development in Northern Quebec and Labrador* (University of British Columbia Press, 2001), based on research during the 1990s by the AGREE (Aboriginal Government, Resources, Economy and Environment) research team, which he directed. Other recent publications include "Land and Sea Tenure at Erub, Torres Strait: Property, Sovereignty and the Adjudication of Cultural Continuity" (*Oceania* 70[2]), 1999); "*Mare Nullius*: Indigenous Rights in Saltwater Environments" (*Development and Change* 31[3], 2000); and "Science for the West, Myth for the Rest? The Case of James Bay Cree Knowledge Construction" (in L. Nader (ed.), *Naked Science: Anthropological Inquiries in Boundaries, Power and Knowledge*, Routledge, 1996).

Marilyn SILVERMAN (Ph.D. McGill, 1973)

Professor of Anthropology, York University (Toronto, Ontario, Canada).

Professor Silverman's research interests are in political economy, local-level politics, agrarian processes and historical anthropology. She has carried out field work in Guyana (1966, 1969-71), Ecuador (1978) and the Republic of Ireland (1979 to the present).

Recent publications include a volume edited with P.H. Gulliver entitled *Approaching the Past: Historical Anthropology through Irish Case Studies* (New York: Columbia University Press, 1992) and, also with P.H. Gulliver, she wrote *Merchants and Shopkeepers: A Historical Anthropology of an Irish Market Town, 1200-1991* (University of Toronto Press, 1995). In 2001, she published an historical ethnography entitled *An Irish Working Class: Explorations in Political Economy and Hegemony, 1800-1950* (University of Toronto Press). Earlier books include In the *Valley of the Nore: A Social History of Thomastown, County Kilkenny, 1840-1986* (Dublin: Geography Publications, 1986); *Rich People and Rice: Factional Politics in Rural Guyana* (Leiden: Brill, 1980); and, co-edited with Richard F. Salisbury, *A House Divided: Anthropological Studies of Factionalism* (St John's: ISER, Memorial University of Newfoundland, 1977). She is now working on the third volume of the Irish ethnographic trilogy: *"Home Places": Agrarian Class and Kinship in an Irish Parish since 1820*.

INDEX

internal economy 315ff
political economy 320ff
reaction to James Bay project 260-1, 313-4
service provision 309ff
Crocombe R. & Hogbin G. 170, 176

Dalton G. 157, 159, 179, 185, 192, 193, 195, 163
Danks B. 221, 229
Darnell R. 345, 351
Davenport W. 155, 163
de Josselin de Jong J. 61
de Lepervanche M. 104
Dene 48, 49, 50
Development. See Anthropology of development; Economic development;
    Politics of development
Dewey A. 169, 176
DuBois C. 331
Dunning R. 298, 307

Ecological anthropology 155-6, 211
Economic anthropology 156ff, 165ff, 206-8, 296ff
    archaic economy 168
    capital in peasant societies 170
    entrepreneurship 170
    labour input 170
    markets 169
    and model building 172
    substantivism 167, 173
Economic development 1, 17, 98, 99,100, 107, 116, 123, 129, 156, 162, 166, 167-8,
    215, 224, 368
    failure of plans 213, 237, 259. See also Innovation, failure of
    and the individual 161, 217
    models of 113, 171, 222, 237, 246
    and political independence 284ff
    and provision of services 120-1, 246-7, 309ff, 368. See also Cree, service provision
    role of the anthropologist 346-7
    theories of 216ff
    and use of courts 242, 313
Economic rationality 107, 218
Economics and anthropology 165ff
Edwards D. 169, 176